High Hopes

High Hopes

The Clinton Presidency
and the Politics of Ambition

Stanley A. Renshon

Routledge
New York and London

Published in 1998 by
Routledge
29 West 35th Street
New York, NY 10001

Published in Great Britain in 1998 by
Routledge
11 New Fetter Lane
London EC4P 4EE

Originally Published in 1996 by
New York University Press
New York, New York

Printed in the United States of America on acid-free paper.

9 8 7 6 5 4 3

Errata
Chapter 1
P. 24, line 22: "election 1976." should read "election in 1976."

Library of Congress Cataloging-in-Publication Data

Renshon, Stanley A.
  High hopes : the Clinton presidency and the politics of ambition / by
Stanley A. Renshon
      p.   cm.
  Includes bibliographical references and index.
  ISBN 0-415-92147-3 (pb)
  1. United States—Politics and government—1993- 2. Clinton, Bill,
1946-   . I. Title.
[E885.R464 1998]
973.929—dc21   98-11840
                                                      CIP

To my children, David and Jonathan, with love,
in the hope that they realize their dreams,
find comfort in their ideals,
and are surrounded by love throughout their lives

CONTENTS

Foreword   *ix*
Preface   *xxiii*
Acknowledgments   *xxv*
Introduction   *1*

PART I. PRESIDENTS, PSYCHOLOGY, AND THE PUBLIC

CHAPTER 1   Public Psychology: The Legacy of History   19

PART II. THE CHARACTER OF BILL CLINTON

CHAPTER 2   Character and the Presidency   37
CHAPTER 3   Ambition   51
CHAPTER 4   Character Integrity   69
CHAPTER 5   Relatedness   93
CHAPTER 6   Character and Presidential Psychology   119

PART III. GROWING UP, COMING OF AGE

CHAPTER 7   His Mother's Son   145
CHAPTER 8   Adoration and Abandonment: The Clinton Family   166
CHAPTER 9   Some Consequences of Hope: A Tale of Two Women   183
CHAPTER 10 Vietnam and the Draft   200
CHAPTER 11 A Life's Choice: Hillary Rodham Clinton   216

PART IV. THE POLITICAL CONSEQUENCES OF CHARACTER

CHAPTER 12 Judgment and Leadership: The Core of Presidential
Performance   245
CHAPTER 13 Clinton's Presidency   259

PART V. CONCLUSION

CHAPTER 14 Lost Opportunities: President Clinton's First Term   285

APPENDIX   Bill Clinton's Character and Presidency:
A Note on Method   307

Notes   319
References   367
Subject Index   391
Name Index   399

★ ——

FOREWORD

THE CONTINUING PARADOX OF CHARACTER
AND THE CLINTON PRESIDENCY
Stanley A. Renshon

He is many a mother's dream and most fathers' nightmare—a smart, educated, disarmingly sincere and decidedly charming suitor, but with a moral compass frozen at self-interest. He is the most skillful politician to occupy the White House since Lyndon Johnson, and one of the toughest. And he remains a man of puzzling and inconsistent political principles—announcing that "the era of big government is over" even as he unveils dozens of new initiatives.

In the two years since *High Hopes* was published, the unintended ironies resulting from these paradoxes have reached extraordinary levels. This most empathetic of presidents has been credibly accused on national television of the crude sexual groping of a woman in difficult emotional and financial circumstances seeking his help. While deciding whether to launch a military attack against Iraq, his administration has worried out loud that a dark, humorous, and unnerving movie satire in which a president starts a phony war to distract attention from a sex scandal might give the public the wrong idea.[1] And the president who promised the "most ethical administration" in history has presided over one in which resignations for ethical cause, indictments, convictions, judicial reprimands, appointments of special investigative prosecutors, and continuing questions about ethical and possibly criminal behavior have played a defining role.

Paradoxically, the president has simultaneously enjoyed strong public approval for his performance in office. His approval ratings rarely broke 45% before the 1994 election, one which resulted in huge Democratic losses. Thereafter, faced with the enforced bipartisanship of a Republican majority in both houses of Congress, his poll numbers began to rise. By July of 1995, stimulated in part by a massive "issue ad" campaign conducted away from major northeastern metropolitan markets,[2] the president's approval ratings broke 50%, held and rose.

So, while a majority (53%) of the public believe that the president lied when he said he had no sexual relationship with 21-year-old White House intern Monica Lewinsky, most (60%) thought it not an important matter, and 65% wanted him to remain in office even if he did.[3] After Kathleen E.Willey appeared on *60 Minutes* and described in graphic language the president's crude behavior toward her, his job approval rating rose four points to 67%.[4]

CHARACTER ABOVE ALL? OR, CHARACTER PERMEATES ALL?

In a book of essays on modern presidents entitled *Character Above All*,[5] ten well-known presidential biographers argue that a president's character ultimately trumps his politics and policies. However, if character is narrowly equated with consensual sex outside of marriage, or even lapses in sexual impulse control which lead to an unwanted sexual advance, this view is not widely shared by the American public. Nor, apparently, are Americans willing to put aside their satisfaction with economic success[6] in order to make stern judgments about these matters.[7]

So, is it true then that a president's personal life, and the psychology it reflects, has no bearing on his presidency? In a word, no. Still, if character above all doesn't describe the relationship between a president and the office, or to the American public, what does? *High Hopes* attempts to provide an answer. It views character not as a president's supreme virtue (or failing), but rather as a set of psychological patterns that he brings to every circumstance. Character, from this perspective, is the answer to the question of how we can best understand a president's, or any person's psychology. It is the foundation of one's stance toward the world. It reflects the fundamental elements at the core of a person—their basic ambitions, the ideals and values they live by, and their relationships with others.

Although character runs deep, knowledge of it doesn't necessarily require "couch questions." We get to know a person's character in the presidency, as in ordinary life, by paying attention to the steady accumulation of choices we see them make, both in and away from the public spotlight. Character is reflected as much in a president's observable behavior as it is in the deepest recesses of his psyche. All that is needed is some knowledge of where to look and how to understand what you see.

The public evidence regarding Bill Clinton's character after an adulthood in public life is fairly clear. He is a man of enormous ambitions. There is nothing inherently wrong with having ambition, even lots of it. It is the lifeblood of achievement and no modern president has been without ample amounts of it. The problems with this president's ambition do not lie in its quantity.

He is also amply endowed with the talents and skills that realize ambition. He is extremely charming and intelligent, enormously resilient, and a loquacious but eloquent advocate of his views. Yet, it cannot be emphasized too strongly that a president's skills and talents, as substantial as they might be, are embedded in, and not independent of, his interior psychology. They do not exist independently of his character structure and overall psychology—his ambitions, ideals, and connections with others.

Neither ambition nor the talents which support it can be understood without asking to what purposes they are put. To answer this central question we must look to the ideals and values that guide a president, and when they do so. We must not be misled by what presidents say of their lofty ideals. Rather, it is the ability to maintain fidelity to their ideals when to do so risks personal or political losses that defines character integrity. In short, for a president to have the courage of his convictions, he must have both.

Character integrity helps to answer a central question about presidential ambition. How can we distinguish between dangerous and necessary ambition? Ambition is dangerous when it is unguided by ideals and values and the capacity to be faithful to them. And, alternatively, the dangers of ambition are defused when firmly guided by ideals, a strong sense of values, and the willingness to stick with them through adversity. Indeed, the larger the ambition, the more consolidated a president's ideals and values must be in order to anchor it.

The question, simply put, is this: Is the president's ambition in the service of his ideals, or are his ideals subservient to his ambitions? This is the great linchpin of character that has eluded Bill Clinton in his public and private life. Even those who worked most intimately with him have failed to discern what, beyond his own self or political interest, he is willing to stand fast for and in doing so accept his limits and his losses. George Stephanopoulos told Elizabeth Drew that he was "unable to discern the real Clinton," and later referred to him as a "kaleidoscope, where what you see is where you stand." "It was real," he continued, "but it could change in an instant, as soon as Clinton turned." Of course, a deeply held set of ideals and values can't "change in an instant." If they are a core part of a person, they will not be dependent on perspective and favorable or unfavorable political views will have difficulty distorting them. Even the president's most rabid advocates have wondered about his real commitments. James Carville told Bob Woodward that he once took out a piece of paper, drew a square and began tapping his pencil and asking, "Where is the hallowed ground . . . where does he stand?"

THE PRESIDENT'S POLITICS

The public, understandably, has even less grounds for being clear. Mr. Clinton ran for office promising to be a "New Democrat," but upon being elected, reneged and governed like an old one. After the direction of his administration was overwhelmingly repudiated in 1994, he survived by temporarily borrowing the policies and premises of his opponents. In 1996 he won reelection by promising, again, to govern from the political center.

Yet, his 1996 State of the Union Address, in which the president announced that "the era of big government is over," contained a substantial list of new government initiatives for his second term. He has been adding to them ever since. His 1998 State of the Union Address continued this trend by proposing a large expansion of government responsibility for areas traditionally taken care of by the states including regulating private health insurance and the nation's child care arrangements (cost, over $20 billion over five years).[8]

His 1998 State of the Union speech was, however, more than another new and expanded list of Clinton administration initiatives, itself a reflection of the president's most elemental governing impulses. It was the key to solidifying his job approval ratings and providing the public with reasons other than the economy to worry about changing presidents in midterm. If his presidency endures, this speech will have played a critical role in shoring it up.

The speech took place amidst swirling sexual accusations about the president and a former intern. Americans, ordinarily not highly attentive to political speeches, were this time. Nielson Media Research estimated that the speech reached 36.5 million homes and over 53 million viewers. *The Washington Post* estimated an audience of over 75 million viewers. Of all of this president's State of the Union speeches only his first one in 1993 exceeded these figures.[9]

And what did Americans hear? The deficit? Gone. A balanced budget? Here earlier than expected. The problems with social security? The surplus will be pledged to fix it. Small wonder that before the speech Mr. Clinton's approval rate stood at 59%, and afterward rose to 67%. Nor is it surprising that before the speech 44% of the public thought the country was heading in the right direction; afterwards 61% did.[10]

So, policies do trump character after all, right? No, not really.

Character *in* Presidential Leadership

Mr. Clinton is not the first president to take full credit for any good that happens during his term, whether he is wholly responsible or not. Nor is he the first to be given public credit for accomplishments only partially his.

High Hopes argues that there were no countervailing forces within the president's psychology, and few in his administration, for the political restraint of his ambitions. Therefore, paradoxically, the best hope for his presidency was a Republican Congress. And it has been the post-1994 Republican Congress that has played a critical role in reducing spending and in balancing the budget, both of which were instrumental in America's economic buoyancy, and in insuring smaller, more moderate policy initiatives. President Clinton has become a policy-moderate by political necessity, not by personal inclination.

The fact that a Republican Congress has restrained this president's psychology does not disprove that character counts. It underscores it. And with this president, examples of the importance of character in leadership are never hard to find. Consider the president's State of the Union pledge to "reserve 100% of the surplus—that's every penny of any surplus—until we have taken all the measures necessary to strengthen the social security system for the twenty-first century."[11] Seventy-five percent of the public thought this a good idea. Yet, in reality, the president's words were deceptive.

Administration officials later testified that "reserving" the surplus didn't actually mean putting it into the Social Security Trust Fund. Moreover, in using the word "any" to modify surplus, Mr. Clinton neglected to make clear that a surplus is what's left if revenues exceed spending, and that the many new administration initiatives would help to place social security last in the budget process, not first. Not mentioned either was that administration plans for new spending exceed by $40 billion the 1990 budget caps which were themselves the basis the Congressional Budget Office's optimistic predictions of a surplus. At first, the new spending is less than revenues, but after 2001 when the full impact of the president's proposals are realized, the new spending would be more than the added revenue, leaving no "surplus." And, finally, there are the administration's plans for new taxes—on cigarettes, high-income individuals, and corporations. Since they have not yet been formally proposed, they are not counted in the budget estimates, thus enabling the president to propose spending these revenues while at the same time claiming that he is not spending any of the (currently projected) "surplus."[12]

One is reminded here of Mr. Clinton's promise in the 1992 campaign not to raise taxes on the middle class to "pay for my programs," and then doing so by relying on the sly distinction between tax increases that were specifically targeted for new programs and increases that would just add to government revenues and indirectly fund new programs. Indeed, as Chris Bury of NBC's *Nightline* put it, "Mr. Clinton has a rich history of extraordinarily careful answers, splitting semantical hairs and avoiding the question that is asked." When asked about using drugs, Mr. Clinton replied, "I've never broken the state law and . . . when I was in England, I experimented with marijuana a time or two and I didn't like it and didn't inhale and never tried it again." When asked whether he tried to avoid military service, he replied, very incompletely, and misleadingly as it turned out, "I was against the Vietnam War, but I gave up a deferment and put myself back into the draft." When asked whether the Clintons got a sweetheart deal on their Whitewater land purchase, he replied, again misleadingly, "It turned out to be a bad investment and we lost what was for us a lot of money."[13]

So, not surprisingly, when asked by Jim Lehrer about his relationship with the young intern, to which he replied, "There is no improper relationship," questions immediately arose about the meaning of the word "improper," and his choice of tense. And when the president absolutely denied having a sexual relationship with Ms. Lewinsky, many wondered whether he believed that oral sex didn't count.

What does it mean that Americans are required to carefully scrutinize, to parse, each presidential explanation or denial, without ever being certain that the words he uses have any shared meaning? What can we say of a president who looks the public directly in the eye, enlists his wife to bolster his deceit, and then flatly denies what he has now confessed to in the semi-privacy of sealed court testimony: that Gennifer Flowers was telling the truth, and he wasn't.

Well, one thing we can say is that his famous empathy and charm have not kept him from trying to deceive the public who, as citizens, depend on his candor. The president's defenders have argued that any sexual allegations are irrelevant to his performance and insist on a distinction between his private, very human failings, and his public virtues. The fatal, and unbridgeable, flaw in this argument is the insupportable assumption that he has been any more honest with the public in his policy dealings than he has been in explaining his personal behavior:

- Was it honest to mislead the public about a then nonexistent health care crisis of a world-class medical system, albeit one with pockets of problems?
- Was it forthright to design a solution behind illegally closed doors, "regional alliances," that were consciously designed to mask a wholesale federalization of the health care system?
- Was it straightforward to promise that we would send troops to Bosnia for only one year?
- Was it sincere when, after his reelection, he changed this policy to say that he had not prepared the American people for this shift, which had been planned for some time, because the public already knew about it as he had mentioned it once, in passing?
- Was it candid to promise a real dialogue on race that from its inception was crafted to exclude and marginalize those who disagree with him?

In so many cases, personal and political, this president has camouflaged, misdirected, failed to fully respond to the question asked, concealed or otherwise obscured his purposes and knowledge. Mr. Clinton's personal and public behavior argues strongly against the idea that you can separate a president's character and psychology from the ways he chooses to address his public responsibilities.

No Damage?

The president's advocates point with undisguised glee to the dismissal of a Paula Jones suit and with great relief to the president's still high approval ratings. However, the president's high approval ratings do not extend to him personally.[14] For example, a majority of Americans do not believe the president's denials about Ms. Lewinsky any more than they believed his explanation that a "bureaucratic error" was responsible for explaining how a longtime Democratic Party political operative wound up with sensitive FBI files on Republican leaders. Only a quarter of the American public believe him to be a man of high personal and moral standards, while a Yankelovich Partners poll in mid-January 1998 thought that only 37% of the public found Mr. Clinton "a leader you can trust." Still, his advocates are now convinced that the president, though wounded, will survive—and he may. But he has lost much, and we have lost more.

Some have argued that Americans no longer look to, or expect, the president to provide moral leadership, but rather ask in essence, can he fix the sink?[15] This new view of the president as plumber-in-chief is said to be a reflection of public sophistication. It could as well reflect public cynicism and the loss of hope for anything better.

Historically, moral leadership in the presidency and the character integrity that underlies and supports it, has played an enormous role in American public life. A president, or administration, whose moral authority has been sapped by dishonesty cannot speak legitimately or authoritatively on the many matters that count. What practical difference does this make? Consider the credibility of Lyndon Johnson's presidency during and after Vietnam, or Richard Nixon's during and after Watergate. Ask Mr. Clinton's national security advisors who ran into substantial and fiery public skepticism in Ohio while giving somewhat facile explanations of administration policy toward Iraq.[16] Or, consider the fate of Hillary Clinton's not inaccurate observation that the content of television advertising is helping to undermine the ethic of delayed gratification that sustains capitalism and democracy. In response, someone publicly asked whether, "she'd be willing to show she's not really a hypocrite and donate her $100,000 commodities profit to charity."[17]

But the costs of dishonesty are found not only in the substantial diminishing of this president's ability to achieve his goals or promote his policies.[18] They are found in the erosion of public trust, the psychological cement of democracy. In 1958, six years into Eisenhower's presidency, the number of Americans who believed they could trust the government to do what's right stood at a now astounding 75%. However, starting with 1964, years of presidential carelessness with the truth or less than sparkling performance caused that key index to take a nosedive, from which it has not, with one exception—the presidency of Ronald Reagan—ever recovered, even partially.

High Hopes argues that this basic public dilemma, the decline of public trust and confidence in government was the single most important policy issue that Bill Clinton faced. When Bill Clinton assumed office the number of Americans who trusted the government to do what's right was down to a bare 23%. Two years later, it had declined further to about 18%. Mr. Clinton's solid approval ratings have done little to elevate these dismal levels of public trust in the face of continuing personal and political scandal.

PRESIDENT CLINTON'S LEGACY

The President has been much concerned with his public legacy and place in history. Frustrated by the public and later by the Republican Congress they elected to check him, he has been denied the chance to create grand policy monuments to his own ambitions. However, our best presidents are not remembered primarily for the number and expansiveness of their programs. Who remembers George Washington's policy initiatives, or thinks that FDR's greatness lies in the creation of big government?[19] These, and other modern presidents—Harry Truman, Dwight Eisenhower, and Ronald Reagan come to mind—are well regarded historically for one of two primary reasons: Either, like Washington, Truman, and Eisenhower, they exemplified in their conduct an honesty and a steady, competent reliability that made them trustworthy anchors during turbulent political times; or, like Roosevelt in response to the Depression, or Reagan in response to widespread public malaise, they were able through the force and example of their characters to help change the political climate—for Roosevelt from despair to optimism, for Reagan from alienation to confidence.

President Clinton will not be recalled as having accomplished either. He will be recalled most as a president who presided during a prosperous period, and perhaps, if people forget the role that the Republican Party and his reelection needs played, as the president who transformed welfare. In foreign policy, the successful risks he took to help start the Irish peace process must be balanced against the decidedly mixed results and legacy of admin-istration policy in Haiti, Somalia, Rwanda, Bosnia, Iraq, and his pressure on Israel for ever more concessions to achieve "peace."

The tragedy of this president is not to be found in the latest sex scandal. It is that his promise to be a "New Democrat" correctly reflected what the country desperately needed—policies that were fair across the board, and *not* only to those who supported the Democratic Party; smaller targeted policies that solved old problems without creating new ones; and a presi-dent who could and would honestly explain his thinking in ways the pub-lic could understand and support. Those promises were discarded at the beginning of Mr. Clinton's presidency.

Mr. Clinton will be remembered as being a supremely astute politician, but a man whose personal psychology both fostered and indelibly stained his presidency. His untempered ambition for large governmental policy monuments, a reflection of his own highly self-confident view of what's best, ran counter to the public's mistrust of such grand designs. Faced with this dilemma, Mr. Clinton attempted to finesse the public's reticence by masking his intentions. He will also be remembered for managing to remain in office through many scandals by a combination of guile, deter-mination, and the benefits of public cynicism which he was instrumental in propagating. Looking out for number one may be advantageous, but it is not publicly inspiring. Worse, it breeds cynicism and destroys hope.

NOTES

1. In Barry Levinson's biting satire, *Wag the Dog*, the president has a problem. He has been accused of fondling a young campfire girl, part of a visiting group delegation, in the privacy of the Oval Office. Faced with a meltdown of his campaign for a second term (his rival runs com-mercials to the tune of "Thank Heaven for Little Girls"), the president does what any modern president would (and the one currently in office has)—he calls in his fixers and spin doctors. In an opening scene that is astounding in its prescience, Stanley Motss (Dustin Hoffman), recruit-ed from Hollywood to help rescue the president, walks past a large cardboard picture of the president greeting adoring crowds. In the pic-ture, very clearly visible, is the darkhaired "campfire girl" who later found herself in the Oval Office. She is wearing a jaunty beret and smil-ing admiringly at the president—a picture eerily parallel to the one of

Monica Lewinsky admiring President Clinton that graced the cover of *Newsweek* and numerous other news outlets. Nor do the uncanny parallels stop here. What is the one event guaranteed to turn the public's attention away from presidential fondling, asks Hollywood consultant Motss. The answer: A war, with Albania. Why Albania? Why not, answers Conrad Bean (Robert De Niro), the president's chief fixer. Besides, the war will be produced solely for television—a fake Albanian battle scene, an inspirational "We Are the World" type song specifically concocted to arouse public patriotism and, of course, a fake war hero. Wicked satire, you say, until you realize that, as the movie was being screened, President Clinton, in the midst of his own unfolding "campfire" scandal, was considering launching a war against Iraq. Clinton aides publicly fretted about the effect of this coincidence on the president's ability to rally the public, should war be necessary. Saddam Hussein insisted that the only reason for the president to attack would be to divert attention from his personal troubles, and showed a bootleg copy of the movie on Iraqi television. And *The Wall Street Journal* argued that the president should ignore both, and attack. See Janet Maslin, "'Wag the Dog': If the Going Gets Tough, Get a Pet or Start a War," *The New York Times*, 26 December 1997, B10; Bernard Weintraub, "A Prequel? Wag the Tongue," *The New York Times*, 30 January 1998, E10; Paul A. Gigot, "War Is Hell if Nobody Believes You," *The Wall Street Journal*, 20 February 1998, A18; Frank Rich, "Dying in Columbus," *The New York Times*, 21 February 1998, A22; editorial, "When Character Matters," *The Wall Street Journal*, 27 January 1998, A22.

2. Dick Morris, *Behind the Oval Office: Winning the Presidency in the Nineties* (New York: Random House, 1997).

3. *The Washington Post*, "1998 State of the Union Poll Results," 1 February 1998. Tracking polls of the president's approval ratings, and responses to specific aspects of the allegations against the president can be found at http://www.washingtonpost.com/wp-srv/politics/polls/polls.htm.

4. Donald Lambro, "Latest Charges Don't Damage President's Poll Numbers," *The Washington Times*, 18 March 1998, A1.

5. Robert A. Wilson, ed., *Character Above All* (New York: Simon and Schuster, 1995). For a review of issues raised, and lessons learned, in examining the ten presidents treated therein, see Stanley A. Renshon, "Review of Robert A. Wilson's *Character Above All: Ten Presidents*

from FDR to George Bush," in *Presidential Studies Quarterly*, 26:2, pp. 606–09.

6. Dan Barry and Jennifer Preston, "Clinton Finds Support in a Town's Prosperity," *The New York Times*, 26 February 1998, A18; Richard Morin and Claudia Deane, "Poll Shows Americans More Satisfied with U.S.," *The Washington Post*, 21 January 1998, A6.

7. This does not seem to apply, however, to allegations of lying under oath or suborning perjury, if proved. When asked whether they would want Clinton to remain in office as president if he did tell someone to lie in a legal document, 54% said no. When asked whether Clinton should remain in office if he himself lied by testifying under oath that he did not have an affair with the woman, 53% said no. And, finally, when asked which was more important—the allegation that Clinton had an affair with a 21-year-old intern, or the allegation that Clinton had lied under oath about this relationship—82% said that lying under oath was more important. See "1998 State of the Union Poll Results," *The Washington Post*, 1 February 1998.

8. William J. Clinton, "Address before a Joint Session of Congress on the State of the Union (January 27, 1998)," *Weekly Compilation of Presidential Documents*, 2 February 1998, 34:5, pp. 129–39. See also Robert Pear and Adam Nagourney, "White House Concedes Voter Appeal of Agenda," *The New York Times*, 29 January 1998, A15.

9. "Clinton's Troubles Built TV Ratings," *The New York Times*, 29 January 1998, A19; Richard Morin, "How Clinton Confounded the Polls," *The Washington Post*, 8 February 1998, C04.

10. *The Washington Post* poll found a seventeen-point jump (from 44% to 61%) in the number of people who thought the country was going in the right direction, after the speech was given. See "1998 State of the Union Poll Results," *The Washington Post*, 1 February 1998. See also Richard Morin, "How Clinton Confounded the Polls," *The Washington Post*, 8 February 1998, C04.

11. William J. Clinton, "Address before a Joint Session of Congress on the State of the Union (January 27, 1998)," *Weekly Compilation of Presidential Documents*, 2 February 1998, 34:5, pp. 129–39; p.131.

12. On these and related points, see John F. Cogan, "Social Security and Abracadabras," *The New York Times*, 18 February 1998, A20; Martin Feldstein, "Let's Really Save Social Security," *The Wall Street Journal*, 10 February 1998, A18; Paul A. Gigot, "How to Beat Clinton at His

Own Game," *The Wall Street Journal*, 6 February 1998, A23.

13. Transcript, *ABC Nightline*, Report on the Clinton Crisis, 23 January 1998.
14. The data which follows is drawn from Dan Baltz, "Willey's Story Gets a Shrug from Public," *The Washington Post*, 19 March 1998, A01; Everett Carll Ladd, "Nixon, Clinton, and the Polls," *The Wall Street Journal*, 1 April 1998, A18; Richard Morin and Dan Baltz, "Bad News Travels Fast," *The Washington Post, Weekly Edition*, 8–14 July 1996, p. 14.
15. See, for example, Dennis Farney, "Clinton's Support Remains Strong Because Voters View Him as Successful CEO, Not Moral Example," *The Wall Street Journal*, 6 February 1998, A24.
16. See Steven Erlanger, "Top Clinton Aides Find Doubt on Iraq at Campus in Ohio," *The New York Times*, 9 February 1998, A1; Robert S. Greensberger, "Clinton's Iraq Stance Draws Hostility in Ohio," *The Wall Street Journal*, 9 February 1998, A2; transcript, "War of Words: The Administration, Its Critics and Questions of Moral Right," *The New York Times*, 19 February 1998, A9.
17. Kim Weissman, "Testing Mrs. Clinton: Letter to the Editor," *The New York Times*, 16 February 1998, wk15.
18. Observers on both sides of the political spectrum have commented on the effect of the loss of the president's authority on his policy agenda. See Paul A. Gigot, "Scandal's Price," *The Wall Street Journal*, 1 May 1998, A14; Frank Rich, "Lame Lame Duck," *The New York Times*, 29 April 1998, A25.
19. Arthur Schlesinger, Jr., a distinguished liberal historian, argues that it was not bigness but experimentation that made Roosevelt a great president. See his "The Real Roosevelt Legacy," *Newsweek*, 14 October 1996, p. 43.

★ ————————————————————————————————

PREFACE

A president's personal strengths and limitations are the foundation of what he will accomplish in office. His ambitions, ideals, and sense of who he is and where he wants to lead all matter enormously for the direction and effectiveness of his presidential leadership. The presidency is clearly an office where psychology counts.

It counts all the more in Bill Clinton's case because his presidency spans a critical period in American and world history. The Cold War is over. Yet, Americans face daunting economic and social problems and are increasingly divided about how to address them. Many Americans were hopeful that Bill Clinton would resolve these divisions. He is an engaging man and a talented politician. But Clinton has emerged as a president of extremes, combining immense personal and political flaws. Not surprisingly, his presidency has been characterized by substantial accomplishments and equally substantial difficulties. This pattern has followed Clinton throughout his public life.

Political analysts are deeply divided about his presidency, as is the public. Many admire him. He is clearly smart, is knowledgeable about the nuances of many aspects of domestic policy, and has focused on and tried to resolve long-standing public problems like health care. He is determined to leave his personal and political imprint, and has proposed the most ambitious schedule of policy initiatives in thirty years. Indeed, Clinton may be the most ambitious and knowledgeable president in the last two decades.

Yet he is also widely distrusted and in some quarters vehemently disliked. Such widely divergent feelings toward a political leader are uncommon. Only Richard Nixon—whom, in some interesting ways, Clinton resembles—generated such passionate and diverse feelings. Clinton is, and is likely to remain, a controversial president.

There are also puzzling contradictions in his presidential accomplishments, and in the public's response to them. In the first three years of his presidency he accomplished a substantial amount. Yet voters overwhelmingly repudiated his leadership, and his party, in the 1994 midterm elections. Many question whether he can be reelected and, if he is, whether he will be able to accomplish many of his goals. Even if he is reelected, Clinton may ultimately be judged to have failed as a president and leader. Such intensely divergent evaluations of a president whose administration is unfolding during such a critical period in our history, coupled with the apparent contradictions in his character and personality, make understanding this complex, controversial man all the more important.

These strong and conflicting popular views have limited what we understand about Clinton and his approach to political leadership and social policy. For a man who has been in elected public office almost all of his adult life, there is surprisingly little understanding of the forces that have shaped him, and certainly no consensus about his accomplishments.

Like other presidents before him, Clinton has supplied a number of details about his life and career. However, presidents' views of their own development are not necessarily the most reliable guide to understanding them. Reporters and other analysts covering the Clinton presidency have tended to focus on particular policy victories or setbacks. Did the budget and NAFTA pass? Did President Clinton backtrack on his commitments to Haiti or to reform military policy toward homosexuals? Will he manage to gain reelection after the sweeping midterm election successes of the Republicans in 1994? While each of these issues is important, focusing on discrete issues in terms of winning or losing obscures the patterns underlying presidential performance.

This book steps away from the day-to-day scorecard analyses and places Clinton's performance in a broader context. My goal is to examine Bill Clinton's psychology—and how it developed—and to trace its influence on his approach to presidential leadership. I do so by drawing on theories of political leadership and psychology. More specifically, I make use of psychological theories of character and personality, theories of presidential leadership and performance, and theories of public psychology.

A psychologically framed analysis of Bill Clinton and his presidency will not resolve every question raised by his performance. But neither can his puzzling contradictions, his missteps, and his accomplishments be fully understood without it.

★ ——

ACKNOWLEDGMENTS

In the effort to clarify and refine my analysis, to address and where possible integrate the various strands of evidence, and to develop frameworks that do them and the questions asked of them justice, I have benefited enormously from the help of many others.

I would like to thank the following people who have read and commented, sometimes more than once, on successive versions of this book. My sincere thanks to John Fiscalini, Lloyd Etheredge, Alexander L. George, Fred I. Greenstein, Edwin P. Hollinder, Bruce Mazlish, Jerrold M. Post, William McKinley Runyan, Peter Suedfeld, Sheldon Zalkind, and Stephen J. Wayne, Their comments, questions, and disagreements have been most helpful.

I was also very fortunate to have had the stimulation and excellent theoretical observations afforded by two doctoral seminars I recently taught on the presidency at the City University Graduate Center, one specifically on the Clinton presidency and the other on the modern presidency. I would like to thank the students in those classes, and especially Beth Brofee, Dan Cook, Robert Geary, Tom Kono, and Andrew Sway.

I presented this work in several contexts as it evolved. I would like to single out for special mention my colleagues at the Training and Research Institute for Self Psychology (TRISP), especially Harry Paul, Doris Brothers, and Richard Ulman. They were helpful in refining my thinking regarding ambition, idealization, and the object relations implications of the theory of character presented herein.

I had a number of opportunities to present and discuss my work on the Clinton presidency during a sabbatical spent as a Visiting Fellow at the John F. Kennedy School of Government, Harvard University during the 1995 academic year and wish to acknowledge, with appreciation, that opportunity. Dean Alan Altschuler helpfully facilitated my time there. While at the Kennedy School, I was associated with the Leadership Development Project directed by Ronald Heifetz, M.D., from whom I learned a great deal about that subject.

Several graduate students assisted me in the development of this book. I would like to thank Suzanne DiMaggio, Jasmine Farrier, and Ann E. Zemaitis for their diligent research and retrieval skills.

This work was also supported by two grants to the author from the City University Faculty Research Award Program. I am very appreciative of the help those grants provided in conducting my research.

Charlotte Sheedy, my literary agent, encouraged me and this work, and I am very appreciative of her confidence in both.

Niko Pfund, editor in chief at New York University Press, was extremely supportive of this project. His skillful suggestions and collaborative working style make him an author's true friend. I thank him. Despina Papazoglou Gimbel, managing editor at the press, supervised the copyediting and production of the book with attention, care, and dispatch. The copyeditor, David Updike, did a superb job of copyediting the manuscript.

My family, Judith, David, and Jonathan, have been the sustaining force and the great pleasure of my life. Their support was my constant companion throughout my writing.

Finally, but centrally, I would like to thank my wife Judith, whose sharp editorial eye and equally sharp logical mind were immeasurably important to this work.

INTRODUCTION

This book's title, *High Hopes,* refers to the public's investment in the success of the Clinton presidency, an investment borne of increasing anxiety and mounting frustration with the American political process in the last few decades. A *New York Times*/CBS News poll taken just before Clinton's inauguration suggested that "Americans await Bill Clinton's presidency with revived optimism about the nation and its economy and a pre-inaugural burst of confidence in him as an effective leader who cares about them" (Clymer 1993b). The phrase "high hopes" refers as well to Clinton's own ambitions, and reminds us that presidential leadership is, in reality, a triangular relationship consisting of the president, the public, and the problems they both face and wish to resolve.[1]

In the subtitle, "the Clinton presidency" refers both to the man, Bill Clinton, and the institution he occupies. Each presidency unfolds in an institutional setting whose history, development, and resources require consideration on their own grounds, as well as for their effects on the particular person who occupies the office. This broadened concept of the Clinton presidency is an important vehicle for analyzing Clinton's ability and success in using the powers, and addressing the responsibilities of the office.[2]

The phrase "politics of ambition" reflects a key element of any modern president's psychology, but one especially prominent in Clinton's character. Yet character, however conspicuous, gains its importance not so much from

1

its prominence as from its effects. Hence, the term "politics of ambition" reflects not only the importance of ambition per se, but its direct relationship to the carrying out of presidential responsibilities.

The Clinton administration is a presidency of many words. Much has been said by the president himself about his policies, his leadership, and his prospects. Much more has been said by others on these same subjects, including, at the end of the first term of his presidency, a substantial number of books, some of which are quite good. Any author or reader must therefore ask: Why another study of President Clinton and his administration? What rationale is there for one specifically framed by the theories of political psychology?

Given the office's growing responsibilities, vast resources, and central location in governance and public decision-making, every modern presidency is consequential. However, some presidents, because of the particular historical period in which they seek and gain office, face a particularly striking range of opportunities and challenges. Their presidencies unfold in particularly acute historical times, domestically, internationally, or, on rare occasions, both. The Clinton presidency is just such a presidency.

Clinton's is the first presidency to fully unfold in the post-Cold-War period. The competitive, hostile Cold-War rivalry between the Soviet Union and the United States no longer dominates and structures international politics. However, no comparable set of dominant relationships in the international system has emerged to take its place. The role of the United States in this emerging context is, as yet, unclear. So are the rules of engagement and the circumstances in which it is necessary to become involved. Every action, or decision not to act, therefore, runs the risk of becoming a premature or inappropriate precedent.

In the domestic arena, the Clinton presidency is also unfolding at a time of great political uncertainty and conflict. The institution of the presidency itself has been attacked both as overreaching and imperial (Schlesinger 1973) and as ineffective, its powers and potential unrealized (Lowi 1984). Of the six presidents who occupied the White House between John F. Kennedy's assassination and Bill Clinton's inauguration, four (Johnson, Ford, Carter, and Bush) were unable to gain another term, and one (Nixon) gained another term but was forced to resign. Clinton, as the 1994 midterm elections made clear, is in danger of becoming the sixth of seven presidents who have failed to accomplish this limited reflection of adequate presidential performance.

Public identification with the major parties has continued to decline, as the rise of a serious third party challenge in 1992 underscored. Rather than fading away, Ross Perot and his followers continue to play an important public role. Speculation about third party candidates in the 1996 presidential campaign, such as Senator Bill Bradley or retired General Colin Powell, whose "character—solidity, strength, effectiveness—is his main selling point" (Gates 1995, 77), reflect, even as they further encourage, an unstable political climate.

Moreover, confidence in the government's ability to resolve public problems has declined, as has the public's faith in its political institutions. The major political frameworks on which public consensus has traditionally rested now give every appearance of having irreparably broken down. The question is, What will take their place?

The times are right for the presidential politics of reconstruction (Skowronek 1993, 36). The 1992 presidential campaign revealed "a deep yearning for charismatic leadership . . . in substantial parts of the American populace" (Mazlish 1994, 751). Such a situation is full of opportunity for an ambitious, smart president like Bill Clinton. But it also contains a number of dangers, not the least of which is having to both lead and govern a suspicious and volatile public. The opportunities for Clinton to forge a new political framework are matched only by the consequences if he fails to do so.

WHY A POLITICAL PSYCHOLOGY STUDY OF PRESIDENT CLINTON?

I have already suggested why a study of the Clinton presidency is important. But why is an analysis specifically framed by the theories and perspectives of political psychology useful? The reasons are to be found in the nature of the office and the man who occupies it.

Clinton is a man who evokes strong feelings, both for and against him. He is also a man whose inconsistencies have profoundly puzzled reporters, pundits, and academics alike. Thus far, there has been little theory to guide us in making sense of these contradictions. Much of what is puzzling about Clinton "stems from inner complexities that do not figure in . . . any classification" (Greenstein 1993–94, 597). In this study I seek to provide just such a theory, one that looks at Bill Clinton's character from the perspectives of ambition, integrity, and his relationships with others.

Character and psychology are important in shaping presidential performance, including the president's responses to particular circumstances. The purpose of a psychologically informed analysis, however, is not to prove that character or presidential psychology explains everything. It will rarely do that in any event. Rather, the challenge of such an analytical focus is to specify what psychological aspects of functioning affect which aspects of presidential performance, and to further clarify the circumstances under which they do so.[3]

Character is a vertical as well as a horizontal psychological concept. That is, the effects of character are evident throughout an individual's psychological functioning. Character is found not only in the deepest recesses of an individual's psyche, but in the everyday world of accessible and observable behavior. A president's ambition, sense of who he is (identity), the level and means by which his ambition manifests itself, and how he organizes his interpersonal relationships are often plainly evident, even to untrained observers.

In examining Bill Clinton's character and its relation to his performance as president, I do not assume that the latter is reducible to the former or that psychological factors are determinative. Clinton's character and psychology do shape his presidency; however, both are mediated through a number of important filters, including his beliefs, his political and personal skills, and the political calculus of the circumstances he must confront.

This last item is crucial. No president operates in a psychological vacuum. He must contend with the conditions he faces. A president's understanding of and response to the circumstances he inherits or makes provide important opportunities to better understand his psychology. Most presidents try to shape or respond selectively to circumstances in order to accomplish their purposes. This presents the president, as it would any person, with a range of possible ways to act. By examining the range of choices available to the president as well as those he selects, both within and across circumstances, one can begin to discern the underlying patterns of psychology that shape his behavior. Such an examination of Clinton's responses is thus an important part of this book.

PSYCHOLOGY IN THE PRESIDENCY

No president controls all the forces he faces, which has led some to question whether any president can be a true "event-making" man.[4] However, the importance of a president's character, judgment, and leadership does not rest on any "great man" theory of presidential impact. A president does not have to change history in order for his presidency to have consequences.

The presidency has become a highly developed and institutionalized fulcrum of governmental activity. It is the combination of public expectation and the vast resources and sophisticated governmental procedures under the president's command that have institutionalized presidential impact, not the greatness of the men who have occupied this position.

The presidency is an office in which the individual psychology of its occupants, their personal strengths and limitations, has a pronounced effect.[5] Some presidents seek more power; others are satisfied with less. Some presidents are skillful in exercising the powers of their office and making use of the leadership resources available to them; others are less able. Some, like Clinton, appear to combine both tendencies.

The importance of a president's psychology is augmented by the fact that few presidential behaviors are formally mandated. The more general descriptions of the president as commander-in-chief, titular head of his political party, or, more recently, as "interpreter-in-chief" (Stuckey 1991) describe role *constructions* that leave a great deal of personal leeway to a president as to whether, to what extent, and how he chooses (or is able) to carry them out. Moreover, the fact that Clinton's presidency is unfolding in the midst of complex and uncharted shifts in domestic and international circumstances oblige us to consider his psychology more seriously. Contextual ambiguity and a lack of clear norms increase the importance of a leader's psychological attributes (Greenstein 1969, 50–51).

Few circumstances that a president faces dictate one, and only one, response. Even among narrowly constrained options, a president's choices make a difference. These choices ultimately rest on the man—his vision, convictions, and ideals. The adequacy of his choices rest on the powers of his social and political analysis and, ultimately, on the quality of his judgment. His ability to translate his choices into policies rest on his political skills—his capacities to mobilize, orchestrate, and consolidate public acceptance of his views of what needs to be done. Ultimately, his ability to lead and govern rest on his ambitions, courage, and integrity. In short, a president's capacity to shape circumstances, even those he has inherited, into opportunity, and opportunity into accomplishment, is powerfully affected, though not fully determined, by his psychology.

CLINTON'S CHALLENGES

On gaining office President Clinton faced a substantial array of problems. In foreign affairs the basic question is how exactly the United States should view and respond to its responsibilities and interests in a paradoxical environment where it is the remaining superpower in an increasingly interdependent world. Domestically, the question is whether, and on what basis, government can effectively carry out its responsibilities when its very legitimacy to do so is in public doubt, and when its traditional solutions to social problems have not worked.

Each of these issues is enormously complex and important. Together they represent the most profound set of challenges to a president since Franklin Delano Roosevelt, and even Roosevelt had to deal *first* with an economy in severe decline, and only later with the gathering storm of European fascism that resulted in World War II.

President Clinton faces extraordinary challenges in both areas at the same time. Even under less trying circumstances, the modern presidency requires of its occupants strong, well-refined political skills, a temperament able to deal effectively with the frustrations and demands of the office, and a strong characterological foundation for the psychological resources that he brings to bear on his presidential responsibilities. Times of great challenge require of a president that he have more, not less, of these characteristics. Exceptional challenges require of presidents who come to office during those periods exceptional attributes.

The question before us, therefore, is not whether Clinton's psychology affects his presidential performance. It undoubtedly does, but, as I will show, that in itself is only the first step in answering two more compelling questions: Does President Clinton possess the requisite qualities of political judgment, vision, character, and skill to meet the daunting challenges he faces both domestically and internationally? And if he has these qualities, does he also have the capacity to utilize them?

A MAN OF PUZZLING CONTRADICTIONS

These questions are not as paradoxical as they might first appear. Clinton is a man of enormous appetites—for information, for attention, for food, for activity. Consider two of Clinton's "most frequently uttered words":

> What else. What else. What else. He was always working the telephone in search of outside information. . . . Clinton wanted the latest reading on Clinton's political futures, up or down. . . . He was a young man of oversized appetites. Any aide who spent time with him could tell stories of his inhaling apples in a few massive bites, swallowing them core and all.

Hot dogs went down so fast they barely touched his teeth . . . what else. What else. What else. (Maraniss 1995, 383)

Clinton's appetites made him an exciting man to work for. Many found the experience exhilarating. "Life around him seemed more vital, closer to the edge, less routine, more physically and intellectually challenging" (Maraniss 1995, 382). Clinton is clearly a man with a substantial psychological presence; the question has always been whether he brings with it equally large psychological flaws.

There is considerable consensus that Clinton brings substantial personal and political talents to his presidency. One unfortunate by-product of this consensus is that his undeniable talents have often been taken as a given. As a result, they are more often the subject of admiration (when he succeeds or among those for whom his success is important) or lament (when he fails to live up to what is seen as his promise) than analysis.

Why do his talents need closer examination? Because for all the substantial talents he possesses, he has too frequently been on the brink of failure or busy recovering from it. While many agree he is extremely talented, many of his major setbacks seem primarily an avoidable result of his own behavior.

Clinton's personal and political strengths have often been overshadowed and undercut by his character and psychology. His strengths cannot be adequately considered in a psychological or political vacuum. They coexist with other elements of his psychology, some of which reinforce, others of which may inhibit, his capacities.

Political strengths are geared toward accomplishing specific purposes. Are Clinton's particular skills, however impressive, the talents necessary for a successful presidency in this political period? Are the skills and talents that might allow Clinton to pass new expansive government programs necessarily responsive to what Americans are asking of their president in this historical period?

Even if we were to find a good match between Clinton's talents and what present political circumstances appear to require (domestically or internationally), the question remains whether he has applied, or is fully able to effectively apply, his talents. This is not a splitting of conceptual hairs. There are very intelligent people who would be able to lead far more satisfying and productive lives were it not for other elements in their psychologies. Presidential talents and skills are embedded in, influenced by, and even grow out of an interior psychological constellation. Sometimes a president's psychology reinforces his talents; sometimes it inhibits their full use.[6]

This helps explain some puzzling anomalies in Clinton's pattern of learning. There is a generally held view among political analysts that Clinton is a man who learns from his mistakes. Assessing the Clinton presidency after a difficult first year, one observer noted, "Bill Clinton is incapable of sustained error, as some say, and I tend to agree, he will learn the lessons" (Brummett 1994, 273; see also Greenstein 1995, 143). But Clinton can also be a slow learner. Two years into his presidency, for example, after his battle over the nomination of Lani Guinier for attorney general, Clinton was again struggling with a controversial performance in nominating Dr. Henry W. Foster, Jr., for surgeon general. Writing in the *New York Times*, R. W. Apple (1994a) noted that many Democrats were blaming the Clinton administration for "bungling" the appointment.[7] Representative Tom Sawyer of Ohio, who won a tough reelection fight in 1992, complained that the administration "has a long, long learning curve." Senator J. Bennett Johnson, a four-term Louisiana Democrat, said, "What people are saying about the Foster thing is: There he goes again. Can't he learn how to run his office, even after two years? Why can't he be more competent? He has such towering strengths, but also such appalling faults."

The complaints about Clinton's performance, however, appear alongside accolades to his enormous talents. John Brummett, a reporter who covered Clinton for many years in Arkansas, writes that,

> he was the best politician of his era and a man of dizzying brainpower and awesome policy command. There was his disarming charm; he was almost impossible to dislike in a personal meeting. There was his mind-boggling accomplishment; he rose from the middle class and a backwater culture to become a Rhodes Scholar, a governor by thirty-two, and a president by forty-six. (1994, 4)

Meredith Oakley, an Arkansas reporter and author of a recent political biography of Clinton, asks,

> Do you want to see a political genius? Turn on the television and watch the evening news. Chances are you'll be looking at him. Here in Arkansas it happens all the time: Bill Clinton dominates the broadcast and print media, but then that has been the case for most of the last eighteen years. (1994, xi)

Ernest Dumas, who covered Governor Clinton as a reporter for the *Arkansas Gazette,* and who recently assembled a compilation of remembrances of Clinton by those who knew and worked with him, wrote,

Few Americans have ever had the exterior gifts of a politician in such abundance.

Bill Clinton was handsome, loquacious, and tireless. He always exhibited a boundless optimism. He met people with grace and facility, and a prodigious memory never let him forget them. He had what seemed to be a compulsive need to meet people, to know them, to like them, to have them like him. . . . Bill Clinton is a case where a man's deepest human instinct perfectly matched, maybe even gave rise to, his most abiding ambition. (1993, xvi)

According to Dumas (and others), there seems to be a remarkable fit between Clinton's talents and ambitions and the capacities needed to be a good, if not extraordinary, president. These talents, extracting from the above list, would include his brainpower (intelligence, memory, verbal facility), his knowledge of policy, personal energy, optimism, and ability to reach out to and engage people (charm, need to like and be liked). Given these talents, several commentators (Alter 1994; Franklin 1995) feel that President Clinton's successes have not been given enough credit.

Others are not so sure. Throughout his public life many have come to distrust and dislike him. During the presidential campaign, he evaded and dissembled when asked about his avoidance of the draft during the Vietnam War, his smoking of marijuana, and his extramarital relations. One year into his administration, Bob Herbert (1994) characterized President Clinton as a "truth sculptor," while Charles Peters (1994) noted "a history of difficulty with the truth." The title and content of Floyd Brown's book, *"Slick Willie": Why America Cannot Trust Bill Clinton*, suggest that admiration for Clinton's capacity for greatness is not universal.[8] Elizabeth Drew concluded her study of Clinton's first two years in office by suggesting that "to the end, Clinton's presidency would be a war between his ambitions and his flaws" (1994, 421).

Nor is the idea that Clinton is a political genius universally shared. Brummett, whose glowing characterization of Clinton was noted, wrote of Clinton's first year in office,

The real story of this horrible beginning is that Clinton wasn't quite the governing genius as had been portrayed. . . . The Congress was seeing the Bill Clinton I had seen in Arkansas: an over-compensator and a strategic blunderer who spent half of his time during state legislative sessions walking a tightrope, wheeling and dealing widely at the end to pass something reasonably bold and meaningful. (1994, 62, 106)

Clinton's record of academic and political accomplishment attests to his strong intellectual abilities, as does his capacity to give detailed, intelligent answers to complex and controversial questions. Moreover, Clinton's capacity to reinvent himself, both over time and within the same campaign, suggests a strong intelligence at work. However, even some of Clinton's talents, like his strong intelligence, are on closer inspection not all that they appear to be. The question begs itself: If Clinton is so smart, why does he take such large and in many cases unnecessary risks, as he did with his health-care plan, or his early moves away from the political center?

UNDERSTANDING THE CLINTON PRESIDENCY

What light can the theories of political psychology shed on the contradictory nature of Clinton and his performance as president? What light can they shed on his talents and limitations and the psychological and behavioral patterns that give rise to them? The answer in brief is that theories of political psychology, especially those that focus on individual psychology, can clarify the nature of Clinton's psychology and help explain his talents, his limitations, and the circumstances in which each are likely to appear.

The psychological analysis of Clinton that follows provides new understandings of his character and his controversial political leadership. That is an important function of any analysis, but it is especially so when the "conventional wisdom" has faltered. But the importance of psychologically framed analysis is to be found not only in its uncovering of new ideas, but in its ability to alter our accepted views when they are mistaken, or to show how some of Clinton's traits, like his supposed need to be liked, are actually much better understood as something quite different.

How does it accomplish this? Political psychology theories extend the analysis of Clinton's psychological patterns in four directions: *inward, horizontally, historically,* and *outward.* By extending the analysis *inward,* toward Clinton's interior psychology, we ask questions regarding the psychological foundation, operation, and meaning of Clinton's behavior as we observe it. Extending the analysis *horizontally,* across other character and personality elements in his psychology, allows us to see how different aspects of Clinton's psychology operate together as a package. Extending the analysis of Clinton's psychology *historically* allows us to trace and account for the development and maintenance of the most important elements of his psychology. Finally, extending the analysis *outward,* toward Clinton's responsibilities and performance as president, allows us to better understand and evaluate his presidency in this important political period.

Such analyses are needed because biographies of Clinton and his presidency have generally been content to portray him through anecdotes.[9] For example, Michiko Kakutani, reviewing David Maraniss's 1995 biography of Clinton writes that

> the portrait that emerges from this biography is not one of a visionary leader or statesman, but of an indefatigable, instinctual politician, driven throughout his life to seek the approval of friends and strangers alike. *By now, of course, none of this is exactly news.* Although Mr. Clinton is only halfway through his first term in office three other books on him or his presidency (Woodward, Drew, Brummett) have already appeared. (1995, emphasis added)

Kakutani is certainly correct in one sense: these traits have been much observed. However, in examining Clinton's presidential psychology one should not necessarily equate old news with having understood the *meaning* of that news.

Biographies and other accounts that develop a portrait of the president based primarily on the accumulation of characteristics suffer from several drawbacks. They often are not clear about the range and meaning of the traits they uncover. It is not enough to document that Clinton is intelligent. Rather, we must also ask what evidence do we have of how Clinton uses that intelligence. How is it applied, for what purposes, and with what results? Or consider Clinton's often observed and reported personal and political energy. Yes, it is true that Clinton invests a great deal of himself in pursuit of his public ambitions. Stories of Clinton's endlessly long working days are, as Kakutani suggests, well documented. But what does this trait actually *mean?* Does it reflect a man single-mindedly pursuing the public's good, his own good, or some combination of the two? Or does it reflect an attempt to ward off through activity thoughts or feelings with which Clinton would rather not contend? Is it some combination of both, or even something else entirely?

Observing and documenting a particular trait is the start, not the conclusion, of a firmer understanding of Clinton and his presidency. The *meaning* we are able to find, after suitable analysis, of a well-documented trait can inform our understanding regarding both the trait itself and the larger picture with which it is connected. Political psychology can help us more fully appreciate the meaning of the particular traits we observe or uncover, but also to see how they fit with other aspects of Clinton's psychology. Consider again Clinton's high level of energy and commitment. How is it related, if at all, to his so-called "need for approval"? Do the two exist independently of each other, like disembodied ghosts wandering though

Clinton's psyche, or is there some theoretically and psychologically plausible relationship between them? Simply to ask this question is to underscore the point that it is not only specific traits, but their relationship to each other that allows us to more fully understand Clinton and his presidency.

Many observers of Clinton have rounded up the usual suspects—his need to be liked, his intelligence, and so on. Other important aspects of Clinton's psychology have been entirely overlooked or noted in passing. A case in point is Clinton's enormous difficulty in setting and maintaining boundaries. I will argue that this is a major element in Clinton's character and overall psychology. But it has not yet made any biographer's list of important traits.

Consider also Clinton's propensity to verbally abuse aides, and his frequent angry attacks on the news media and assorted targets (special interests, greedy doctors, and muscle-bound labor unions). Some of his biographers have noted his tendency to get angry at aides and the press (Drew 1994, 96, 218), but no one has attempted to link his private and public displays of anger, or to account for them. What do they mean? Where does his anger come from? Is it the result of political or personal frustrations, or something more chronic? More pointedly, how do proponents of Clinton's so-called "need to be liked" explain this? For a man who supposedly needs to be liked by all, he certainly does not shrink from displaying anger and using potentially alienating stereotypes.

A number of the traits used to describe Clinton, such as his need to be liked, his energy, or his intelligence, may on closer inspection be more complicated. If Clinton does in fact need to be liked, he is clearly able to tolerate being disliked by some. Could there be some other psychological dynamic that better explains this and helps us make fuller sense of Clinton? In chapter 5 I will argue that there is.

Documenting Bill Clinton's traits is one thing; making judgments about them in connection with his presidency is another. Is having a smart president better than having one of average intelligence? Intuitively, it would seem so. However, this view assumes a president's performance is primarily governed by intelligence. If this is so, what role does a president's integrity, convictions, and judgment play? Are these elements as important, less important, or perhaps even more important than intelligence? Before we express too strong a preference for particular traits in a president, we had better be clear about which psychological elements are crucial and which merely preferable in enhancing a president's performance.

Finally, there is the issue of explaining how the traits and their associated personal and political characteristics came into being. Most biographies of Clinton, even the most useful of them, are content to detail his path from Hope, Arkansas, to the presidency. Along the way, one can learn important biographical details about Clinton's life. However, what has been missing thus far is a well-grounded understanding of how, specifically, the two are *psychologically* related. We know, for instance, that Clinton lost his biological father in a car accident. We also know that his stepfather was a verbally abusive alcoholic,[10] and that his mother was a "character." To date, however, these facts have been more often repeated than analyzed. There has been little attempt to connect these and other biographical facts, and to put them into an explanatory framework that links Clinton's past with his present.[11]

Clinton himself has focused public attention on his stepfather, and many have followed this lead. I will argue, however, that this focus has obscured a more important set of understandings about Clinton's childhood experiences, those having to do with an adoring but abandoning mother and a strong-willed but more ethical grandmother. This is not a plea for some kind of reductionist analysis in which everything that Clinton is, or will be, is explained by his childhood. On the other hand, we can hardly ignore Clinton's childhood. If the child is father to the man, how are we to understand Clinton's childhood experiences?

If we don't more fully appreciate the real nature of the elements that shaped Clinton's character and personality, or their role in Clinton's overall psychology, we will be hard pressed to explain the inconsistencies that seem to characterize the man and his presidency. Moreover, we will be at a disadvantage in following the zigs and zags of his administration's daily political strategy, or his shifts in public political identity. Theories of political psychology provide a framework in which we can consider and try to resolve these issues.

ADDRESSING THE BASIC PUBLIC DILEMMA: THE CONTEXT OF CLINTON'S PRESIDENCY

This study proceeds along two overlapping levels. The first, and most general, is the evolving psychological and political context in which the Clinton administration gained office and governs. Ironically, this context, instrumental to his successful campaign, has been equally instrumental in his difficulties as president.

The second level of this study is Clinton himself—his policies, his personal and public identity, leadership, and judgment. My purpose in this book is to develop a psychologically framed portrait of Clinton's interior and interpersonal psychology with the aim of accounting for how he has approached his presidential responsibilities. The rationale for such a study is to clarify the particular ways in which Clinton's psychology has shaped his success or difficulties in addressing the basic public dilemma with which he was elected to deal.

The stakes are high:

> On Clinton's capacity for leadership rested not only his political fate but also that of the country. Another failed presidency, for whatever reason— another dose of disillusionment, more cynicism could poison the political well to the point where the country could . . . give up trying to deal with its problems. The high hopes that were invested in Clinton were his opportunity and the nation's danger. If these hopes were dashed, anything could happen. (Drew 1994, 18)

Clinton's presidency is a pivotal one, unfolding at a particularly sensitive period for domestic public psychology and for America's place in the world more generally. If political psychology cannot fully resolve all the questions raised by this volatile mixture, neither can these questions be adequately framed and addressed without it. In the work which follows, I hope to demonstrate why.

In part I, I examine the international, domestic, and psychological issues that faced Clinton upon taking office. Internationally, the end of the Cold War raised many new issues, but I argue that the most important challenges Clinton faced were domestic. Chief among these were the decline of public confidence in policy solutions and a loss of confidence in political institutions and leaders. I argue that Clinton faced a basic public dilemma, a fundamental dislocation between citizens and government, and that it is this problem, rather than more specific issues like health care or Bosnia, that will frame his success or failure as president, and thereby his place in history.

In part II, I analyze Bill Clinton's character. I begin in chapter 2 by explaining the nature of character in the presidency and its three primary elements: ambition, character integrity, and relatedness. Ambition speaks to a president's aspirations and his ability to accomplish them. Character integrity reflects a president's ideals, values, and his fidelity to them. Relatedness concerns the nature of the president's relationships with others. In the three chapters that immediately follow, I examine each of these character elements in some detail with regard to Clinton. In chapter 6, I trace the effects of Clinton's character on some other elements of his psychology that have been evident in his presidency. I examine the basis and consequences of his persistence, impatience, high sense of achievement, and competitiveness. However, I argue that among the most important elements in his psychology is a dislike of boundaries, and a sense of himself as being special.

Character is formed and developed through experience. Part III, "Growing Up, Coming of Age," explores experiences that were critical to Bill Clinton's development. In chapters 7, 8, and 9 I examine more closely the Clinton family myth and the facts behind it. I explore more fully Clinton's relationship with his mother, the loss of his father, his relationship to his stepfather, and the ways in which they helped to shape his character. Clinton's memories of his childhood and his mother's autobiography present very different views of his family life. Clinton had an inconsistent childhood in which he was both adored and disregarded. A fuller understanding of the difficult nature of Clinton's early childhood is essential to understanding the man he has become.

In chapters 10 and 11, I turn to Clinton's later developmental experiences. In chapter 10, I explore Clinton's attempt to avoid the draft and the consequences of doing so. In chapter 11, I analyze his marriage to Hillary Rodham and the effects of her own psychology, which has sometimes helped and other times hurt his political career.

In part IV, "The Political Consequences of Character," I explore the relationship between Clinton's psychology and his performance as president. In chapter 12, I discuss some difficulties in assessing Clinton's performance as a political leader and suggest two broad, primary tasks every president must successfully master: making high-quality decisions and mobilizing the public in support of political purposes. I argue that intelligence alone does not guarantee good judgment, and that elements of character can either facilitate or hinder good judgment, even if the president is, like Bill Clinton, very smart. Further, I argue that candor is a critical leadership ingredient, especially in times when the public distrusts its institutions and leaders. In chapter 13, I focus on Clinton's performance as president in the two broad areas of decision-making and political leadership. I examine the outstanding characteristics of the Clinton presidency, its ambitious policy agenda, its discontinuous, episodic nature, its ambiguous policy stances, and a range of issues having to do with Clinton's approach to decision-making and the effects of his character on the quality of his judgments.

In the final chapter, I consider the meaning of the 1994 elections and

Clinton's performance as president. I draw some conclusions about his performance as president during his first term and suggest some issues that are likely to be important should he be reelected. An appendix briefly examines some methodological issues that arise in connection with a psychologically framed analysis of Clinton and his presidency.

I

PRESIDENTS, PSYCHOLOGY, AND THE PUBLIC

★ ───────────────────────────────────────

PUBLIC PSYCHOLOGY: THE LEGACY OF HISTORY

The analysis of every presidency is a story consisting of four overlapping parts. First, it is the story of a particular historical context and political time. Second, it is a story that unfolds within a particular institutional setting, a presidency which has either been strengthened or weakened by the actions of those who have occupied the office in the past. Third, it is a story of the public and its psychology—how people feel about their institutions, their lives, and their prospects. Finally, it is a story whose central character is the president himself—with his abilities and limitations.

Each of these four elements plays an important part in shaping the challenges and opportunities that face a president. It also affects the public and institutional resources he can draw upon to meet these challenges, and the extent to which his own psychology will either help or hinder him in accomplishing his and the public's purposes. While I focus in this work on Clinton's psychology as it affects his approach to exercising the powers of the office, his presidency itself cannot be well understood without a clearer grasp of the contexts, material and psychological, in which it is unfolding.

THE INTERNATIONAL CONTEXT

Every presidency takes place in times of change, but some historical periods involve managing change within a more stable framework, while other times require the president and his advisers to develop the framework itself. These two contexts call for different kinds of judgments on the part of a president and his advisers.

Decisions that define a major problem and place it in a context, I term *framing decisions*. Framing decisions are crucial because they represent key, and sometimes starkly contrasting, alternatives, each of which will point to different paths, open up some options, close others, and bring about different results. I use the term *judgment framework* to denote the major conceptual organization that a president brings to bear on the analysis of a problem. However, the major problem for presidents and other policy makers in new circumstances is that there are no specific frameworks. Therefore, in new, emerging circumstances the president and his advisers must be able to (1) see the framing decision for the crucial choice that it represents; (2) understand the essential elements of a problem and their significance, and place the problem within an appropriate judgment framework; and (3) develop a policy that preserves, and perhaps extends, the major values at issue.

The major defining international frame of the period stretching from the late 1940s through the late 1980s was, of course, the Cold War. The Truman presidency faced the task of devising a basic strategy to respond to challenges from the Soviet Union. Truman thus helped define every presidency that followed. Presidents Eisenhower, Kennedy, Johnson, Nixon, Ford, Carter, and Reagan all had to manage a Cold War that dominated the international system, alternating between rivalry and outright hostility.

The international challenges facing the Clinton presidency call for different policy making and judgment skills. The first and most obvious challenge is to define America's role in the world. The collapse of the former Soviet Union has presented the United States with a series of dilemmas and opportunities that are in many respects unprecedented. What structures for international relations can develop now that the former Soviet Union and the United States are no longer locked in a dangerous but stabilized worldwide conflict-management paradigm? What role can and should the United States now play in these circumstances?

These basic questions raised by the demise of the Soviet Union lead to many other questions, which have been explored by a number of other writers. What are the implications of the possibility of American hegemony (Layne and Schwarz 1993)? Is it possible to develop a "New World Order," and, if so, what would it look like (Hames 1994)? Should it be based on traditional standards of enlightened self-interest (Walt 1989), an attempt to make the world safe for democracy (T. Smith 1993), neo-Wilsonian pragmatism (Tucker 1993–94; Zoellick 1994), principles of human rights (Burkhalter 1993; Manning 1994; Posner 1994–95; Tonelson 1994–95), or economic considerations (Parker 1994; Stemlau 1994)? What role will force play in the "New World Order"? Is the United States too quick to become involved in circumstances that could lead to conflict (Stedman 1992–93), or too reluctant (Mandelbaum 1994; Tonelson 1993)? Should the United States become involved in peacekeeping operations (Evans 1993; Weinrod 1993), and if so, should it necessarily be done under U.N. auspices (Berdal 1994)? Related to these issues are the more specific questions of whether, and how, the United States should have become involved in such conflicts as Somalia (Bolton 1994; Clark 1993, 1992–1993; Stevenson 1993), Bosnia (Binder 1994–95; Freedman 1994–95), and Haiti (Martin 1994). And, of course, many have questioned how President Clinton dealt with these and other matters[1] (Maynes 1993–94; Meyerson 1994; Szamuely 1994; Wolfowitz 1994).

THE DOMESTIC CONTEXT

The list of emerging and unresolved issues in the international context are themselves daunting. Yet Clinton assumed the presidency at a time when the basic paradigms of domestic American politics were also in disarray. In the 1992 presidential election Clinton received just over 43 percent of the popular vote. His Republican rival George Bush received just over 37 percent of the vote, and the third party candidate Ross Perot received 19 percent of the vote. Perot's total was the best showing for an independent or third party candidate since Teddy Roosevelt's 1912 run for the presidency on the Bull Moose Ticket.[2] These statistics reflect long-term declines in support for the traditional parties, party-line voting, and the level of party identification (Wattenberg 1991, 47–65; see also Wattenberg 1990).

Political parties have traditionally served as a filter through which citizens assess presidential candidates (Campbell et al. 1954; Campbell et al. 1960). In the past, a major party nomination conferred a stamp of approval on the candidate. Voters could be assured that such a person had been selected and had obtained the approval of many party regulars who knew and presumably trusted him to lead and represent them. However, the rules of the nomination process have dramatically changed. Generally, control has passed from a cadre of party officials to party activists. The increasing importance of presidential primaries have allowed candidates' organizations and support to bypass traditional bases of party support. As a result, the traditional apparatus of the major political parties has become increasing less important to candidates attempting to secure their party's nomination. It has also had consequences for successful candidates once they attempt to govern. Party discipline and coherence, rarely exceptionally strong, have been further weakened by these developments.

At the same time, the major political parties have retreated from their traditional role as ideological and policy guides. Knowing that a presidential candidate was running as the standard bearer for one of the political parties once conveyed something concrete about a candidate. It reflected his political identity, suggesting for whom and for what he stood. Political party affiliation keyed the public to a presidential candidate's policy positions. Moreover, the candidate's political identity and his party's ideology were mutually reinforcing. Making a choice for the Democrat (Lyndon Johnson) or Republican (Barry Goldwater) party in 1964 or choosing Ronald Reagan (the Republican) or Walter Mondale (the Democrat) in 1984 were essentially related choices. Each candidate's political philosophy and persona were reflected in the official and unofficial policy views of the party. The coherence and stability of this link provided the public with a broad, but nonetheless accurate, indication of how the successful presidential candidate would proceed and where he would lead if elected.

Over the past two decades, the link between presidential candidates and their political personas, on the one hand, and party ideology and policy, on the other, has become attenuated. Political circumstances have caused political parties to move toward the center. Political parties whose platforms and candidates reflected too narrow an ideological spectrum, as did the Republicans in 1964 and the Democrats in 1984, suffered electoral losses. This is a powerful political incentive toward moderation.

What is true for political parties has also become true of the presidential candidates themselves. The threat of electoral loss is a powerful political incentive for candidates to blur ideological and policy distinctions. This development can be traced to the presidential campaigns of Richard Nixon. Nixon was a Republican, but he rejected discussions of whether he was "conservative" or "liberal." He saw himself as "pragmatic" rather than ideological, and his policies tended to follow from that perception. Nixon was a conservative anticommunist, and yet he was prepared to engage in strategic negotiations with his adversaries. Nixon's anticommunist views did not keep him from forging a new relationship with China. His domestic policy shows the same blending of ideological strands. Nixon was "tough on crime," in both rhetoric and policy. But Nixon the conservative Republican was not a mortal foe of liberal welfare programs. In fact, he attempted to reform and improve several of these programs. In answer to whether Nixon was a moderate, liberal, or conservative, one would have to answer, "It depends on the issue."

One can see similar trends in the Carter candidacies in 1976 and 1980. Jimmy Carter, a Southern Democrat, ran on a personal platform in which supporting a "strong defense" and being "tough on criminals" played prominent roles. Was Carter a traditional Democratic liberal? No, not really. Was he a "conservative?" In some respects yes, but in others no. Carter, like Nixon before him, campaigned and governed as a pragmatist, not an ideologue.

In the presidential election of 1988, the same trends are observable for both candidates. George Bush had so blended and moderated his views on many policy issues that many asked, "Who is George Bush?" In the area of civil rights, for example, Bush was known to be generally supportive, though he opposed quotas and other preferential systems for minorities. His Democratic opponent, Michael Dukakis, completely disavowed any political ideology, liberal or conservative, Democratic or Republican. His campaign slogan that the election was "about competence, not ideology" reflected in the most pristine form attempts by presidential candidates to bypass ideology, and the labeling and filtering function that it served.

That trend continued in the 1992 presidential campaign. President Clinton's campaign promised a candidate who reflected a "new Democratic party," presumably one unlike its predecessor. His policy positions, expressed in general terms, continued the trend of blending ideologies. Thus, candidate Clinton was for "a strong America," but also promised to drastically reduce the military budget. He was a supporter of social welfare programs, but promised to "end welfare as we know it" during his presidency. His 1996 State of the Union Address continued this strategy.

THE PRESIDENCY: A POWERFUL OR DEFLATED INSTITUTION?

American political culture reflects a deep ambivalence regarding the exercise of executive and especially presidential power that dates back to the framing of the Constitution. Delegates to the Constitutional Convention, in the process of breaking away from oppressive executive power in the form of the King, fiercely debated just how much power to give to the new institution of the president. The dilemma then, as now, was clear. On the one hand, a president needs sufficient power to govern effectively. On the other hand, too much unrestrained power might lead to the very excesses that fueled the American Revolution.

This same ambivalence permeates the modern presidency. Scholars have worried that the presidency is too powerful, too imperial (Schlesinger 1973). Richard Pious notes that "the presidency may be an instrument of representative democracy, benevolent autocracy, or malevolent Caesarism—depending on the interplay of constitutional interpretation, institutional competition, and *personality and leadership qualities of the incumbent*" (1979, 14, emphasis mine). Others have worried that it was not powerful enough to accomplish all its public purposes (Lowi 1984). At the same time, the presidency is still seen as the engine of the American political system (Mansfield 1989) and, in many ways, still imperial (Lind 1995). Whether in domestic or foreign affairs, presidents are routinely expected to be conversant with an enormous range of issues. Small wonder that some fear that no institution or person could survive the expectations that surround the modern presidency.

Consider the electoral fate of the last seven presidents. Lyndon Johnson won election in a landslide in 1964 but did not have the political capital to stand for reelection in 1968. Richard Nixon won election in 1968, was reelected in 1972, but was forced to resign from office under threat of impeachment. Gerald Ford became president upon Nixon's resignation, but was unable to gain election 1976. Jimmy Carter won the presidency in 1976, but was not reelected in 1980. Only Ronald Reagan was able to manage reelection, in 1984. George Bush was elected in 1988, but rejected by voters in 1992. Bill Clinton was elected president in 1992 with only a 43 percent plurality of the vote and was handed a stinging rebuke in the 1994 midterm election when his party lost control of both the House and Senate in the equivalent of a political earthquake.

What accounts for the difficulties presidents have had in sustaining public support? Has the growth of public expectations simply transcended any president's ability to accomplish them? If this is true, how did Ronald Reagan manage to get elected and reelected when the four presidents who preceded him and the one who immediately followed him did not?

Changes in public psychology represent a part of the answer, but the focus on increased public expectations misses a central point. *Public psychology has become unhinged from its foundation.* It has done so because trust, the psychological cement which secures the attachment between the public and its leaders and institutions, has weakened and seriously eroded. The central issue now is not the growth of expectations for presidential and public performance, but its opposite, a decline in confidence and trust in public leadership and institutions.

THE DECLINE OF PUBLIC CONFIDENCE IN
POLICY SOLUTIONS

Americans have traditionally been optimistic about their ability to solve problems and are consequently great believers in the idea of progress. It seemed only reasonable, therefore, to believe, as was the case in the 1960s, that an emphasis on aggressive government policies coupled with a growing command of developing social technologies would usher in a period of prosperity. In domestic politics, it was believed that this combination would address and eradicate major social problems such as poverty. Internationally, superior military power would assure the triumph of our policies where the virtue of our positions was not otherwise persuasive.

From our present perspective this view seems somewhat naive, but it is worth asking how it became so. In the international arena from 1948 to 1988, Americans were forced to face the fact that there were limits to the nation's ability to accomplish its policy purposes abroad. A partial list of the historical experiences that reinforced the idea of limits include the fight to stalemate in Korea, the (apparent) rise to scientific and military parity of the Soviet Union, the decline of colonial systems, the failure of U.S. policy in Vietnam, and the failure to bring about a comprehensive Middle East settlement.

Even after the demise of the Soviet Union, American power has come up against limits. American interventions in Somalia, Rwanda, Bosnia, and even Haiti have proved ample evidence of these limits. While the existence of the Soviet Union no doubt played a major role in limiting American power in the 1948–88 period, its demise suggests there was more to these limits than the efforts of one major adversary.

The paradox of enormous formal power coupled with limited ability to effect outcomes has also had its counterpart in domestic public policy. It was the hope of many that important domestic problems such as poverty and race and class divisions would yield to a combination of technical solutions and large-scale government intervention. However, this has not proved to be the case. No doubt one reason is that these policy problems have complex causes that are not easily amenable, even to complex, comprehensive solutions. Homelessness, for example, does not simply reflect a lack of housing but rather results from a complex series of causes having to do with economic and skill marginality in relation to shifting economic and employment trends, as well as with drug and alcohol abuse (Jenks 1994). Each of these problems, in turn, are complex, difficult, and not easily resolved.

Not only have social problems proved difficult to eradicate, but large-scale government policy programs have sometimes brought with them paradoxical and perverse effects. One illustration of this is the dependency and the institutionalization of the poverty cycle that have accompanied income-maintenance programs for the poor (Murray 1984). An analysis of New York City's policy of providing housing to anyone who said they needed it found that the city's initial generous policy had the perverse effect of encouraging many less well-off New Yorkers to declare themselves homeless, so that a new system was needed to make sure that only the truly homeless were served (Dugger 1993a, 1993b).

Addressing complex social problems is difficult enough under any circumstances. However, the approach of some public officials and advocacy groups charged with dealing with social problems have exacerbated already difficult situations. For example, it was well known in policy circles that drugs and alcohol abuse were a serious problem among the homeless, yet advocates persisted in minimizing this problem to win public sympathy. Marsha A. Martin, who served on the board of New York City's Coalition for the Homeless, recalled that "there was a discussion that went on amongst us all. Do you market it as a problem of shelter, or do you tell people about alcoholism, drug addition, mental illness, and concerns about child abuse?" (Dugger 1993a). The problem was marketed as one solely of housing, with the result that escalating demands were made on the city for developing new shelters. Paradoxically, advocates continued to press for more of the very mass shelters they severely criticized as inhumane and inefficient "as part of a calculated strategy" based on the belief that "the terrible conditions in the shelters would embarrass the city into giving homeless permanent apartments."

Many social programs that began as presidential initiatives were put into place without adequate evaluation or monitoring or even basic data. Christopher Jenks, in his study of the homeless, noted that inflated estimates of over three million homeless were repeated as fact when they had no empirical basis. The purpose of these numbers was not to provide a basis for realistic policies but to stimulate a sense of crisis. One researcher has characterized this as "lying for justice." As Jenks notes, "Big numbers are politically useful" (1994, 2).

Along similar lines, Thomas Cronin notes of the large-scale social programs initiated in the 1960s that "former White House aides now admit that these [diagnostic and evaluative] capabilities were overtaxed and ineffective throughout the nineteen sixties. Alternatives seldom were evaluated carefully, and effectiveness was rarely calculated accurately"

(1975, 242). One result was that costs were substantially underestimated and expected, and actual results overinflated. A little noted but prophetic 1980 report by the Advisory Commission on Intergovernmental Relations noted "an unmanageable, wasteful and unaccountable system of domestic aid programs," which it concluded had been partially responsible for the "rising public discontent with government at all levels" (Herbers 1980).

Not only was there little recognition that social problems take many years to address, but officials tended to downplay the problems or to acknowledge them only with enormous reluctance. The frank public discussion of many issues became (and continues to be) difficult. When Daniel Moynihan (1969) released his report on how social and economic strains affected minority families, he was denounced by many as a racist. So while there was a growing sense among the public that policy solutions were failing to accomplish their purposes, real discussion of the issues as a foundation for introducing meaningful changes was stymied by a lack of candor.

As a result of these and similar problems, the public has increasingly questioned the legitimacy of large-scale social programs. Welfare spending has acquired a steadily rising negative connotation; public support for it declined dramatically (Wattenberg 1991, 108). A 1994 Times Mirror poll found a "striking decline in public support for social welfare programs," with a 12-percent decline from the previous year in the number of people who thought it was the government's business to take care of people who can't take care of themselves (Berke 1994b).

Another result has been a dramatic decline in the public's confidence in the government's ability to solve social problems. In the absence of faith in the government's ability to provide policy solutions, the public has turned increasingly toward the search for leadership, which, it is hoped, will prevail where particular programs have not. However, public leadership has been disappointing. Since 1964, presidents have attempted to solve large-scale public problems with large-scale public programs, largely without success. Perhaps because of this lack of success, they have increasingly substituted optimism for candor. As a result, government and policy itself have become suspect.

THE DECLINE OF PUBLIC TRUST IN GOVERNMENT

Presidential leadership, like governance, reflects a set of relationships between presidents and citizens. In the American system, citizens temporarily cede to presidents the power to make decisions and implement them. However, they do so with certain basic implicit and explicit understandings.

It is assumed that the president will act, to the best of his ability, for the public's interest and not solely his own. The public does not expect the president to be devoid of self-interest, only that he be able to put it aside when it counts. It is assumed that leaders will initiate meaningful debate and clearly lay out the alternatives they and the public face, as well as their implications. The rationale for this assumption lies not only in the concept of legitimacy based on the public's consent to be governed. It also lies in the basic psychological fact that the more people are aware of the risks and options they face, the more prepared they are to deal with the inevitable difficulties that accompany any effort to effect improvements.

Finally, it is assumed that presidents will use the vast powers that have been ceded to them while in office in a responsible, competent, and thoughtful way. These may sound like textbook expectations, but the consequences of a failure to meet them are weighty. The public's confidence and trust in its leaders[3] and institutions are the psychological cement of leadership and governance. The more closely the behavior of leaders and institutions approximates implicit and explicit public expectations, the more legitimacy they have and the more easily they can develop and implement their policy initiatives.

The perception that presidents are acting, in their best judgment, in the *public's* interest and not their own is the basis of a very important psychological connection. Such a president earns a large measure of discretion with which to initiate policies, not because citizens are guaranteed, or even expect, full effectiveness, but rather because they have *enough* confidence in a president's judgment and skills to take allow him to take the chance. Public trust and confidence also provide a president with time for his proposals to take hold and a cushion against the inevitable ups and downs of policy success.

The level of confidence and trust the public has in a president reflects their view of his stated and actual intentions, his skills and competence, his candor in discussing issues, the solutions he proposes, and his past record with the public on these matters. The link between confidence and trust is not accidental. Trust implies a leap of faith. Confidence implies a more objectively based assessment. Both figure in the public's support for a president.

Trust alone, without attempts to make more objectively based judgments, runs the risk of substituting wish for reality, and thereby increasing the risk of disappointment and cynicism. Addressing complex policy dilemmas, however, requires of citizens that they support plausible policy initiatives in the face of uncertainties. A president must encourage hope even as he candidly addresses doubt. To focus only on the former at the expense of the latter also runs the risk of increasing disappointment and cynicism.

The public's confidence and trust in its leaders and institutions is a major psychological component of the context in which a president initiates policy, responds to challenges, and in general governs. The more confidence and trust the public has in a president, the more latitude he has to shape the policy agenda. Clinton entered his presidency with his own trust deficit, but his personal issues with public trust are best analyzed in the context of the long-term declines in public confidence.

When researchers at the University of Michigan's Survey Research Center asked a national sample of Americans in 1958 how much of the time they could trust the government in Washington to do what is right — just about always, most of the time, or only some of the time — 78 percent of the public said they could trust the government all or most of the time.[4] In 1964, at the start of Johnson's presidency, that number remained at 78 percent. However, two years into the Johnson administration the number had dropped to 69 percent, and by the end of Johnson's presidency it had reached 63 percent (Miller 1974, 952, 989).[5] By 1976 that number had halved to 35 percent!

The number of people who trusted government to do what is right "always" or "most of the time" rebounded somewhat, to 43 percent, during President Reagan's first term in office, then declined and leveled off at about 40 percent during his second term. Thereafter, the index began to drop dramatically again. By the 1992 presidential election, only about 23 percent thought the government could be trusted to do what's right all or most of the time. After two years of Clinton's presidency, that number had further fallen to about 18 percent.

When a January 1993 CBS/*New York Times* poll asked whether "you think that in general, the government creates more problems than it solves . . . [or] solves more problems than it creates," 69 percent chose the former and only 22 percent the latter (Ladd 1993, 16). Not surprisingly, in a Voter Research and Surveys exit poll taken on the day of the 1992 election, which asked voters whether they wanted a government that provided more services but cost more in taxes, or a government that cost less while providing fewer services, 55 percent of the voters opted for less government (Ladd 1993, 16).

The decline of the public's confidence and trust in its leaders and institutions has enormous consequences for governing. Martin P. Wattenberg notes that "candidate-centered politics may dominate the process today, but candidates have become less and less popular in recent elections." He characterizes this as "one of the great ironies of the candidate-centered age" (1991, 12; 159). The 1992 presidential election was no exception. Voters "cast troubled ballots, evidencing only limited approval for the candidates as individuals. For most of the campaign, voters' evaluation were unfavorable to the candidates" (Pomper 1993, 143–44).

While many voters expressed the view during the 1992 presidential campaign that they were tired of character attacks, they continued to be influenced by them. A CBS/*New York Times* poll taken in mid-October found that 57 percent of independents and 32 percent of Democrats felt that Bill Clinton could not be trusted to deal with the problems a president might face (Ladd 1993, 17). Voters in 1992 selected a president *in spite of* their personal misgivings about the candidates, not because they didn't have them. And while the voters ultimately gave Clinton a plurality, the undercurrent of public discontent and uneasy feelings about the choice had as many implications for his ability to govern as they did for his election. The decline of the public trust and confidence in its leaders and institutions plays a critical role in understanding the 1992 presidential campaign, Clinton's success in it, and his subsequent difficulties as president.

THE PSYCHOLOGICAL CONTEXT OF THE CLINTON PRESIDENCY: THE BASIC PUBLIC DILEMMA

This book focuses on Clinton's psychology and its relationship to his performance as president. In the calculus of public choice and evaluation, however, judgments regarding presidents are a joint function of a president's strengths and weaknesses, on the one hand, and what the public perceives it needs and wants, on the other. Therefore, context cannot be ignored in assessing any president's performance.

Context has both a historical and a psychological component. The first reflects the legacy of the past, the second its meaning. Presidential candidates are selected and evaluated in part by their response to both dimensions. As a way of conceptualizing this contextual legacy, I have suggested that each president is selected because he is perceived as the best person to address and resolve the *basic public dilemma*. The basic public dilemma is a fundamental unresolved question concerning public psychology that faces a president on taking office.[6] It is not a specific question about public policy, but rather the public's psychological connections to its institutions, leaders, and political process. This unresolved public concern underlies and frames more specific policy debates.

One such dilemma among modern presidents was Franklin D. Roosevelt's facing whether and how the government would respond to major national economic and social dislocations in 1932. For Lyndon Johnson, in 1964, the question was whether and how the government should be the implementor of major programs designed to further civil rights and economic opportunities for disadvantaged and politically marginal groups. For Gerald Ford (after Richard Nixon), and for Jimmy Carter (after Johnson, Nixon, and Ford), the basic public dilemma was whether a president could accomplish his policy purposes honestly as well as competently. For Ronald Reagan in 1980, the question revolved around whether public faith could be restored in the office of the president after the flawed presidencies of Lyndon Johnson, Richard Nixon, and, as the public perceived it, the well-intentioned but ineffectual presidencies of Gerald Ford and Jimmy Carter.

Some presidents appreciate the nature of this major public dilemma and respond successfully, as did Roosevelt and Reagan. Others realize the dilemma but lack the skills to respond successfully, as was the case with Carter. Still others, like Johnson, appreciate the major question but become distracted by other issues and wind up being unsuccessful.

What is the major public dilemma that faces the Clinton presidency? It is not his policy toward Bosnia, Iraq, or the former Soviet Union. It is not the problem of the deficit, or trade, or health care—as important as all these problems are. In my view the major public dilemma that Bill Clinton faces is the dilemma of trust in public policy. At its base, this dilemma reflects a fundamental public question about whether government policies, even those which are constructive in intent, can be fair in formulation and successful in result.

Americans' belief in the competence and fairness of government has been repeatedly challenged in the last three decades. Policies of government intervention designed to redress economic and social imbalances, constructive and even laudable in intent, have often not realized their goals. Moreover, they have often resulted in unanticipated and unsatisfactory consequences. More recent government policies designed to let the market accomplish laudable social purposes have not yet proved adequate to the task, as the persistence of problems of poverty, crime, and the environment attest.

Wilson McWilliams has argued that "the clearest message of 1992 was the majority's demand for active government engaged to relieve America's discontents and reclaim the future" (1993, 194). Perhaps so. But this public aspiration has a number of more specific expectations connected with it.

Clinton campaigned on a personal platform that stressed government's ability to develop and implement public policies that are fair to groups across the political spectrum, and not just those that have traditionally supported the Democratic party. He promised that his policies would solve old problems without creating a host of new ones. And he promised to do so in way the public would understand and support. In short, he promised, in Osborne's and Gaebler's ambitious phrase, to "reinvent government."[7]

The stakes are high. How high is suggested by a preliminary analysis of the implications of the 1992 election by Peter Nardulli and Jon Dalanger (1993; see also Ladd 1993). They examined three possible implications of that election: whether the election could be considered a "deviating" election with continuing strong prospects for the Republican party, a critical realignment election at the presidential level, or an election that continues the process of electorate "dealignment." They conclude that the election might have enduring electoral consequences, but that the consequences depend in part on perceptions of [Clinton's] success in office. These perceptions, they argue, will depend not only on what he accomplishes, but also on what he is expected to accomplish: "Clinton has promised much, and many groups who have been outsiders during decades of Republican rule are expecting much from him. In addition, expectations will be fueled by speculation that his victory, which is sizable given the historical measures we have used, marks the beginning of a Democratic realignment" (1993, 166).

TOWARD AN APPRAISAL OF THE CLINTON PRESIDENCY

The Clinton presidency faced a basic set of public questions at the outset regarding its real intentions, strategies, and competence. These questions have persisted through the first three years of his presidency. Many of Clinton's policy initiatives have been controversial, some extremely so. Some voters question whether the change they wanted was the change they are getting. They are concerned that Clinton is not being entirely candid with the public either about the real costs of his policies or their impact, a concern that has been fueled by the elastic estimates of the costs and savings of some administration initiatives. Related to this is the concern that Clinton's new language may mask old commitments. New government programs are touted as "investments," payments to government entities such as health alliances are listed as "premiums," and so on. The question remains unanswered as to whether Clinton is really a "New Democrat," and if so, what that really means. Remarkably, in 1995, after more than three years in the public eye, Clinton is still seen as a president who needs to define who he is and what he stands for (Kelly 1995, 42).

In his approach to ordering military intervention in Bosnia, in his policies towards Haiti, and in the difficulties he encountered in Somalia, Clinton has often said one thing and done another. Is this the cool strategic calculation of tough-minded president, a reflection of indecision and ambivalence, or an attempt to accomplish goals without clearly examining the potential difficulties and costs?

Similar questions have been raised regarding many of Clinton's domestic policies. He has backed away from a number of his domestic campaign promises. Moreover, he has compromised or abandoned major parts of his policy initiatives. Is this a reflection of a mature, pragmatic leader settling for what is obtainable, or does it reflect deeper inhibitions or concerns? How do we explain the puzzling discrepancies between his talents and performance? How will the public, other political actors, and professional analyzers of his administration come to view and evaluate the Clinton presidency?

The answers to these questions ultimately rest on two related factors. The first depends on the psychology of the president himself, his character, thinking, judgment, vision, and leadership skills. The second depends on his ability to successfully address and begin to resolve the basic public dilemma.

II

The Character
of Bill Clinton

CHAPTER **2**

CHARACTER AND THE PRESIDENCY

At its center, the powers of the presidency are set into motion by its occupant. His goals, ideals, skills, judgments, and responses to circumstances drive and define his time in office.[1] Above all other psychological factors, it is character that shapes a presidency.

President Clinton has conceptualized character as "a journey, not a destination" (Kelly 1995). It is, he says, a lifelong passage, always "in process." In conceptualizing his character in this way, he makes both a plea and a point. His point is that character is neither static or frozen. His plea is that his political lapses and mistakes be seen as the normal and expectable by-product of someone who, like everyone else, has made mistakes but who, unlike many, is not afraid to learn from experience. His character, he asks us to remember, is still developing.

In contrast, character, in my view, is not an open-ended expanse of developmental possibilities, but a consolidated psychological foundation that frames a person's responses to circumstances and is often responsible for the person's circumstances themselves.[2] Can character develop? In a word, yes.[3] Character development may enhance a person's opportunities, but character also imposes limits. Character, in its consolidated form, is not an ode to unlimited choice. It is a reflection of choices already made, of establishing emotional priorities, and of the methods one has developed to satisfy them. The consequences of character choice accumulate, and certainly by mid-adulthood, who one is carries more psychological weight than who one might become.

The term *character* is derived from the Greek word meaning "engraving."[4] In his classic work on personality theory, Gordon Allport defined it as "a person's patterns of traits or his lifestyle" (1937, chap. 1). He distinguished character from personality. Personality denotes "appearance, visible behavior, surface quality," while character implies "deep (perhaps inborn), fixed and basic structure."[5]

The early understanding of character reflected several basic clinical observations. First, character operates across a number of key areas of psychological functioning. Second, character elements produce observable, consistent patterns. A person who speaks in measured tones, uses precise words, is meticulous about arriving on time for appointments, and perceives the world in detailed terms is not likely to be given to wild displays of public emotion. Third, because character is basic to psychological functioning, it is present in a variety of social situations.[6]

Character differs from other psychological elements in that it is pervasive not only across time and circumstance, but across personality itself. Beliefs, attitudes, and even neuroses typically represent only small parts of the total personality system. Each may be relevant to and therefore engaged only in limited areas of functioning. Character, in contrast, stands at the core of the person's psychology and is the basic foundation upon which personality structures develop and operate. Character shapes beliefs, information processing, and, ultimately, styles of behavior. It is therefore deeply embedded in the foundation of psychological functioning.

Another important aspect of character is that it is usually more fully experienced by others than by the individual himself. Because character is so fundamental to a person's functioning and develops over so many years, it is taken for granted. From our own perspectives "we are who we are," "have always been that way," or cannot say why but "that's just how we feel." All those phrases, and others that could be added, simply reflect the fact that for most people their own character structure is an unexamined given. Few people spend much time in characterological introspection.

One way in which people do become aware of their character is when aspects of it result in continuing difficulty. A person who takes reckless risks, and who loses often and substantially, may become motivated to do something about it, or to listen to others who call attention to self-defeating patterns. Success, however, tends to diminish any tendency to look inside oneself, and large successes diminish any such possibilities even more so. In Clinton's case, when one adds a tendency toward high levels of activity (see chapter 3), there is even less inclination, not to mention time, to look inward.[7] Clinton's enormous successes have been a mixed blessing for him in that regard.

THE ELEMENTS OF CHARACTER

Character represents a person's integrated pattern of responding to three basic life spheres or domains: what they will do with their lives, how they will do it, and their relations to others along the way. There are, therefore, three corresponding core character elements: ambition, character integrity, and relatedness. These three character elements are the psychological foundation upon which the superstructure of personality develops. They are also critical to understanding Bill Clinton's presidency and, I would argue, any presidency.

Ambition

The first character domain is that of purposeful initiative and action. This is the sphere of ambition. The basic concerns in this domain are the capacity, desire, and ability to invest oneself in accomplishing one's purposes. A consolidated sphere of ambition gives rise to a sense of self-confidence and personal effectiveness.[8] It reflects the development and consolidation of a set of skills that can be successfully engaged in the pursuit of one's goals and the realization of one's values.

In both academic and ordinary discourse, ambition carries with it negative connotations. To be characterized as ambitious is to be labeled as essentially self-serving, unmindful of others, and manipulative. This negative connotation is evident in studies of presidents and other leaders whose ambition has primarily been viewed as being in the service of compulsively accumulating power. Heinz Kohut (1971, 1977) reminds us, however, that ambition is the normal by-product of a healthy narcissism. Ambition is, along with ideals and the talent to achieve it, one foundation of a well-realized life. Without ambition there is no achievement, and without achievement there is little basis on which to consolidate self-regard. In Kohut's theory, ambition, even substantial ambition, is not problematic. On the contrary, a substantial lack of ambition would denote a developmental arrest. Childhood grandiosity is the foundation of adult ambition. As long as it is gradually and successfully modulated by empathetically attuned others and "optimally frustrating" experience, ambition does not run the risk of careening out of control and interfering with judgment and behavior (Kohut 1971, 8–9, 107).

Both too much and too little ambition are brought about by the empathetic failures of parents. In one case, the parent fails to respond positively to the child's budding grandiosity, causing it to falter. This undermines the development of healthy narcissism, which is a foundation of ambition. In the case of too much ambition, childhood grandiosity is reinforced rather than modulated. In this case, one or both parents overstimulates the child's "grandiose self," reinforcing unbounded expectations. The parent *seemingly* gives love without limits to the child, stimulating the child's sense of specialness and entitlement. I will show in chapters 7, 8, and 9 that this framework provides a useful way of understanding some important aspects of Clinton's formative experiences.

While Kohut attributes most of the sources of difficulty in the sphere of ambition to parental failures of empathy in one direction or another, external circumstances can also play a reinforcing role. These, too, are helpful in understanding the development of Clinton's ambitions. For example, being a "big fish in a small pond" may facilitate ambition. In these circumstances, the developing child may experience relatively easy success (compared to others whose achievements come less easily), which reinforces rather than modulates expectations of getting what one wants.

For people like Clinton—with the substantial talents, skills, and the success they bring—there is a danger that their success will reinforce their sense of being special and therefore entitled. In short, it may facilitate their grandiosity.

Integrity

At the center of the three elements of character lies the domain of character integrity. It is the central character element, not only because of its own fundamental importance, but because of its crucial role in shaping the other two character domains. The ideals that are the basis of character integrity also help to shape and guide ambition and define how we relate to others. It is an absolutely critical basis for evaluating the character and political performance of presidents.

In ordinary usage, the concept of character sometimes carries with it the connotation of honesty, as in the observation that a person "has character." So, too, the concept of integrity carries with it not only the connotation of honesty, but also of adhering to commendable values. We do not ordinarily equate integrity with the unbridled pursuit of ambition or wealth. The term *character integrity* shares these perspectives but approaches the term's meaning from a more psychologically grounded perspective.

Character integrity actually involves three interrelated sets of psychological elements. First, it reflects the person's acquisition of a set of ideals and values that are both practical and ethical. Second, it reflects the development of a consolidated identity, buttressed by ambitions and skills, but encased in a framework of ideals and values. Third, it reflects a confident sense of oneself as a worthy person.

I define character integrity as the consolidated capacity for fidelity to one's ideals even as one works to fulfill one's ambitions. What are ideals? In one respect they are standards; in another respect they are goals. Ideals are the framework for interpersonal and personal ethics. They are the bases upon which individuals believe they should conduct themselves—in their dealings with others, in economic and other material matters, and ultimately in their relationship with themselves. One result of a well-developed and substantially realized set of ideals and values is a consolidated personal identity and sense of self-esteem.

Early ideals are somewhat abstract, primitive, and grandiose. They often attempt to incorporate levels of virtue and even perfection, based upon how others would like to be (but are not) or would like us to be.[9] Ideals that will stand the test of the real world are affirmations developed over time, through experience, of the ways in which we would like to and, in the best cases, actually do live our lives. They represent a person's sense of appropriate and ethical behavior, built upon the ideas and modeling of others but ultimately of one's own construction.

It is important here to distinguish between holding ideals and being faithful to them. The two are often confused when examining presidents and other political leaders. Ideals are aspirations that are often easier to hold in the abstract than they are to live by in the face of real-world temptations and disappointments. Yet the experience of having remained true to one's ideals, and to have done so under circumstances of adversity, is fundamental to the development of character integrity. Erik Erikson nicely captures this particular aspect of ideals and their refinement in his observations on the difference between *ego identity* and *ego ideal*. He notes that the former "can be said to be characterized by the more or less *actually obtained but forever to be revised* sense of the reality of the self within social reality; while the imagery of the ego ideal could be said to represent a set of *to-be-strived-for but forever-not-quite obtainable ideal* goals for the self" (1959, 160).

The process of developing ideals and values begins early in life. Early ideals come primarily, but not exclusively, from parents and the other early models who try to guide and help us. This is one reason why in examining Clinton's early experiences, it is important to focus not only on what others have said of him, but on what the people who influenced him, such as his mother and stepfather, were really like.

Ideals develop from what individuals see, what they are told, and what they experience (these often are not synonymous). In favorable circumstances, they provide the foundation to develop the ethical frameworks within which one's ambitions can be pursued. The different ideals by which one might live become refined and consolidated in part through the process of addressing, with the help of others, the dilemma of translating ideals into values [10] that adequately address the circumstances we face while still reflecting who we are and wish to be.

Parents play an important role in the process of refining ideals because it is they who are, in good circumstances, closest emotionally and psychologically to the child. The child naturally looks to them when puzzled about the ways in which ideals and values operate in the real world. This role is ongoing and requires of parents a sensitivity to the child's psychology, a willingness to put aside when necessary their own concerns and pursuits, to be available, and above all a strong core of ideals and values in their own psychology.

There are many ways in which this process can falter. Parents may have high or otherwise unrealistic standards for the child. The child may be expected to act as the parents have not. There may be a strong and noticeable discrepancy between what parents say and how they act or treat the child. Or parents may be content to espouse ideals without providing guidance in the difficult task of putting ideals into action. These were issues in Clinton's early experiences.

Without parents who provide boundaries, love, and guidance, ideals can falter. A person may never develop ideals that go beyond securing what he or she wants. Or a person may never be able to resolve the many conflicts that occur among ideals in a way that provides a sense of the basic integrity of one's fundamental ideals, aspirations, and unfolding identity. Or a person may have developed and refined his or her ideals and values but lack the capacity to realize them in a manner that maintains fidelity to them. A developmental failure at any of these levels compromises a person's sense of having a purpose guided by ideals and not solely by self-interest. Failure to consolidate one's ideals also undermines the development of a sense of authenticity and self-esteem. One can always justify self-interest to oneself. However, it is a measure of the power and importance of ideals that the selfish often feel obligated to provide some less self-referential reasons (to themselves as well as others) for their behavior.

Once one has developed a set of ideals and refined them in a way that does justice to the person one feels comfortable with and aspires to be, there remains the step of actually living by them. Ideals, even refined ones, are not always easy to live by. Circumstances may make it difficult to live by one's ideals without substantial penalties. However, as difficult as it may be, it is crucial to the consolidation of one's ideals within one's identity to try to live by them. This does not require perfect virtue or total fidelity, regardless of circumstances.

From the psychological perspective, what does it take to live in accordance with one's ideals and values? First, it requires a capacity to endure loss. The choice to live as fully as possible by one's ideals must be governed by the realization and acceptance of the fact that it will, on occasion, prove costly to ambitions or other personal pleasures. Second, one must be able to endure conflict and a degree of separateness from others. This is especially important for those in high political office, since much of what they do requires decisions that will make some people unhappy.

It is perhaps clearer now why the concept of integrity is so important to an understanding of character and why it has played such a crucial role in evaluations of presidential candidates. Character integrity does not involve a president's public identification with the virtues and ideals that most would find laudable. No one would expect him to say otherwise. Rather, a president's integrity or lack thereof is confirmed by examining his behavior, over time and through difficult circumstances, to see how he has handled the complex dilemmas involving ambition and ideals. The development of integrity suggests a president has integrated his basic psychological motivations, skills, and ideals into an authentic, coherent, and consistent sense of who he is and what he stands for. It follows that in this case, there will be little substantial difference between the person he sees himself to be and would like to be seen as, and the person that he really appears to be.

What is the relationship between ambition and integrity? Is ambition incompatible with ideals? Traditionally, strong ambition has been seen as underlying a drive for power at any cost. (For early but still representative views, see Lasswell 1930; 1948; George and George 1956.) This model clearly fits some presidents, but does it fit all? This question is particularly important because Clinton's personal and policy ambitions are such a clear part of his character and political identity. Ambition in the pursuit of ideals, many of them socially valuable, is an integral part of the development of a strong and favorable sense of self (Kohut 1971, 248). In other words, in Clinton's case, we must attempt to distinguish between ambition in the service of ideals, and ideals that are primarily in the service of ambition.

Personas and Identity: The Crucible of Character Integrity

As the construction of politically desirable personas becomes more common in presidential politics, it becomes increasingly important to distinguish *persona* from *identity* and examine the integrity of that relationship.

A president's identity reflects the confluence of his motives, ideals, values, skills, experiences, and views. At its best, it is a consolidated constellation of motivational, emotional, and cognitive elements that have solidified in the course of development. Psychologically, the presence of a firm personal identity reflects the fact that a president has been able to combine his ambitions, skills, and style productively and has found a way to do so that maintains his integrity.

A solid, coherent *political* identity reflects a president's successful attempt to combine his particular talents, ambitions, and ideals in a political role that does justice to each.[11] It is an important psychological accomplishment because it allows a president to act upon his personal ambitions, skills, views, and style in a way that satisfies not only himself but the public. The failure to develop a strong sense of either personal or political identity is therefore cause for concern not only on psychological grounds, but also on political ones.

A solid political identity is necessary for effective presidential leadership. The president with an established political identity stands for particular personal, political, and policy values and an acceptable style of pursuing them. His political identity plays an important role in his connection with the public, by allowing the electorate to define and understand what he is likely to do and how he is likely to do it. A president can ask the public to take him as he appears only if how he appears reflects, for the most part, who he is. Thus, the concern with who Clinton really is and what he stands for is not an idle one.

Personas, by contrast, are constructions that are often developed to present the candidate as he wishes to appear. The term *persona* in Latin originally meant "mask." Many presidents have attempted to substitute political personas for political identity, but this does not mean that all personas reflect deceit.

There are various reasons why presidents adopt personas. They can use personas to reframe circumstances. Candidate Bill Clinton's self-described persona as the "comeback kid," after placing second in the New Hampshire primary, was a deft twist. It built on something he had accomplished and reframed it in a way that allowed a second-place finish to look like a victory.

Personas can be used to generate political support or as a tool of political leadership. President Eisenhower's persona as a genial, not quite hands-on president apparently masked a clear and incisive mind that was very much concerned with the specifics of presidential decision-making. Eisenhower's "hidden-hand Presidency" (Greenstein 1982) allowed him to do the hard work of presidential leadership and decision-making while giving the impression that not much urgency affected his day-to-day-routine. By not going public, Eisenhower was able to govern with a freer hand.

The difference between the public persona and the "real" president behind it is obviously critical. Persona can reflect a president's identity, but it can also be developed to mask unflattering characteristics. How do we distinguish between the two? One clue lies in the solidity of a coherent, stable, identifiable, and authentic political identity. Eisenhower appears to have used his public persona both to reassure the public and to provide room for himself politically. His political identity, however, was well established and authentically represented many of his personal and political values, including his preference for accomplishment over getting public credit.

One way to distinguish between authentic and masking personas is the degree of consistency between personal and political identities. The ability to develop multiple (and divergent) personas in response to the press of circumstances is, to some, a valuable aspect of "post-modern identity" (Gergen 1991). However, it raises the legitimate suspicion that at the core of these various personas is a person whose only consistency is his attempt to manipulate perception in the service of ambition. The use of the word *new* before a president's name (e.g., the "new" Richard Nixon in 1972 and the "new" Ronald Reagan in 1984) invites the assumption that the president has learned something important from experience and will now be appreciably different. This often proves not to be the case, however, and the reason is simple: It is hard to be a "new" person after so many years of being the "old" one.

Relatedness

The third basic character domain concerns one's stance toward relationships with others and the psychology that shapes it. This sphere contains a continuum of interpersonal relationships, ranging from antagonistic, un-friendly relationships at one pole, through various kinds of friendships, to intimate relationships at the other pole.

From the start, analytic theory stated that others are always central to an individual's psychological development and functioning. In 1921 Freud pointed out:

> The contrast between individual psychology and social or group psychol-ogy, which at first glance may seem to be full of significance, loses a great deal of its sharpness when it is examined more closely. . . . In the individu-al's mental life someone else is invariably involved, as a model, as an object, as a helper, as an opponent: and so from the very first individ-ual psychology . . . is at the same time social psychology as well. (1921, 69)

Somewhat later, psychoanalyst Karen Horney (1937) suggested that as a result of early experience, people develop an interpersonal style in which they move either toward, away from, or against people. In the first case, an individual reaches out toward others, gaining psychologically from relationships. In the second, the individual moves away from relationships either because they are less important than other needs (like those for autonomy or solitude [Storr 1990]) or because of disappointments. In the third, the individual wants contact but engages in a way that ensures distance, not intimacy or friendship. Each of these general orientations toward relationships is accompanied by specific constellations of personal needs and skills.

The successful development and consolidation of ambition and ideals rests in large part on productive experiences with others. Character integ-rity, for example, is involved with the domain of relatedness in a number of ways. Ideals develop out of our relationships and experiences with others (parents, siblings, mentors, friends, and even those who dislike us). The emotional responses of others are instrumental in developing, refining, and consolidating our own ideals. Our sense of self is intimately tied to our relationships with significant others, ranging from the intimacy of parent and family bonds to the other important relationships that develop as a person matures, especially marriage partners and close friends.[12] Our sense of effectiveness and self-confidence also derives in part from our experi-ences with others. The realization of our ambitions always has a direct interpersonal component, whether it involves competing with others, coop-erating with others, or simply measuring our own accomplishments against others.[13]

CHARACTER AND STYLE

Character forms the foundation of a president's overall psychological functioning. It also shapes his personality, and a set of stable psychological orientations that I term *character style*. Character style develops along with character itself out of the specific ways in which the three basic character elements come together and are linked with the individual's personal skills and resources. *Style is the operational enactment of character.*

Character style consists of the ways in which a particular person's strengths and limitations become integrated over adolescence and adulthood into patterns of behavior meant to navigate the circumstances he addresses. Character style is the mediator between character and the external world. The particular character style a person evolves will be shaped by his skills and their success and reception in the world. Intelligence may be strongly valued in one family, charm in another. Once a particular mix of skill, circumstance, and need have come together and brought success, this mix will become consolidated as a character style.

People vary in their genetic and psychological gifts, and hence in their ability to develop specific aspects of style. People who are inclined to move away rather than toward others, for example, are limited in their ability to develop charm. For analytical purposes, we can distinguish three broad areas of endowed or developing stylistic skills: the cognitive/analytic, the interpersonal, and in the characterological.

Character Style and Presidential Performance

Character style allows us to uncover patterns in a president's behavior. Not every president is smart. Not every president is charming. Not all presidents are equally secure and self-reliant. Some presidents are stylistic specialists. They rely heavily on their charm, their intelligence, or their strength of character. Most successful and effective presidents develop more than one of these traits.

The importance of a president's relationships has been long recognized. Richard Neustadt (1990), for example, argues that the essence of presidential power lies in persuasion, an ability that depends on one's relations with others. Ronald Reagan's political success was certainly related to his administration's ability to develop and maintain good working relationships with key Washington power centers as well as with broad segments of the American public (Jones 1988). On the other hand, the failure to develop a good interpersonal style is frequently suggested as one reason that the Carter presidency floundered (Buchanan 1987). Apparently, if Presidents Carter and Nixon hold any lessons for us here, successful presidents move primarily toward people, not away from or against them.

The second set of skills instrumental in developing a character style rests on strong analytic capacities. A person with these skills may be attuned not so much to persons as to problems. He is a skillful problem solver, able to abstract, conceptualize, and analyze. When these skills are not combined with interpersonal strengths, the person may find himself somewhat ill equipped for political life, which, after all, requires the solution of problems within a context of relationships with others.

Barbara Kellerman (1983) notes that Jimmy Carter was an able decision-maker who had difficulty with the interpersonal aspects of exercising power because he was introverted. But Carter also ran into troubles because of his high confidence in his own decisions. Superior intelligence is not enough; it must be combined with an ability to connect emotionally with people. The title of Carter's campaign biography, *Why Not the Best?*, reflected the view that he knew what the best was. In such circumstances, strong intelligence may prove to be the enemy of an effective presidency, which, after all, is precisely about adjudicating different views of what's best. Michael Dukakis, when asked during a presidential debate how he would respond to a criminal who attacked his wife, gave an intelligent answer that focused on due process but left his feelings unaddressed. This conveyed the impression that he was in control, a cool—possibly too controlled—man and thus perhaps unable to empathize with the real-life plight of others.

The third set of skills, characterological strengths, refers to those aspects of the self that emerge from the successful development of the three character elements (ambition, character integrity, and relatedness) and help presidents overcome the inevitable difficulties and setbacks that arise as they make their way in the world. These strengths can include a capacity to endure setbacks or disappointments. Or it can include a capacity to be somewhat self-contained and not too dependent on others for validation, support, or judgment.

The Question of Motivation

Another essential step in analyzing presidential character is to uncover the ways in which the elements of character style are related to the underlying character elements that shape them—that is, what *motivates* his style.

In short, we need to analyze *how* the president's style fits in relation to his overall psychological and behavioral patterns. Is a president's relational style motivated by the hope of being accepted, admired, respected? Does the view of the president as particularly smart and well informed help define his personal and political identity? Is his persistence driven by the need to be validated? Does the president's style flow from developed and consolidated characterological elements, or does it operate primarily to compensate for what he does not have or cannot count on getting?

Consider interpersonal relations, which are clearly so central to Clinton's political style. It is important to know how skilled he is, but also *how* he uses those skills. Lyndon Johnson is often credited with being a masterful president in this regard. His skills at cajoling, manipulating, flattering and, where necessary, threatening are legendary. James David Barber calls this the famous "Johnson Treatment" (see also Evans and Novak 1966, 95–117) and argues that Johnson "exemplifies, as no other president in history, an emphasis on personal relations" (1992, 67).

Doris Kearns (1976, 371–72) writes that Johnson

> obligated his followers by providing them with services or benefits that they desired or needed. But the line between obligation and coercion was often thin. In return for his gifts, Johnson demanded a high measure of gratitude, which could only be acceptably demonstrated by the willingness to follow his lead.... These demands for submission invariably worked against him.

There can be no doubt that Johnson had strong interpersonal political skills. But these skills were in the service of an even stronger psychological need, that of getting his own way at whatever cost. The very array of information he possessed about the strengths and weaknesses of others and the range of his approaches to them reflect that Johnson had a specialized and well-developed skill. But this is not the whole story. Johnson could be demanding, forceful, and, more than occasionally, personally abusive to those who balked at his wishes. The intensity and frequency with which these tactics surfaced suggest that the skills were in the service of a very strong psychological motivation to get his way, in many cases at the expense of others' self-esteem.

Such behavior and the psychology behind it, however, will not always appear in such a stark guise. A "narcissistic character" might well ultimately be interested in exploiting people for his own ends but might nonetheless have developed gracious social skills to do so. There are very practical political reasons for presidents to mask the operation of certain character elements, even from themselves.

What are the three major core elements of Bill Clinton's character? I suggest they are (1) his substantial level of ambition; (2) his immense self-confidence, coupled with a somewhat idealized view of his fidelity to the ideals he espouses; and (3) a distinct and powerful turn toward others in his interpersonal relationships, motivated by his strong need for validation of his somewhat idealized view of himself. Individually and collectively, these elements shape Clinton's approach to his presidency.

In the chapters that follow I will examine each of the three character domains separately, and then go on to examine how they developed over the course of Clinton's childhood, adolescence and early adulthood. Let me first turn to the cornerstone of presidential accomplishment, ambition.

★ ───────────────────────────────

CHAPTER 3

AMBITION

President Clinton's character has been as controversial as his administration. While his capacity to persist in the face of adversity is an important political asset derived from his character, the continuing questions about his integrity represent a character-based liability. His character was an important campaign issue in 1992 and will no doubt be critical in assessing his performance as president in 1996, and in calibrating his place in history.

Clinton's ambition has fueled questions about his character and integrity. His 1992 election as president is widely viewed as the culmination of his (and his wife Hillary's) public ambitions. Many people believe "he has been running for the presidency for most of his adult life" (Oakley 1994, xiv). Yet Clinton himself has publicly disowned any deep ambition. During the 1992 campaign when a heckler accused him of being driven by ambition, Clinton responded angrily, "If I were dying of ambition, I wouldn't have stood up here and put up with all this crap I've been putting up with for the last six months" (Toner 1992; *New York Times,* 28 March, D9).

The evidence, however, strongly points in the opposite direction. There can be little mistaking Clinton's substantial ambition. His path from Hope, Arkansas, to Washington, D.C., is a chronicle of and testament to his personal and political ambitions (Oakley 1994; Maraniss 1995). Clinton was an outstanding student at Hot Springs High School, an accomplished student at Georgetown University, a Rhodes Scholar, and a graduate of Yale

Law School. These accomplishments precede his substantial and upwardly directed political career, which include winning the post of attorney general of Arkansas in 1976 at the age of thirty, becoming the youngest governor in the country in 1978 at the age of thirty-two, and successive reelections to that position in 1982, 1984, 1986, and 1990. He was named cochair of the National Governors Association in 1986 and chairman of the Democratic Leadership Council in 1990. He was prominently mentioned as a possible presidential candidate in 1988. He became a declared candidate in 1992, won his party's nomination, and defeated a sitting president to gain the White House.

The basic dilemma surrounding Bill Clinton's ambition is that presidential ambition is both necessary and suspect.[1] We worry that too much ambition on a president's part reflects deep psychological flaws. On the other hand, ambition, the brother of what might be considered normal narcissism, is, as noted, along with ideals and the talent to achieve its goals, one foundation of a well-realized life (Kohut 1971, 1977). A more focused examination of ambition is needed to help distinguish between ambition that is more concerned with self-aggrandizement and ambition whose personal functions are subordinate to larger public purposes.

In this chapter I develop a psychological and, more specifically, a psychoanalytically framed analysis of President Clinton's character, focusing on his ambition.[2] Indeed, it would not be possible to construct a serious or plausible account of Clinton's development, his political life, and certainly his presidency without examining this core element.

CLINTON'S AMBITIONS: INITIATIVE AND CAPACITY

Many of Clinton's acquaintances along the way recall and can attest to his ambition. Virgil Spurlin, a high school teacher and band director with whom Clinton was extremely close, recalls, "One of the things that will always stand out about Bill is his unique combination of abilities, ambitions, and talents" (Levin 1992, 24). Edith Irons, Clinton's high school teacher and adviser, recalls Clinton "as a man who set his goals and *never* deviated from them" (Levin 1992, 34). Dru Francis, a friend of Clinton's from his days at Georgetown, recalls that "Bill exhibited all the signs of someone who was on the way to somewhere else and in a hurry to get there" (Levin 1992, 5).

His mother, Virginia Kelley, dated Clinton's political ambitions to the time he attended Boys Nation as a sixteen-year-old and shook hands with President Kennedy. Clinton himself dates his political ambitions to the same period. He told *Georgetown Magazine*, "By the time I was seventeen, I knew I wanted to be doing what I'm doing now" (Levin 1992, 35). After his defeat for reelection as governor in 1980, he was asked by a political science student why, given all the choices open to him, he chose to continue his political career. "His response revealed that his urge [towards politics] was so deep and strong that he never saw it as a choice. . . . 'Why politics? It's the only track I ever wanted to run on,' Clinton replied" (Maraniss 1995, 390).

During his political career, which now spans more than three decades, he has lost only two elections. He lost, but barely, in his first try for public office, a campaign for a congressional seat in 1974 against a well-established incumbent. He gained the governorship in 1978 but was defeated for reelection two years later. He has not lost an election since, in spite of controversy, allegations of scandal, and accusations that he cannot be trusted.

In traveling this path, he has made good use of family connections (his uncle Raymond Clinton, a well-connected civic power broker, arranged for him to get a Navy ROTC slot), political connections (Senator J. William Fulbright helped arrange his ROTC deferment at the University of Arkansas and nominated him for his Rhodes Scholarship), and an increasingly sophisticated computerized filing system listing every person he has met, the subject of their conversations, and other data pertinent to maintain contact and political support. However, he has also made good use of some prodigious talents.

TALENTS AND SKILLS

Without talents and skills, ambition is an empty vessel. Therefore, no account of successfully realized ambition can dispense with a consideration of them.

In doing so, however, one essential point must be kept in mind: *A president's skills and talents, as substantial as they might be, are embedded in, not independent of, his interior psychology.* They do not exist independently of his character structure and overall psychology—his ambitions, ideals, and connections with others. This is why talents and skills, even those that would ordinarily be considered virtues,[3] can lead to difficulties. In the analysis that follows I examine both the usefulness and limitations, when they are relevant, of these skills and talents as they affect Clinton's approach to his presidency.

At least four skills and talents have facilitated Clinton's ambition. Two are substantially physical and motivational, one is primarily cognitive, and one is primarily interpersonal. They are (1) a high level of available physical and emotional energy, (2) an ability to invest himself in his work and purposes, (3) high-level cognitive capacities, and (4) a capacity to engage people and convey the impression that he is committed to them and understands their concerns. I will examine the first three here and the fourth in chapter 4.

PERSONAL ENERGY AND STAMINA

There can be little doubt of Clinton's enormous energy and high activity levels (Clift and Cohn 1993). Long before Governor Clinton was impatiently demanding of his staff, "What else. What else" (Maraniss 1995, 383), there were numerous accounts of his high levels of activity, beginning with his high school years and extending through Georgetown, Oxford, and Yale Law School. For example, in high school Clinton, in addition to compiling a strong academic record, was a member and/or president of numerous school organizations.[4] He was also extremely active at Georgetown, although his activities there had a more decidedly political cast to them.[5]

The energy to "fund" his psychological investments was evident during the 1992 presidential campaign. One typical description of Governor Clinton's frenetic campaign schedule noted,

> Enormous energy. . . . His schedule defied human tolerance. . . . On February 17, the day before the New Hampshire primary vote, he made 17 stops over the state.
>
> At 11:30 that night, schedule completed, he asked, "Isn't there a bowling alley that's open all night? We need to shake some hands." (Pryor 1992, xx)

After the election, Clinton's frenetic pace continued. Consider the following representative story by a reporter covering President Clinton on his trip to the Group of Seven (G-7) meeting in Tokyo. In discussing why Clinton might well make some small social gaffes, the reporter notes,

> It's little wonder that the President was feeling silly when you consider his schedule today. Mr. Clinton shuttled from a breakfast and news confer-

ence with Boris N. Yeltsin to an announcement with Prime Minister Kiichi Miyazawa. By mid-afternoon he was in South Korea where he met with President Kim Young Sam and appeared before news reporters for the third time today. By this evening he and his wife Hillary were toasting their hosts at a state dinner at the Blue House. (Ifill 1993h; see also Drew 1994, 90)

Ifill went on to note that the Clintons planned to meet their daughter, Chelsea, in Hawaii for a brief vacation but did not plan to rest immediately: "unable to resist the chance to shake a few more hands, Mr. Clinton has scheduled a rally in Honolulu for Sunday afternoon."

INVESTING IN HIMSELF

Clinton's ambitions have been facilitated by his ability to invest himself in activity and his commitment to accomplishment, as we can see from his academic and political career and the many other activities he was involved in along the way. Clinton was president of so many high school clubs that the principal of Hot Springs High School, Johnnie Mae Mackey, limited the number of organizations a student could join, "or Bill would have been president of them all" (Levin 1992, 30). Edith Irons, an influential teacher for Bill Clinton, recalls that at one point the principal was forced to limit Clinton's community service activities because she feared they were distracting him from his schoolwork (Levin 1992, 32). Clinton was also active in a range of activities at Georgetown, while he worked for Senator Fulbright, and throughout his political career in Arkansas.

In these activities, Clinton was not only a participant but an invested one. In high school, for example, he not only played in the band but made all-state, a recognition of talent but also of practice and commitment. Carolyn Staley, a high school friend with whom Clinton practiced for state music competitions, recalls, "We met several times a week at my house to perfect his solo. We never sat around and chatted. The rehearsals were intense. Bill was always serious about his performances and worked hard to win first place" (1993, 36).

At Georgetown, Clinton worked in a student service organization that greeted new freshman. The first blind student accepted at the university's School of Foreign Service recalled how Clinton personally helped him learn his way around campus by guiding him through various routes until he had mastered them (Levin 1992, 46–48). In 1970 Clinton did the same thing when this student came to Oxford as a Rhodes Scholar (Levin 1992, 67–

68). Clinton appears to be someone who served as well as joined many organizations.

The same pattern of intensive personal involvement characterized his drive for the presidency. Woodward quotes Alan Greenspan as remarking of President-elect Clinton after they had met for three house of intense economic discussions, "He wouldn't need a chief of staff. He would be his own. The president-elect was not only engaged, he was totally engrossed" (1994, 69).

President Clinton was personally involved in trying to win support for almost all of his first-term initiatives (some more than others). Accounts of his attempt to win passage of his first budget make clear that he was involved in a day-to-day and hour-to-hour, hands-on attempt to acquire the necessary votes. The same was true of his attempt to secure enough votes to pass the North American Free Trade Agreement (NAFTA). In late September, "Clinton threw himself into the fight—meeting members of Congress in one-on-one sessions, making many phone calls to them, giving speeches, meeting with opinion leaders, meeting with individual members" (Drew 1994, 340). Upon gaining the presidency, Clinton "essentially extended the campaign through the first nine months of the presidency, taking up the battle with all the urgency of FDR during the depression or a president in war" (Woodward 1994, 329).

Intense Presidential Activity: Virtue or Flaw?

High levels of presidential activity are generally considered a virtue. Presidents who are active convey a sense of commitment to their goals and even a sense of mastery. After all, the reasoning goes, they are doing something so they must have a plan to accomplish their purposes. A president who appears psychologically removed from his administration raises the issues of whether he is really committed to the goals he has espoused and whether he is really in charge of the things being done in his name.

However, high activity levels and personal investment by a president are not unalloyed virtues. Extraordinary levels of activity, especially when the president is psychologically motivated to sustain them, are likely to result in a deepening sense of fatigue. A president who feels he *must* do it all, or worse, feels he *can* do it all, runs the risk of overextending himself both physically and psychologically. The problem is not so much that he will suffer some form of emotional or physical breakdown, but rather that it will begin to affect the quality of his judgments.

A president's use of his time is crucial. The demands for it are enormous. Programs must be touted, allies consulted, Congress lobbied, and the public informed. Added to this are the demands on the president by aides—especially if there are diverse ideological factions within the White House who want his approval of their views and, if possible, his commitment to endorse them publicly. Finally, there are the demands that a president creates for himself, by his agenda, his strategy of leadership, and his approach to organizing and exercising the powers of the presidency.

These issues have emerged with force in the Clinton presidency. There are many indications that Clinton has difficulty in limiting himself and his involvement, even when doing so might be productive. The lag in filling administration positions, for example, was a result of several problems: "Foremost was the President, who, in the midst of everything else he had to do, insisted on signing off on the appointment of every assistant secretary, and sometimes deputy assistant secretaries" (Drew 1994, 99).

Nor did Clinton limit himself in other ways. After the first budget had passed, Bob Woodward reports the following conversation between Secretary of the Treasury Lloyd Bentsen and Clinton:

> "Mr. President . . . You want to make every decision. You can't. You've got to delegate more. . . . Mr. President it's not the quantity of your decisions. It's the quality. I've sat beside you when someone else is talking at one of these meetings, and I watch your eyes just fog over." Bentsen half closed his eyes in imitation of impending sleep. "You're gone. It's because you're tired. You think you can go without sleep. You can't."
>
> "I know you're right," Clinton replied mournfully. "I know you're right, Lloyd."
>
> Things seemed to get better briefly. But they did not change. (1994, 329)

The demands on a president require a capacity to delegate, a consolidated personal and political identity that facilitates the choices a president must ultimately make, and a strong sense of boundaries and limits. A president who feels he can or must do everything will not be able to delegate and will have problems setting appropriate limits for himself and others. A president who is still struggling with where he stands will have difficulty deciding between strongly held but conflicting views. A president who hopes that he won't ultimately have to make those choices or attempts to avoid them by finessing the differences runs the risk of appearing insubstantial or disingenuous, both of which can prove politically fatal.

Clinton's Peripatetic Activity in Psychological Perspective

President Clinton's history of intense peripatetic activity demands scrutiny. Many have said "wonderingly that he was the most frenetic president the nation had ever seen" (Kelly 1992a). However, it is not enough to admire Clinton's high level of activity, we must also understand it. Does it serve any further psychological functions other than the obvious one of furthering his policy ambitions?

Clinton has characterized himself as "almost compulsively overactive" (Moore 1992, 35). There is a relentless, driven quality to him. Whether he is staying up late after a grueling day of campaigning to search for more people to meet, engaging in speed diplomacy, or frenetically relaxing on vacation,[6] Clinton is not only a man in motion, but a man for whom motion is clearly an important psychological element.

There are several possible ways to understand the importance of activity in Clinton's psychology. High activity levels serve ambition and achievement and are thus clearly "functional" for him in that respect.[7] However, compulsive activity is different from being active, a difference captured by the common label "workaholic." These are people for whom work is not merely a means to an end, but a functional end in itself. For them, work does not coexist easily with other interests or pleasures. The need to be driven that pervades such intensive levels of activity suggests that we must search elsewhere for fuller understanding.

Clearly, one important function of intense activity levels is to provide stimulation. A person so motivated relentlessly searches for new experiences ("What else. What else.") to provide stimulation. Clinton's behavioral pattern suggests that he frantically pursues not just work activity, but activity itself.

A major consequence of relentless action is that it displaces quiet. Intensive activity by its very nature precludes thoughtfulness and introspection. It is an effective method of avoidance and therefore may function psychologically in that manner. Even intense discussions or debates about issues or strategies can be seen as part of the search for activity and the avoidance of quiet. The person who uses activity in this way has difficulties being alone. To be alone would be to be thrown back on oneself, perhaps to be put in touch with thoughts, feelings, or experiences one would prefer to avoid.

Does this explanation help account for Clinton's intensive levels of activities? There is evidence that it does. A number of observers have noted that Clinton cannot easily tolerate being alone. He has been characterized by a number of associates as "the consummate social animal—unless engrossed in a good book, he becomes very restless when left alone and seeks out conversation, however, mundane or inconsequential" (Oakley 1994, 41). Speaking of Clinton's aversion to spending time at Camp David,

John Brummett observed, "The quiet (at Camp David) bothered him too. Clinton is not proficient at being alone; if nothing else he'll pick up a telephone" (1994, 196). Meredith Oakley notes that Clinton

> is almost compulsive about seeking people out; many of those midnight calls for which he is famous have no bearing on politics or business of any kind. Sometimes he has no more on his mind than contact with another human being, as evidenced by the time he called a local reporter whose father had just died. Clinton moved through the entire conversation without ever offering his condolences or even indicating any specific reason for having called, but rather giving the bereaved journalist a summary of a book he had been reading. (1994, 93)

This characteristic apparently developed early in Clinton's life. In high school, David Maraniss observes, the many clubs that Clinton joined, and even his intense involvement with the school band, "played to Clinton's personality. He never wanted to be alone. He enjoyed working a crowd, whether old friends or new. He made many close friends in high school, but he seemed more comfortable in crowds" (1995, 47). One clue to why Clinton took and practiced the saxophone in high school was "to fill up the lonely, uncertain hours of childhood. He had always hated to be alone, and playing the sax was one of the few ways he could tolerate it" (1995, 45).

Maraniss goes on to relate this to Clinton's "troubled home," presumably referring to his stepfather's abusive alcoholism. The evidence supports Maraniss in his general observation. However, as I will document and analyze in chapters 7, 8, and 9, which deal with Clinton's childhood, he was alone earlier and in a much more profound way than simply being the child of an alcoholic stepfather.

CLINTON'S COGNITIVE CAPACITIES

Clinton's ambitions have been bolstered substantially by his impressive intelligence. At Hot Springs High School his grades earned him a place in the National Honor Society. At Georgetown they earned him a spot on the dean's list in addition to his political and campus activities. His intelligence is reflected in his selection as a Rhodes Scholar and his performance at Yale Law School. It is also evident from his performance as a professional practitioner of public policy during his ten years as governor of Arkansas.

Clinton has displayed the same intellectual skills as president in such public contexts as the "economic summit" he chaired in December 1992. Many commentaries at the time noted the mastery displayed by "Professor Clinton" as he questioned and discoursed at length on complex economic matters (Friedman 1992; Rosenbaum 1992). The general impression conveyed by his performance was of a president who not only understood but had mastered the complex interpretations needed to address the increasingly interdependent domestic and international economic systems. Alan Greenspan, chairman of the Federal Reserve, who met with the president-elect for a long and detailed discussion of the complex economic issues that faced the new administration, had the same view. Greenspan came away from that meeting thinking that "Clinton's reputation as a policy junkie was richly deserved" and that Clinton was "remarkably knowledgeable" (Woodward 1994, 69).[8]

Clinton's press conferences as president have also displayed a mastery of detail and subject matter on a wide range of issues. He is able to answer a variety of questions on diverse policy topics with an array of information and a sophisticated appreciation of the issues involved. Indeed, after one particularly effective press conference, one of his aides remarked that he ought to do them more often since they showed off his intellectual and verbal skills to such good advantage. Clinton has not only mastered a wide range of information, but has also developed meaningful categories in which to organize it. Whether these categories reflect deep or creative integration of this information in ways that point toward the successful resolution of policy dilemmas is a question I will address in chapter 13.

Another indicator of Clinton's substantial cognitive capacities is his ability to do several things at once. Hillary Clinton has said of her husband, "He'll be watching some obscure basketball game, and he'll be reading and talking on the phone all at the same time and knowing exactly what is going on in each situation" (Allen and Portis 1992, 169). According to Elizabeth Drew, "Not a man to do one thing at a time, Clinton often watched an old movie on television while talking on the telephone" (1994, 90). When Clinton was governor, "When someone went in to brief him on a subject or an upcoming event, his habit was to keep doing some other activity, either reading or writing, at the same time that he was being briefed" (Maraniss 1995, 383).

Clinton, however, on occasion has been capable of unexpected and basic errors of information and understanding. When told of the important relationships between federal deficit reduction, reductions in interest rates by the Federal Reserve, and increased business confidence resulting in an improved economic climate, Clinton turned red with anger and disbelief, asking, "You mean to tell me that the success of the program and my reelection hinges on the Federal Reserve and a bunch of fucking bond traders?" (Woodward 1994, 84). The same information had been conveyed to Clinton a month earlier in a meeting with Greenspan, who, as noted, left the meeting impressed with Clinton's grasp of his tutorial.

The most dramatic illustration of this occasional, but important, lapse concerned the impact on the Clinton budget of caps agreed to during Bush's presidency. After the House slashed the administration's "investment package" from $231 billion over five years to only $1 billion in the first year (1994) rising to less than $6 billion the following year (1995), a meeting was quickly convened to discuss this crisis.

> It was instantly apparent that the president didn't grasp what had happened. The magnitude and importance of the House's action had never sunk in. . . . The president began to yell and shout questions. . . . Clinton let loose a torrent of rage and frustration. Why hadn't they ever had a serious discussion about the caps? . . . Why didn't they tell me? (Woodward 1994, 161)

Many of those at the meeting believed that they had let the president down. Secretary of Labor Robert Reich thought, "All of them should have seen this coming" (Woodward 1994, 162). In fact, Reich had a point, but it applied equally, perhaps more so, to Clinton as it did to the others. After all, the 1990 budget accord was well known to Clinton since it had helped his election by allowing him to portray Bush as going back on his "Read my lips, no new taxes" pledge. Moreover, Clinton had immersed himself in domestic politics and budgets for decades. The spending caps imposed by Congress surely were a large and conspicuously relevant consideration for his spending plans. If it was an oversight, it was a rather large one.[9]

Looking back over Clinton's impressive performance as an adolescent and young adult, one element emerges that may help to explain his having been taken unaware in the two circumstances described above. Being very smart has clearly been advantageous for Clinton. However, through the years it has on occasion led him to be either overconfident or underprepared. An early example of this is related by childhood friend Joe Neuman, who was Clinton's partner in an eleventh-grade science assignment. As Neuman recalls, "Bill . . . told me he would take care of everything. That was good since I sure had no idea what we'd do. . . . The day before the fair he came up with a curved, shiny piece of sheet metal and put a hot dog on it. Our project was a solar hot dog cooker . . . we got the 'D' we deserved" (Levin 1992, 28–29).

At Oxford Clinton was known to read a lot, but was also "known to be lackadaisical about his studies, often skipping class lectures" (Oakley 1994, 62). At Yale Law School, "he was less devoted to his studies than most because of his consuming interest in politics and his amazing ability to memorize many facts and figures quickly and store them for use at will. His class attendance was sporadic" (Oakley 1994, 102; see also Maraniss 1995, 233–35). His last term at Yale, "he studied little and attended few classes" (Oakley 1994, 121). To prepare for his final examinations, he borrowed a friend's notes and disappeared for a few days to memorize the material. He was, according to William T. Coleman III, a friend of Clinton's at that time, "a classic quick study" (1993, 121).

The same tendencies were also evident when Clinton took a teaching position at the University of Arkansas Law School after graduating from Yale (Oakley 1994, 128; Moore 1992, 40). One faculty colleague of Clinton's there recalls, "On the morning of exam day, colleagues knowingly chortled at the sight of Clinton in a frenzy because he had waited until the last minute to prepare the exam. Students were answering the first question while Clinton was writing the next. Clinton always seemed to be juggling too many things at one time" (Maraniss 1995, 292).

One of Clinton's top aides during his first term as governor, Stephen Smith, recalls that when Clinton returned to Arkansas from Yale, he "impersonated a law professor and pondered his political future" (1993, 5). A student of Clinton's at Arkansas Law School who went on to become a reporter in Arkansas recalls, "It was clear to us all that his interest was in politics and not in teaching, but he was a good teacher in his own way" (Bassett 1993, 74). A senior faculty member, Mort Gittleson, asked to prepare an evaluation of Clinton's teaching, wrote that "he was very good at engaging students . . . but a lot of times he was off-the-cuff. . . . He was not the kind of person who would prepare a class meticulously" (Maraniss 1995, 293; see also Moore 1992, 40).

As governor, one of the two most frequent complaints about Clinton from state legislators was that he was never prepared for legislative sessions (Oakley 1994, 333). Typical was the 1987 session, in which Clinton's proposal for the state's two-year budget, which was to begin in July, was not introduced until late February. Oakley notes, "Each day seemed to bring a new round of criticism from lawmakers who were upset because the governor's proposals were late in coming, or came to them poorly drafted and requiring extensive rewrites" (1994, 335). The same pattern of too many proposals, not clearly enough thought through, has been a problem at the Clinton White House.

Clinton's substantial intelligence has been a tremendous advantage, but it has also paradoxically resulted in some difficulties. It has enabled Clinton to perform at high levels of accomplishment. It has also apparently led him on occasion to rely on his ability to "wing it." He sometimes appears to believe that intelligence can substitute for preparation. This belief has been *relatively* successful for him in the past, which has no doubt reinforced his confidence that he is not bound by conventional cognitive limits. However, for a president this is a potentially dangerous psychology.

CHARACTER AND THE LIMITS OF INTELLIGENCE

Like his activity levels and capacity to make personal investments in achieving his goals, Clinton's intelligence has much to recommend it as a presidential attribute. The presidency demands a capacity to deal with complexity. Intelligence is one, but not the only, tool that facilitates meeting this demand. Intelligence, however, like activity and personal investment, is not a virtue without limits, nor is it unconnected to other parts of his psychology.

Consider Clinton's substantial policy knowledge, which, when coupled with his verbal ability, would make a desirable set of presidential skills. Clinton's substantial verbal facility includes the capacity to produce a "perfectly grammatical 100-odd word sentence . . . extemporaneously" (Greenstein 1993–94, 593). While we can acknowledge the verbal skill associated with such capacities, the real question is whether this skill is used to facilitate or diminish public understanding.

In an interview with Ted Koppel on *Nightline* (September 24, 1993) in connection with Clinton's appearance on a nationally televised "town hall," Clinton gave a particularly long answer to a question Koppel asked. Koppel then commented, "Mr. President, this is a curious criticism to make, but sometimes I think you're so specific in your answers, that it's a little hard to know what your answer is." As one reporter characterized the exchange, "Mr. Koppel lost patience with the torrent of words at one point and complained that the President was being glib to the point of obfuscation" (Ifill 1993c, A1).

Intelligence facilitates policy understanding by allowing the president to grasp the meaning of complex substantive material. It is also an important tool for weighing evidence and making appropriate inferences. However, intelligence is not synonymous with good decision-making, nor does the level of a president's intelligence tell us much about the uses to which he puts it. These are matters of judgment and character.

When Clinton's advisers met during the campaign to discuss the middle-class tax cut, there was disagreement about whether it would operate as an economic stimulus (Woodward 1994, 30–31). In private, Clinton ultimately came to side with the arguments of Rob Shapiro, an economist and one of Clinton's early economic advisers, that it would not. However, Clinton nonetheless included language in his book *Putting People First* that promised publicly what he had come to doubt privately. In thus choosing, Clinton made a political decision rather than a substantive one.

The role that character can play in inhibiting the usefulness of intelligence is perhaps most obvious in the case of learning. Intelligence does not guarantee that a president will not make mistakes, but it can increase the chances that he will not make the same (or a similar) mistake twice. Many think this is an area in which Clinton's intelligence has helped him. Commentators have said that Clinton seems incapable of sustained error.[10] Fred Greenstein (1995, 143) thinks Clinton's ability to rebound in the face of adversity, his essential pragmatism, and his ability to admit his own errors help to account for this.[11]

It is perhaps useful to distinguish here between being incapable of *sustained* error and making *repeated* errors. Making sustained errors would require the president to persist in a course of action that appears to be, or is obviously, causing harm to his administration. That is, it requires that the president pursue a damaging policy to its ultimate damaging end regardless of strong evidence of its potential consequences. This failure to heed the obvious is illustrated by Lyndon Johnson's pursuit of a victory in Vietnam, Woodrow Wilson's failure to compromise to get his League of Nations Treaty through the Senate, and Richard Nixon's handling of Watergate (Barber 1992, 23–54).

In contrast, Clinton has been extremely dexterous at changing direction in response to changes in political circumstances. His turn toward the center with the selection of David Gergen as White House counselor midway through his first term and his return to New Democrat themes after the Democratic party debacle of the 1994 midterm elections are two illustrations of this skill. In that sense, he does address the political harm caused by his policies or actions. In making necessary corrections to preserve his political standing and viability, he also demonstrates the pragmatism (even if it was in this case somewhat obligatory) that many have noted.

However, acknowledging that one's policies or tactics are not working and must be changed to ensure continued political viability is a limited definition of political learning. Only a fool would continue to march straight ahead to his own political demise, and Clinton is no fool. But his short-term flexibility masks a more profound set of questions. Why is he so frequently in the position of needing to correct what he has been doing? What does his flexibility suggest about his core personal and political identity? Political flexibility is often discussed as if it were an unalloyed virtue, when in fact its virtue rests on the presence of a core personal and political identity that provides the boundaries within which it is exercised.

Moreover, a *repeated* need for shifting political direction is an important performance issue in its own right.[12] Greenstein observes that Clinton's pragmatism "appears to come into play only after outside forces have humbled him" (1993–94, 596). Why does he need to be humbled in order to do politically what he might have easily done in the first place?

Clinton may be incapable of making sustained errors, but he is not incapable of repeating profound ones. As a case in point, consider Clinton's difficulties during the first two years of his presidency in the context of his performance in his first term as governor in Arkansas. As is now common knowledge, Clinton was defeated in his reelection campaign for governor in 1980. Explanations for the defeat abound. There was Clinton's decision to raise taxes on automobile registration in a way that was especially hard on those with older, heavier cars, that is, those less able to afford new cars. There was the issue of Cuban exiles housed at Fort Chaffe who rioted and broke out of the camp. Others have mentioned the negative impact of Hillary Rodham's decision to keep her own name. Hillary herself is quoted as attributing Clinton's defeat to the fact that he "had not communicated a vision or described the journey he intended" (Woodward 1994, 110).

However, the best key to understanding Clinton's defeat comes from his advisers and the path they selected for his successful comeback. Almost immediately after the loss, Clinton began to plan his reelection with consultant Dick Morris (who has also been brought in to head President Clinton's reelection campaign in 1996). Morris suggested that Clinton ask forgiveness from the state's voters, but Clinton was reluctant to do so. Clinton preferred instead to say that he had made errors and to "explain and justify what he had done" (Maraniss 1995, 398). In the end he agreed to apologize, but not directly. Rather, he told the state's voters that his "daddy had never had to whip him twice for the same thing," and that "he would never make the same mistakes again" (1995, 399). Just what these mistakes were was left unspecified, allowing Clinton to do what his consultants told him was necessary in order to be reelected, while satisfying his view of himself as having done nothing wrong and his tendency to "justify every specific action he had taken" (1995, 398). This was one of a long string of efforts by Clinton to have it both ways.

His campaign slogan was "You can't lead without listening," which reflected the view that he had lost because he had attempted too much, too soon, without adequate public preparation. Even Levin, a very friendly biographer, admits that Clinton's staff "was brilliant, young, reform minded, and . . . convinced that they knew what was best for the state" (1992, 133). Rudi Moore, Jr., Governor Clinton's chief of staff during his first term, writes,

> Some of the personalities [of Clinton's advisers] did seem to abrade people, even inside the administration. It was *one of the elements* that contributed to the perception that many people began to have of Bill: that of an arrogant young man who was going to impose his ideas on Arkansas people whether they were ready from them or not. (1993, 89, emphasis mine)

David Osborne, in his book *Laboratories of Democracy,* quotes Clinton as saying after his loss that he learned "a reformer must find a way to do what his constituents want, not what he thinks they need" (1988, 89). After losing his bid for reelection in 1980, Clinton told John Brummett, "If I ever get the chance again, I'm not going to force people to do what's good for them" (1994, 68). The conviction that he knew what people needed, even if they didn't, may be one source of the view that Clinton was arrogant, or at least presumptuous.

On the eve of his successful 1982 comeback, in an interview for *Current Biography Yearbook 1988,* Clinton himself said, "I made a young man's mistake. . . . I had an agenda a mile long that you couldn't achieve in a four year term, much less a two year term. *I was so busy doing what I wanted to do that I didn't leave time enough to correct mistakes"* (Moritz 1988, 120, emphasis mine).

One can make a strong case that the repudiation of the Democrats and President Clinton in the 1994 midterm election was a result of similar factors. In his first inaugural address as governor on January 9, 1979, Clinton began his term of office by stressing the limits of government:

> In the recent past, we have learned again the hard lessons that there are limits to what the government can do—indeed, limits to what people can do. We live in a world in which limited resources, limited knowledge and limited wisdom must grapple with problems of staggering complexity. (Levin 1992, 127)

Once in office, however, he immediately initiated an ambitious plan for change. In his first term, "He had not one or two priorities, but scores of them, encompassing virtually every area of public policy" (Oakley 1994, 198). In his first appearance before a joint session of the legislature he laid out proposals in which

> virtually every area of public policy was covered: economic development, education, energy and environmental policy, health and human services, improvements in the infrastructure, taxation and tax incentives. Clinton threw into the pot several extremely controversial measures, too, most of which . . . he doubted would pass. (Oakley 1994, 197)

Hillary Clinton's understanding of her husband's defeat noted above— namely, that he "had not communicated a vision or described the journey he intended"—is validated by these facts, but perhaps not in the way she intended.

A similar dynamic can be seen in the first years of the Clinton presidency. Clinton campaigned as a New Democrat, a president who would return to traditional values and who, in discussing the importance of personal responsibility, seemed to be conveying an appreciation of the limits of government. Yet the first year of the Clinton administration was marked by the proposal of several new large-scale government programs in the area of national service, a complex, large-scale free vaccine program that ran into substantial difficulties, and an enormous expansion of government regulation of and involvement in the health-care system. At the same time Clinton's support of abortion, his championing of homosexuals in the military, his apparent preoccupation with the appearance of diversity in his administration, and his support for affirmative action seemed to many inconsistent with the themes on which he campaigned.

He also assembled a young, inexperienced staff (not cabinet) of aides and advisers who had strong ideas about what the country needed. Their lack of experience coupled with the their strong views of the country's needs, which they saw as self-evident, led to excesses. One of Clinton's aides, upon being greeted at the White House by a military official, responded "I don't talk to the military" (Drew 1994, 45). In July 1992 one of Clinton's senior advisers prepared a memo for White House officials entitled "Hallelujah! Change Is Coming." The memo, which dealt with the new administration's economic and political plans, urged members of the administration to use everything, including their body language, to convey the message, "This is good, and this is change" (Woodward 1994, 261).

Are Clinton's first terms as governor and as president comparable? In a word, yes. In both cases, Clinton started by saying he understood the limits of government, but, upon gaining office, immediately launched an ambitious personal and public agenda. In both cases, he recruited inexperienced but ideologically committed aides who reinforced his own tendencies to believe he could solve almost every problem with a program, and had a personal and public responsibility to do so. In both cases, he pushed causes and policies inconsistent with both the promises on which he had been elected and the preferences of a substantial portion of the citizens he had been elected to serve. In Arkansas, as in Washington, Clinton's real views were a constantly moving target as he tried to finesse a fundamental and ultimately irreconcilable inconsistency: You cannot maintain a promise to respect limits and do less by blurring boundaries so that you can do more.

Learning from mistakes requires more than intelligence. It requires a capacity for introspection, an ability to see what you are doing and how it *really* affects people, as opposed to how *you* think it affects them, or how you think they *should* be affected. It requires a president to move beyond the search for smarter tactics to accomplish his purposes and to consider, even if only briefly, the possibility that his basic premise might be somewhat mistaken. This in turn requires of a president that he truly step away and momentarily reconsider his own ambitions, his confidence that what he is doing for people is right even if they don't yet appreciate that, and his own view of himself as working only for their benefit.

There is no strong evidence that this process has taken place for Clinton. In his first press conference after the November 1994 midterm elections, Clinton publicly voiced his view of what the election results meant:

> What I think they said is they still don't like what they see when they watch us working here. They still haven't felt the positive results of the things that we have done here that they agree with when they hear about them. . . . They are still not sure that we understand what they expect the role of government to be. . . . They want us to do more. (Clinton 1994a)

In these remarks, Clinton acknowledges that the public wants a smaller government that more clearly reflects their values. However, his point about the public not appreciating what he has done on these issues suggests that he believes he has been accomplishing these purposes, and that what stands between his and the public's view is perception, not reality. From Clinton's assertion that the public wants him to do more of what he has already been doing, it is clear that he believes he is already on the right course.

CHAPTER 4

CHARACTER INTEGRITY

Character integrity lies at the core of presidential performance. Psychologically, character integrity reflects our fidelity to our own ideals as we pursue our ambitions and forge our identities. Politically, it is reflected not so much in where a president stands as in what he ultimately stands for. It is not only about his stated political goals, but *how* he chooses to accomplish them. While character integrity does not guarantee that a president will not make costly political and policy mistakes, its absence almost certainly guarantees that he will, especially in a political climate of public skepticism with government and leaders.

Ultimately, character integrity reflects a president's ability to maintain boundaries. It reflects the lines he draws and maintains regarding his ethics, his treatment of others, and the political positions he favors. It is important psychologically that a president be committed to his ideals and values. It is not enough simply to have ideals; they must also be worth fighting for, and worth enduring loss to maintain.

Character integrity has been a recurring issue for Clinton—as governor, as presidential candidate, and as president. What does he really stand for? Are personal ambition and political viability his basic concerns? Is he consistent in his stated commitment to being a New Democrat? Ultimately, these questions can be reduced to two basic questions: Is Clinton honest? Can Clinton be trusted?

Questions of honesty and integrity go to the heart of Clinton's presidency. If by honesty one means that Clinton almost always says what he knows to be true and almost always doesn't say what he knows to be untrue, that he is substantially candid about all the implications of his policies and not just their advantages, then the preponderance of evidence points in one direction. Judged by these standards Clinton has not been honest with the public, and his behavior to date does not give confidence in his trustworthiness. There is much evidence to support these views,[1] but that is not the end of the issue by any means. Like Clinton's high levels of activity, it is not enough to document what, at this point, has become fairly obvious; rather, we must also try to account for and understand it.

OBJECTIONS TO A FOCUS ON CLINTON'S CHARACTER INTEGRITY

One can argue that by focusing on lapses in character integrity we run the risk of overlooking all the good that President Clinton has done or might do. That is a risk; however, our role here is not to pass moral or final judgments[2] but to account for the patterns that are essential to understanding Clinton's presidency and political career. To fail to address what is clearly a reoccurring, even persistent, pattern of behavior would be the intellectual equivalent of malpractice.

A second objection attempts to transfer the argument from psychological to political grounds, arguing that a president shows "character" or rectitude in championing programs that help people. Clinton himself, responding to an interviewer who asked whether questions regarding his character had devalued the moral authority of his office, made that exact argument: "I think it demonstrates character when you're going immunize every kid under two years of age. I think it demonstrates character that in spite of all this rhetoric and hate-filled stuff, we fought to expand Head Start and let people go to college [through the National Service Program]" (Clinton 1995b, 22).

This argument is attractive on the surface, but it falters on several grounds. First, it is unclear whether the president is saying that he should be given credit for the content of his programs (e.g., it shows character to immunize children because that is a good deed), because others have opposed his plans (and he has gone ahead anyway), or both. One problem with assigning "character" to the content of particular policy positions is that their utility and even necessity are often in the eyes of the beholder. Is

Clinton's passage of a National Service Program a plus in the character column? Conservatives and liberals would have different opinions. The existence of opposition is a difficult basis on which to assign character because few policies generate no opposition. Moreover, criticism of *aspects* of a policy doesn't necessarily reflect opposition to the policy itself. Critics of the Head Start program, for example, have called attention to the dangers of investing too much in a program whose widely touted results rest on a narrow empirical base. In other words, suggesting caution is a mild form of opposition, one that accepts the basic worth of the policy.

In standing his ground a president can show fidelity to principle and demonstrate character. However, policies are a result of many personal and political factors, which makes it more difficult to assign the virtues of "character" to them. When President Clinton put forward his economic stimulus package in his first budget, it was as much in response to the strong urging of Democratic members of Congress and Democratic mayors in the country's major urban centers as it was to any economic rationale (Woodward 1994, 70, 110; Drew 1994, 114–20). Moreover, the stimulus package contained funding for a number of programs—such as a beach parking lot in Ft. Lauderdale or student drawings of "significant structures" for deposit in the Library of Congress—that were of questionable value. In one of his first acts as a New Democratic president who had promised to reinvent government, "quality control, or even coherence wasn't even a consideration" (Drew 1994, 115). Clinton's proposals overrode the concerns of more moderate Senate Democrats who wanted to delay spending the money placed in the stimulus bill until comparable budget cuts were put in place (Brummett 1994, 100). Anyone who wants to link character to policy might have a hard time scoring this bill on a character ledger. Would trying to do things for people count as a plus, regardless of how much need there was or how inconsistent the package was with the promise to be a New Democrat or to work with the opposition party? As these questions suggest, the calculus for assigning the virtues of character to policies are far from clear.

It is true that most, perhaps all, presidents have occasionally misled the public. It is also true that President Clinton is not alone in stressing the virtues, and not the limitations, of his plans. Why, then, focus on Clinton in this regard? Isn't he just like every other president? No, not really. Questions about candor, integrity, and fidelity to ideals conveyed by a political identity did not emerge with any great force in the Truman, Eisenhower, Kennedy, Ford, Carter, Reagan, and Bush presidencies,[3] whatever specific policy controversies might have taken place during their administrations. They emerged with greater force, and for better reasons, in the Johnson and Nixon presidencies. The "every president does it" argument ignores vast and important differences in the *frequency* and *patterns* of such behavior among presidents.

Moreover, this argument neglects the basic public dilemma that many hoped the Clinton presidency would address, namely, the decline of the public's trust in its presidents, policies, and institutions. It is one thing for Eisenhower to have misled the public on a national security issue but maintained and earned the public's trust otherwise. It is another for a president to come to office during a time when people hope to have their trust restored in their leaders and policies, to promise to do so, and then to fail to act consistently with that promise.

It is of course true that all presidents believe their plans are best. Presumably no president would put forward policy plans that reflected a preponderance of limitations over advantages. But that is not the point. The point is that in a climate of public distrust, honesty regarding the relative benefits and possible limitations of one's policies is more than a luxury, it is a necessity. Here again, presidents differ. When Franklin Delano Roosevelt assumed the presidency in 1934, he frankly told the American people that he had no guaranteed answers. But what he promised them was that he would immediately start implementing what he thought were good ideas and see if they worked. If they didn't work, he would discard them.

It is also possible to argue that presidents cannot always see the effects of their programs and thus cannot be held accountable for those that turn out differently than they intended. This is accurate to some degree, but it fails to address a very critical point. A president who does not ask of the programs he would like to propose what their possible consequences are and give some time to considering them has chosen optimism over candor.

Presidents can develop good reasons for continuing a particular course of behavior. They may come to believe strongly in their good intentions or in their own vision of how their policies will work. Believing strongly that he is right, a president can easily rationalize avoiding candor as temporarily necessary or justified by the ultimate results he envisions. This can be based on his own intimate knowledge of his good intentions, the identification of his wishes with those of the people, the bolstering of these feelings by the persons he surrounds himself with, or all three. These are especially important issues for President Clinton.

Examining these issues for any president requires us to focus on the four interrelated dimensions of character integrity. The first are the president's ideals and values—where he draws the lines that separate yes from no, right from wrong and ethical from questionable. The second concerns his fidelity to his ideals and values, his ability to follow through on them even in difficult circumstances. (I will examine some aspects of Clinton's fidelity in this chapter, and also in chapter 5 and elsewhere.) The third area concerns the president's own views of his fidelity to the ideals and values he espouses. The fourth area concerns the president's degree of self-confidence both in himself and in the personal and political identity he has developed and consolidated.

IDENTITY, IDEALS, AND CHARACTER INTEGRITY

Among any person's most important psychological accomplishments is the development and consolidation of an identity that allows both expression and satisfaction of one's ambitions and ideals.[4] A consolidated political identity reflects a president's personal and political ideals, values, and psychology. The public looks to a presidential candidate to present his political identity in a clear and forthright manner because it provides them with an understanding of his vision of his presidency. This identity thus becomes part of the implied and expressed political contract between the president and the public.

A president's public expression of his ideals and values provides a benchmark against which we can examine his actual personal and political choices. We cannot rely on the expression of laudable sentiments since these are to be expected on political grounds, and also because presidents are likely to view their own behavior in the best light. An intelligent and articulate president like Clinton has even more tools available to justify his actions, both to himself and others.

A consolidated political identity does not require that a president rigidly adhere to any ideal, value, or position regardless of circumstance. A president who operated that way would soon raise legitimate psychological issues of another sort. Nor does it obviate the need or desirability for a president to maneuver to accomplish his purposes. All successful presidents do so to some degree. What it does require, however, is a clear, generally consistent set of ideals and values, expressed not only in words for public consumption but in choices made and actions taken. Fidelity to one's choices and honest means to obtain them are not functions of political ideology. From the psychological standpoint, authentic political identities as "traditional Democrat," "New Deal liberal," "Goldwater conservative," or "New Democrat" all have equal standing.

A president with a solid political identity will establish a range of accommodation within which his ideals and values (including ethical standards) operate, and outside of which he will refuse to move, even if it decreases his chances of getting what he wants, and even if his personal and or political positions suffer. In short, it requires a president to be willing to make difficult choices and to accept their consequences.[5]

Clinton's Political Identity: Ambiguity and Controversy

At one level the controversy over Bill Clinton's political identity has revolved around which label most accurately defines him. As noted in chapter 1, presidential candidates (and some presidents) have, in the last decade, attempted to blur the sharper edges of their ideological convictions. So an argument can be made that Clinton's self-identification as a New Democrat, one who transcends traditional Left—Right politics, is merely a continuation of those trends.

However, even though some past presidents have resisted ideological labels, it was still fairly easy to get an accurate fix on their political identity and the personal ideals, values, and beliefs at its foundation. While Richard Nixon, for example, took some moderate domestic positions, few would mistake him for a liberal Democrat. So, too, while Jimmy Carter took some moderate conservative positions on issues like defense, few would mistake him for a Goldwater Republican. The political identities of Presidents Johnson, Kennedy, Reagan, and Bush were all easily and comfortably placed within the frameworks of their respective parties.

Central to Clinton's expressed political identity as a New Democrat in the 1992 campaign was his assertion that he was neither a liberal nor a conservative, but a president who would transcend traditional Left-Right politics. In the introduction to his campaign book (with Al Gore), Clinton noted that "our policies are neither liberal or conservative, neither Democratic or Republican. They are new. They are different. We are confident that they will work" (Clinton and Gore 1992, viii). At a representative speech to the Urban League, Clinton said, "Your plan and my plan . . . do not involve liberal versus conservative, left versus right, big government versus little government. That's a load of bull we've been paralyzed by for too long. Your plan and my plan are about big ideas versus old ideas" (Ifill 1992c).

Some disagree and argue, "Nuance and lengthy analysis aside, Clinton in his soul is a fairly conventional liberal Democrat" (Brummett 1994, 26). Others see a moderate and argue that

> the notion that Bill Clinton began his political career as a radical and moved inexorably rightward over the decades is misleading. He was a cautious defender of the establishment in his student days at Georgetown. In his Oxford and Yale years, he was in the moderate wing of the anti-war movement. From the beginning of his assent in Arkansas, he would attack organized labor and court corporate interests when it served his political purposes. (Maraniss 1995, 451)

Clinton's behavior as president has amplified rather than resolved the issue. Clinton has supported racial preferences, a stimulus bill loaded with antipoverty social action programs, and such cultural issues as allowing declared homosexuals to serve in the military. On the other hand, Clinton has supported NAFTA, federal debt reduction, and a crime bill that included a "three strikes" provision. The disparate nature of his positions coupled with his numerous policy shifts have left many arguing that Clinton has no authentic center, no real political identity, and thus no real core of ideals or values to organize and consolidate his presidency. One reason for this view is that "Clinton . . . tends to envelope people and ideas rather than confront them, and so he remains slightly out of focus" (Klein 1993b, 33). Others argue, "What is worrying about Bill Clinton is the possibility that something very fundamental is lacking in this very smart man. He may have inadvertently said it in his comment on dropping Lani Guinier: 'This is about my center, not about the political center' " (Lewis 1993b). Another observer writing about the difference between candidate Clinton and President Clinton, worried that Clinton "doesn't challenge people to take responsibilities for their own lives as he once did; he offers them programs. He lists towards moral relativism; he doesn't talk about what's right or wrong anymore. And the suspicion grows that he didn't really mean it the first time" (Klein 1993a).

Clinton himself has bridled at the these concerns. In an interview with *Newsweek,* Clinton had the following exchange with the correspondents,

> NEWSWEEK: One rap against you is that you're not sure what you stand for. David Gergen has said there's a struggle for the soul of Bill Clinton. You disagree with that?
> CLINTON: Absolutely. . . . I find it amazing that anyone could question whether I have core beliefs. . . . This idea that there's some battle for my soul is the biggest bunch of hooey I ever saw. I know who I am; I know what I believe. . . . Maybe (the problem is) my so-called New Democrat

philosophy has some liberal elements and some conservative elements. Most thinking people, particularly the older they get, have liberal convictions and conservative convictions. (Clinton 1995b, 43)

Controversy about Clinton's real political identity is not confined to the public and outside political observers. His actual political identity, core ideals, and values are a matter of confusion and concern to even his closest aides. Bob Woodward reports that James Carville and Paul Begala, two aides very close to the president during his campaign and in the White House,

> still had one fundamental question about Clinton. . . . Once Carville took out a piece of paper, drew a little square, and tapped it with his pen. "Where is the hallowed ground?" He asked. "Where does he stand? What does he stand for? For Begala, too, that was the most perplexing question about the man." (Woodward 1994, 125)

George Stephanopoulos, another extremely close Clinton adviser, was unable

> to discern the real Clinton. . . . One moment he wanted more costly investments, the next moment more cuts. Stephanopoulos referred to the conflict as the "unbridgeable chasm" in Clinton and the economic plan: the investment, populist, soak-the-rich side versus the deficit reduction, slash-the-spending side. Clinton's conflict rather than being resolved, seemed only to deepen with time. (Woodward 1994, 225)

At another point Stephanopoulos says that

> he knew it was a mistake to assume that any one moment with Clinton, any one conversation, day, or even week reflected Clinton's true feelings or fundamental attitude about something. With a particular audience or person Clinton was generally consistent. . . . But he could articulate a totally different, even contradictory rap to the next audience with genuine sincerity. (Woodward 1994, 185)

FIDELITY TO IDEALS: PROMISES MADE, KEPT, AND ABANDONED

Fidelity to ideals is a critical dimension of character integrity. It reflects a person's willingness and capacity to follow through on the commitments he has chosen to the best of his abilities. A president's ideals and values, and his commitment to them, are particularly important resources. The fact that a president has a strong, coherent set of ideals, that he does not lightly undertake actions that put those ideals on the line, and that once committed he *will* follow through, are the elements that underlie the meaning of *gravitas* or stature in a president.

Of course, this does not mean that a president can't compromise, or that he must follow every one of his initiatives to the end, no matter what. But it does require the president not to commit himself lightly or easily. It requires a seriousness of purpose, which in turn requires that a president carefully consider what he wants to do so that his commitment is real, not just expedient. The reason is not that expediency is always to be eschewed, but rather that a carefully thought through commitment that the president comes to believe is *really* important not only underscores his seriousness, but also provides him with a small but important psychological basis for enduring adversity. A president who has come to the conclusion that a policy, an initiative, an appointment, a promise *is* important, given his ideals and values, will find it easier to endure the political or personal hardships that might accompany commitment to it.

Fidelity to ideals and values is not only manifested in a president's commitment to his policies. It is also found in his personal and professional ethics, his candor, his willingness to accept responsibility where it is war-ranted, and his treatment of others. Here, as with a president's policy commitments, the standard is not perfection. A president may get angry at a mistake that costs him personally or politically, or at what he perceives are misstatements about him or his policies. A president may occasionally approach an ethical line too closely, or allow a subordinate to give him the ability to deny he knew of or authorized some questionable act. Being human, presidents are all subject to imperfections.

However, having said this, it is not such isolated incidents that draw our attention, but the patterns that reflect a president's character integrity. Does the president promise too much, with a questionable basis for doing so? Does he give his commitments after fully thinking them through, or are they given less seriously and thus subject to relatively rapid modification? What of his treatment of others? Does he treat them honestly, respectfully? What of his ethical standards? Is he a man of probity, or does he tend to skirt the ethical edge and occasionally go off it?

Consider, for instance, campaign promises. They come in all forms: sweeping rhetorical pledges, such as John Kennedy's vow to "get the coun-try moving again"; pledges of more specific good intentions, such as the promise by Clinton to "focus on the economy like a laser beam"; or very specific pledges like Lyndon Johnson's never "to send American boys 9,000 miles away from home to do what Asian boys ought to be doing for themselves."

General promises commit a candidate to very little of a specific nature and allow him wide latitude should he gain office. The Clinton campaign and Clinton himself took another tack. Rather than making only general promises, they chose to commit themselves to specifics. George Stephanopoulos told a reporter during the campaign, "Specificity is the character issue this year" (Stencel 1993). Many advisers warned Clinton against being specific, but he gave the go-ahead to Stephanopoulos (Woodward 1994, 39). The result was an unprecedented number of extremely specific promises covering almost every area of domestic and foreign policy. Using just the Clinton/Gore campaign book *Putting People First* and Clinton campaign press releases, the *Washington Post* (Stencel 1993) published a list of the Clinton campaign's "main" proposals that consisted of 170 specific pledges in at least twenty-six different areas. My own count, using campaign speeches, as well as the two sources cited above, totals over two hundred specific promises in thirty-nine different policy areas.

In an editorial appropriately titled "A Dawn of Promise," the *New York Times* (1993b) noted, "There seems little doubt of Clinton's sincerity. But his record as governor and candidate show that he occasionally confuses mere assertion with real accomplishment." The issue actually goes somewhat deeper than that. In Arkansas, one of the two chronic complaints of state legislators about Clinton when he was governor was "that he could not be trusted to keep his word" (Oakley 1994, 333; see also 419–40). For example, in proposing a sales tax increase to finance educational reform in 1983, Clinton promised that all of the revenue would go to primary and secondary education, but over a third of it ultimately went to higher education. Worse, although Clinton had conveyed the impression that the revenues raised by the tax increase would be forever exclusively committed to education, in mid-1985 they reverted to the state's general fund, which Clinton could then use for other purposes (Oakley 1994, 290).

However, Clinton's record of promises made and not kept brought him even more trouble in Washington than in Arkansas. By choosing to commit himself to so many promises, Clinton almost guaranteed that his lack of follow-through would become an issue. An incomplete list[6] would include: his pledge to appoint ambassadors only on merit (Greenhouse 1994); his failure to follow through on the middle-class tax break he proposed, substituting instead a new tax on the middle class (Kelly 1993f); his position on Haitian refuges; his supporting and then backing away from a constitutional amendment to allow school prayer (Verhovek 1994); his promise to be tougher on dictators like Syria's Hafez al-Assad; his promise to link most favored trade status for China with substantial human rights progress; his pledge to get Congress to cut their staffs by 25 percent; his promise to cut his own staff by 25 percent (Friedman 1993a); his promise to be strongly committed to universal coverage for any health-care reform (Jehl 1994d); his support of a proposal to freeze social security payments (Rosenbaum 1993d), followed quickly by a decision not to do so (Ifill 1993g); his campaign promise to oppose a federal excise tax on gas, followed by a decision to seek such a tax, which was quickly abandoned when strong opposition arose (Wines 1993b); his support for allowing homosexuals to serve openly in the military, followed by his backing away from this pledge; his backtracking on the pledge to "end welfare as we know it," leading Senator Daniel Moynihan to complain during the confirmation hearing of Donna Shalala as Secretary of Health and Human Services that he "heard the clatter of campaign promises being thrown out the window"; his supporting and then backing away from an attempt to raise grazing fees (Cushman 1994), and so on. Clinton did follow through with some of his campaign promises, such as repealing the Bush administration's rule restricting abortion counseling in clinics, passing a family leave bill, banning the replacement of striking workers, increasing the funds available for drug treatment (Treaster 1994), and passing the "motor voter" bill, among other things.

Obviously, candidates before Clinton have backed away from campaign promises. Abraham Lincoln promised not to abolish slavery. Franklin Roosevelt promised to balance the budget. Ronald Reagan promised never to negotiate for the release of American hostages from Iran. George Bush promised not to raise taxes. However, like the issue of candor, the issue of broken promises must be viewed in the context of their numbers, the degree of fidelity or lack of fidelity in other aspects of the president's behavior, and the nature of the basic public dilemma underlying the 1992 election. Interestingly, in the period between Clinton's election and his inauguration, when national surveys reflected renewed hope that Clinton could and would restore confidence in the government (Clymer 1993b), there was also an undercurrent of disappointment with Clinton and renewed cynicism arising from his failure to follow through on his commitments *even before he assumed office.* A series of seventy-five interviews conducted just before Clinton took his oath of office found,

> Without any prompting in conversations over the last four days, voters cited the campaign pledges that Mr. Clinton already seemed to be pulling

back on, like a tax cut for the middle class, and easing the immigration of Haitians. Some people were angry about that, but most seemed resigned, with looks that said, "What else can you expect?" (Schmalz 1993)

In giving these specific policy promises, the Clinton campaign committed its candidate to a very large number of undertakings if elected. In allowing the campaign to release these promises in his name, Clinton was in fact telling the public that he had seen and approved this list, that they were all things he felt strongly about and would fight for if elected. The list of promises that Clinton made and backed away from is startling from a number of perspectives.

First, there is the sheer number of them. Other presidents have backed away from pledges or positions, but the number of times Clinton has done so is striking. The fact that he began to do so even before he took office, and that he continued even after his backing away became a public issue, only highlights this tendency. Concern over his flip-flopping is not a matter of ideological preference. Some of the positions Clinton backed away from pleased moderates and dismayed those on the Left. Others did the reverse. Clinton backed away from positions that played both prominent and less consequential roles in his campaign pledges. Not only did Clinton retreat from his pledges, but sometimes he did so more than once. For example, after first demanding universal health-care coverage, Clinton then backed away and said that 95 percent might do, then backed away from that and returned to demanding universal coverage.[7] Another Clinton campaign promise was to raise the minimum wage. The administration then decided not to do so. After the 1994 midterm election, in his State of the Union message to Congress, Clinton said he would propose raising the minimum wage, only to back away again from his position the very next morning.[8] Some of Clinton's promises were simply extravagant, like the pledge to provide college loans to all students in return for some form of national service, or to provide drug treatment on demand. Others, like the promise to commit military forces to stop ethnic cleansing in Bosnia, were overly audacious. These and similar commitments were larger and more grandiose than any thoughtful review of their implications might allow. Their extravagance suggested an inability to draw lines or create and keep boundaries.

Finally, there was the way in which Clinton handled some of these changes. In changing his position from a middle-class tax cut to a middle-class tax increase, Clinton relied on a sly distinction (Drew 1994, 60). His advisers pointed out that every time Clinton said he would not raise taxes on the middle class, he always added the phrase "to pay for my programs."

By this logic, an adviser stated, "Mr. Clinton's legalistic construct was a 'distinction with a difference' " (Kelly 1993f). The loophole created by the additional phrase was itself a revision of a flat-out pledge made by Clinton not to raise taxes on the middle class (Kelly 1993f). Technically, Clinton had created a loophole for himself, but he might also have chosen to speak honestly and directly to the public about what had changed and the basis for his new thinking. The fact that Clinton chose to deal with this issue as he did paralleled his approach to the draft and marijuana controversies during the campaign.

Clinton's lack of forthrightness with the public stems from a basic set of contradictions at the heart of the Clinton presidency. The unprecedented number of campaign promises reflected not only his own policy ambitions, but a massive commitment to federal government programs. That commitment was in many respects directly contrary to another major commitment Clinton had made, to be a New Democrat.

As John Brummett notes, Clinton

> continued his campaign mode of over-promise and sleight-of hand. Outside of defense, he wasn't curbing spending: he was reducing the projected rate of spending growth. He wasn't raising taxes merely to reduce the deficit; he was raising taxes partially to reduce the deficit and partially to pay for new programs. . . . Confident in his cleverness, he followed an instinct to be disingenuous; rather than explaining to the American people what has just been explained here, and the reason and virtue of it, he leaned on the political selling points . . . and tried to veil the full meaning of his amalgam of proposals. (1994, 6)

Does Clinton really have a central core of political values? Dick Morris, who engineered Clinton's successful comeback in Arkansas in 1980, thinks he does. During the presidential campaign in 1992, he said that while Clinton's political maneuvering often obscures his core ideals and values,

> I think Bill Clinton has a very true compass. I don't think that varies much with public opinion. But within the general proposition he wants to go north, he will take an endless variety of routes. He's constantly maneuvering, constantly picking the routes he wants to get there, maneuvering his opponents into positions where they can't get a clear shot at him. That is what leaves a legacy of "Slick Willy." (Kolbert 1992)

Another observer explained that

> his difficulty in articulating [his positions] stemmed in part from the ambiguity of his own beliefs, in part in getting past the complexities in his

own mind, and the fact that there were too many cooks involved in almost every significant speech he made and every important action he took. Clinton didn't have the confidence to simply dismiss the cooks often enough and say what he wanted to say. Sometimes he didn't know what he wanted to say. . . . His efforts to keep conflicting constituencies in his corner sometimes confused his purposes and muffled the sounds coming out of him. (Drew 1994, 128)

Still a third explanation is put forward by Stephanopoulos who compares Clinton to "a kaleidoscope."

What you see is where you stand. . . . He will put one facet toward you, but that is only one facet. Every time, the kaleidoscope would reflect the fragment of stone at the bottom in a unique way, showing a different facet; every person would see a different pattern. It was real, but it could change in an instant, as soon as Clinton turned. (Woodward 1994, 186)

Clinton's view of himself is radically different. In the *Newsweek* interview quoted earlier, he took strong issue with those who say he doesn't have core values. He offered as evidence of his character his support for particular policy programs. He then allowed that there may be come confusion over where he stands and suggested it may be caused by the fact that his philosophy has "some liberal and some conservative elements," without giving any specifics. He ended with a slight putdown of those who don't share his philosophy and, at the same time, expressed approval of himself by noting that "most thinking people, . . . the older they get" share his philosophy.

In defining his New Democrat political identity through a "some of this and some of that" approach, Clinton appears to be arguing that he defines his beliefs on a case-by-case basis. This leaves him vulnerable to the concern that he lacks any guiding core ideals or values that help him to organize and weigh the myriad facts that surround each policy case. That even his close advisers have great difficulty discerning where he really stands raises serious questions in this regard. It is less surprising that the public is unclear than it is that Clinton's advisers—who see the president close up, day after day—would be so. That fact that there is apparently as much debate within Clinton's inner circle about where he stands as there is outside of it does not suggest that Clinton has a clear, relatively consistent set of core ideals, values, or principles.

A longtime friend of Clinton's attributed his difficulties to the demands of the oval office itself and to Clinton's lack of a system to deal with them: "There is no system. He has a decision making method which is a postponement process" (Drew 1994, 232). Under these circumstances, the ambiguities of Clinton's *behavior* with regard to administration policies are not surprising. Stephanopoulos's metaphor comparing Clinton to a kaleidoscope whose views "could change in an instant" is extremely revealing in this regard. A set of deeply held ideals and values that can "change in an instant" is a logical and psychological oxymoron. This metaphor implies that Clinton is a man of many facets, and this may well be true. Clinton does appear to find some identification with all the views that are brought before him. However, it is not impossible for a president to find some merit in divergent views and still be able to apply his own developed framework of ideals and values to sort through them. Not all views can have equal weight, and not all can claim equal worth. The ability to make these distinctions is ultimately what distinguishes judgment from empathy. The latter is no substitute for the former.

A flexible political identity gives Clinton a great deal of political latitude. By choosing this strategy, however, he raises several critical issues. Is Clinton unwilling or unable to articulate the real basic principles that guide him across instances or integrate his philosophy? If so, why? Is he unwilling to do so because it will cost him politically? Then he is masking his views for political advantage. That may be a clever short-term tactic, but for a president about whom issues of honesty and integrity have been raised so often, it is a dangerous one. By failing to articulate his fundamental views and the basis on which he reconciles the liberal and conservative elements in his political identity, he has abdicated the very important presidential responsibility of educating the public about his solutions to their problems.

It may be that Clinton has not yet reconciled and integrated these elements himself. Perhaps he does not articulate the core ideals and values that shape his political identity because he hasn't yet been able to find a consistent way to do so. Alternatively, they may be impossible to synthesize. Recall Drew's observation that Clinton appears not to have resolved ambiguities in his mind regarding how his liberal and conservative views actually fit in a given situation, and that he is pulled in different directions by his advisers.

In spite of being in elected public life since 1976 and having dealt with domestic policy for over twenty-five years before assuming the presidency, Clinton seems not to have developed a real synthesis and integration of the ideals, values, and principles that would make it possible to proceed on other than a case-by-case basis. Had he done so he would be able to hear conflicting advice and then go on to make his decision, secure in the understanding of how his already-held convictions shaped the diverse considerations at hand.

Specific policy debates conducted in the context of a firmly established set of personal ideals and values are very different from political debates whose function is to help define such ideals and values. Ideally, a president's political identity flows directly from his own personal values and commitments. The characterological foundation of this integrity should already be in place *before* a president assumes office.

However, the real problem may be not be so much with Clinton's intellectual or policy abilities as with the nature of what he has attempted to accomplish. Is it possible to reconcile the smaller, more efficient government promised by the "reinventing government" initiative with the massive federal program he proposed to regulate the nation's health-care system? Is it possible to reconcile "ending welfare as we know it," smaller government, a stress on personal responsibility, with the welfare reform proposal put forward by the administration that would make the government the employer of last resort for any person who could not find a job? It is difficult to see how.

By almost all accounts, Clinton has a strong disinclination to draw lines, to say yes or no, and otherwise to make the hard choices that are part of a president's responsibilities. There exists a very good psychological explanation for this: Clear-cut decisions run directly counter to his ambitions and his somewhat idealized view of himself and his purposes. For Clinton, making choices means accepting limits, which is extraordinary difficult for a person with such substantial ambitions and a high level of self-confidence in his ability to accomplish his irreconcilable purposes.

Character Integrity: Clinton on Clinton

The concept of character integrity reflects a dual perspective. First, it reflects others' assessments of the degree to which someone does in fact possess a set of genuine, deeply held ideals and values that inform his choices and commitments on a consistent basis. An equally important dimension of a person's interior psychology, however, is how he comes to view himself, his own estimation of the degree to which he possesses and acts on deeply held ideals and values.

Clinton's view of himself is essential to understanding his psychology and his presidency. What is perhaps most striking about Clinton's view of himself is how few doubts he entertains about his own motives, values, and candor. He responded to the press and others who raised questions about him during the campaign by presenting himself as a man of conviction, determination, integrity, and principle. He presented himself as fair, open, honest, and genuinely interested in and responsive to others' points of view and concerns. Critical to his self-image (as well as to his campaign strategy) was a view of himself as a victim.[9]

I don't list these characteristics because I believe them wholly untrue. Rather, I note them because they reflect a strong component of *self-idealization*. Most people wish to think well of themselves. However, Bill Clinton appears to have come to believe the *best* of himself, and to either avoid or discount evidence from his own behavior that all is not as he believes it to be. He attributes to himself the most sincere and best of motives. His errors, when acknowledged, are the result of basically correct efforts gone temporarily awry, misunderstandings that, if one knew more of what *he* knew, would disappear or be mitigated, or else are attributable to naiveté and inexperience. The latter is, of course, another way of attributing to oneself good intentions gone awry, this time because of the faults of others. Any attention called to a number of discrepancies between Clinton's real behavior and his view of it, as was done by the press during the campaign and first years of his presidency, is met with denial, exculpatory explanations, answers, often long ones, that do not deal directly with the point, or, when all else fails, unconcealed frustration and anger.

When questioned by a college student about his lack of candor in handling questions about the draft, extramarital relationships, and smoking marijuana as a young adult, Clinton offered a "rambling, insistent defense of his own character," which "at times resembled a tirade" (Ifill 1992a). In his response, Clinton said, "There is no trust issue, except the press again trying to make a mountain out of a molehill," and "One of the things that amazes me is that if I don't say something they say I'm not being candid, and if I tell the whole truth I'm not being candid."

When challenged by a homosexual rights advocate about his ambition during another campaign stop, Clinton lashed out:

> And let me tell you something else. Let me tell you something else. . . . The reason I'm still in public life is because I've kept my commitments. That's why I'm still here. That's why I'm still standing here. And I'm sick and tired of all those people who know nothing of my life, know nothing about the battles I have fought, know nothing about the life I've lived, making snotty nose remarks about how I haven't done anything in my life and it's all driven by ambition. That's bull, and I'm tired of it. (*New York Times* 1992b, D9)

One of the most striking pieces of evidence along these lines is contained in a 1993 *Rolling Stone* interview. The interviewers asked why, if Clinton supported Jean Bertrand Aristide's return to Haiti, he allowed the Central Intelligence Agency to testify before Congress about a very unflattering CIA profile of Aristide:

> GREIDER: But can't you direct the CIA either to shut up or support your policy? In another administration, the director of the agency would have been gone by that evening if he had done that to the president.
>
> CLINTON: The director didn't exactly do that. The guy who expressed that opinion—or at least revealed the research on which it was based— was a career employee. He did that work in a previous administration under a previous director. Under the rules of Congress, when someone is called to testify and asked their personal opinion, they have to give it.
>
> GREIDER: Yeah, but the CIA, come on. They're the last agency to believe in free speech.
>
> CLINTON: All I'm saying is, *consider the flip side.* What if the story is, today the president suppressed information from the CIA . . . information that [North Carolina Sen.] Jesse Helms knew about because he's been on the committee.
>
> GREIDER: He had you either way.
>
> CLINTON: He knew he had me either way. He knew I'd been given this information when I became president. . . . So what was I to do? Try to jam it? Eventually it would have come out. . . . So I reasoned that since I knew it was out there before I took office, and it was a matter of fact, and Congress had a legal right to know it, that rather than gagging this guy or playing games with him the best thing to do was to let it happen. . . .
>
> WENNER: *What's the most important thing you've learned about yourself since you've become president?*
>
> CLINTON: *All the old rules are still the ones that count. I feel better every night when I go home if I've done what I think is right.* (Wenner and Greider 1993, 81, emphases mine)

There are many interesting aspects to this exchange. The president, in answer to the question of why he didn't suppress an unfavorable report, essentially responded that it wasn't possible to do so since others already knew of it. (He also appears to be arguing that he shouldn't be blamed for failing to suppress information because he had no choice.) One can view this as simply an illustration of "hardball politics" or, alternatively, as reflecting a good grasp of "political reality." However, it also appears to reflect a strong element of expediency. Clinton's ethical calculus here appears very responsive not to what is right, but to how it would look in the morning papers.

The other striking aspect of this exchange occurs directly afterwards, when he is asked what the most important thing is that he has learned about himself in the presidency. He points to the importance of old, traditional virtues which, he clearly believes, were reaffirmed by his behavior in the Aristide case and, more generally, as president. He then adds that he could sleep better knowing he had done what he thought to be right. This comment comes immediately after he has outlined the most basic kinds of political calculations that went into his decision not to attempt to squelch the damaging profile of Aristide. It implies that these kinds of political calculations are what Clinton thinks of as "doing right."

President Clinton showed no indication that the two sets of statements, one immediately following the other, might somehow be related. Political expediency was clearly one part of his decision to allow the testimony. So was the fact that others already knew about the study. But having established the decision on these grounds, Clinton felt a need to cloak it in a more virtuous frame.

One important and related consequence of Clinton's enormous accomplishment coupled with his self-idealization is a belief in his own essential goodness and *correctness*. It is a sense that he has about himself, about what he does, and about what he wishes to accomplish. The importance of maintaining this view of himself is at the heart of Clinton's interpersonal relations, which are organized, in my view, around his need for validation. (I will take this up in chapter 5.)

The Element of Self-Confidence

While much attention has been devoted to the effects of low self-esteem on presidents, the influence of unusually *high* self-esteem has been left largely unexamined. It is critical to distinguish between self-esteem and self-confidence. Self-esteem refers to the overall sense that people have about themselves, whether they like themselves and think of themselves as essentially good. Self-confidence, a component of self-esteem, is the degree of assurance people place in their own skills, values, and choices. Or to put it another way, self-esteem refers to the degree that one feels one is worthwhile; self-confidence reflects the degree of certainty that one's view is correct.

Generally, people gather more self-confidence by specializing in what they do well, and these successful choices tend to bring further opportunities. However, there is another situational element to self-confidence in political leaders. Both governors and presidents do not in many respects live in the real world.

> The mansion, the entourage, the aides, the pampering, the currying of favor, the deference—they are addressed as "governor" [or Mr. President] by one and all—produce a similar phenomenon. . . . They come to see themselves, and are treated, as awfully important people. Governors are no strangers to arrogance. The smart, serious ones—a Michael Dukakis, a Bill Clinton—come to believe that they know more about national issues than they do. (Drew 1994, 234; see also Renshon 1996, chap. 3)

The issue of self-confidence is particularly relevant for a president like Clinton, who is smart, persistent, and charming. One would expect to find in such a president a strong degree of self-confidence, and in President Clinton one does. Clinton's extremely high levels of self-confidence apparently developed early, and there is ample documentation of them throughout his life. Edith Irons, Clinton's high school adviser suggested Georgetown University to him but warned him that admissions were very competitive. In an interview, she recalled, "Because of the great difficulty in getting into Georgetown, I suggested he apply to a couple of others. He did everything he was told but did not apply to another college. . . . This was typical of the confidence that Bill had in himself" (Levin 1992, 36–37). Rudi Moore, Jr., Clinton's campaign manager during his first run for governor and also his chief of staff during his first term, recalls that Clinton "always had *boundless confidence* in his ability to forge a consensus and work out *any problem*" (1993, 92, emphases mine). Part of Clinton's confidence in this area rests on his considerable interpersonal skills.

Clinton's high levels of self-confidence have been noted frequently throughout his career. The adjectives "supreme" and "extreme" often precede descriptions of it. Brummett notes Clinton's "supreme confidence" (1994, 42). Another observer commenting on Clinton's performance at a televised "Town Hall" on health care noted, "Mr. Clinton is supremely confident in this sort of setting" (Dowd 1993). Gwen Ifill, a reporter for the *New York Times,* writes after interviewing Clinton, "Less than a month into his Presidency there are subtle changes evident in Mr. Clinton, but one thing has not changed. As the brief visit to the Oval Office revealed, the extreme self-confidence—almost inexplicable in the face of political disaster—is still there" (1993a).

Another piece of behavioral evidence is Clinton's willingness and ability to talk publicly, at length, without notes, on a range of subjects. Clinton was one of the most verbal presidential candidates in modern history. Few candidates have felt so secure talking at length in a variety of settings. Yet another indication of Clinton's confidence was his performance in addressing a joint session of Congress about his health care plan. This was, by any calculation, an important event for Clinton and his proposals, delivered in front of a nationwide audience during prime time. When the wrong speech began to unfold on the teleprompter, Clinton did not hesitate. He did not wait until the right speech could be placed in the machine. Rather, he forged ahead and delivered it extemporaneously, drawing on his notes. His response to an unexpected technical glitch, which could have been a cause of a major public embarrassment in full view of a national audience, suggests and reflects a very high level of confidence.

Clinton's self-confidence is not invulnerable. There is some volatility to his moods, which seem especially susceptible to setbacks. Elizabeth Drew notes that by June 1992, after a series of setbacks and administration mistakes, David Gergen, a senior aide to the president, said that "Clinton's . . . confidence was shot . . . he had lost confidence in his staff, and for all his smiling in public, himself" (1994, 232). Another source said,

> It's amazing to me how many things turn on his mood. . . . If he's thrown off stride, he loses confidence. One of Nancy Hernreich's (Clinton's appointments director) jobs is to assess his moods and adjust the pace according[ly]. . . . I don't know how many former presidents were on such a sharp edge of emotion. (Drew 1994, 232)

A longtime friend of the Clintons said, "He's used to having things come fairly easily. In Arkansas you can make mistakes and get away with them" (Drew 1994, 232). Drew goes on to note,

> This person wasn't the only close observer who thought that Bill and Hillary Clinton had been somewhat spoiled and also self-indulgent. They had been huge frogs in a small pond, a couple with a large, nation-wide framework of supportive friends. They were special. (1994, 232)

These setbacks to Clinton's ordinarily high levels of self-confidence appear to be the exception to the rule. Yet they do point to a vulnerability in Clinton's generally high levels of self-confidence. Clinton is able to recover from setbacks but his temperament[10] and psychology leave him vulnerable to mood swings. It is obviously easier to maintain your emotional balance when things are going well, but this experience will be episodic in most presidencies.

Some might argue that Clinton's high level of confidence masks a deeper sense of insecurity. As evidence they could point to Clinton's difficulty in making decisions. Ordinarily, people with high self-confidence do not have great difficulty reaching decisions. However, as I argue when I take up this question in chapter 13, I believe Clinton's reluctance to make decisions has more to do with his dislike of limits than his lack of confidence. This idea also ignores the psychological fact that high levels of self-confidence based on substantial talents and successes will have a strong reality base. In other words, high self-confidence that developed from repeated experiences of success can take on a psychological life of its own. The gap between grandiose ambitions and the ability to realize them may still be a problem for a president like Clinton who has talent and high self confidence. But any argument about Clinton's "underlying" lack of self-confidence must explain the many strands of evidence that point to his high self-confidence.[11]

Some Limitations of Self-Confidence

Self-confidence, like intelligence, has important consequences for a president's performance, many of them positive. It is a personal resource that can be reassuring to the public, especially during difficult periods, and it can buttress the president as he attempts to grapple with complex political or policy issues.

However, there are dangers to a president with too much self-confidence. The chief danger is that self-confidence will evolve into grandiosity and overconfidence.[12] When Drew asked Bruce Lindsey, Clinton's close friend and senior adviser, whether the president's problem was the size of his agenda or the way his time was allocated, Lindsey replied that Clinton "would say it's the way he's been scheduled, because he never thinks he has taken on too much" (Drew 1994, 135). Any president, even a very smart, ambitious one like Clinton, needs to be aware of limits. The inability or disinclination to do so reflects an element of grandiosity.

"Grandiosity" may seem an odd term to apply to a man who started life in a small rural enclave and has overcome many obstacles to attain the nation's highest elected office. Aspirations for gaining the White House, given Clinton's background, might seem somewhat grandiose. Yet it happened. I use the term, however, to reflect expectations that are not in keeping with one's level of talents or a realistic appraisal of the circumstances. Having reached the top after a long journey is no barrier to grandiosity; it can in fact encourage it. Unless the person is guided by a consolidated set of ideals, a grounded identity, and a realistic appraisal of the obstacles facing him, success may reinforce grandiosity rather than restrain it.

Perhaps the most public manifestations of this danger took place in an interview Clinton gave before his inauguration regarding the possibility of a new relationship with Saddam Hussein. His comments on the matter reflect a remarkable self-assurance about his ability to change the Iraqi leader and his pattern of behavior. After talking about the need for Hussein to change his behavior, and about his not being obsessed with the man, he goes on to state:

> *I think that if he were sitting here on the couch I would further the change in his behavior.* You know if he spent half the time, just a half, or even a third of the time worrying about the welfare of his people that he spends worrying about where to place his SAM missiles and whether he can aggravate Bush by violating the cease-fire agreement, what he's going to do with the people who don't agree with him in the South and in Iraq, I think he'd be a stronger leader and be in a lot better shape over the long run. (Clinton 1993b, emphasis mine)

In this interview president-elect Clinton appears to believe that he personally can bring about this change.[13] Moreover, and in keeping with the political skill that Clinton emphasizes, he believes that he can do so by persuading Hussein that he would be a better leader and be better off if he followed Clinton's advice. The expectation that people can be won over by words is an understandable and plausible premise given Clinton's experience in the presidential election, but it is a potentially dangerous misapplication in this context.

There is an element of naiveté, but also grandiosity, to be found in Clinton's apparent belief that he would be able to overcome, indeed reverse, the character patterns that have been evident throughout Hussein's career, and that he could do so, in a chat with him, by appealing to what he sees as Hussein's long-term interests. The danger in the high confidence that Clinton expresses, in this and similar cases, is not that he will discount Hussein's shrewdness, but that he will overestimate his own potential impact.

Consider, for instance, that although Clinton came to Washington with a large, even massive policy agenda, he did not develop a plan of action after the election that would have allowed his administration to hit the ground running. At a meeting that took place at a weekend retreat at Camp David during the second week of his term, Clinton laid out an agenda that included "an ambitious list":

> a stimulus program to reinvigorate the job base; an economic program that reduced the deficit and shifted priorities from consumption to investment; a political reform bill, including reform of campaign financing and

new restrictions on lobbying; a national service bill; welfare reform; comprehensive reform of health care. Beyond this list, Clinton said there were other things that the government could do; work on politics that protect the environment and sustain jobs; teach everyone who works to read; stress training and apprenticeship programs; adapt a trade policy that recognizes the competitive dimensions of world realities; reduce the homeless population. (Drew 1994, 52)

Aside from the scope of this list, what is striking is that there was no real plan in place for what the new administration would actually do once it got to Washington (Drew 1994, 36). Stephanopoulos told Drew "that a memo covering the first two weeks had been drawn up before the Clinton people left Little Rock. And that was it" (1994, 36). Another senior White House official told Drew,

> There was a legend developing from the fact that we won. . . . [However] it was only in part because we were smart. . . . Some of the campaign people were glorified in *Time* and *Newsweek,* and it carried over into the administration. . . . We just weren't ready—emotionally, intellectually, organizationally, or substantively. (1994, 37)

The euphoria of victory is an understandable feeling. Yet susceptibility to it and the inability to temper it with a realistic appraisal of what the administration's goals might require is not a distinguishing characteristic of every first-term presidency. Ronald Reagan's victory over an incumbent president did not keep his administration from getting off to a very fast start in implementing its policy and political agenda.

No doubt many factors contributed to the lack of preparation, fatigue among them. However, it was certainly unrealistic to expect that Clinton's vast agenda could get off to the fast start he desired without a well-grounded plan in place. Once the administration took office, the decision to go ahead with all these plans, without a secure foundation in place, seems to reflect a triumph of confidence over prudence.

CHAPTER 5

★ ───

RELATEDNESS

There have been few presidents for whom interpersonal relations have played such an important political and psychological role as they have for Bill Clinton. Some presidents have been more socially skilled than others, but the Clinton presidency is unique in its emphasis on interpersonal relations.

In psychological theory, the *affiliation motive* is the most common way of examining a person's connections to others. To be affiliated means to want to belong. People with affiliation motives tend to be joiners and to spend a lot of time in the company of others. Character theory, however, paints a more complex picture of a person's stance toward others. Rather than asking, as affiliation theory does, *if* people want to be connected, character theory also asks *why*. It examines the array of a person's relationships—from antagonistic, unfriendly relationships through various kinds of friendships to intimate relationships—and asks what psychological functions each serves for the individual.

Affiliation does not *begin* to adequately describe the nature of Clinton's interpersonal relations. Clinton is a man for whom interpersonal relations and "chemistry" are critical, but his relationships to others are more complex—and, like other aspects of his character, controversial—than has generally been acknowledged. Clinton is, by many accounts, a charming, gregarious, and friendly man. Unlike Gary Hart and Richard Nixon, two

men with a tendency toward interpersonal isolation, Clinton is often surrounded by a group of admiring friends.

Many find Clinton an attractive man and leader. He is outgoing and
conveys the sense that he cares. Indeed, he has been characterized as a man
with a profound need to be liked, and criticized by some for caring too
much what others think. I believe these views to be mistaken, and in this
chapter I will put forward an alternative explanation for Clinton's need to
be surrounded by people. Like other aspects of Clinton's character, this one
too contains many puzzles, contradictions, and ambiguities. Clinton is both
strongly disliked and strongly admired for his talents, sometimes by the
same people. He is seen as a person capable of the deepest empathy with
others, yet also capable of profoundly disappointing the expectations he
has led them to have. He is often disliked from a distance but is able to win
people over in person. In this chapter, I attempt to explain some of these
puzzles and ambiguities by examining the nature of Clinton's relationships
and analyzing some of their implications for his approach to the presidency
and his political leadership more generally.

RELATEDNESS IN PRESIDENTIAL PERFORMANCE

There are few positions in which a leader's methods of dealing with other
people are more important than in the presidency. The presidency is a
highly personal and personalized institution. However, while the president
is *the* single person at the top, he is never alone. Everywhere the president
turns, there are people: people whose sole responsibility is to ensure that he
is taken care of, protected, informed, appraised, advised, bolstered, kept on
track, reminded of deadlines; people to speak for him; people to find out
for him; people to do what he can't do and, sometimes, what he shouldn't.
The president's world is filled as much with people as it is with policy.

His relationships with Congress, with the press, with the public, with
his own party, with the opposition, and with those who support and
oppose him abroad all reflect the profoundly intense relational nature of
the presidency. It is not only that this one man is at the center of this
Archimedean institution, but that his ways of dealing with all these relationships are central, too. It is a fact so obvious that its significance has not
been fully appreciated.

The president's relationships with others are often perceived in terms
of a series of external concentric circles. At the center is the president, in
the first outer ring are his most intimate and trusted advisers, and so on.

However, another way to approach the relational presidency is to examine the function of others in the president's inner psychology. Here too, we deal with a series of concentric circles measured by a proximity-distance radius, with the important difference that here they are organized according to their internal psychological meaning and significance to the president.

Events, experiences, and especially people that have special emotional valence for the president are part of his internal world. In clinical theory, the study of these internal images, how they got there, and what they mean is called *object relations*.[1] Among the important dimensions of this internal world of objects is whether a particular object is "good" or "bad"—that is, whether or not it provides available memories and images of warmth, support, firm and loving care, and so forth. A person can rigidly categorize particular objects as "good" or "bad," or he can see objects as having qualities of both.[2]

The individual's internal representational world serves important psychological functions.[3] "Bad" objects are constant reminders of what might (or perhaps is likely to) befall the person if he doesn't take appropriate steps. They are associated with difficulty in developing one's ambition; in maintaining fidelity to realistic, satisfying, and self-selected ideals; and in fully trusting others. "Good" objects provide examples of worthwhile ambitions and ideals and help the individual to develop and sustain them. A fear of the harm that others might do (as bad objects) can lead a president to try to control them in various ways. He may use his position and talents to overwhelm others, to disarm them through charm, or to avoid them to the extent that he is able to do so.

The nature and functions of a president's internal world of object relations shape the external world of the relational presidency. For example, the degree to which a president has a consolidated, realistic sense of himself as an able, honorable person who stands for what he is makes a considerable difference in how he approaches others. A president whose internal object world includes people and experiences supportive of his reaching for his ambitions will be more able to do so. A president whose internal object world has not included, for whatever reason, persons or experiences that form the basis of principled adherence to ideals will be much more susceptible to the lure of results, regardless of the process. A president whose internal world is populated by warm, supportive experiential objects has something to sustain him in tough times, apart from what others on the outside, even his closest advisers, might say. He can listen to a variety of other views, but know how each view fits in (or doesn't) with his own, and feel comfortable with doing so.

The president's primary experience with others is critical to how he treats his staff, his advisers, his appointees, and, ultimately, the public. What is the function of these people for the president? Are they *selfobjects,* that is, persons whose primary role is to provide something psychological for the president? Or are they independent persons whom the president feels comfortable asking for their best (views, work, etc.) even if it might not always be fully in accord with his positions and views? When the president's own sense of self is secure and consolidated, he can afford, psychologically, to allow people to be who they are rather than who he emotionally needs them to be.

A skeptic might ask: How is it possible to know anything regarding a president's internal object relations? The answer is not found by putting the president on the metaphorical couch. Rather, it consists of knowing what to look for and asking the right questions about a president's temperament, relatedness, decision-making, and leadership. A president's interpersonal relations are fairly visible and consistent, and they leave a long and easily documented trail.

Another important set of clues comes from the president's earlier developmental experiences. A president's early family life is very important in the development of his object relations. In this respect he is no different from anyone else. But we cannot depend on presidents to provide this information, especially those inclined to present themselves as they would like to be seen. On resigning the presidency, Richard Nixon, in his nationally televised farewell, twice recalled his mother as a "saint." Knowing that his father, Frank, was a stern, argumentative man, one wonders about the connection in Nixon's mind between sainthood and martyrdom. But at a level of analysis even closer to the surface, one can wonder what effects being raised by a "saint" may have left. We need not wait for presidential resignations to ask "what might it have been like" questions. I address the questions of the impact of Clinton's early family experiences on his character development in some detail in chapters 7, 8, and 9. However, in this chapter I focus on some observations and puzzles regarding Clinton's relationships with others.

THE PRIMACY OF OTHERS IN CLINTON'S PSYCHOLOGY

Clinton's interpersonal style clearly reflects a movement toward people, and this tendency is remarkably consistent in every stage of his development. George Wright, Jr., a childhood friend of Clinton's, recalls that at age six, Clinton "wanted to be everybody's friend" (1993, 29). Donna Taylor, who first met Clinton when he moved to Hot Springs in 1954 at the age of eight, recalled that he would "light up" when he was around other children, and that "some people like to be with other children; Bill was like that" (Maraniss 1995, 32). Carolyn Staley, Clinton's next-door neighbor in Hot Springs and a close high-school friend, recalled the many special friendships that Clinton developed during those years and how they always traveled in a group (1993, 39). One reason was that "group activities seem to hold special appeal for Bill; friends say he rarely dated, preferring instead the company of many, against whom he would invariably emerge as the center of attention" (Oakley 1994, 32).[4]

At Georgetown, Tom Campbell, Clinton's first-year roommate, recalls, "Bill wanted to meet everyone. I was willing to limit my circle. . . . But he wanted to meet *everyone*" (1993, 43).

At Yale Law School, fellow student William T. Coleman III recalls, "There was a 'black table' in the cafeteria. This self-segregation was readily acknowledged by the majority student body, with one notable exception. A tall, robust, friendly fellow with a southern accent and a cherubic face unceremoniously violated the unspoken rule by plopping himself down at the 'black table' " (1993, 55).

In 1968, traveling to Europe to take up his Rhodes Scholarship, "Clinton immediately set out to make friends with everyone" (Levin 1992, 63). Stephen Oxman, a fellow Rhodes Scholar and now a foreign policy adviser to Clinton, recalls that Clinton "displayed an unusual ability to engage people from many different backgrounds in friendly, substantive conversation" (Levin 1992, 64). Woody Bassett, a former law student of Clinton who worked on his early campaigns, said he has spent fifteen years waiting for Clinton "to finish talking with the last person he could find," and that Clinton "never wants to leave anyone who wants to talk to him" (1993, 71).

THE FRIENDS OF BILL

Central to Clinton's political success has been the network of friends and contacts he has accumulated with systematic intensity over the years. The "Friends of Bill" (FOB), a network that Clinton began developing early in his life, has reached proportions without precedent in the modern presidency. For the most part, these friends are extremely supportive of Clinton and his accomplishments. In a number of cases, one sees strong tendencies toward uncritical idealization (see, e.g., Levin 1992; Dumas 1993). A number of them "have dedicated a large portion of their lives to building and enhancing his image as a presidential candidate" (Oakley 1994, 11).

Bassett has said that Clinton "wanted to know people, wanted to know their names and to know about them, and once he knew he never forgot" (1993, 72). Clinton's memory is prodigious in certain areas, but in building his network of supporters he did not rely on memory alone. Jim Moore, an FOB who has written a political biography about Clinton, recalls being at the governor's residence for a reception, "and jostling with hundreds of other guests. . . . Before we left, the governor handed each of us a small card, and asked us to write down our names, addresses and phone numbers" (1992, xi).

Maraniss describes in more detail the 10,000–plus-card data base that Clinton had assembled as of 1978:

> Each card recorded a piece of his history and reflected his relentless campaign style. On the top right hand corner was the county where the subject of the card lived, or, if the name was from out of state, the era in which the person came into Clinton's life: Georgetown, Oxford, Yale, McGovern campaign. Running down the left hand side of the card were dates, starting with the first time Clinton had met the person and every important contact that they had since. . . . In the middle were names, telephone numbers, addresses, sometimes contribution amounts. Another row of dates noted when that person had received a letter from Clinton or his aides known as GTMY: for Glad to Meet You. (1995, 392)

Clinton has always been extremely skilled in using the parley, in which one set of circumstances and experiences are made use of in the next step. For example, Clinton made use of family connections, in this case his uncle Raymond Clinton, who was a player in local politics, to gain entry into Frank Holt's campaign for governor. Clinton was first introduced to the Holt people as "Raymond Clinton's young nephew—a bright boy who goes to school up East" (Maraniss 1995, 75). In fact, Frank Holt's father, Jack Holt, Sr., was the head of a powerful political family and had himself twice run for governor. It was to the latter that Clinton turned in the final days of the campaign to provide him with an introduction to Senator J. William Fulbright's office in Washington. Holt called Fulbright's administrative assistant Lee Williams to recommend Clinton for a position, and Williams in turn called Clinton and offered him one (Maraniss 1995, 81–82). According to Clinton's friendly biographer, Robert Levin, it was Fulbright to whom Clinton turned for a recommendation for a Rhodes

Scholarship, an endorsement that Clinton said was "crucial to his acceptance for the honor" (1992, 54).

Clinton did not get where he is simply by pull; his impressive talents and accomplishments are real. However, both Clinton and his supporters have tended to downplay or otherwise omit the good use to which Clinton put his connections. In discussing the Rhodes Scholarship, for example, Levin notes that "Bill was self-made," which is true but not in the sense that Levin conveys (1992, 55). Levin acknowledges that Senator Fulbright was a "prominent political connection," but he adds, "it was a connection though, which he had made on his own, without any family influence." In support of this, Levin quotes Clinton as saying, "They gave me that job [in Fulbright's office] when I was . . . nobody from nowhere, my family had no money, no political influence—nothing" (1992, 55).

Well, not quite. Clinton's politically powerful uncle provided him with an introduction to the Holt campaign, and was also powerful enough to have a slot in the Navy Reserve created for his nephew who was searching for an alternative to being drafted. Clinton also made extensive use of his political connection with Senator Fulbright and others in the Arkansas political establishment to secure a slot in the state's ROTC system, thus helping to stave off induction during the Vietnam War.

There is nothing inherently sinister about these efforts. Clinton's extensive data base, for instance, is no different in many respects from the list of contributors kept by many organizations. What they do show, however, is that in meeting others, whatever else the basis of their relationship, Clinton was aware of an individual's potential usefulness to him. The "ah, shucks," lip-biting persona of Clinton, the naive ingenue, masks a very skilled and knowledgeable political strategist.

A NEED TO BE LIKED?

Much has been written about Clinton's difficulty in saying no and his eagerness to please.[5] Both are often attributed to Clinton's compulsive need to be liked. Indeed, the brief biography of Governor Clinton that appeared on the front page of the *New York Times* on the day of his election was entitled, "A Man Who Wants to Be Liked, and Is" (Kelly 1992d).

However, this image of Clinton as needing to be liked is, in my mind, mistaken. At least two theoretical and factual difficulties stand in the way of this argument. First, there is Clinton's very high level of self-confidence. Ordinarily, the need to be liked would not be associated with such personal confidence. Second, the idea of a "need to be liked" does not fully come to grips with Clinton's well-documented tendency toward public and private displays of anger. During the presidential primary campaign, when Clinton was told (erroneously) that Jesse Jackson had come out in support of a party rival, Clinton, not aware that he was speaking near an open microphone, angrily denounced Jackson as a "back-stabber" (Berke 1992a, A14). After the election, when news reporters followed the president-elect onto a golf course, he lost his temper, cursed them, and complained to the manager of the club (Kelly 1992j). When out of the public's eye, Clinton's anger can often turn to rage.

The "need to be liked theory" also fails to address another psychological aspect of Clinton's political leadership style—his tendency to demonize, build up, and then lash out against those who oppose his policies. The press is one example, but there are others, including "lobbyists," "special interests," "profiteering" drug companies, "greedy doctors," "musclebound" labor unions, and—increasingly after the 1994 elections—Republicans.[6] Presidents, like others, can be known by and benefit from having certain kinds of enemies. However, for a man who is said to have such a strong need to be liked, the list of enemies is rather long and his characterizations of them often harsh. Moreover, Clinton's tendency to develop enemies, even if partially for political purposes, runs counter to another important theme that he has often publicly expressed—the need to bring Americans together and stop practicing the "politics of division."

If it is not a need to be liked, then what does motivate Clinton's interpersonal relationships? I think the central emotional issue for Clinton is a strong need to be *validated*.[7] The need for validation is reflected in a person's efforts to be acknowledged for the specific ambitions, skills, and accomplishments by which he defines himself. It is important that these specific aspects of oneself be met with appreciation and acknowledgment from important others. Validation and self-regard are closely connected under normal circumstances, but they are even more critically joined in cases such as Clinton's where self-regard and idealization are firmly entwined.

Meredith Oakley says that Clinton "cannot tolerate anyone's displeasure, *particularly people of a certain standing in their community or field,* and he will attempt to ameliorate their disapproval whenever possible" (1994, 4, emphasis mine). Clinton's angry outbursts suggest, however, that there are some people he doesn't care to placate. They also point to the fact that there are areas that appear particularly sensitive to Clinton. Through the presidential campaign and first three years of his presidency at least two such areas have emerged. The first is Clinton's view of himself as a man of accomplishments. The acknowledgment that he is doing things and succeeding is very important to Clinton. Criticism that he is doing too much was considered briefly by Clinton, then summarily rejected. Criticism that he is not doing what needs to be done results in extensive lists of how many more things he has done than his predecessors and how well he compares to presidents, like Franklin Delano Roosevelt, with whom he personally identifies and wishes to be compared (Blumenthal 1993a; Samuelson 1993a). For example, in a May 1993 news conference (Clinton 1993e), he asked, "Who else around this town in the last dozen years has offered this much budget cutting, this much tax increases, this much deficit reduction . . . asks the wealthy to pay their fair share,[8] gives the middle class a break,"[9] and so on. Clinton then went on to complain that he was being held to an impossible double standard, "one day people say he's trying to do too much . . . and then on the other day says, well, he's really not pushing very hard."

If Clinton doesn't receive validation from others in areas that are central to his self-view, he validates himself. In such circumstances he has a strong tendency to say "look how much I've done." For example, at a press conference in which he was asked about his first hundred days in office, Clinton recited a list of accomplishments and then said, "So I think it's amazing how much has been done. More will be done" (1993c). One could translate this as saying, "Not only have I accomplished an amazing number of things but I will do even more!" In a session with reporters, Clinton asked them to "Look what's happened in four months" and then went on to say of his own performance, "It's pretty impressive" (1993c, A14).

The second sensitive area concerns any questions about a difference between how Clinton sees himself and how others see his behavior. During the presidential campaign, charges that he had been less than forthcoming about his marital difficulties, the draft, and other matters led Clinton to complain angrily that he was being unfairly and inappropriately targeted by the press. The *New York Times,* which ordinarily supports President Clinton in its editorials, noted that Clinton "exhibits a self-righteous streak and a quick temper when reminded that his performance has sometimes failed to climb as high as his promises" (1993b). Oakley notes that

> when charm and affability have been pushed to their limits, he erupts in anger, scattering people and papers in his wake. . . . When Clinton loses, he quickly assumes the role of injured party, going to great lengths to explain his good motives and the self sacrifice and altruism with which he has invested his efforts, while all the time marveling that, despite this, he is so misunderstood. (1994, 4–5)

Aside from the relatively mild public displays of anger (when contrasted to the severity of his anger in private), a rare public glimpse into this aspect of Clinton's character emerged in a *Rolling Stone* interview that appeared near the end of Clinton's first year in office. At first, Clinton's responses to the questions posed to him appear to indicate a man who has invested a lot in his work and enjoys it: [10]

> WENNER: Are you having fun?
> CLINTON: You bet. I like it very much. Not every hour of every day is fun. The country is going through a period of change . . .
> WENNER: But are you having fun in this job?
> CLINTON: I genuinely enjoy it. (Wenner and Greider 1993, 40)

At the end of the interview, one of the reporters told Clinton of a call he had received from a young person invited to the Inaugural as part of Clinton's "Faces of Hope." The interviewer told the president that this young man was very dejected and disappointed with Clinton's performance. The interviewer then passed on to Clinton a question from the young man: "Ask him what he's willing to stand up for and die on."

The second reporter describes the subsequent exchange as follows (Wenner and Greider 1993, 81):

> WENNER: The President, standing a foot away from Greider, turned and glared at him. Clinton's face reddened, and his voice rose to a furious pitch, as he delivered a scalding rebuke—an angry emotional encounter, the kind of which few have ever witnessed.
> CLINTON: But that's the press's fault, too, damn it. I have fought more damn battles here for more things than any President in the last twenty years . . . and have not gotten one damn bit of credit for it from the knee-jerk liberal press, and I am sick and tired of it and you can put that in the damn article. I have fought and fought and fought and fought. I get up here every day, and I work till late at night on everything from national service to the budget to the crime bill and all this stuff, and you guys take it and you say, "Fine, go on to something else, what else can I hit him about?" So if you convince them I don't have any convictions, that's fine, but it's a damn lie. It's a lie. Look what I did. I said the wealthy would have to pay their fair share, and look what we did to the tax system. [Clinton then mentions another accomplishment.] Did I get any credit for it, from you or anyone else? Do I care if I get credit? No. Do I care that man has a false impression of me because of the way this administration has been covered. . . . I have fought my guts out for that guy and if he doesn't know it, it's not all my fault. And you get no credit around here for fighting and bleeding. . . . And if you hold me to an impossible stan-

dard and never give us any credit . . . that's exactly what will happen, guys like that will think like that. But it ain't my fault, because we have fought our guts out for 'em.

In this exchange Bill Clinton sounds more like Richard Nixon than John Kennedy. It certainly contradicts his earlier assertions of how he is enjoying his role. The sense of being "done in" in spite of good deeds, of receiving no acknowledgment for hard, indeed almost Herculean efforts ("fighting my guts out," "fighting and bleeding"), and being held to "an impossible standard" (in a sense, being set up) are all consistent with the bitter sense of futility ("no matter how much I do, it's never good enough") that is pervasive in the psychology of some presidents.

Which is the real Bill Clinton? One possibility is that the first ("I like my job") is the real one and the second ("I can't get any acknowledgment for my immense and good efforts") a temporary outburst of frustration. Or the reverse may be true—that is, the angry, frustrated Bill Clinton that is rarely seen is the real one, and the friendly, charming Bill Clinton is in some respects a combination of how he would like to feel and be seen.

In this age of the strategic manipulation of presidential character, it is well to recall that Jimmy Carter, on meeting James David Barber, who wrote a book on presidential character, told Barber that he had read his book and wanted to be an active-positive president—that is, one who invested himself in his work and drew pleasure from it. Clinton, who as a presidential candidate mounted an extraordinary plan to market a new persona to the public to answer their doubts about him during the campaign (Kelly 1992c; Bennett 1995), is not beyond such a strategic manipulation of character in order to enhance his public image.

The real test of a president's enjoyment of his work is rooted in a sense of overall personal satisfaction and public contribution, not in the episodic joy that comes when things are going well. After all, even Richard Nixon in a pre-Watergate interview seemed to be relaxed and enjoying his presidential role. The real test is how the president responds when things are not going his way.

It is quite possible, even likely, that Clinton represents a "masked active-negative" type—that is, a person who looks on the surface as if he draws satisfaction from his efforts, but in reality is driven by a need to have things his way and a willingness to adopt a number of methods, some questionable, to ensure that he does. In short, Clinton appears to be a person whose surface psychology has been constructed and operates in one way, but whose deeper psychology operates quite differently.

In clinical work, analysts have long been familiar with masked character traits and types. There is, for example, the phenomenon of "masked depression," which presents itself as normal functioning until the person feels safe enough to be in touch with what amounts to an underlying depression. Similarly, the concept of the "false self" reflects the clinical understanding that individuals will sometimes cloak or mask certain character or personality traits, either because they are socially or personally unacceptable, or because they do not feel safe enough to express who they really are. Clinton's attractive, outgoing, charming outer psychology appears to coexist with or be built upon a more angry, demanding, entitled inner psychology.

THE PRIMACY OF OTHERS: A USEFUL ILLUSION?

Charm and Its Uses

By many accounts of those who have met him, Clinton can be a charming man.[11] Indeed, as Brummett notes, he "is almost impossible to dislike in a personal meeting" (1994, 4). Clinton has developed and made good use of his charm as a political resource. The quality is well captured by Anna Quindlen: "over and over you hear about folks who are uncomfortable with him, who think he's too slick or too polished or just not quite. And then they meet him. And their opinion changes. Bill Clinton is a guy who does better up close and personal" (1992). Brummett writes that "Clinton always prefers contact; he believes that he can persuade you intellectually and seduce you interpersonally, and often he can" (1994, 23).

There are many other illustrations of this tendency in Clinton.[12] Brummett details Clinton's attempt to get him to not to write any more about the famous "unveto" story (1994, 14–17; see also below, Appendix) and says, "Bill Clinton thought he could undo everything if he could only get your ear" (1994, 14). The same behavior can be seen in Clinton's comments regarding Saddam Hussein and in his tendency while abroad to give a speech each day to some group in the host country trying to get them to pressure their governments to respond to his policy views. "As usual," writes Elizabeth Drew, "Clinton seemed to believe that there was no one he couldn't persuade" (1994, 245).

Charm, of course, differs from sincerity and fidelity, and it is the latter that have been major issues for Clinton throughout his political career. Some long-time Clinton observers note, "The Arkansas landscape was strewn with people who believed that Clinton had lied to them, double crossed them, or left them out to dry" (Brummett 1994, 70). Many Clinton admirers "have remained staunchly loyal to a man not known for returning the favor" (Oakley 1994, 10). Pat Flanagin, a Democrat from east Arkansas who worked with Clinton, said, "I came away with the feeling that loyalty was a one way street, that if it was good for Bill Clinton, everything was chummy. . . . But if you needed something in the other direction, don't count on it" (Oakley 1994, 11–12).

Yet, like other controversies concerning Clinton, there is evidence on both sides of the debate. Meredith Oakley believes there is "ample evidence that Clinton has often remained steadfast when he should have feinted. For every political appointee he deserted, there were two or three whose tenure caused embarrassments" (1994, 10).

These two views are not necessarily inconsistent. Loyalty to Clinton may be the factor that explains his willingness to keep some people in his administration when their behavior has become controversial. It is also clear that Clinton has been able to withdraw his support from aides or nominees when they have become too controversial. The cases of Lani Guinier and Kimba Wood provide ample evidence, and there are a number of others. While Clinton has been faulted for doing so, a president would appear to have every right to back away from any nominee whose views or behavior might cause him difficulty. However, in other areas, Clinton's difficulties with fidelity and commitment appear less understandable or defensible on political grounds.

Charm facilitates relationships, but obviously it can also be used as a method of getting what one wants from others. That is one reason why Clinton's charm and the question of its sincerity have become issues. Yet there is another aspect to Clinton's charm that has been largely overlooked, namely, what its continuous use reveals about his trust of others. Clinton has been characterized frequently as a man who is too trusting, but his persistent use of charm suggests otherwise. The use of charm can also stem from the belief that if you don't use it, you cannot depend on others to respond to you. Clinton's tendencies to mislead and equivocate, to market and sell his policies rather than deal with their costs and implications honestly, and his rages at those who don't share his view of the virtues of his plans, and especially his views of himself, suggest that he doesn't trust others to respond on the basis of substance or hard work to find common ground. When you believe you can't depend on others to be responsive, charming them into doing so is one obvious strategy for a man like Clinton, who has such strong interpersonal skills.

The Dual Nature of Empathy

One of the major controversies regarding Clinton is the question of whether his interest in others and the sympathy and understanding that it conveys are genuine. The controversy is well summarized by Douglas Eakeley, a friend of Clinton's who met him on their way to Oxford, and whose first impression of Clinton was, " 'Is this guy for real?' It didn't take long to find out. He was (and remains) one of the more naturally gregarious persons I have ever met. Bill's interest in others conveyed a sense of understanding and sympathy" (Levin 1992, 64).

During the presidential campaign, at "town meetings" and similar formats that brought him directly in touch with the public, "People told him their problems and he would bite his lip; occasionally a tear would appear. He would express his sympathy with their plight—and then spell out some program he had proposed that would deal with it. Clinton's empathy, actual or feigned, became one of his trademarks" (Drew 1994, 95). Some friends compare Clinton "to a character in the television show 'Star Trek: The Next Generation.' The character is an 'Empath,' one of a race of beings born with an ability to empathize and absorb the feelings of others" (Friedman 1993d).

The *New York Times* (1993c) editorialized about Clinton that "of all the candidates, he alone felt almost a primal connection with the pain of the American people." Others note that Clinton "will do everything in his power to persuade those around him that he understands their wants and needs and will work his heart out to meet them" (Oakley 1994, xiv).

This characteristic was perhaps most publicly displayed during the second round of presidential debates. A woman asked President Bush how the national debt and economically difficult times had personally affected him. Bush did not quite understand what the woman was really asking, which appeared to be whether the president, because he was well off, was or could really be in touch with the suffering of others. The moderator then called on Clinton to respond. For a brief moment his mind was clearly elsewhere, but then he quickly refocused his attention on the woman and said, "Tell me how it's affected you again. . . . You know people who have lost their jobs and homes." The woman repeated her point and Clinton responded by walking over to her, refocusing his attention directly on her, and answering her question by telling her of the many people he knew *personally* in his state who were experiencing hard times and how personally upset he was for each of them.

In evaluating a president's psychology, we need to distinguish *strategic empathy*[13] from *empathetic attunement*—which is a temporary, limited, but nonetheless real attempt to enter into the world of another.[14] The primary purpose of the former is advantage rather than understanding. In reality, most persons and presidents combine some aspects of both in their interpersonal relationships.[15] The role empathy plays in an individual's psychology depends upon the range of circumstances in and degree to which it is employed.

Strategic empathy may serve a number of purposes, each of which has a somewhat different implication for understanding a person's interpersonal relationships. One purpose is to get something from others they might not otherwise offer. Strategic empathy in this instance is a sophisticated form of manipulation for direct personal gain. A person who makes use of this form of empathy sees others essentially as objects whose primary function is to provide what he wants or needs. There is little real consideration of others, since such consideration might interfere with their use.

A second form of strategic empathy shares some aspects of the first, but is based on a different set of relationships with others. The president using this form of strategic empathy begins from narcissistically projected feelings of self-identification with "the people." In these cases, a leader has less a real empathetic connection with the people than a belief that his rule embodies their aspirations and needs.[16] In its most extreme form this version of strategic empathy reflects a severe absence of interpersonal connectedness, since *real* individuals are rarely considered—the president already assumes that he knows what they need.

Strategic empathy can also be motivated by a desire to receive validation or approval from others. Here empathy is put in the service of knowing what others want so that one can be appreciated for providing it. The primary motivation in this instance is not so much to take as it is to give for the purpose of receiving.

There are reasons to explore strategic empathy in connection with Clinton, which I do more fully below. This does not imply that he *is* necessarily manipulative, only that the view of Clinton as being selflessly attuned to others is somewhat overdrawn and idealized.

There are clearly areas where Clinton's empathetic attunement does not extend. His repeated failures to follow through on his promises as governor and as president can be seen as one example of empathetic breach, namely, a failure to consider fully how others will feel when his promises are abandoned. Clinton's tendency to berate his staff can be seen as another failure to curb behavior that can have an adverse impact on others.

After his gubernatorial campaign loss in 1980, Clinton

invited several aides to lunch . . . and launched into a melodramatic soliloquy on what he should do next. Should he practice law in Little Rock? Should he compete for the chairmanship of the National Democratic Committee, which would entail a move to Washington and a six figure salary? Should he take another high visibility public interest job being dangled in front of him? (Maraniss 1995, 388)

No one else at the table had any plans or job offers because they had not expected to be out of work so soon. One of his aides, Randy White, then yelled at Clinton, "You sonofabitch! You've got every offer. You can do all those things. What are we going to do?" (Maraniss 1995, 389). Clinton hadn't thought of that. Chastened, he promised to help his aides find work.

This anecdote points to another element in Clinton's psychology that limits his capacity for empathy, namely, his self-absorption. It is a trait noted by others who have observed and studied Clinton (Oakley 1994, 4).[17] He reportedly spends many hours on the telephone in search of "the latest reading on Clinton's political futures, up or down" (Maraniss 1995, 283). He can also spend endless hours discussing his current circumstances or future prospects and the tactical mistakes he may have made. In such cases, there is "a fine line between self-absorption and humility" (Maraniss 1995, 389). Self-absorption, of course, places powerful limits on empathy.

Empathetic limits may result not only from self-absorption, but also from too much self-confidence about one's personal or political views. Before Clinton attempted to reverse by presidential edict a ban on openly homosexual men and women serving in the Armed Forces, he was warned by Senator Sam Nunn and General Colin Powell, among others, that there were strong feelings on this issue. Clinton chose not to have more discussions about the issue, but rather to figure out how to implement what he had already decided. The issue here is not the wisdom or ultimate correctness of the policy, but rather Clinton's failure to address the feelings held by those who had concerns about it. Clinton may have been aware of these feelings, but he never suggested during his campaign or before the controversy broke out that he had considered them and discussed the reasons he found them unpersuasive. He appears not to have given them much thought. Congressional and Pentagon opposition essentially forced Clinton to consider them more seriously and to integrate them into his policy design. He himself appears to have accepted that some of these concerns, like group cohesion and close quarters, were legitimate issues on which people might hold different and legitimate views.

CLINTON'S ANGER

While Clinton is a charming man, he is also frequently an angry one. There are by now many accounts of President's Clinton's outbursts. Bob Woodward reports a number of instances of Clinton's anger, as does Elizabeth Drew.[18] Clinton's temper has also frequently been on public display. When asked about the decision process that resulted in the nomination of Ruth Bader Ginsburg to the Supreme Court, Clinton angrily rejected the question and abruptly terminated the news conference, saying: "I have long since given up the thought that I could disabuse some of you from turning any substantive decision into anything but political process. How you could ask a question like that after the statement she just made is beyond me. Good bye. Thank you" (1993k, 1083). Publicly, Clinton "has trouble concealing his exasperation when things do not go his way" (Ifill 1993d).

The volatility of Clinton's temperament seems most directly tied to setbacks to his ambitions or questions that challenge his view of himself. Clinton seems to have a strong expectation that things will go his way and a *very* strong reaction when they don't. The expectation of success is in keeping with Clinton's experience, but also with his view of himself. Not only has he worked hard all his life against great odds to accomplish what he sees as noble public purposes, but he has, in his view, often succeeded as well.[19]

Almost all of the many incidents of Clinton's rage concern his explosions when things do not live up to his expectations. Privately, Clinton can be extremely harsh with aides who have made errors or are simply associated with events that do not go well. Indeed, given the descriptions of some of these outbursts, *rage* is a more appropriate term than anger. On a campaign stop in Macon, Georgia, on September 1, 1992, Clinton became enraged when he learned that some local people had inadvertently been kept from the event. He demanded to know who was responsible. When no one could tell him, he directed a senior aide to return to Little Rock and discover who had made the mistake: " 'I want him dead, dead,' Clinton said in a blind fury. 'I want him killed. I want him horsewhipped.' Clinton was in a steady rage for three days" (Woodward 1994, 54).[20] Mark Miller, a reporter from *Newsweek* who was given extraordinary access to the inner working of the Clinton campaign, reports that when Clinton was told that the Bush campaign was arguing that his economic program would mean higher taxes for everyone making over $36,000 a year, Clinton flew in a rage, yelling, "I want to put a fist halfway down their throats with this. I don't want subtlety. I want their teeth on the sidewalk."

When it became clear, at one White House budget meeting, that their plan was not detailed enough to sell their proposal,

> Clinton was seething, and he just started yelling.... Stephanopoulos almost tuned out. He had seen and experienced Clinton's temper tantrum so many times before. Others called them "purple fits" or "earthquakes." Stephanopoulos simply called it the wave, an overpowering prolonged rage that would shock an outsider, and often was way out of proportion to what had caused it. (Woodward 1994, 255)

As a result, few aides question the propriety and accuracy of Clinton's view of himself in front of the president. But the *Rolling Stone* interview gives some indication of how powerful Clinton's responses are to people who question his views of himself or his intentions. Another indication of this occurred in June 1994, when Clinton, apparently on impulse, dialed a conservative radio call-in program and "unleashed an unusually bitter 23-minute attack on the press, the Rev. Jerry Falwell, conservative radio talk shows in general and Rush Limbaugh in particular" (Jehl 1994b; see also *New York Times* 1994g). The report goes on to note that the White House "later sought to soften the tone of the remarks" and that "Mr. Clinton had spoken loudly so that he could be heard over the noise of the engines on his jet and that it sounded a lot harder than it was."

Others presidents (Eisenhower, Johnson) have had bad tempers, but, according to Drew,

> The real significance of Clinton's temper was what it said about his deeper nature. There was a self-indulgence about Clinton's tantrums, an immaturity, a part of him that never grew up and a part—shared by other politicians who took advantage of their powers over others—that felt free to chew out aides, who couldn't argue back and weren't likely to quit. (1994, 96)

Clinton's rages and the situations that trigger them suggest that the concept of *narcissistic rage* developed by Kohut (1972) might be useful. Kohut used the term to describe extreme and emotionally violent reactions to "narcissistic injuries." Such injuries are either empathetic failures or, more to the point here, challenges or experiences that tend to deny the person's intense narcissistic striving or call into question an idealized (grandiose) self-image. Kohut notes that all narcissistic rage shares "the need for revenge, for righting a wrong, for undoing a hurt by whatever means."

Once this rage is triggered, "there is utter disregard for reasonable limitations" (1972, 383, 385).

Eisenhower had a temper, but he learned to modulate it. Clinton has apparently been unable or unwilling to do so. However, the presidency requires a person who understands his own emotional strengths and limitations, and has learned to build on the first and address the second. Clinton's behavior in these circumstances suggests that his public reputation for empathy needs to be placed in a more balanced perspective. His repeated rages directed at staff members suggest that his empathetic attunement with others can be derailed by threats to his own ambitions or a need to measure up to his own high views of his correctness and performance.

CLINTON'S FIDELITY: EXPEDIENCY OR EXEMPTION?

Campaign promises are, in one sense, an interpersonal agreement between a candidate and the public and thus are very much in the relational domain. However, there is a more direct, interpersonally immediate arena in which to examine Clinton's relatedness to others. Clinton has a well-documented decision-making style that conveys the impression to each party he talks with that he understands and is in touch with their views (even if the views of the parties he talks with are in strong opposition). A corollary assumption, which Clinton does nothing to dispel, is that he will act favorably on that agreement.

A small-scale illustration of the issue is reported by Brummett, to whom the president had promised a number of interviews. Clinton aide Thomas "Mac" McLarty called Brummett a few days after Clinton's promise: " 'You understand the President,' McLarty said as a way of dismissing Clinton's unsolicited offer of frequent meetings. Yes I understood. At that moment, in his desire to please, Clinton had meant what he had said. But he forgot it as soon as the moment passed" (Brummett 1994, 20).

More serious, however, is Clinton's behavior toward members of his own party who have put themselves on the line for him and his policies. This issue first arose in connection with the stimulus bill introduced by Clinton early in his administration. The administration enlisted the support of Democratic House members, who passed the bill, only to have Clinton first offer to reduce its size and then abandon it altogether in the face of Republican opposition in the Senate. This left House Democrats feeling "they had voted for things that the administration had then offered to give away in the Senate," which led them to wonder "was this the way the administration would handle the big ones?" (Drew 1994, 120).

The administration's next backtrack occurred shortly afterward, in connection with its proposal for an energy tax. On January 25, 1993, the administration said it would propose a broad new energy tax to raise revenues. That tax became part of the reconciliation bill that set targets for revenues and spending the following year. That bill was reported out of the House Ways and Means Committee on a straight party-line vote. However, there were grave doubts that the bill would pass in the Senate. One reason was that "numerous House Democrats didn't trust him [Clinton] to stay with the controversial tax after the House had voted for it. House members had, after all, voted for the stimulus package only to see it die in the Senate" (Drew 1994, 167). Clinton then met with members of the House Democratic Caucus and

> assured them that he wouldn't abandon them if they voted for a BTU tax. Clinton told Charlie Wilson, a ten-term Democrat from Texas, "If you are out there on a limb, I'll be out there with you." The House Democrats left the meeting feeling that they had been assured by the President that if they voted for the BTU tax he wouldn't make a deal with the Senate that undermined them. "I'm not going to leave you out there alone," Clinton said. (Drew 1994, 167)

He did. On June 8 he backed away from the BTU tax in the face of Senate opposition (Rosenbaum 1993b). The next day he backed away from any broad-based energy tax (Wines 1993b). Outraged members of his own party in the house accused him of selling them out. Representative Patricia Schroeder remarked that Democrats who had voted for the tax were "doing a tap dance on the end of the plank and then it was sawed off underneath us" (Hilzenrath and Marcus 1993). Others were equally angry.

The White House took the position that changes in the tax were always a possibility. Certainly that was true. The administration also noted that such changes are always part of the political process. Again, that is accurate. However, what about the president's word to his fellow party members? Clinton gave his promise of support directly and personally to House members in a face-to-face meeting in order to get them to vote as he wished. He did not meet with them again, however, before he changed his position to let them know or prepare them. Representative Charles Rangel said, "It is embarrassing that we were going to censure those who walked away from the president, and now it's reported the president walked away from us" (Hilzenrath and Marcus 1993).

While change to accommodate new circumstances is certainly part of presidential bargaining, Clinton's behavior in these two incidents damaged him both politically and personally. By backing completely away from both the stimulus and BTU tax proposals he suffered two large political losses without any offsetting political gains. Clinton's abrupt reversals didn't gain him any credit with the Republican opposition—and indeed helped to solidify it. Nor did he get any credit for waging a valiant, but losing, battle on behalf of his beliefs and principals. And his quick abandonment of congressional allies when he had specifically promised that he would stand by them cost Clinton their willingness to take any political risks for him on other administration proposals.

At the time of the BTU tax reversal Robert Torricelli, a Democratic House member from New Jersey, said that Clinton's retreat created "a credibility problem with Congress that makes it harder for him to ask lawmakers to cast tough votes on major legislation in the future" (Hilzenrath and Marcus 1993). Clinton's famed flexibility "in some cases accounted for his legislative success, but it also made it increasingly difficult to convince a number of legislators—at least twice burned—to take a chance for him. His abandonment, early in his presidency, of the stimulus bill and the BTU tax haunted his legislative efforts from then on" (Drew 1994, 420). One major illustration of this reluctance took place when, as a result of the administrations's earlier reversals, House members were loathe to vote yes on Clinton's health-care plan (Drew 1994, 435).

It seems evident that Clinton's treatment of his fellow Democrats in the House was damaging to his relationships with them, as well as to others who drew lessons from these incidents. Beyond the question of whether or not his behavior was politically astute, what is striking from a psychological standpoint is the fact that Clinton felt no need to prepare and alert his allies to his impending reversal *before* it happened. Would they have liked the reversal? No. Would they have argued against it? Probably. Would they have understood the political need to make a change? Perhaps. Would they have felt less betrayed by a president who asked for their understanding and patience? Absolutely. However, Clinton gives the impression that his consideration of his allies became very much less important after they had given him what he wanted. For a president who is said to have such tremendous empathy for others, his behavior represents a significant empathetic breach.

What accounts for this empathetic failure? Others who have followed Clinton have noted a strong element of expediency in his behavior. Clinton works hard to convince others that he will work his heart out to get them what he has promised he will deliver.

> Perhaps he even means it at the time. But then that person or that group leaves and another with a new set of wants and needs take its place, and irrespective of the previous encounter, Clinton again says that he understands and will deliver, even if his promises to the second group contradict those he made to the first. Appease for the time being. Expediency's the thing. (Oakley 1994, xiv)

Expediency, of course, is the opposite of fidelity. Fidelity requires commitment even after you have obtained your goals. Expediency that begins with expressions of fidelity is often more troubling than simple expediency. The latter presents itself with no apologies. The former presents itself in the guise of commitment, but then doesn't work out for reasons that are obvious to the expedient person but not so clear to those who feel betrayed.

This tendency came up several times in the recollections of those who worked for Clinton when he was governor. Stephen Smith, a friend, political adviser, and assistant to Governor Clinton, notes,

> Many times I saw groups that got a full and fair hearing subsequently feel betrayed by a lack of support for favorable action on their request because they assumed that the absence of "no" meant "yes." That happened partially because supplicants for support are always more inclined to hear what they wanted to hear and partially because *they were not explicitly or immediately told what they did not want to hear."* (1993, 14, emphasis mine; see also Moore 1992, 92)

Over a decade later, with Clinton in the White House, a senior presidential aide made the following comments:

> Sometimes when the President says "That's a great idea" or "I really like that," that doesn't mean "Go do it." It means "Let's think about it." He'll say, "That's incredible," or "I really like that, we ought to think about that," and then launch into another subject. You had to edit out the last phrase. . . . It's like a conversation tic, but people hear the part they want to hear." (Drew 1994, 241)

This behavior has come up several times in Clinton's presidency. When his secretary of labor, Robert Reich, suggested that the new Republican Congress more closely examine "corporate welfare," Clinton publicly stated this was a good idea. However, when his secretary of the treasury, Lloyd Bentsen, dismissed the idea, President Clinton backed off it too.

Drew calls Clinton's behavior "well-intended equivocation" (1994,

241). Others are not so charitable. J. Bill Becker, a labor organizer and leader who worked with Clinton, gave one reporter a number of reasons why he had come to think of Clinton as a "liar." That reporter then wrote, "The full thrust of the word 'liar' bothers me as applied to a man who means no harm with his chronic tendency to finesse and waffle out of commitment. I'd gladly call him weak, over-promising, and dissembling, but then, maybe I'm merely clinging to softhearted euphemism whereas Becker tends to be brutally candid" (Brummett 1994, 218).

Is Clinton "a decent person . . . a man whose glaring foibles, while exasperating and making him not at all likable, were neither dark nor malignant?" (Brummett 1994, 269). Can the chronic tendencies documented above really still be thought of as "well intentioned"? Perhaps, *if* Clinton were beginning his adulthood, and not yet had the experience of seeing the results of his behavior. Yet many years separate Smith's observations of Clinton's first term as governor (1978–80) and Drew's observations of his first years as president (1992–94). There was ample time for Clinton to appreciate his adverse impact on others and take steps to change it. Clinton's failure to do so is especially striking because it has caused him, first as governor and then as president, much trouble and ill will. The complaints about Clinton have been loud and persistent in this area and have been partially responsible for the label "Slick Willie."

In spite of Clinton's reputation as a fast learner and a man incapable of sustained error, he has persisted in this practice. Why? Perhaps Clinton continues his equivocations because they allow him to avoid telling people what they may not want to hear, thus mitigating their potential political opposition. However, this argument falters when one considers that many come away from the experience more angry with and opposed to Clinton than they might have been if they agreed to disagree.

Nor does the contention that Clinton has adopted this style because of a "desire to be liked" (Brummett 1994, 70) make much sense. Leaving individuals with the (erroneous) impression that he agrees with them, only to find out shortly afterward that his agreement doesn't necessarily correspond to his subsequent behavior, is a recipe for disaster. Whatever role a need to be liked may have played in the early stages of this career, the actual effects of his behavior have been clear for many years. They are unlikely to have been lost on someone who, like Clinton, is so keenly aware of his standing with others.

Betsey Wright, a long-time Clinton aide and fervent booster, insists, "But he *wants* to keep his promises, and he thinks at the time he can" (Brummett 1994, 263). This is an argument that pleads for forbearance because of Clinton's good intentions. However, it also points to another set of explanations having to do with Clinton's belief that he can accomplish things that different groups want, even when those things are diametrically opposed. Clinton here has seemed to operate by a "myth of nonideological politics" based on the premise that "conflicting ideas could be brought rather easily, *through the agency of himself,* into something that would pass for agreement" (Kelly 1993a).

Clinton believes that he can easily accomplish, through his own personal talents, something that many others would view as difficult and uncertain, perhaps even impossible. According to Wright, Clinton as governor actually thought he could reconcile polar opposites. He apparently still does. The question is why this belief persists in spite of the fact that it has gotten him into serious trouble in Arkansas and throughout his presidency. The answer, in short, is that a person who, against all evidence, persists in beliefs and behavior that unduly harms others does so for *his own* reasons.

What are these reasons for Clinton? One is very likely his dislike of limits and his belief that, in the end, it may be possible not to be bound by them. It is the same issue that underlies his tendency to agree with opposing positions, his difficulties in focusing, and his energetic pursuit of his substantial personal and policy ambitions. Clinton truly believes that he—and, to some degree, *he alone*—can accomplish what other smart, talented, motivated people have not been able to. In that heightened sense of his own capacities there is also a sense of being special, even unique. Part of the feeling of being special is the feeling of entitlement. Other people may have to toe the line, other people may have to be considerate of others, of the hopes they raise or dash, of the promises they make and keep, of the way in which they treat others, but the specially entitled person feels exempt from these ordinary rules and holds himself to a different standard, one that only he can truly define since he knows the good he is trying to accomplish and the price he is paying for trying to do so.[21]

CLINTON AS ROOSEVELT?

Clinton sees himself as a modern Roosevelt (Blumenthal 1993a; Samuelson, 1993a) and has also publicly identified himself with Kennedy (Alter 1993). Others have seen him differently. Some have compared him unflatteringly to Jimmy Carter (Gelb 1993) and to Lyndon Johnson (Baker 1993). Others have seen Clinton as resembling presidents as diverse as Reagan, Bush,

Ford, Carter, and Kennedy (Solomon 1993). The diversity of these perceptions reflects Clinton public ambiguity and the difficulty that many have had in distinguishing Clinton's many personas from his basic character and psychology.

While it is true that one can find elements of Roosevelt and Kennedy in Clinton, there is less there than meets the eye. Clinton does not share Roosevelt's "first-class temperament." While both are associated with social and political change, their approach differs dramatically. Both presidents promised bold, persistent experimentation, but only Roosevelt carried through on his promise to discard what didn't work. In his first two years in office, Clinton has been committed to change but not to experimentation, especially when it comes to his new programs. In fact, the president whom Clinton most psychologically and politically parallels is not Roosevelt or Kennedy. It is not even Carter and Johnson. The president Clinton most resembles in a number of basic psychological and political ways is Richard Nixon. They share high ambition (along with the skills to realize it), problems with character integrity, and questions about the authenticity of their interpersonal connections. Both have invested enormous energy in their ambitions, but have not gained great satisfaction from their results. Both have expressed their resentment at the lack of credit they have received.

Both also share important background experiences. Both grew up in difficult economic and emotional circumstances in small rural towns. Both had difficult fathers and both idealized their mothers. Both overcame these experiences through talent, hard work, and ambition. Both made serious mistakes and fought back repeatedly in successful attempts to overcome them. Indeed, Nixon, after his defeat for the governorship in California, his defeat by Kennedy, and his rehabilitation after his resignation, can accurately be considered the first "comeback kid." Nixon himself commented on the similarities. After meeting with Clinton, Nixon said,

> You know he came from dirt and I came from dirt. He lost a gubernatorial race and came back to win the Presidency, and I lost a gubernatorial race and came back to win the Presidency. He overcame a scandal in his first campaign for national office and I overcame a scandal in my first national campaign. *We both just gutted it out.* He was an outsider from the South and I was an outsider from the West. (Stone 1994, emphasis mine)

Not only have both presidents "gutted it out" to win back a measure of their reputations, they have even used similar public techniques to do so.

Nixon's famous "Checker's Speech," given to diffuse public concern about his moral character, is not too far removed for the Clintons's appearance on *Sixty Minutes* to do the same.

Further, Clinton and Nixon are among the two most intelligent modern presidents. Both have blurred their ideological leanings—Nixon defining himself as a pragmatist not driven by ideology (Renshon 1996, 39), Clinton as a "New Democrat." They both have tended to blame others, and especially the press, for their problems. Indeed, at the White House Correspondents dinner in 1994, one columnist usually very favorable to the administration noted that Clinton delivered a testy monologue that "ushered in ghosts of the 1962 'last press conference' . . . [in which] Clinton failed to cover his feelings of anger and resentment (Rich 1994b)." Both have been given to using private profanity. Both presidents shared an explosive temper as well as a tendency to villainize those who don't agree with them. Indeed, the importance of "enemies" for both presidents is striking, especially in view of the fact that the extroverted Clinton seems on the surface so different from the introverted Nixon.

The striking correspondence in Nixon and Clinton's basic character psychology is paralleled by the public's response to both men. Through the years, both have elicited extremely strong public emotions. Many hated Nixon. Many too have "a visceral, personal animosity against Clinton" (Engelberg 1995a), a response that Clinton has acknowledged exists. Both, throughout their careers, have had great difficulties with issues of public trust. Nixon's "Checkers Speech" was a response to accusations that he had a slush fund. Clinton, as governor, in his relations to those who helped he and his wife financially, engaged in a number of questionable practices. And of course, there are the developing parallels between Watergate and Whitewater which several reporters, who have been either supportive of Clinton or fair and professional in their reporting of the administration, have noted (Quindlen 1994; Apple 1994b).[22]

Do these parallels mean that Clinton is like Nixon in every respect? Obviously they do not. But their similarities can help us better to understand Clinton more fully. "Tricky Dick" and "Slick Willy" are characterological siblings.

★ ——

CHAPTER 6

CHARACTER AND PRESIDENTIAL PSYCHOLOGY

A president's psychology is not synonymous with his character. Each president has a number of personality traits that help to define him as a unique person. Some presidents are restless, others patient. Some are drawn to getting things done, others enjoy the ceremonial aspects of the role. Some seek out responsibility, others avoid it. Some traits are central to a president's performance, others peripheral.

In this chapter I identify those personality traits central to understanding Clinton's approach to his presidency—those directly linked with his ambition, character integrity, and relatedness. Since character represents the foundation of a person's overall psychological functioning, it is generally associated with the development of a stable set of psychological characteristics clearly evident in the person's behavior. These characteristics, which I call *character-based personality traits,* originate in the specific ways in which the three basic character elements have come together in an individual.

Most of a president's personality traits are not by themselves either "good" or "bad." Their value depends on their strength and their relationship to other aspects of the president's psychology and character. The evaluation of a president's traits must therefore rest on the ways they function in particular circumstances. The trait of "affiliation," for example, is critical for Clinton, but its actual use can be either positive or negative.

Being able to deal effectively with others is clearly one important element of presidential leadership, but it can also serve keep a president from making tough but needed decisions. What may appear at first to be a useful political resource can also be a source of difficulty (Heifetz 1994, 764). While this is true in theory for all presidents, it has particular importance for Clinton who, throughout his career, has both prospered and faltered, often as a result of the very same traits.

PERSISTENCE

Persistence, an excellent example of a character-based trait, reflects a capacity to tolerate disappointments, frustrations, and setbacks and not be deterred from continuing attempts to achieve one's goals. Persistence is partly a function of ambition. The greater a president's ambition, the more likely he is to continue trying to realize it. Persistence is also related to self-confidence. The greater one's self-confidence, the more capacity one has to persist. A no less powerful association is to be found in the reverse— namely, the more important success (however defined) becomes to maintaining or validating one's self-regard or identity, the more determined a person may become to obtain what success provides. Persistence is also related to a president's capacities and skills. The more developed a president's skills, the more resources he can bring to bear on achieving his goals. Finally, the capacity for persistence is related to the emotional and (often) material support of others in times of need.

Clinton is both determined and resilient, and his persistence has been a great political asset. In his political life, Clinton has experienced a number of setbacks from which he has recovered and gone on to new achievements. Clinton lost the race for class secretary his senior year of high school (Moore 1992, 26). He lost his bid for student council president at Georgetown in his junior year but won it in his senior year (Levin 1992, 51). He narrowly lost his first run for public office, for a congressional seat in Arkansas in 1974, but then won election for attorney general in 1976 and governor in 1978. He lost his reelection bid in 1980 but ran again in 1982 and won. In the 1992 presidential campaign, he recovered from major questions raised about his character to capture the presidency. In an article entitled "Grace Under Pressure? It's Working for Clinton," one reporter noted that Clinton's apparent "serenity" in the face of these accusations had been an important aspect of his campaign's ability to weather them (Tierney 1992). A less self-confident and determined candidate, it was reasoned, would not have been able to do so. Clinton also used the "come-back kid" persona with some success in trying to rebound from a difficult and rocky transition from president-elect to president, and from major and minor difficulties during his first two years in office.

How can we account psychologically for this capacity? One factor clearly seems to be Clinton's unusually high levels of self-confidence and ambition. The *exact* mixture of personal and policy ambitions is difficult to specify in many people and is particularly so in Clinton, who insists, when confronted with accusations of personal ambition, that his ambitions are solely in the service of others.[1]

If Clinton's capacity to recover is obvious, the question begs itself: Why has he had to do it so often? His tendency to become involved in situations from which he has to extricate himself permeates his career and has repeatedly been a problem in his presidency. The answer to this question is closely related to Clinton's difficulties with boundaries of all kinds— of ambition, of propriety—and, ultimately, to the characteristics associated with character integrity (see chapter 13).

IMPATIENCE

Clinton is a man in a hurry. When he was asked by Dan Rather what his biggest disappointment in the presidency has been, he responded, "How hard it is to do everything I want to do as quickly as I want to do it. . . . I still get frustrated. . . . I'm an impatient person by nature, and I want to do things" (Clinton 1993i).

A certain degree of impatience can be politically helpful in advancing a president's agenda. It is likely to cause him to press more firmly for results and can speed up the policy process. It is crucial for a president to act when his appeal and influence are high. The president's party tends to lose congressional seats in off-year (nonpresidential) elections, one of the reasons offered for the rapid pace of Clinton's early political and policy efforts (Drew 1994, 94). However, Clinton's combination of a large policy agenda and an impatience to accomplish it precedes his presidency. David Mathews, who has known Clinton for over twenty years, observed of his first term as governor, "When he began his administration in 1979, Bill was like a man in a hurry to accomplish many things in a short time. . . . I think somehow Bill felt that, through his sheer energy, he could change our state overnight" (quoted in Levin 1992, 133).

Clinton himself has traced his impatience to the early and tragic death of his father in a highway accident. He told one of his early biographers, Charles Flynn Allen,

> I think I always felt, in some sense, that . . . I should be in a hurry in life because it gave me a real sense of mortality. Most kids never think about when . . . they're going to have to run out of time, when they might die. . . . I thought about it all the time because my father died at 29 before I was born. . . . And I think it's one reason I was always in a hurry to do things—which is both good and bad. . . . And I also think I . . . thought I had to live for myself and him too. (1991, 20–21; see also Maraniss 1995, 79)

It is certainly plausible that the early death of his father left Clinton with a sense of the fragility of life. Strong ambition coupled with a sense of life's fragility would increase the pressures to accomplish things more quickly. So would Clinton's sense that he has substantial talents and skills. In other words, what one can do (because of talent), one *must* do (because of time).

How might Clinton's view of himself as a highly moral and somewhat selfless man, whose ambitions are not primarily for him but to serve others, be related to his sense of not having enough time? Could it lead to a tendency to cut some corners in the pursuit of one's ambitions? After all, if one has little time, much important work to do, and the talent to accomplish it—mostly for the good of others—then it will perhaps be understandable if one can't touch all the bases, or square all the corners.

One factor that argues against the fragility-of-life explanation for Clinton's impatience is the large number of public deadlines he has placed on himself and his administration. For example, Clinton publicly vowed to pick his whole cabinet by Christmas, a promise that led to a "mad scramble" (Drew 1994, 31). Appearing on *Larry King Live* on June 4, 1992, Clinton said, "I know I can pass a sweeping package of legislation during the first hundred days of my administration." In the May 1992 issue of *Fortune* magazine, Clinton promised to "put together a transition team to 'hit the ground running,' resulting in one of those great 100 days in which Congress would adopt my health care and education policies, my energy and economic initiatives." [2]

While these promises may simply represent the rhetorical expansiveness of a new, untried administration, the degree of public expansiveness is striking in comparison to other transitions. And the tendency to make unrealistic promises occurred not only during the transition but after the administration had been in office and ought to have known better. For instance, Clinton told Senator Orrin Hatch on June 7, 1993, that he would have a Supreme Court nominee within forty-eight hours; White House officials were forced to backtrack on this pledge because not enough ground work had been accomplished (Berke 1993a).

Or consider the Clinton health-care plan. Clinton appointed the health-care task-force chaired by his wife on January 25, 1993. He charged them to "prepare health care reform legislation to be submitted to Congress within one hundred days of our taking office" (Pear 1993b). Up until the last minute, White House officials continued to insist that it would be ready by May 3, 1992. That date was later pushed back to May or June; some said July or August was more realistic (Pear 1993f). However, because of the scope and complexity of the developing plans, top administration aides, including then budget director Leon E. Panetta, urged the president to delay submitting the plan, a suggestion that first Clinton and then his wife rejected. The White House then backtracked again and agreed that there would be a further delay in presenting the administration's health-care plan. The following month the task force disbanded without preparing comprehensive health-care legislation for submission to Congress. A further delay was then announced.

The point of documenting the above sequences[3] is not to criticize Clinton because of delays or slippage in the schedules he announced, but rather to underscore that the time limits placed on Clinton were of his own making and strictly speaking not necessary. Clinton's time frame was clearly unrealistic given the complexity of what he was undertaking. Such premature public commitments were unnecessary and counterproductive. The public did not expect, nor was it demanding, that Clinton produce detailed legislation in a variety of areas, some of which would be complex and contentious, and have it passed or submitted to Congress within his first hundred days.

The public nature of Clinton's self-imposed deadlines are inconsistent with the fragility-of-life theory. Clinton could have felt the pressure of that early loss and decided to push hard in all these areas without publicly promising to perform these expansive feats of accomplishment. The public nature of the promises seems more closely tied to Clinton's desire to tell people how much he is doing and will do than to a sense that life is fleeting. Clinton could have felt the pressures of time without feeling the need to publicly tout how much he would do.

Character questions raised by such impatience aside, there are political questions as well. Institutions like Congress[4] that have their own important and historical legislative role cannot simply be expected to perform as uncritical conduits for large numbers of presidential initiatives with far-reaching consequences. A president who does not recognize this invites frustration. He also invites the question of how he could possibly have expected it to be otherwise. Frustration, after all, is a function of expectation as well as impatience.

ACHIEVEMENT

A desire to achieve, like affiliation, is most often examined on the basis of whether a president has more or less of it. By a number of different measures, Clinton is highly motivated to achieve. A standardized measure of Clinton's achievement motivation scores in his inaugural address was a very robust score of 71, compared, for example, to a score of 57 in George Bush's 1989 inaugural speech (Winter 1995, 119).[5] Ordinarily, a strong aspiration for achievement is a desirable trait in a president. A president who lacks a desire to achieve will also lack a strong sense of what he wants to accomplish and the conviction to do it, resulting in presidential drift.

However, there are costs associated with having too much motivation to achieve (Winter 1995, 127–28). While high-achievement leaders such as Ross Perot do well in business, they may not do as well in politics, due to the "command and compliance" culture of business in contrast to the "debate and convince" culture of American politics. *Why Not the Best?*, the title of the campaign biography of another high-achievement president, Jimmy Carter, makes the point explicitly. Presidents with high achievement motivation can come to believe in the theory of a single best solution: theirs. A president's view that he has found the single best solution may reflect over-expansiveness (grandiosity) as well as arrogance. A strong desire for achievement by itself, unsupported by a grounded sense of boundaries and ethics, can cause a president serious problems.

One result of the inevitable compromises that politics requires is that high-achievement presidents may "be tempted to go over the heads of politicians and take the case directly to 'the people' (as did achievement-motivated Woodrow Wilson), to take ethical short cuts (as did achievement-motivated Richard Nixon), or to exhaust themselves in micromanagement (as did achievement-motivated Jimmy Carter)" (Winter 1995, 128). Or, like Clinton, they may do all three. Clinton has repeatedly sought to bypass other centers of power and political responsibility (the press, the Congress) and appeal directly to "the people." He has immersed himself in a wide range of policy, personnel, and administrative details. In his educational role as president and in his private behavior, he has taken short-cuts that often skirt ethical boundaries.

How does Clinton define accomplishment? How much is "good"? How much is "enough"? What functions does accomplishment serve in his overall psychology? The combination of intense ambition, high self-confidence, and strong self-regard lead Clinton to be very directed toward achievement, but achievement of *a particular type*. Modest successes are not what he has in mind. Clinton defines his own achievement at extremely high, even grandiose, levels. The passage of *some* major policy initiatives is not enough. Some—even many—can still be too few given Clinton's definition of success.

The ambition to achieve large ends coupled with a determination to see that ambition through can sometimes result in achievements that would have seemed unreachable at their inception. Expansive ambitions can also be consciously employed as a political tool. A president who wants to promote social or policy change may reason that change, even moderate change, is difficult to accomplish. Given this, one strategy is to attempt large change with the expectation of getting at least some change. Some have even argued that this is precisely what Clinton has done.

And yet I doubt Clinton's expansive policy aspirations are merely a strategic artifact. This view falters when we consider such events as the Clinton health-care plan, where more moderate versions of reform (e.g., the Cooper plan) were attacked by the administration in the hope of getting its extremely ambitious version through Congress (Ifill 1994a; Pear 1993g). Moreover, even if Clinton had been able to achieve only some aspects of each policy he proposed, the result would have remained one of the most ambitious and expansive policy agendas brought into the presidency since 1964.

COMPETITION

Clinton's psychology combines an intense desire to accomplish with a highly competitive nature. Clinton's competitiveness has been part of his behavior from childhood and has been observed over many years of Clinton's life in differing contexts. His mother attributes it to her influence. She says of herself that "I play any game to win," and goes on to note, "Bill is the same way," and "I'm proud to say that Bill inherited my competitiveness" (Kelley 1994a, 138). She also recalls that when her son Roger expressed disappointment about not winning a football competition, Bill wrote to him encouraging him to keep trying because "determination will finally pay off—*if* you want to win badly enough" (1994a, 164, emphasis in original).

In the second grade, one teacher gave Clinton a D in deportment because he talked too often in class, spoiling an otherwise perfect report card (Oakley 1994, 27–28). Why give him a D instead of talking with him or using some other method? According to Clinton's mother, his teacher said, "I have to get his attention one way or the other and this is the only way I know how to do it, because he is so competitive that he will not be able to stand this D" (Allen and Portis 1992, 6).

Clinton's competitiveness extended to many areas. His childhood friend Carolyn Staley recalls that Clinton, upon receiving a higher math grade than another very smart student, ran into the house holding his test paper and screaming about what he had done (Allen and Portis 1992, 10). She also recalled of Clinton in another interview: "He had to be the class leader, he had to be the best in the band. He had to be the best in his class. . . . And he wanted to be in the top . . . in anything that put him in the forefront of any course" (Allen 1991, 12). After another student outper-formed him in a Latin translation, Clinton "brought it up for weeks there-after and . . . behind the smiles . . . was upset . . . [he] always wanted to win" (Maraniss 1995, 43). As governor, Clinton had a pinball machine installed in the basement of the governor's mansion. When the son of one of his staff ran up a score of 800,000 points, breaking Clinton's record, Clinton stayed up until two in the morning trying to reclaim his record from the seven-year-old (Maraniss 1995, 383).

Isn't it to be expected that a president with high achievement motiva-tion would also be very competitive? Not necessarily. To be sure, almost all achievement is gauged in relation to others. However, individuals vary substantially in the degree to which they derive satisfaction from tri-umphing over others rather than from the actual accomplishment itself or, simply enjoy winning. For some people the enjoyment of what they accom-plish outweighs whatever satisfaction they receive from winning or beating others. For other people the reverse is true. In Clinton's psychology all three appear to play a role.

What role does competitiveness play in a president's performance? A competitive president who does not like to lose may be more likely to do what is necessary to win. In certain circumstances this may be politically beneficial to him or to the public more generally. A competitive president challenged by an enemy abroad, for example, may be prone to respond forcefully. Certainly a competitive president can improve his position domestically, with regard both to his rivals and to his own policy agenda, by wanting and trying to win.

One drawback to an emphasis on winning—specifically triumphing over others—is a lessening of satisfaction with one's real accomplishments. Here the mentality is "I haven't won enough, therefore I can't be satisfied with what I have accomplished." In Clinton's case his competitiveness is buttressed by his idealized sense of doing good for the right reasons and being very confident that his views are right. One may eventually have to compromise with the devil, but not before one has tried to beat him.

This combination can easily lead to a tendency to make others into enemies, sometimes unnecessarily. This seems to have played a key role in Clinton's deteriorating relationships with Republicans in Congress and with some moderate and conservative members of his own party. Although he pledged a bipartisan effort to break congressional deadlock, Clinton's first budget was drawn up and submitted with little, if any, consultation with Republicans. As a result, Senator Robert Dole told Clinton that no Republicans would vote for his bill because, in his view, it raised too many new taxes and did too little for deficit reduction (Woodward 1994, 104). Rather than seeking to follow through on his promise to work with Republicans, Clinton went ahead with a "Democrats-only strategy." It is perhaps understandable that Clinton submitted his budget without trying to enlist any Republicans. However, in doing so he set the stage for what happened next. The budget resolution passed in the House 342–183 with not a single Republican voting for it. The same party-line vote occurred in the Senate. It is possible, of course, to argue that no Republican would have voted for anything the administration put forward, but this did not prove to be the case in other votes—NAFTA for instance—when the president was forced to abandon his Democrats-only strategy.

The administration pursued the same strategy with its next budget item, the stimulus bill. Here again Clinton chose not to involve the Republicans, and in doing so, according to some, made a "tremendous blunder" (Drew 1994, 116). Democratic Senator David L. Boren, for instance, thought that a Democrats-only strategy was a grave mistake and that "Senate Republicans were there for the asking if they could give the stimulus package a conservative cast" (Woodward 1994, 178). He was rebuffed by the White House. By the time the Budget Reconciliation Bill arrived in the Senate, the die was largely cast. At a meeting between the president and Democratic members of the Senate Finance Committee, George Mitchell and David Boren argued for trying to bring in the Republicans. Al Gore asked that all present agree not to work with Republicans, and that is how the meeting ended (Woodward 1994, 181). The bill passed in the Senate with Vice President Gore casting the tie-breaking vote.

The administration followed the same fifty-one-vote strategy in attempting to move its health-care proposal through the Senate. Given a choice between working with Republicans and excluding them in the hope of getting a bill closer to what they had proposed, the White House and especially Hillary Clinton chose "to proceed with a fifty-one vote strategy; getting enough votes from Democrats (with one Republican ally, Senator James Jeffords of Vermont)" (Drew 1994, 434). Even Democrats were not excluded from being placed on the enemy list. When moderate Democratic Senator Jim Cooper proposed a health-care plan that was less ambitious than the Clinton plan, he and his plan were publicly attacked by Hillary Clinton (Pear 1993g).

Clinton's desire to win by having things totally his way suggests that his reputation as man too ready to compromise is not always deserved. In these cases the strategy he chose violated his campaign promise to conduct his presidency in a bipartisan manner. It was also costly to him in other ways. Having been elected with only 43 percent of the vote, he clearly needed to expand his political base, either by pursuing moderate policies or by staffing his administration in a somewhat bipartisan way. Instead Clinton did neither. For example, although he briefly considered offering the U.N. ambassadorship to Condoleeza Rice, who had served in the Bush administration, he again decided to go with a Democrats-only strategy (Drew 1994, 28).

This strategy helped to unite and solidify opposition to his vast agenda among Republicans, but also among moderate and conservative Democrats. It thereby set the stage for other setbacks, the most spectacular of which were the results of the 1994 midterm elections. Who knows what would have happened had Clinton chosen to work with moderates and conservatives of both parties as he had promised, instead of pursuing a win-it-all-my-way strategy. Here again, Clinton's own psychology helped him get into a position from which he has been fighting to extract himself ever since.

The Need to Be Special

Clinton will most likely continue to be a very public president. For him to be appreciated, others, especially the public, *must* know all he is doing.[6] Clinton is a man with strong analytic capacities and a mastery of facts that comes from decades of immersion in policy, and he *wants the public to know it.* He believes in his abilities to solve the public's problems, and it is crucially important to him that others know and appreciate what he is doing. Clinton's wish to impress the public with how much he would accomplish and how quickly he would do it is one likely source of the unnecessary public deadlines he imposed on himself at the start of his presidency.

Consider, for instance, the economic conference staged by the newly elected president and his staff in Little Rock in December 1992, during the transition period. Some advisers argued against it, believing—correctly, it turned out—that it would take time away from other important matters of planning and implementation. However, Clinton wanted to make a strong impression as someone who had mastered the complexity of the American economy. "Professor" Clinton demonstrated at length his grasp of policy detail, putting his intelligence on display in a setting structured to be supportive of ideas he had presented during the campaign: "Clinton got to do what he loves most: talk policy and show off his knowledge" (Drew 1994, 27).

When the new administration sat down behind closed doors in the White House Roosevelt Room to hammer out its first budget proposal, Clinton again was "the star": "he both conducted . . . and dominated the discussion . . . It was Clinton showing how much he knew. Clinton seemed to have a compulsion about this—though, as he must have known, no one who dealt with him doubted that he was a very smart man" (Drew 1994, 66–67).

This compulsive need to showcase his skills—dating back to his D in second grade—is also evident in the large number of public venues in which he appears and in the enormous extent of his public commentary. These include, but are by no means limited to, news conferences, formal interviews, local radio and television interviews, talks, town meetings, and other specially constructed dialogues such as his health-care meetings. It is also evident in his desire to speak in public at length about so many things, in many cases more than is needed, and sometimes more than can be educationally absorbed.

This tendency to display his technical knowledge to the public may have a political as well as a personal payoff for Clinton. Certainly the demonstration of policy knowledge is an asset to a president interested in policy leadership. So too, educating the public is an important part of effective political leadership in a democracy. However, information can confuse as well as enlighten. Too much information, or a bewildering barrage of information, may disguise purpose as well as reveal it.

It is not be surprising that someone with Clinton's large and successful ambitions, sometimes realized against great odds, would come to think of himself as special and unique.[7] And I believe that Clinton does see himself as uniquely experienced and qualified to provide this country with leadership.

Interesting in this regard are Clinton's inaugural speeches as governor and president, specifically his frequent use of identification words such as "we," "us," and "our" in his gubernatorial and presidential speeches (English 1993, 13). Of course, many politician use such symbols of inclusion. However, when we compare Clinton's inaugural addresses with Reagan's addresses, Nixon's first address, and Eisenhower's first address, "Clinton's speech proportionately identifies its vision with that of the American people to a significantly greater degree" (English 1993, 22).

This sense of being special can also be expressed in the belief that one has been singled out and treated differently, for better or worse. Clinton often points to the impossible standards to which he is held. For example, when the issue of his marital fidelity was raised during the campaign Clinton was suffused with a sense of his own victimhood and being singled out for martyrdom. He complained loudly to his traveling companions, "No one has ever been through what I've been through in this thing" (Goldman et al. 1994, 118). In the *Rolling Stone* interview he complained of being held to "an impossible standard" and of "never" getting credit for his accomplishments in spite of having "fought my guts out" (Wenner and Greider 1993, 81). A year into his presidency, Clinton complained, "I sometimes think I get the worst of both worlds. I lay out real ambitious agendas and try to get them done. And the people who don't agree with me are threatened by it and really don't like me. And the people that do agree with me sometimes hold it against me if I don't get it all done, or have to compromise" (Brummett 1994, 278).

The sense of having been singled out *because of* the important, major, or unusual nature of what one is trying to accomplish calls attention to one's efforts and to the valiant struggle one is waging. It has the effect of underscoring the unique and selfless nature of one's efforts. Both of these views are consistent with Clinton's idealized view of his own behavior and motives.

WANTING TO HAVE IT BOTH WAYS

Due largely to his idealized view of himself, Clinton often seems unaware of the discrepancies between what he says and what he does. In matters large and small, there is an element in Clinton of not wishing to, or perhaps thinking that he does not *have to,* make the ordinary choices that individuals and presidents do. Whether this comes from the sense of not wanting to be limited in any way personally or politically[8] (itself a possible manifestation of grandiosity), or whether it comes from a sense of being special and therefore entitled to operate differently, or both, is not yet clear. However, even a very partial list of such discrepancies bears testimony to Clinton's dislike of boundaries.

The most obvious and basic reflection of Clinton's wish to have it both ways is in his portrayal of himself as a New Democrat, one who will transcend the boundaries of Left and Right. There was an inherent contradiction between Clinton's pledge, made throughout the campaign, that he was a new kind of Democrat, one who looked to create a smaller, smarter government, and the implications of his promises. Elizabeth Drew has remarked, "Clinton's self-definition as 'a new kind of Democrat' was designed, among other things, to camouflage his big government tendencies, which were real enough" (1994, 60). That is one reason why Clinton's deficit reduction pledges didn't square with the large amounts of money that would be required to fund his new programs (Drew 1994, 59, 64). George Stephanopoulos has similarly observed that Clinton "knew exactly what he was doing. He put himself on the path of significant budget reduction . . . at the same time he sought increased spending for his 'investments.' . . . It turned out to be a troublesome combination" (Drew 1994, 64). Why? Because it was not really possible to accomplish all of what Clinton wanted to do in both areas *at the same time.* Stephanopoulos realized that "Clinton's promises didn't hang together. He couldn't cut middle-class taxes, cut the deficit in half, and finance a big investment program" (Woodward 1994, 95).

This contradiction represents a fundamental incongruity in the logic that underlies the Clinton administration and is a direct result of Clinton's attempting to have it both ways. Realizing that the public is cautious and concerned about the efficacy and appropriateness of large-scale government programs, but personally committed to that approach to solving social and public problems, Clinton has tried a number of tactics. He has sought to relabel government programs as "investments," thereby shifting the focus from who is doing the spending and mandating to viewing their purposes in a way consistent with Clinton's view. One drawback of this tactic is that it has tried to finesse the terms of the debate rather than taking the opportunity to explain how his investments differ from previous big government efforts and thus to build public support for his programs.

Another dilemma posed by this fundamental contradiction was how Clinton was going to get the money to fund his programs without being labeled a traditional tax-and-spend liberal.[9] Clinton's wish to have it both ways is at the heart of many of his subsequent attempts to finesse and otherwise mask his proposed expenditures (e.g., by calling government-mandated payments for health care "premiums" rather than taxes).

This, then, is the fundamental contradiction at the heart of the Clinton administration. But there are others. For example, Clinton is for public education but sends his child to an exclusive private school. He is "pro-choice" in education, but only within the public school system. His own behavior coupled with his public position seems to suggest that more wide-ranging choice is acceptable for his family but not for other families.[10]

As regards ethics, Clinton has spoken of his commitment to setting a high moral tone and tough standard of ethics for his administration. Yet from the start, he has allowed for important exceptions. While pledging high ethical standards, the administration found reasons to make exceptions for Vernon Jordan and others so that they could serve on the president's transition team (Berke 1992b). Clinton's nominee for secretary of commerce, Ronald Brown, a Democratic party official with extensive lobbying interests, was at one point set to throw a party for corporate lobbyists charging ten thousand dollars a person (Labaton 1993a). That party was canceled in the face of mounting criticism (Labaton 1993b).

The administration skirted the laws regulating campaign contributions by inviting big contributors to the Democratic party to a "breakfast with president." This plan was dropped after word of it became public (Ifill 1993h). The president has consistently decried the pernicious role of lobbyists but visited a large fundraising dinner for lobbyists while not allowing the press to take pictures of him doing so. When criticism of this "stealth visit" mounted, Clinton promised to be more open in the future (*New York Times* 1993c). The president has vocally denounced the pernicious impact of "soft money," yet as a candidate, Clinton received record amounts (Wines 1993c).

Clinton pledged to cut the White House staff 25 percent as a symbol of his commitment to smaller, more efficient government, a commitment that ran into trouble almost as soon as it was announced (Berke 1993e). Clinton first backed away from the commitment by citing the semantic difference between "goals" and "commitments" (Friedman 1993a). When 25 percent cuts were announced, the figure excluded a large number of individuals whose offices are part of the executive office of the president and who work for the White House (Friedman 1993a). These included hundreds of military communications workers, as well as workers in the trade representative's office and the Office of Management and Budget. When these individuals were included in the White House staff, the actual cuts were about 16 percent. Many workers "cut" from the White House staff were simply reassigned to their home government departments. In short, these cuts reflected the politics of symbolism and perception, not substance (Hart 1995).

Clinton presented himself during the campaign as a middle-class man of the people. He stressed the modest economic circumstances of his childhood. However, he seems quite different in this regard from Harry Truman (to whom Clinton is sometimes compared), who came from modest origins and remained in touch with them. In his social and personal trajectory, Clinton more clearly resembles Gary Hart. Clinton plays golf at exclusive, all-white country clubs (A. M. Rosenthal 1993), gets two-hundred-dollar haircuts (Friedman and Dowd 1993), hobnobs with Hollywood stars (Dowd 1993; Drew 1994, 182), and goes to high-powered retreats (Jehl 1993). The projected image and the reality are quite different.

When he was criticized for going to the "elitist" Renaissance weekends that he had attended for ten years, did he stop going? No. Did Clinton simply go ahead, saying that he enjoyed them and had a right to go? No. Rather, "sensitive lest he be seen as too cozy with the elite, he planned to stay barely 24 hours—a much shorter stay than his typical past visits of several days" (Purdum 1995e, A18).

Clinton has presented himself to the public as having a close and loving relationship with his wife. Yet his campaign produced a memorandum detailing the ways that the couple should act in public (contrary to how they had acted towards each other in public previously) to convey this image (Kelly 1992c). It suggested "events where Bill and Hillary can go on dates with the American people" and outlined the arranging of such events as "Bill and Chelsea surprise Hillary on Mother's Day," and so on.[11]

The point here is not that there are differences between President Clinton's words and behaviors. Few people are totally consistent. Nor is it that there are not some possible, even plausible, explanations for some of these matters. It is quite simply the *sheer volume* of such discrepancies that draws attention. (I have specifically excluded from this list many substantive policy discrepancies between words and deeds on issues such as homosexuals serving in the military, sending back Haitians who attempt to reach the United States by boat, the conflict in Bosnia, and so on.) Cumulatively, they give the unmistakable impression of a president who has difficulty following through on his professed commitments. Further, they suggest a president who wishes to give the appearance of following through on commitments, while acting in a manner that is not wholly consistent with adhering to them. Put another way, Clinton repeatedly does something publicly for which one would receive credit, while taking steps to ensure that he satisfies personal, less public-minded motives.

The tendency to believe that one can "have it all" or "have it both ways" is marvelously distilled in the 1969 letter that Clinton sent to Colonel Holmes about his draft status, which suggested that Clinton wanted both to have what he wished for (deferment of military service), and to be seen (and see himself) as doing the right thing (see chapter 10). The wish not to be limited in any way, personally or politically is understandable. However, in ordinary developmental experience, an individual's grandiose wish to "have it all" becomes modified by the acceptance and appreciation of realistic limits.

TAKING RISKS

Clinton's risk-taking, like his character, contains inconsistencies. In some areas, Clinton is not reckless and many of his risks are hedged. Clinton's attempt to have it both ways is one strategy for managing these larger risks. On the other hand, the combination of strong ambition, high self-confidence, and feelings of being beyond the rules that govern others frequently combine to push Clinton toward substantial risk-taking, often of a self-absorbed type. Said one friend of Clinton, "Bill has always been someone who lived on the edge, both politically and personally, for better or for worse" (Drew 1994, 387).

Outsiders have sometimes misjudged Clinton's behavior as risky when it was not. Consider Clinton's run against President Bush. It may have seemed very risky but was not, given the circumstances. Some polls had suggested Bush was vulnerable. Moreover, in running against him, Clinton was not taking the risk of falling on the sword of his ambition. He was, after all, still a sitting governor. And his calculations might well have included the belief that a strong run against Bush, even if unsuccessful, would have made him a frontrunner in 1996, when no strong Republican contender (like a widely respected vice president) was immediately obvious.

In his presidency, many of Clinton's risks—his economic package, the NAFTA agreement, or his welfare reform plans—reflect a mixture of ambition and self-protective hedging. For example, the budget package first proposed in August 1994 called for increased government spending (during his first term in office) and cuts in government spending to reduce the deficit in 1996 and after (once he had already stood for reelection). He followed the same strategy in his second budget.

Yet on occasion Clinton has taken bold policy gambles. For example, Clinton viewed the NAFTA agreement as marking the kind of new international economic relationships that Americans had to be ready for. However, he took up the issue of NAFTA at a time when his presidency was already floundering from a series of missteps and the perception that he backed away from his commitments too easily. Having invested his prestige in winning at a time when his presidency was in trouble, Clinton was forced to pull out all the stops. Stephanopoulos was speaking of NAFTA but might well have been speaking of Clinton's presidency more generally when he said, "We're always stuck in the small crawl space between 'must win' and 'can't lose' " (Drew 1994, 345). Unlike other, more ambiguous commitments, Clinton "kept shoving more and more chips into the pot on an issue that few Americans understood, [and] it paid off handsomely," at least as far as passing the legislation [12] (Apple 1993).

While some applauded the administration's much-needed victory (Lewis 1993a), the method by which it was accomplished is troubling. A large number of industries were offered special deals to ensure that they would be treated well under NAFTA. There were tariff breaks for citrus growers, for sugar, peanuts, bed frames, wine, wheat, and manhole covers (A. M. Rosenthal 1993). The titles of two news accounts tell the story: "Clinton's Shopping List for Votes Has Ring of Grocery Buyer's List" (Bradsher 1993) and "A 'Bazaar' Way of Rounding up Votes" (Wines 1993a). Some of the deals involved were equivalent to making changes in the trade agreement, which was supposed to be voted on up or down without amendments. Indeed, "the deals were so numerous that it seemed as if a For Sale sign had been hung over the White House" (Drew 1994, 342). Clinton gained a much-needed short-term victory, but his methods cost him credibility and made his getting votes in the future more difficult. After NAFTA even lawmakers who are inclined to take Clinton's side "first often state their price" (Myerson 1994). By making so many side deals with particular congressmen and their constituents, the administration succeeded in having it both ways—they got an up or down vote without amendments but were able to make side deals that amounted to amendments. But this tactic also carried a price for Clinton's credibility because again he was seen to have acted inconsistently with what he had demanded of others.

On occasion, Clinton's belief that he can accomplish what has eluded others and that he knows more than they did leads him to take large risks and attempt to mask rather than hedge them. One prime example is the president's ambitious, complex health-care plan. It should be kept in mind that this plan represented a risk not only for President Clinton but for the public. Clinton was willing to take a large policy gamble—that his untried plan would work as promised, that it would not result in damaging consequences, and that it would be fair—in the public's name. Many of Clinton's aides and allies were not as confident as he was. Yet, he and his wife overrode a number of his aides' concerns and went ahead anyway. Why? One answer lay "in their sense that they were smarter than anyone else. For people who considered themselves masterly politicians with a fine feel for the public, and people who were of considerable political talents, they misjudged probable public reaction" (Drew 1994, 305).

In other words, strong ambition and too much self-confidence can lead to poor judgment. President Clinton not only underestimated the public's response to his health-care plan but overestimated his ability to overcome it. Moreover, the method he chose to help him win acceptance of the plan, emphasizing security (which became the selling point after polling had indicated it would be effective) instead of dealing directly with the many complex and difficult issues his plan raised, exacerbated the difficulties.

Throughout his career, Clinton has engaged in behavior that has skirted the ethical line and sometimes bordered on crossing over it. This behavior has taken the form of his extramarital relationships,[13] Whitewater, his personally calling an Arkansas state trooper as president when allegations emerged about his sexual misconduct while governor, and other similar matters. In each of these cases, Clinton engaged in behavior that was extremely risky from the standpoint of his personal and political ambitions.

People have attributed such behavior to Clinton's "large appetites," which is another way of saying he has difficulties with impulse control. He seems to have the sense that the limits he draws are alright because *he* knows what he is doing (as opposed to how it looks to others), and that if his behavior is revealed he can always find some way to diffuse the situation. All of these are elements that emanate from Clinton's character. From ambition comes the sense that you go after what you want. From character integrity comes his highly idealized view of himself, a view he has come to believe he can convince others to hold. And from his skills at relatedness comes his sense that he can and will do what it takes to get others to see things his way. It is a self-indulgent form of risk-taking, all the more striking in Clinton's case because of how much the continued realization of his ambitions were at risk.

Clinton's attention to foreign policy is characterized by the same self-indulgent risk-taking. Clinton is well known for his interest in and knowledge of domestic rather than foreign affairs. He is not the first president to feel more at home in one than the other. But Clinton's presidency unfolds in a particularly important transitional period in foreign policy. The Cold War is over, but high-intensity, local conflicts are on the rise. The United States clearly has as many world leadership responsibilities as it did before this transition period, perhaps more. Yet it is still addressing the nature and implications of changes in the international system and debating its response. No president in such a period can afford to neglect these facts, regardless of his level of comfort or preference in dealing with them.

Yet from the start, Clinton has tried to finesse foreign policy to concentrate on his domestic agenda. There are different ways to characterize this tendency, but few disagree it is a fact. The *Newsweek* team that was given behind-the-scenes access to the White House observed that "Clinton's disengagement from foreign policy was an exercise in self-discipline and realpolitik." Why? Because he "didn't see a winner in the whole lot" (Mathews 1993, 38). On the other hand, some thought Clinton's lack of attention to foreign policy was a costly form of self-indulgence traceable to the fact that "his pollsters had told him the public didn't want their president spending a lot of time on foreign policy" (Drew 1994, 419).[14]

How neglectful has Clinton been of foreign policy? Both Anthony Lake (Clinton's national security advisor) and Warren Christopher (his secretary of state) were given the same general assignment: "keep foreign policy from distracting the president from his domestic agenda" (Drew 1994, 28). Lake admitted "that in an effort to conserve the time of the president, he might not have been brought into enough of the larger contemplative discussions on issues not of the highest rank, including Somalia" (Friedman 1993b).

In reality, foreign policy meetings were infrequently scheduled and often canceled.[15] Lake's meetings with the president were scheduled for every morning but were often postponed, a process that led the normally cautious Christopher to tell the president "point blank that he had to become more engaged in foreign policy by spending at least *an hour a week* with his national security advisor" (Sciolino 1993, emphasis added). Although Clinton agreed with the suggestion, between October and the end of the year there were only two such meetings, one of which was constantly interrupted by calls to the president (Drew 1994, 336).

Has Clinton's approach changed? Has he learned by painful experience that even if he prefers domestic policy, foreign policy cannot be avoided? Perhaps, but the lesson appears to be a difficult one. While talking with reporters in an attempt to explain a remark he had made that Americans seemed to be in a "funk," Clinton went on at some length. When his spokesman, Michael McCurry, tried to get him to break off to attend a scheduled national security meeting on Bosnia, "Mr. Clinton testily brushed him off. He said: 'That meeting's at 2:15. That's when I called it for.' Mr. Clinton stayed so much longer to talk that Mr. McCurry desperately tried again, saying, 'Let's go, boss.' Mr. Clinton . . . ignored him" (Rosenthal 1995).

TAKING RESPONSIBILITY

A president who sees his own behavior in an idealized manner, who believes that he has been unfairly held to high or inconsistent standards, and who wants to be publicly validated for his accomplishments would have difficulty acknowledging his mistakes in a straightforward way. Not surprisingly, this has been an area of great difficulty for Clinton.

While he is sometimes able simply to take responsibility when something goes wrong, this is by far the exception to the more general pattern.[16] That pattern, evident in the marijuana, draft, and marital fidelity controversies, consists of denying, avoiding, blaming others, and misrepresenting or not fully disclosing information that, if disclosed, would put a different and less benign cast to his behavior. During the draft controversy he diced the truth into small bits, which were only served up after investigation and disclosure by the press forced a response (see chapter 10). During the 1992 campaign, when Clinton was first asked whether or not he had used marijuana, his response was that he had not broken the laws of this country. It then turned out that he had experimented with marijuana while in England. Thus, his answer, while technically accurate, was unresponsive and evasive. Clinton further tried to downplay what he thought would be a damaging admission by claiming that while he had tried marijuana, he had not inhaled. This effort might have been more amusing than troubling had it been an isolated incident. It was not. This pattern has repeated itself throughout his presidency.

Although President Clinton was briefed periodically on developments regarding the Branch Davidian crisis in Waco and was in fact told that a final assault was to be attempted, he disclaimed any responsibility. The morning of the assault Clinton told reporters, "I was aware of it, I think the Attorney General made the decision." Pushed by reporters, he then said, "I knew it was going to be done, but the decisions were entirely theirs" (Clinton 1993k). By singling out the official who actually made the decision, thereby discounting his own knowledge and final authority—

which he could have exercised to stop the operation, but did not—he invites the public to believe that he was ill-served by those whom he hired and trusted to know better. For a day after the Waco attack, the president said nothing and his aides insisted that in letting his attorney general take all the blame herself, he was not ducking responsibility, but "only letting Janet Reno do her job" (Friedman 1993e).

Clinton used the same stance in responding to the mishandling of the White House Travel Office investigation: "I had nothing to do with any decision, except to try and save the tax payers and the press money . . . that's all I knew about it" (Clinton 1993f, 942).[17] Here Clinton both takes credit for his action and disclaims the knowledge that led to it. Later, Clinton said, "Ultimately, anything that happens in the White House is the responsibility of the President," thereby again both assuming and defusing his responsibility (Friedman 1993e). In the absence of a more specific statement, this aphorism, meant to recall the political courage of Harry Truman, is at once both an acknowledgment and a disclaimer. It acknowledges that the president is ultimately responsible for everything that goes on in his administration, but at the same time it invites the public to be understanding of the fact that no one person can really be expected to be on top of everything that government does.

Sometimes, in his desire to avoid responsibility, Clinton has seriously misrepresented the facts. In his first weeks in office he indicated that he intended to lift the ban on homosexuals serving in the military, which was consistent both with his campaign policy book, *Putting People First,* and with his statements to reporters during the campaign.[18] Shortly after his election, Clinton was asked by Andrea Mitchell of NBC News whether he intended to honor his campaign pledge to lift the ban and he replied, "Yes" (Drew 1994, 43). During the transition Clinton directed his secretary of defense, Les Aspin, to meet with military leaders to plan the *implementation* of that policy. As a result of that controversial meeting the joint chiefs requested a meeting with the president, which was equally stormy. Thereafter, the controversy broke out publicly, negotiations with Senator Sam Nunn ensued, and Clinton's reputation was damaged because of the position he originally took regarding the lifting of the ban and his failure to accomplish his stated purpose.

What was Clinton's response? He blamed the Republicans who had threatened to add language to a family leave bill preserving and writing into law the current military policy, saying, "The issue was not put forward . . . by me; it was brought forward by those in the U.S. Senate who sought to make it an issue early on . . . they control the timing of this not me"

(Clinton 1993j). This is simply untrue. The Republicans had made such a threat, but Clinton had introduced the subject and told his secretary of defense to meet with the joint chiefs to plan the policy's implementation. A Clinton adviser who had helped propagate the claim that the Republicans were the ones responsible later privately told Elizabeth Drew that the claim "was a lie" (Drew 1994, 48). Three years later, Clinton was still blaming the Republicans for his own policy initiative (Rosenthal 1995).

Even when Clinton appears to take full and unequivocal responsibility for a difficult decision, further information often emerges that casts a different light on his behavior. For example, in discussing his decision to pull the controversial nomination of Lani Guinier, Clinton seemed to be unequivocally taking "full responsibility for what has happened here" (Clinton 1993l). What was Clinton taking responsibility for? He "admitted" he had not read Guinier's controversial racial views. However,

> rather than simply announcing that the nomination was being withdrawn, Clinton and his advisors put on an elaborate charade. The public was later told that Gore had "confronted" Clinton on Thursday morning and told him he must read her writings. But as Clinton had said on more than one occasion, he was already familiar with her writings. (Drew 1994, 207)

Moreover, even as he was taking "full responsibility," Clinton also stated that his friendship with Guinier played a role because "the adequacy or the inadequacy of the briefings I received about this issue is partly based on the assumption that I must have known everything she had written about since I knew her as a lawyer. I think that's probably true" (1993l). In other words, "My staff failed to inform me."

Has Clinton learned to accept more responsibility? Perhaps, but like other areas that are deeply embedded in his character structure, this one seems resistant to change. In his first news conference after the devastating 1994 midterm elections, Clinton suggested that his problem was that he didn't communicate his accomplishments well enough. The assumption was that if people only understood how much he was doing they would not be upset. Ten months later he repeated that view, claiming that "I may have a marketing problem, I do not have a substantive problem" (Rosenthal 1995).

What, then, *is* the real problem? Why are his accomplishments not getting the credit they deserve among the public? In the past, he has blamed the press for misrepresenting him, or even Americans themselves for being in a "funk" out of which it was his responsibility to lead them (Purdum 1995c). Too much information and not enough understanding of the "big picture" were at the root of this problem. Clinton alluded to his ambitious agenda during his first two years in office and suggested that he and the country might have been better served if "we'd done *slightly less,* if people understood some of the big picture more" (Purdum 1995c, emphasis mine). Here again Clinton takes some responsibility for not having spent more time providing a "big picture," that is, educating the public. However, the basic message remains the same, if people knew what Clinton knows about what he is doing, they would approve. As Clinton says, he has a marketing, not a substantive, problem.

THE PAST AS PROLOGUE

Taking Clinton's early experiences into account, his character and personal traits as president come into sharper focus. Reflecting on one's behavior and taking responsibility for its consequences were never strong traits in Clinton's early family life. His mother, stepfather, and brother all avoided this type of introspection.

It is, however, naive psychology to simply say "like family, like son" and stop there. Family experience can help account for the origins of Clinton's character and psychology, but their development need not merely be a replica of his family's. Clinton had a much more complex and difficult childhood and adolescence than has been generally recognized. One cannot fathom this complex man without a more accurate understanding of what he experienced, survived, and built on.

III

GROWING UP,
COMING OF AGE

★ ──

CHAPTER 7

HIS MOTHER'S SON

An analysis of the Clinton family myth requires us to focus in particular on his mother. Therefore, after briefly laying out the Clinton family myth, I will present a brief annotated overview of the major events in Clinton's early family life. This will provide a chronological framework within which we can develop a more psychologically framed analysis of Clinton's early experiences and their impact on him. Toward this end I will present a detailed psychological portrait of his mother, Virginia Kelley, as the basis for a more extensive examination of Clinton's family life and its implications in the following chapters.

THE MAN AND THE MYTH

The basic story of Bill Clinton's character is contained in a number of pre- and post-election interviews and comments by Clinton himself, his friends and supporters, and his family members (primarily his mother). Crucial to understanding Clinton's story is the carefully orchestrated film biography that introduced him to the American public during the 1992 Democratic convention, entitled "The Man from Hope." [1]

The major themes of the Clinton narrative presented in "The Man from Hope" are of tragedy endured and adversity overcome by courage and persistence. It is a story of a family struggling and ultimately succeeding against great odds, but not without costs. It is, in short, a story of human courage and, above all, character.

Within these major themes lie other associated narratives. It is a story of a hard-working and dedicated mother, who suffered the tragic loss of her husband and was forced to fend for herself and her new son. It is a story of her successful struggle against great odds to get an education that allowed her to support and raise her son. It is a story of a mother whose struggles did not diminish her love of life and her faith in people, traits that left an enduring legacy for her young and beloved son. One analysis of "The Man from Hope" argued that Clinton's mother is "presented as a pillar of small town values, [who] ostensibly held the family together" (Rein 1994, 196).

It is also the story of Bill Clinton, a young boy left fatherless by a tragic accident that gave him a special appreciation of the fragility of life and the need to live it fully. It is the story of a young boy, growing up in a small rural town in difficult (but not dire) economic circumstances, who sat at the feet of a beloved grandfather and a nurturing and devoted mother, who together instilled in him the basic small-town values that guide him today. It is also a story of hard work and talent, of a young man whose intellectual and interpersonal gifts were evident to all who came in contact with him and which, along with his determination and hard work, helped to propel him from a small, rural Arkansas town to the most powerful political position in the world.

Like many myths, the Clinton family myth (and I intend that term to be descriptive rather than valuative) is based on some fact. Like other myths, it both exaggerates virtues and blurs the sharper, controversial edges. And, like other myths, it is meant to serve public purposes, one of which is to present Clinton as he wishes to be seen, and perhaps as he sees himself. In these respects, Clinton's attempt at constructing his own public image is no different in kind from other attempts that surround the nomination and campaign process in the modern presidency. But there was another critical, perhaps overriding, motive to the myth propagated in the film: to counterbalance doubts about Clinton's character that were raised during the presidential campaign of 1992.

My purpose here is not primarily to debunk this myth, although that is one likely result of the more systematic analysis of any myth. Rather, my purpose is to construct an alternative narrative. That narrative, like the Clinton family myth, focuses on Clinton's biography and its associated developmental experiences. Like the Clinton family myth, it focuses on the implications of Clinton's experiences to help us more fully understand and appreciate what we know of his character. It is an attempt to look behind the events for their psychological meaning.

THE CLINTON FAMILY: AN ANNOTATED CHRONOLOGY

The basic outline of Clinton's family history is by this time familiar. Clinton's mother, Virginia Kelley, went to high school in Hope and nursing school in Shreveport, Louisiana. It was there in July 1943 that she met William Blythe. They married on September 3, 1943. It was, as Kelley recalls, "a textbook definition of a whirlwind romance" (1994a, 42).[2] After her marriage, Kelley returned to her nursing studies. Blythe had enlisted in the army in Shreveport several months before he met Kelley, although she was apparently unaware of this. After finishing her training, Kelley returned to Hope, moved in with her parents, Edith and Eldridge Cassidy, and began to work as a private nurse.

Blythe returned home from the war in November 1945 and the couple moved to Chicago, where he had secured work as a heavy equipment salesman. They lived in a hotel in anticipation of finding a house, which proved difficult in the postwar housing market. The couple eventually found a house, but its sale was contingent on the owners finding another house. In the meantime, Kelley had become pregnant, and she temporarily moved back to Hope with her parents until the housing issue was settled. On his way back to pick up his wife in Hope, Blythe was killed in a car accident. His son, William Jefferson Blythe, was born three months later, on August 19, 1946.[3]

Kelley, twenty-three years old, widowed, a single parent, lived with her parents in Hope and worked as a nurse until the spring of 1947. In that period, two important events in her and young Bill Clinton's life occurred. First, she met and began to date Roger ("Dude") Clinton, a seemingly well-heeled man about town whose family owned a Buick dealership in Hot Springs. Then, in the fall of 1947 Kelley left Hope for New Orleans to train as a nurse-anesthetist. She was gone from Hope for approximately two years, during which time young Bill Clinton was left in the care of his grandparents, Edith and Eldridge Cassidy.[4]

After completing her training Kelley returned to Hope and her family's home and settled into a work and social life that increasingly revolved around Roger Clinton. They were married on June 19, 1950, at which time young Bill was just shy of his fourth birthday, his mother twenty-seven, and Roger forty. The marriage was a tempestuous one. A major reason was Roger Clinton's alcoholism, but there were other problems as well.

In 1953, when Bill was six, the family moved to a farm just outside Hot Springs but had difficulty making a go of it. After the first winter, the family moved to Hot Springs proper, where Roger took a job in his brother's thriving Buick dealership. Roger Cassidy Clinton, Bill's half brother, was born on July 25, 1956, just before Bill turned ten.

The marriage continued to deteriorate in a series of drunken fights. Roger Clinton was verbally and sometimes physically abusive. In 1962, Virginia Kelley filed for divorce. She was now thirty-nine, Bill was sixteen, and his brother was six. The divorce, like the marriage, was messy. Kelley requested a court order to keep Roger from the family home. Three months after their divorce Mr. and Mrs. Clinton reconciled and were remarried, on August 6, 1962. The marriage lasted until Roger died in 1967 of a cancer that had been diagnosed shortly after his remarriage.

Approximately six months after Roger died, Kelley received a call from George J. "Jeff" Dwire, her former hairdresser, and they began to see each other. In 1961, Dwire had been indicted on twenty-five counts of stock fraud and had served nine months in prison. In 1969 they were married. Five years later, in 1974, Dwire died. In January 1982 Virginia Kelley married a retired food broker, Richard W. Kelley, and remained married to him until her death in January 1994.

Bill Clinton spent his early years with his grandmother and grandfather, who gave him his first introduction to letters and reading. He visited his mother once in New Orleans, a trip that made a lasting impression on him. Like other children, he played, went to school, and had his share of childhood mishaps, breaking his leg in 1952 while jumping rope in his cowboy boots and being repeatedly knocked down and butted by a ram on the farm that the Clintons moved to when Bill was almost seven.

In Hot Springs, he attended a Catholic school for two years and began to distinguish himself academically. In class he raised his hand so often to give the answer that one of his teachers gave him a poor grade for deportment. He started a new school in fourth grade "and within days seemed to be running the place" (Maraniss 1995, 35). A student at the school when Bill was there recalled that "He just took over the school. He didn't mean to, but he just took the place over" (Maraniss 1995, 36).

By the time Bill completed Little Rock High School he was the school's golden boy. Gifted in his studies, an accomplished participant in extracurricular activities ranging from music to student politics, and surrounded by a large circle of admiring friends, Bill Clinton's adolescence was in most outward respects a developmental success.

The Clinton Family: A Psychologically Framed Narrative

Biographical elements help account for the character elements so evident in the adult Bill Clinton: his ambition, his ideals and sense of himself, and his relationships with others.[5] Since character and psychological development begin in the family, our task requires us to focus squarely there. In large part this requires us to focus on his mother, Virginia. It is clear that Virginia Kelley was a critically important emotional center of Bill Clinton's life both as a child and as an adult. "By any measure . . . Mrs. Kelley's legacy was especially strong, in part because she was the only blood parent this President knew" (Purdum 1994).[6] Many of Clinton's childhood friends "say that his mother was probably the most influential person in his life" (Allen and Portis 1992, 16). Elizabeth Drew observes, "Clinton seemed to have loved her without reservation" (1994, 403). James Carville, Clinton's campaign strategist, recalled to a reporter, "Any time he was asked who the most influential in his life was he would say without a doubt, 'My mother' " (Purdum 1994).

That emotional centrality persisted well into adulthood, indeed, until his mother's death. Bill Whillock, one of the first to encourage Clinton to run for Congress when he was looking to start his political career in Arkansas, recalls how Clinton was very appreciative of him since "no one but his mother until then had encouraged him" (1993, 79). When the news about Gennifer Flowers broke and Clinton's presidential campaign went into free fall as he campaigned in New Hampshire, Clinton excused himself from a critical strategy meeting. Later, his aides found him hunched over a pay phone in the lobby calling his mother.

Clearly, Clinton was very emotionally connected to his mother. But what of Virginia Kelley's relationship to her son? What can we tell of her character and values from her choices and behavior? What was her life like? What kind of mother was she to young Bill? How did these factors appear to affect him?

Virginia Kelley: The Persona and the Person

Virginia Kelley has been characterized as "an American original" (Oates 1994, 14). Of herself, she said, "I'm a character, a cut up, kook," noting that "even before Bill became a public official, I had what might be called a 'public persona' " (1994a, 16, 157). Perhaps the best brief summary of her life and persona is as a woman who worked hard and played hard, with an affinity for the nightclubs and the thoroughbred horse-racing tracks. . . . In later years, her flightiness and raucous laughter coupled with her love of flashy and multiple pieces of jewelry and colorful ensembles gave her an Auntie Mame quality as surely as her jutting jaw, spidery false eyelashes, and quarter-moon grin gave her an uncanny resemblance to Bette Midler. (Oakley 1994, 23)

At one level, she was a charming, vivacious woman with a zest for life that sustained her through a turbulent but fully lived—if not fully realized—life. She followed in her mother's footsteps even while trying to avoid them; married then tragically lost the love of her life in a freak car accident; married, divorced, then remarried an abusive alcoholic, whom she lost to cancer; remarried to a convicted swindler, whom she lost to diabetes; and finally found a modicum of stability with her fourth husband. Along the way she raised two boys, one of whom became president and the other of whom spent time in a federal prison for drug dealing. As one reviewer of her autobiography put it, "She survived bad luck with men, petty town gossip and so many family disasters in her seventy years that she writes, 'My life was too much like a country song' " (James 1994).

Virginia Kelley's autobiography is "a celebration of the life of feeling. . . . It is not self-reflective, except in the most modest terms" (Oates 1994). Yet, at the end, having revisited and written of the many tumultuous years of a vivid life, she wonders

why there are so many hills. Is there something about our family, some built-in need to live life as if it were a StairMaster? Then, I thought, *Oh, I'm giving us too much credit for eccentricity. Maybe behind the scenes every family is like ours.* But Dick's [her fourth husband] family wasn't. And Hillary says her family wasn't, either—the Rodhams didn't have crises every four minutes. What then explains our turbulence? I keep coming back to what my friend said about leading with my heart. (1994a, 276)

One cannot help but note the similarity of Kelley's sense of her own life as crisis-driven[7] to that of her son, whose private and especially public life and presidency have also been substantially crisis-driven. While the specific dynamics that help to explain and account for their respective crisis-driven lives differ, the overall process seems remarkably parallel.

In some respects Kelley's insight could be considered an allusion to what psychoanalyst Michael Balint (1979) has termed the "basic fault," an element of deep inner psychology on which life gets constructed, often on shaky ground. Keeping this in mind, Bill Clinton is his mother's son.

Her character had a direct effect on his because it helped to create the circumstances of his childhood and adolescence, which in turn helped to shape his character. In Clinton's case, because he didn't have a father, the mother as well as the child are father to the man.

In the portrait that follows I examine Virginia Kelley from the standpoint of the three basic domains that I have suggested are the foundation of character: ambition, character integrity, and relatedness. I begin with relatedness because I think it is the key element for understanding her.

Relatedness

Virginia Kelley, like her son, tended to move toward people, not away or against them:

> I think that Bill, Roger, and I are all alike in that way: when we walk into a room, we want to win that room over. Some would say we even *need* to win that room over, and maybe that's true . . . if there are one hundred people in a room and ninety-nine of them love us and one of them doesn't, we'll spend all night trying to figure out why that one hasn't been enlightened. (1994a, 38)

She believed that her basic problem was a tendency to "lead with her heart." This she defines as being "so softhearted it hurts. I love people. I trust people" (1994a, 13). One might think that after four marriages that highlighted the perils of unconditional trust, she would have had second thoughts, and she admits, "Sometimes I've consulted my heart, when others might've thought I had to consult my head." But still, she says, "I wouldn't change a thing" (1994a, 13–14).

From a psychological perspective, how is such a feat accomplished? The answer she gives eerily parallels what has been said of her son:

> The way I've gotten through life is by living in the present. I have no concern for history. . . . You know what they say about people who don't pay attention to history: They're doomed to repeat the mistakes of the past. I've done that a time or two. But I've always maintained that whatever's in someone's past is past, and I don't need to know about it. . . . I've trained myself not to worry about what-ifs, either, because nine times out of ten they don't happen. And when bad things do happen, I brainwash myself to put them out of my mind. . . .
>
> Inside my head I construct an airtight box. I keep inside it what I want to think about and everything else stays behind the walls. Inside is white, outside is black: The only grey I trust is the streak in my hair. Inside is love

and friends and optimism. Outside is negativity, can't-doism, and any criticism of me and mine. Most of the time this box is a strong as steel. . . . This is a not the same as denial; this is choosing how you want to live your life. (1994a, 14)

Technically, she is at least partially right.[8] For her it was a strategy of survival that was necessary because "you have to focus, like a laser, as Bill would say, on the good things. That's where your strength comes from, and God knows you need every ounce of strength you can muster in order to get up and face each and every day" (1994a, 14).

The problem, of course, is that the very strategy that gives you strength to face your troubles is also likely to be responsible for them. What forms did her strategy take? One form was a reliance on not asking too many questions. Another was accepting life at face value. In an almost classic illustration, she writes, "I've been accused of being attracted to smooth talkers, and I don't deny that," but then adds, "The smooth-talking men I've fallen for have meant what they said" (1994a, 181).

Kelley knew that her second husband, Roger, had been married and "assumed they were divorced," but "it turns out that Roger was still married—to his second wife—when he and I met" (1994a, 73, 89). For a two-year period after they were married, Roger's ex-wife sued him several times for overdue child support: Kelley "didn't know a thing about it" (1994a, 90). A close friend of hers in Hot Springs told her that Roger "once bashed a Puerto Rican boy in the head with a cue stick" and "had rigged a craps table in Hope and then had the audacity to lure a city official . . . into the game" (1994a, 73). She writes, "I guess if you paid attention to events like these, a certain pattern might begin to emerge. As usual, I didn't pay a lot of attention to such things; I accepted Roger at face value" (1994a, 73).

A similar set of difficulties occurred with Kelley's first husband and Bill Clinton's biological father, William Blythe. It turns out that he was married at least two and possibly four times (Maraniss 1995, 26; Kelley 1994a, 64) and appears to have still been married when he and Virginia Kelley were married (Oakley 1994, 21). He is also listed on several birth certificates as the father of the children even though in one case he was no longer married to the woman in question and in another had never been married to her.

Kelley's reaction to her husband's unrevealed previous marriages is in character—she asks the basic question only to disclaim any interest in the answer:

What did I really know about him? I hadn't met his family and all I knew of him was what he had chosen to reveal to me. For many people that wouldn't have been enough but for me, the important part was not the past or the future. . . . For whatever reason I had come to believe that relationships started from the moment two people met, and that the only acceptable way to judge people wasn't by what they had or hadn't done in the past or would or wouldn't do in the future . . . it's a measurement taken as much by the heart as the head. (1994a, 45–46)

As to the appearance of her husband's name on the birth certificates of children to whose mothers he was not married, she had this to say: "Ultimately, this is the way I feel about it: you can put anyone's name on a birth certificate. Specifically, I don't believe that Bill was married that third time before me, and no birth certificate is going to convince me otherwise" (1994a, 65).

When she found out that Jeff Dwire, who was to become her third husband, had been indicted for fraud, she organized her friends in a letter-writing campaign to attest to his "sterling character" (1994a, 142). After he was convicted and sentenced to jail, she writes that "over time I would finally have to accept that he—*duped by others*—had indeed done something against the law. However, to my mind that one mistake wasn't a reflection of the inner man" (1994a, 142, emphasis mine).[9]

Kelley seemed drawn to men whose charm outweighed their substance.[10] Of her first husband, she writes, "Bill was charming and funny and totally disarming . . . he had a way of saying things that let him get away with saying things that others couldn't" (1994a, 43). When she took her beau home to meet her mother, her mother was unimpressed at first, "but eventually even she couldn't resist his charm—*the ultimate test as far as I was concerned*" (1994a, 45, emphasis mine). Of her second husband, Roger, she wrote, "People fell under Roger's spell. Men seemed to like being around him because he was in a man's business and he talked men's talk and he liked things men liked—speed and money and risk. Women liked him because he was charming. When he asked me out, I said yes" (1994a, 72). In speaking of her first date with Dwire, she mentions all of the "little niceties" he lavished on her, such as flowers, perfume, and dinner, but then notes, "Even if Jeff hadn't spent a dime on all these other things, he would still have been charming, because he gave whomever he was talking to his undivided attention" (1994a, 178).

Kelley was clearly someone who moved toward people—but, perhaps because of the kind of people (especially men) that she was attracted to, she did so in a way that led (or perhaps required) her to overlook much of what she might easily have seen. She responded to charm and apparently did not mind taking risks. She paid a price for not being in touch with what was going on in her life, but her children also paid a price for her insistence on looking on the bright side and suppressing or otherwise downplaying information at variance with her assumptions.

Ideals and Values

What were Virginia Kelley's ideals and values? What things were important to her, what guided her as she made the decisions that would shape her life and her sons'? She gives many clues in her autobiography, which can be organized around the twin themes of being noticed (narcissism) and having a good time regardless of convention (the boundary problem).

Narcissism is a normal part of developmental experience (Kohut 1979, 1984). It is only problematic when a person becomes too preoccupied with him or herself and organizes too much of his or her life around it. One form that narcissism takes is a preoccupation with personal appearance and being noticed. Ordinarily, of course, most people care how they look and like to be noticed, but the person with narcissistic tendencies is overly preoccupied by such concerns. Kelley's autobiography is replete with evidence of her preoccupations, about which she is relatively straightforward. She notes that "ever since I was a girl, when I've showed up some place, I've wanted people to know I'm here" (1994a, 157). Elsewhere she says, "Truth is I like bright colors and I like people to notice me. In fact, I hate for them *not* to notice me" (1994a, 38).

Describing her first date with Jeff Dwire, she says, "It was wonderful having a Southern gentleman sitting there giving me all his attention. Jeff was a master at that. He liked women, and he enjoyed lavishing the little niceties on them—flowers, perfume, dinner, dancing. But all of these are mere symbols of the thing a woman wants most of all: attention" (1994a, 178). In describing her high-living nightlife in Hot Springs, she says that after a couple of drinks, which "brought out the show-off in me," she often joined the singers on the stage, because "I was convinced that I was more talented than most of the singers we heard" (1994a, 48).[11] She describes "prancing up there [on the stage] to hog the spotlight" (1994a, 108). Once she did this with a troop of skaters, one of whom lifted her above his head and began to twirl her. Kelley became so dizzy that she almost threw up. "The crown applauded, but that was one time when the applause wasn't worth it" (1994a, 108).

Everyone likes to be noticed. Few women writing an autobiography, however, spend much time describing their makeup. Kelley, on the other hand, spends several pages describing the details of that process, which are clearly important to her and her persona. Later on we learn that she was disciplined in nursing school because the head nurse, Nurse Frye, didn't like her looks. What did that mean? According to Kelley, "She didn't like the lace handkerchief *that I thought looked so stylish* protruding out of my pocket" (1994a, 38, emphasis mine).

Kelley's concern with looks extended to others. For example, Nurse Frye, it appears, did have a favorite, a girl "who happened to be president of the senior class"; however, Kelley had never understood why Nurse Frye had favored this particular girl because "her shoes and stockings were always dirty. . . . I personally was always scrupulously clean. My uniform was spotless and pressed to perfection. However, I did like a little color in my nail polish" (1994a, 39).

Looks—or rather what she felt was a lack of attention to them—were what she first noticed on meeting her son's wife-to-be, Hillary Rodham. Hillary "wore no make up . . . Coke-bottle glasses . . . [and had] brown hair with no apparent style" (1994a, 191). Kelley recalls that although she and her son Roger were polite, "I guess our expressions gave us away" (1994a, 191). Kelley later attributes their original difficulties to a cultural divide, but it is clear that Hillary's looks were an important element of this discomfort. Her fantasy was to sit Hillary down and give her some makeup lessons (1994a, 199).

Not surprisingly, Kelley also placed a high premium on the looks of the men to whom she was attracted. Of her first husband, she says when she first saw him, "I was stunned. . . . I looked at that tall handsome man . . . and I was weak-kneed" (1994a, 41). The fact that he was with another woman at the time and that Kelley was wearing a friendship ring given to her by a man she had been dating for four years proved no barrier. Of her second husband, Roger Clinton, she recalls, "When I met him again he was thirty-six, and I remember thinking he was attractive, a lot more dashing, in a dangerous sort of way, than most of the men in Hope" (1994a, 71). He was nicknamed "Dude," and Kelley says she could see why: "He dressed fit to kill with sharp creased trousers and fine tailored sports coats and two-toned shoes. He was tall, though not as tall as Bill Blythe had been: I guess Roger stood five feet eleven inches. Tall enough. His hair was dark and curly and his eyes twinkled when he talked" (1994a, 72).

Kelley's third husband, Jeff Dwire, is introduced to readers as "a tall handsome man with movie star looks and flashy clothes to match. He was meticulous about his appearance" (1994a, 131). Later, when describing the first evening he came over for a date with her, Kelley notes that she was surprised at how attracted she was to him. She then asked herself why she felt that way. The answer was: "charm" and "looks." Of the second she says, "He was a handsome man—close to six feet tall, with dark, dark hair, a product of his cajun genes. During this time he wore his sideburns down to his ears. I thought of Rhett Butler" (1994a, 178).

In her first description of her fourth husband, Dick Kelley, whom she saw at a friend's party, she says, "Dick, as usual, seemed to genuinely enjoy being in the middle of such throngs—and people obviously liked being around Dick, too. He's a big bear of a man with an engaging smile, which he uses often" (1994a, 211–12). Introducing her new beau to her friends, she was certain there would not be a problem because "my friends would approve of Dick immediately. Dick just has an aura of solidness about him . . . part of that is due to his six-foot-three frame. But beyond that is his business success, his travel experience, his strong sense of family, and his wide circle of friends" (1994a, 226–27). Here, as elsewhere, the inner qualities of the man seems to take a backseat to the more public qualities.

Ambition

Ambitions are important because they offer the individual a channel through which his or her aspirations, narcissistic striving for recognition, and respect may be met. They offer the possibility of experiencing vitality and aliveness. Kelley's mother and father presented competing models of ambition. Her father, the parent with whom she felt most emotionally connected, is described as "kind and gentle," a man who "loved laughing and fishing and story telling and people" but was "too good for his own good" (1994a, 19).[12] He worked variously as a farmer, a worker in a small manufacturing company, an ice delivery man (which Kelley believed was his favorite), a clerk in a liquor store, and finally as the owner of a small grocery store (1994a, 22). The picture that emerges of her father's ambition as it related to work is of a steady, if unspectacular, worker, devoid of strong ambitions.

Her mother presented a different picture. Kelley believes that her mother's ambition "took the form of wanting to improve herself financially . . . she was very concerned with that" (1994a, 19). She says that one day her mother saw an ad in the newspaper for a correspondence course to become a nurse and announced she was going to enroll (1994a, 27). Both Virginia and her father were surprised. The course took eighteen months to complete, during which time her mother not only pored over her books, but also continued to keep the house, prepare meals, and take care of her daughter. The picture that emerges is of a smart, ambitious woman determined to succeed.

What of Kelley's own ambitions? She reports that in high school she was a member of the National Honor Society and other school clubs. One can assume that as a member of the honor society she received good grades. Attending college, however, "never occurred" to her because she "was too eager to be independent and self sufficient" (1994a, 33).[13] She decided to enroll in nursing school because she wanted to become a nurse anesthetist. "This was an exciting, even romantic, idea to me. I could just *see* myself wearing those *crisp, important-looking* whites" (1994a, 33, first emphasis in text, second and third emphases mine).[14] Notice here the mix of narcissism and ambition. The focus is the uniform and its look. It is the uniform, with its "important-looking whites," rather than her profession, which underlies her pride in accomplishment.

Kelley recalls working hard and being good at her work (1994a, 36–37). While at nursing school she met and married Bill Blythe. After graduation she returned to Hope and began to practice her profession as a private-duty nurse. However, for a person who prides herself on liking people, she didn't like that role. "When you do private-duty nursing, you spend a lot more time with the same patient than you do as a hospital nurse. . . . I found out right away that familiarity breeds—well, annoyance, at least. But of course I wouldn't let the patient know that for anything" (1994a, 53).

Adding to her discomfort was the fact that her mother, who had been a private-duty nurse, was apparently quite respected for her work. Kelley was amazed to find that her mother, whom she considered so strict and domineering, apparently spoiled her patients and took their every wish as her command (1994a, 53). Later, when she got a job at a local hospital, her mother's reputation as a hard-working, caring nurse for a whole floor of patients led Kelley to curse her mother under her breath (1994a, 82).

Self-Esteem

Ordinarily, a stable sense of self-esteem develops when we successfully realize our ambitions in the context of fidelity to our ideals. One of Virginia Kelley's ambitions was to be independent of her mother (while at the same time reflecting an identification with her by also becoming a nurse). Her ambition was also influenced by her narcissism (the crisp white uniform) rather than her fidelity to that profession's ideals (serving, caring, etc.). At the same time, her pursuit of the party life moved her further away from realizing her ambition in a framework of ideals that could have provided a substantive foundation for her sense of self. Kelley's persona as a "character" was very important to her and was the vehicle through which her narcissism was realized.

A stable, secure sense of self-worth is acquired gradually over many years of working to realize one's aspirations in the context of difficult value choices. Absolute success is not required. One need only succeed enough to help develop the sense that one is, through struggling, making real and honest progress.

Kelley's robust sense of her own self-worth apparently began early. In commenting on a picture taken of her during high school, she notes, "The thing people comment on is my facial expression: the camera had caught a look of supreme self-confidence that makes me appear more mature than my years. As one friend says, 'This was before people talked about "attitude," but you had it even then' " (1994a, 30). It is, however, in her professional life that this attitude showed itself most forcefully. Given her decades-long difficulties with the local medical profession, her comment that she thought "nurse anesthetists knew a lot more about modern anesthesia than any general practitioner" seems a recipe for trouble (1994a, 33). So does her admission that when she got out of nursing school, "I was as guilty as some of the doctors I had seen—I thought I knew it all" (1994a, 53).

Her attitude of "supreme self-confidence" shows up in her discussions of how she contradicted hospital policy regarding procedures for patients undergoing surgery because she saw nothing wrong with what she did. In one case, a woman undergoing surgery wanted to keep her makeup: "We were supposed to remove all fingernail polish when we anesthetized a patient, because you look at their fingernails to detect a lack of oxygen. How was I going to stand there and deny someone the use of a little make up? . . . It was just a silly rule" (1994a, 122–23). In another case, a young boy just out of surgery wanted a Coke but the nurse said she would first have to check with the doctor to see if it was alright. Kelley "didn't see a bit of harm in that child's having a Coke if it would make him feel better, so I got him one" (1994a, 122).

Kelley may have been correct in her view that there were many other ways to tell whether a patient was getting oxygen, but hospital procedures are designed to prevent difficulties. She also was correct about the Coke; she notes, "Just so you know, the boy is still alive" (1994a, 122). Of course, the point is not simply whether these patients survived, but rather the degree of risk that was taken. Kelley thought she knew best. It was she who would define which hospital rules she would abide by—and if she thought them "silly," well, as she noted in another connection, she was "not one for rules" (1994a, 91).

Interestingly, when Kelley filed suit against the Hot Springs medical anesthesiologists for restraint of trade, the doctors raised the issue that Kelley had not really kept up with advancing medical understanding. She notes that one of the defendants, Dr. Klugh, when asked whether Kelley resisted keeping up with the times, answered, "I think Virginia thought she was keeping up with the times" (1994a, 246). At her deposition, the defendant's attorneys "asked me medical questions I would have no way of knowing the answer to. It was like he was speaking a foreign language. And while I was stammering, or sitting there dumbfounded and silent, I could see the doctors . . . whispering other questions to the attorney— questions that would leave me twisting just that much more" (1994a, 247). In the end, Kelley dropped her lawsuit.

It is possible to argue, as Kelley does, that the questions she was asked were unfair and that she would have no way of knowing the answers to them. The implication is that she should not have been required to know them in her role. If that were true, it would seem to be a legitimate defense. However, the fact that she dropped the suit suggests otherwise.

Regardless of the merits of the suit, Kelley's immersion in the party life must surely have had an impact on the time and energy she spent keeping up with rapid technical advances in the medical field. Her allegiance to the profession was the independence that it gained for her—besides which, she already thought she knew more than enough. Here, as elsewhere in her life, Kelley purchased her supreme self-confidence for a high price, the price of not addressing disconcerting facts. Her knowledge was not illusionary, but her somewhat idealized view of what she knew and what she needed to know caused her unnecessary damage in her professional life, as it had in her personal life.

Pleasures versus Ideals

Adult life offers many opportunities. In it one may satisfy or frustrate many values and ideals. However, it also offers many dilemmas, since it is often impossible to realize fully all that one might wish to do. One such dilemma for Virginia Kelley, apparently from an early age, was the choice between the pursuit of her own pleasure and the identity that could have been provided by her work. Work appears to have had a primarily instrumental quality for Kelley. She chose nursing for its romantic quality and because it provided a means of being independent of her mother. When she returned to Hope during the last years of the war to await her husband's return, she "worked as much as possible" because "work has always been my salvation" (1994a, 52)—that is, work was something that she turned to when other things she valued were missing. As noted, she didn't like her role as a private-duty nurse; even taking care of patients in the more stimulating setting of a hospital floor was not satisfying, in part because her mother had apparently performed this role too well.

Nowhere in Kelley's autobiography is there any sense of her having taken *pleasure* from her work.[15] Nor, it seems clear, was work a central part of her identity. Certainly it was not an important part of her persona. Why is Kelley's relationship to her work of interest? Primarily because she was a woman who took a bold, ambitious educational step at a time when it was unusual for women to do so. She also built up a highly successful practice over the years. Both of these accomplishments might well have provided a firm anchor for a different identity and persona than the one she chose. They might have also provided an alternative to the sources from which she derived pleasure, but they didn't. What, then, *did?*

In a word, men. Kelley is quick to admit, "I'm friendly, I'm outgoing and I like men. Always have, always will. Men like me too" (1994a, 81). She discovered boys early (1994a, 30). In high school she dated a number of boys and in her class yearbook bequeathed to a junior classmate her "magnetic attraction for boys (help us please if she turns it on full force)" (1994a, 33).

What is relevant here is not the fact that she liked men so much, but the nature of her relationships with them and the kind of men she was attracted to. She quotes her son Bill as saying, "Every man Mother's ever fallen for has been good-looking, smart, aggressive, and a little bit of trouble" (1994a, 227). The last part of that statement is an understandable but nonetheless highly understated characterization of his mother's choices. It is also a keen insight into an important aspect of her psychology.

Kelley was a woman who was not attracted to, or strongly bound by, convention. Like most other characteristics, the importance of this one lies in the use that was made of it. On the one hand, it clearly had some beneficial functions for her. Her persona as a "character," enthusiastically embraced, is one reflection of that. Her ambition and the steps she took to fulfill it were unusual for women of her time. On the other hand, there was another more prominent and more problematic side to it, namely, the lines she was willing to cross, the boundaries she sought to blur, and the social conventions she was willing to ignore in pursuit of fun, stimulation, and a good time.

Here again, our interest is not in the fact that she wanted to, or enjoyed, having a good time. Most people do. But not everyone places the same high value on doing so. In this context, Kelley's experience during her senior year class trip is interesting. Apparently, it was the first time she had traveled out of Hope. She recalls having visited Hot Springs, specifically the Oaklawn racetrack, where "I was awed. I found the horses beautiful, the people glamorous, and the action exhilarating" (1994a, 35).[16] It was her first taste of what, in retrospect, emerges as "the fast life," a life filled with partying, drinking, clubs, gambling, and of course the men with whom she shared these interests. The fact that the action was "exhilarating" is an important clue to, and reflection of, a theme that appears elsewhere in her autobiography. In commenting on her dislike of being a private-duty nurse, she notes that it was "too monotonous for someone with my disposition" (1994a, 53).

Kelley loved to party, and the references to this aspect of her life are found throughout her autobiography. When she was in nursing school she was very upset to be punished by having to stay in her dorm on New Year's Eve because "I *love* New Year's Eve" (1994a, 38). Because she didn't want to miss the biggest party of the year, she and a friend hatched a supposedly foolproof plan to sneak out. It didn't work. During her senior year in nursing school, her class spent six months in New Orleans for advanced study in pediatrics. She writes, "Nursing classes from all over the country would be there. Wartime, New Orleans, and a bunch of twenty-one year old nurses to be let loose in the big city for six months: It had all the makings of a great party" (1994a, 48). Her first husband, Bill Blythe, was "by all accounts a charming fun loving sort who loved to drink and dance and make pretty women laugh" (Oakley 1994, 19). When she returned to Hope to await the end of the war and the return of her husband from military service, she did not do so quietly: "Virginia was, according to several contemporaries, 'a wild one' who wasted little time keeping the home fires burning. She loved to get all dressed up and, shod in the clunky high heels of the day, go dancing and drinking till dawn" (Oakley 1994, 21).

However, her partying really found its level with the arrival on the scene of her second husband-to-be, Roger Clinton, who was "the life of the party, and he partied a lot." Kelley, who thought she "needed a little fun in my life," began going out with him (1994a, 74). Most of the things Roger liked to do, like gambling and drinking, were illegal in Hope but not in Hot Springs. The latter was a wide-open town, "a place where gangsters were cool, and rules were made to be bent, and money and power— however you got them—were the total measure of a man" (1994a, 73).

After returning from her two-year stint in New Orleans to get her advanced nursing degree, she and Roger "were heavy, heavy partyers" (1994a, 84). Almost every weekend they either went to Hot Springs or were joined in Hope by their friends. Kelley recalls that during these times she would climb on the counter, under the influence of Roger's moonshine, and sing.[17]

After marrying Roger, her heavy nightlife continued. Even her developing professional practice didn't affect her partying. As her practice grew, she increasingly burned the candle at both ends.

Kelley recalls that she went to the track *every day* it was in session (1994a, 109). Both the gambling and the "scene" attracted her. The problem was that as a nurse she was frequently on call. The solution? "After I found out I loved horse racing so much I began to schedule my cases for the mornings during the racing season, just so I could be at Oakland every afternoon—in fact the doctors and the nurse used to joke, 'God help the patients after the bugle blows' " (1994a, 109). I can think of no stronger reflection of the relative weight that Virginia Kelley gave to her profession and her personal pleasure than her decision to schedule her patients around the horse races.

VIRGINIA KELLEY IN PSYCHOLOGICAL PERSPECTIVE

Cultivating a persona as an interesting, off-beat character was very important to Virginia Kelley. However, she also had ambition, ability, and a determination to accomplish her purposes. Chief among these was to find a way out her mother's home and the tensions that existed there. She seems to have identified strongly with her gentle, people-loving father and rebelled against any identification with a mother whom she saw as angry and vindictive (especially towards her father).[18]

A central feature of her psychology was her narcissism. One form this took was a great concern with appearances—hers and others. From the vision of how she would look in the crisp white uniform of the profession she chose to her concern with the looks and outward appearance of the men she married and the woman her son brought home from Yale, appearance rather than substance seems to have played a major role in her life. Another form her narcissism took was wanting to be noticed, indeed to be a (if not *the*) center of attention, and doing whatever was necessary to ensure it. From carefully constructing her "Auntie Mame" persona to joining name entertainers on stage, Kelley liked the spotlight. As she says of her partying in Hot Springs, "I was obviously born with a flashy streak inside me, just waiting to burst out, and Hot Springs let me be me with a vengeance" (1994a, 107).

Her narcissism was also reflected in the men she chose, men whose own narcissistic charm masked questionable characters and behavior. Kelley found Roger Clinton's "vast vanity charming. I like a man who likes himself, and Roger Clinton certainly seemed to approve of Roger Clinton. He was always trying to catch his reflection in a mirror or a window. And when he was playing host, you've never seen such strutting in your life" (1994a, 81). Wouldn't this have interfered with her own narcissistic needs? No. Because, according to Kelley, "The thing was, he made you feel like strutting too." Of Jeff Dwire she recalls, "He was also vain, like Roger, and I would catch him looking at himself in a mirror, studying himself to see if he detected a diminishing of his looks. He was in his midforties. . . I though he looked wonderful still, and I repeatedly told him so" (1994a, 200).[19]

What of her values and ideals? Even a casual examination of Virginia Kelley's life suggests that the idea that she, and by extension her son, was the embodiment of "small town values" is a public relations creation. She evidenced no interest in civic affairs and took no part in them, nor did her husband Roger. Actual involvement in civic life was not part of Clinton's early experience, and there is almost no mention in Kelley's autobiography of any political views before her son began to seek public office. Religion is another source of public values in small Southern towns, but Kelley and her husband Roger had little interest in it. They didn't attend church regularly and she couldn't recall the church in which she married him or why they chose it (1994a, 87, 106).[20]

She was drawn to men who tended to skirt legality, convention, and ethics. Her first husband had several wives and a number of children she didn't know about. Her second husband was a sometimes violent man whose behavior got him in trouble with the police. He was also a bootlegger, gambler, and bookie. Her third husband was a convicted swindler. Even her beloved father, it turns out, had a problem with alcohol,[21] and while doing research for her book she learned that her mother sold bootleg whiskey from their house (1994a, 94).

Kelley herself was a willing participant in a number of these quasilegal and socially questionable activities. For example, while most people, including she and Bill Clinton, have focused on her husband Roger's alcoholism, no one has observed that Kelley herself seems to have had a substantial problem here. In her autobiography the sheer number of references (over twenty-six) to *her* drinking is startling.[22] The list begins in nursing school and continues through every phase of her life. In nursing school she and a friend "smuggled a bottle of whiskey into the dorm . . . and we downed it pretty handily" (1994a, 37). In New Orleans she remembers a friend "going fishing in a wading pond late one night . . . after we had way too much to drink" (1994a, 48). In Chicago, after her husband came home from the war they liked to go to the clubs where they could have a couple of drinks, dinner, and hear live music (1994a, 58). With her husband Roger she drove to Texarkana from Hope for nights of drinking, gambling, and nightclubbing (1994a, 74). In Hot Springs she really became involved in heavy partying and nightlife. As Kelley observes of her husband's drinking, without realizing it applied to her as well, "Drinking had become so much a part of Roger and my relationship, that I really hadn't worried about his excesses in any sustained way" (1994a, 91). She still, rather late in her autobiography, describes her drinking as "social" (1994a, 138).

Kelley did on occasion partially acknowledge the effects of her choices and behavior, but usually only years after the fact. Of her husband Roger's jealous rages and violent behavior toward the men she danced with, she acknowledges,

> I'm sure I drove him to anger many nights when we were out. I won't pretend I'm oblivious to the power of female sex appeal and I certainly recognize a handsome man when I see one. I won't deny that I was often put out by Roger and didn't mind seeing him suffer a little. He usually left me to go into the back room and threw dice with the boys. Then he would emerge drunk, to find me dancing with someone else. (1994a, 111)[23]

The result was violence, between Roger and the men she danced with, and sometimes between her and Roger.

Of her decade-long battle against the Hot Springs medical establishment and the lawsuit filed against her over the death of a patient in her care, she noted, "I believe that their lawsuit was a result not just of that one case, but of the poisoned atmosphere in the Hot Springs medical community. Only later would I see that it was a poison I had helped to inject" (1994a, 231). The same belated and ambivalent recognition can be seen in connection with her son Roger's developing drug problem.

Virginia Kelley had a robust sense of self-worth, her "supreme self-confidence." However, this attitude seems to have been relatively unconnected to the experiences that ordinarily generate it—hard work and sustained attention to realizing one's ambitions in the context of ideals and values. Kelley did have ambition, and she pursued it. She was clearly motivated to get the training necessary to build a career. However, her ambition was substantially tempered by her narcissism and her concern with her own pleasure. In the next chapter, I discuss how these characteristics played out in the context of Bill Clinton's early life.

★ ───

CHAPTER 8

ADORATION AND ABANDONMENT: THE CLINTON FAMILY

Adoration is the experience of oneself as a beloved object.[1] Abandonment, at minimum, calls into question how adored you really are. Each by itself has profound psychological and developmental implications. Bill Clinton, however, experienced both, repeatedly.

Beneath the Clinton family myth lies a more complex psychological reality. That reality has been obscured, in part by Clinton, in part by his mother, and in part because pundits covering this story have preferred easy explanations to accurate ones. Clinton is certainly a product of his family life, but not the family life that has emerged in most accounts.

Clinton was born into a family already fractured in many ways. His grandmother and grandfather, with whom his mother lived, were not happily married. His mother had just lost the man who can reasonably be described as the love of her life in a freak accident. That accident widowed his mother, but it also cost Clinton his father before he was able to benefit from the experience of having one. Moreover, his mother, having left home to become a nurse expressly to put some distance between herself and her mother, now found herself back in Hope, living at home, with limited prospects. Worse, there was real antipathy between his mother and his grandmother.

Bill Clinton became president despite his childhood experiences in Hope and Hot Springs, not, as the myth suggests, *because* of them. That the triumph of destiny depicted in the Clinton family myth does not comport with actuality is not surprising. In fact, the myth has obscured a somewhat more poignant reality—the real nature of the struggles that Clinton not only managed to survive, but to some degree surmount. That he has not been entirely successful in overcoming the consequences of these experiences can only be surprising to those who, like his mother, continue to give hope more weight than reality.

While the child is, in many respects, the father to the man, I have no intention here of reducing Clinton's adulthood (or his presidency) to his childhood or the influence of his mother's character on him. Clinton's early years were shaped by four distinct factors: (1) the loss of his father, (2) his mother, (3) his grandparents, and (4) his stepfather. Each of these factors, to different degrees, served substantially to shape the development of Clinton's character. In this chapter I examine the first two.

THE LOSS OF HIS FATHER

From the time of his birth on August 19, 1946, until his mother married Roger Clinton on June 19, 1950, when young Bill was just shy of his fourth birthday, Clinton was without a father. What was the effect of this experience?

Clinton himself has had relatively little to say about the loss of his father. He has talked of visiting the scene where his father died (Baer 1991, 40), and he told Bill Moyers of "looking at the way the road was and wondering what it might have been like and wishing he'd landed the other way" (Levin 1992, 3). He has said, "I guess in ways I never permitted myself to admit, I missed my father terribly" (Baer, Cooper, and Gergen 1992, 29–30). One result of his father's early death was his feeling that "I . . . should be in a hurry in life because it gave me a real sense of mortality . . . and it's one reason why I was always in a hurry to do things—which is both good and bad" (Allen 1991, 20). A statement his mother attributes to him in relation to his abusive and alcoholic stepfather, Roger, serves as evidence of how much Clinton missed his real father: "I loved having a father . . . I loved having a man around the house that I could just be with" (Kelley 1994a, 143).

In the psychological literature on the role of the father in a child's development, two related types of comparisons are made.[2] One stresses a comparison of the influence of mothers versus fathers (father-present homes) in the development of personal characteristics; the other compares children with and without both parents (father-absent homes). The early literature comparing mothers and fathers focused on masculinity, moral development, and academic performance (Lamb 1976b). Several findings are of interest to a study of Bill Clinton. One study found little father-child similarity (in father-present homes) but significant mother-child similarity in levels of moral development (Lamb 1976b, 17–18). Another found that weak identification with the father was associated with lower levels of moral development, and that boys from father-absent homes consistently scored lower than boys from father-present homes on a variety of indices of morality (Biller 1976, 109). In other words, mothers play a central role in the development of different aspects of morality, and the absence of a father can accentuate this role.

Two other suggestive findings emerge from empirical studies of father-son relationships. The absence of a father interferes with a young child's development of trust in other people (Biller 1976, 108). This need not occur, however, *if* the mother is trustworthy. The father is also important because "the boy whose father has set limits for him in a nurturant and realistic manner is better able to set limits for himself" (1976, 110). If a child does not have a father to do this, and if his mother is also unable to set limits, the child can have lifelong difficulties with boundary issues, as Bill Clinton has.

According to the psychoanalytic view, a young boy's renunciation of his mother and identification with his father (at about age five) forms the core of the resolution of the oedipal conflict, which Sigmund Freud viewed as fundamental to his theory of development (1918).[3] A great deal of psychological development occurs *before* a child reaches five.[4] The imitation and internalization of parents begin very early in a child's life and take the form of the child's desire to become more like his parents (A. Freud 1965). These processes become the basis for the child's emerging view of his "ideal self" and the early incorporation of boundaries and limits. Thus, they are important precursors to the development of the super-ego, in which the "ego ideal," the capacity to renounce (some kinds of) gratification, and the replacement of a more primitive dependence on punishment to uphold rules gives way to a more principled and internally motivated capacity to "do the right thing."

What do these theoretical formulations suggest regarding young boys' development in general, and Bill Clinton's in particular? The father provides a number of important functions in a child's early family life that have implications for Clinton's childhood—some immediately obvious, some not (Muir 1989, 47–48). He helps to regulate the mother-child dyad relationship by providing an alternative and differentially responding attachment figure (object). Having two parents ensures that there is someone to love when the other is hated.[5] The father is also a stimulus for individuation. He offers the oedipal challenge and thus the child's initiation into group relations. Finally, he contributes to the relational patterns of the family, which are the basis of much of what the child internalizes. Clinton, of course, did not have a father to regulate his relationship with his mother in this early pre-oedipal period, which means her character, personality, and child-rearing assume much more importance. A father's character, personality, and parenting style often present an alternative to the mother's because most parents are not psychological clones. Here, too, the absence of Clinton's father gives more weight to his experiences with his mother.

One-parent children tend to idealize the missing parent (Neubauer 1960). Idealization is, of course, compounded by absence because the idealized person is never realistically available to make mistakes, correct them, and struggle with decisions and conflicts, and thus present a model of how real people go about resolving dilemmas in real life. Idealization of the absent parent therefore creates a problem with the child's own needs for perfection (grandiosity). When the idealized parent is presented as, and becomes, a model of perfection, the child may internalize this image and measure himself against it.

Was Bill Clinton's father idealized? Virginia Kelley's view of her husband, a view that she steadfastly refused to alter in the face of facts, was clearly less than accurate. There is no reason to assume she passed on to her son anything other than her own idealized view. Indeed, she said her son remembers that she used to sit him down when he was four or five to tell him about his father (1994a, 89).[6] She told him about how they met, how they decided to get married, his citation for excellence in the military, and how he had died coming to get her. She concludes, "To this day Bill Clinton still remembers all of that, and to this day he believes, as I do, in the possibility of love at first sight." Kelley came to believe that one difference between how her two children developed was that "Bill . . . had the memory of a mythical father out there somewhere, one who died young and who had been good and kind and hadn't abused his mother" (1994a, 172). Clinton was apparently unaware of this advantage; in discussing his father with Charles Flynn Allen, he said, "It's hard to be raised with a myth . . . all of my relatives attempted to make it [his father's death] positive, rather than a negative thing" (1991, 20).[7]

Children who lose a parent also long for him or her. They become "object hungry" (Neubauer 1989, 68), which is to say they search for persons able to provide what was missed in experiencing the loss. This may take the form of a lifelong quest for mentors (parenting or fathering figures) or in a more generalized search for attachments.

While the absent parent is idealized, the child tends to minimize conflictual feelings about the remaining parent, and indeed to cling to the remaining parent out of fear that she or he too may abandon the child. If the separation from a parent occurs in the first years of life, the fear of abandonment, the hunger for attachments (objects), and the dislike of conflict may become connected in the child's psychology.

Finally, the child may perceive himself to be (and may well actually be) different in the context of his social group. Joe Purvis, one of Bill Clinton's oldest friends, who attended kindergarten with him, extolled the virtues of growing up in a small town like Hope: "For nearly all of us, it meant that you grew up with both parents, and also had your grandparents, cousins, and others around you" (Levin 1992, 7). Clinton, of course, had only one parent, his mother, until he was five, and for two years didn't even have her. Clinton's knowledge that he was different may well have accentuated his sense of loss and fueled his need to make other connections.

VIRGINIA KELLEY: AN ADORING, DOTING MOTHER?

Views of Virginia Kelley as an adoring, doting mother are an important part of the Clinton family myth. As Allen puts it, "Whether there was a man around the house or not, Virginia was an adoring mother whose relationship with her boys was especially close" (Allen 1991, 10; see also Allen and Portis 1992, 8). Dale Drake, a cousin of Virginia Kelley's, recalls that "Bill was loved above all things by his mother" (Levin 1992, 6). What tangible indications are there that Virginia Kelley was an adoring mother to her son? Perhaps the most straightforward evidence of adoration was "the shrine": "to open the side door and enter the tan brick ranch house . . . where the Clinton family lived during Bill's high school days was to visit a shrine to the oldest son" (Maraniss 1995, 37). Kelley recalls, "By this time I had framed Bill's colorful band medals. . . . They took up a large frame . . . and I combined that with portraits of Bill . . . on the wall just outside of the living room. Carolyn Yeldell and David Leopoulos used to refer to that area as 'the shrine' " (1994a, 152).

It was very clear that Bill "held a special place in Virginia's heart"; indeed "her adoration of Bill was the subject of the jokes and jibes of his friends" (Moore 1992, 22). They "used to tease him because his mother kept so many pictures of him around the house" (Allen 1991, 19). Carolyn (Yeldell) Staley, a very close friend of Clinton's then and now, recalls that in high school "we joked that there ought to be candles around the pictures" (quoted in Moore 1992, 22).

Virginia Kelley, according to several Clinton's biographers and Clinton himself, was a doting mother who paid, if anything, too much attention to her son. For Kelley, "the psychological center of her life seemed to be her son Billy" (Maraniss 1995, 35). Clinton himself recalls that "my mother was probably too protective," a memory consistent with other portraits of her as a doting parent (Baer, Cooper, and Gergen 1992, 31). In her autobiography, she writes of having the feelings associated with being a doting parent: "We mothers—especially when there is no father at home—want *so* for our children. We want to give them the good things and protect them from the bad things" (1994a, 255).

Clinton loved and was very emotionally connected to his mother. However, characterizations of her as both adoring and doting raise a very basic question. Evidence suggests that she was a very self-involved woman, so attuned to her own pleasures that she was willing to ignore that which might cause her to think twice about pursuing them, and whose behavior consistently ignored conventional rules because she had become accustomed to making her own. How can one reconcile this with the perceptions of her as an attuned and attentive mother? Simply, one cannot.

In order to address this rather large discrepancy, we need first to consider what it means, psychologically, to be an "adoring" or "doting" mother. Ordinarily, these terms carry the connotation of being a good parent, but being the child of such a parent is not an unalloyed blessing.

FOSTERING A CHILD'S DEVELOPMENT: ATTUNEMENT, RESPONSIVENESS, AND BOUNDARIES

Born into a world of people as well as objects, the infant struggles with a diverse set of physiological states. He is helped by the presence of a person attuned to his needs in general as a baby (e.g., nourishment), and his particular needs, likes, or dislikes. In thus helping their child parents accomplish two things. First, they allow the child to experience making use of the parent's more mature psychological organization (in more technical terms as a selfobject) [8] to calm the tensions brought about by needs, rather than allowing this tension to spread, thereby causing the child to be overwhelmed. Second, in helping the child, parents provide the important experience of having been appropriately responded to by someone who cares, knows him or her, and is able to help.

All this sounds deceptively simple, but it is more easily stated than accomplished, and its consequences are profound.

> The importance of the two step sequence . . . cannot be overestimated; if optimally experienced during childhood, it remains one of the pillars of mental health throughout life and, in the reverse, if the self-objects of childhood fail then the resulting psychological deficits or distortions will remain a burden that will have to be carried throughout life. (Kohut 1977, 87)

A parent's capacity to be attuned to the infant's, and later to the growing child's, emotional needs and respond in a way that is appropriate to the child's age and psychology is the foundation of his or her empathetic attunement with others. It is also the basis, at least in Heinz Kohut's theory, of the gradual modulation of feelings of childhood grandiosity and entitlement and an important contributor to the child's development of healthy narcissistic ambition, personal ideals, and the capacity to make real and *mutual* emotional connections with other.[9]

Parents need to be attuned, but not perfectly, to the child's emotional needs, as D. W. Winnicott's (1965) reassuring term "good enough mothering" suggests. Empathetic "lapses" are to be expected because family members are likely to have diverse psychologies. What matters, therefore, are not the differences in psychology among family members per se, but how well and in what ways family members respond to such lapses.

While perfect attunement is an unrealizable ideal, parents do need to be aware of their children's changing and developing psychologies and be able to respond to them in a consistent, firm, and loving way. This requires parents' awareness of and attention to a child's needs, often before their own. This is obviously difficult for a parent whose own narcissistic needs are primary. Parents must act in a way that is consistent with the child's chronological, social, and psychological development. Treating a child as a little adult or, alternatively, babying an older child reflects a lack of awareness and attunement to who the child really is and what he might need.

Parents must also have in place a set of ideals and values that allow them to make choices and draw lines. No parent is likely to approve of everything the growing child wishes to do, but in order to convey clearly to the child where they stand, parents must be clear regarding their own convictions. This is difficult for the parent who has not developed a set of values shaped and refined by experience, or who has maintained fidelity to his or her ideals. Such values form the basis for helping the child understand the ways in which his own ideals and values can, in actuality, be made a realistic part of his life. Finally, it requires of parents the capacity to *persist* in their attention to all these matters over time and changing circumstances.

What does being "adoring" or "doting" have to do with the process I've just described? Not necessarily very much. When a parent dotes, he or she presumably is paying attention to the child. The same seems true of a parent who is adoring. But neither term necessarily reflects empathetic attunement. To dote carries with it the implication of indulging—perhaps overindulging—the child, thus possibly spoiling him. In this case, attunement to what the child would like to have is not balanced by the more mature appreciation by the parent of what the child may also ultimately need: some sense of limits, thoughtfully drawn and sensitively applied. Being adored by one's parents is a critical developmental experience for a child.[10] However, it is not a substitute for the process of instilling healthy ambitions and ideals. Why that is the case will perhaps become clearer as we turn our attention back to Virginia Kelley.

Virginia Kelley may well have been an adoring mother, but she was also an abandoning and, in important ways, an unattuned one. However much she felt she loved her children, she was unable to translate those feelings into adequate attunement with *their* needs, primarily because of her own pursuit of pleasure and her tendency to quickly disregard any information she found potentially discordant. Before Bill Clinton went through the adolescent experiences that have led many to focus on him as an adult child of an alcoholic (ACOA), and long before attempts by Clinton, his aides, and others to explain—erroneously in my view—his behavior as having resulted from his status as an ACOA, he was dealing with the consequences of his mother's psychology.[11]

Though often overused as a label, "narcissistic" nonetheless best describes Kelley. I do not doubt that she "adored" her son Bill, but that did not keep her from abandoning him a number of times throughout his formative years. The combination of these two (apparently) antithetical and powerful psychological currents in Bill Clinton's life had important consequences for his development.

THE QUESTION OF ABANDONMENT

The word "abandonment" is a strong one and is not used lightly. In addition to physical absence, it refers to a fundamental emotional unavailability. Virginia Kelley and her mother already had a long history of not getting along. When Bill Clinton was brought home from the hospital these conflicts began to intensify. Edith Cassidy (Kelley's mother) apparently spent a great deal of time with Bill Clinton, which led Kelley to believe she was "monopolizing him" (1994a, 71). Yet in spite of the fact that she felt her mother was "monopolizing" her child, she was quite willing to accept her mother's help so that she could go out: "Mother would take care of Bill and I would go downtown to a movie. I saw a lot of movies during the fall and winter of 1946" (1994a, 71).[12]

Kelley met and started dating Roger Clinton in the spring of 1947, when Bill was not yet one year old. With her first husband not dead a year and her plans of leaving Hope sidetracked, her mother and she were increasingly at odds over her new child. Kelley felt she "needed some fun" in her life (1994a, 74). It was at that time that her nightclubbing, partying, and gambling began. She and Roger Clinton drove to Texarkana to drink and gamble and also spent a lot of time in his apartment engaged in the same pursuits (1994a, 74-76).

In the last chapter I noted that a substantial part of Kelley's wish to become independent as soon as possible had to do with her wanting to get out from under a mother she perceived as trying to control her life. It was this and the idea of that white starched uniform that led her to leave the state to study nursing in Shreveport. Yet she found herself back in Hope. According to Kelley, her son Bill was no more than a week old when she decided to leave Hope to get advanced training as a nurse-anesthetist. She recalls that she looked at her son and said, "You deserve the best I can give you, and nursing isn't going to get it. . . . I decided that it was in his best interest that I go" (1994a, 70). That is certainly one possible factor in her decision. However, given the intensity with which she pursued her own pleasures both before and after returning from that training, as well as her tendency to put the best slant on things, it seems entirely possible that her difficult relationship with her mother—which had caused her to leave town once before—also played a role this time. The first time, she had only a taste of the outside world during her senior class trip to Hot Springs. However, by the time of her return to Hope she had spent four years away from home on her own—three and half years in Shreveport and six months in glamorous New Orleans, a "town that when combined with copious quantities of alcohol had brought out the show off in me" (1994a, 48).

Kelley recalls that she couldn't take her baby with her to New Orleans for "*the year* of additional training" (1994a, 70, emphasis added). While the additional training may have taken a year, Kelley was away from Hope for two years, from the time her son Bill was a little over one year old until he was three. For this period, except for infrequent visits to and by his mother, he was raised by his grandparents.

Whatever the reasons that took Kelley to New Orleans, the fact remains that she was absent from her young son's life for approximately two years. For Bill, this represented the second time a parent left him. The first was involuntary, the second voluntary. The point might justifiably be raised that Bill was too young to remember his mother's absence. However, Clinton has recalled that his earliest childhood memory is of boarding the train with his grandmother to leave New Orleans after visiting his mother: "I remember my mother crying and actually falling down on her knees by the railbed." He recounts his grandmother telling him, "She's doing this for you" (Baer 1991, 40).[13] (Perhaps his grandparents were loving substitutes. I will discuss the role of Clinton's grandparents more fully in the following chapter. Suffice it to say at this point that what Clinton recalls of his grandmother's comment regarding his being the cause of his mother's grief is not promising evidence for that assumption.)

Many have argued that the primary reason Kelley was away for two years was so that she could better provide for her son. This view flounders on several grounds. First, the idea that Kelley loved her son "above all," as her cousin put it, fails to take into account her strong attraction to and involvement in partying and nightlife. Indeed once she returned to Hope from New Orleans and began her life with Roger, her autobiography is replete with indications that Bill was on his own for much of the time. She worked as a nurse and notes it "was a blessing . . . that I had someone to take care of Bill during the day," namely, her mother (1994a, 83). By this time she and Roger were seeing quite a bit of each other. "I would spend as much time as possible at Roger's apartment. . . . Roger and I were spending most of our weekends together. . . . We were heavy, heavy partyers in those days" (1994a, 84).

After she and Roger married in 1950, the party life continued. "Many weekends I would leave Bill with mother and daddy and we would drive to Gabe and Virginia's [in Hot Springs], where the rule was to enjoy yourself—a rule I could handle quite nicely, thank you" (1994a, 90-91). As this part of her life was unfolding, her professional life was becoming more intense. In Hot Springs, where the family moved in 1953, "I was busy night and day" (1994a, 99). She worried about leaving her son with her husband because his drinking buddies might drop by and also because "for much of the time I was married to him, I had no idea of Roger's whereabouts"

(1994a, 124). She hired a nanny who worked for her and her husband for eleven years, starting from the time her son was seven.

During this period her work kept her extremely busy during the day, and her partying kept her very busy the rest of the time. She also began to frequent the racetrack and to schedule her work around it. She liked Hot Springs more than Hope because "there was more to entertain you in Hot Springs, but of course that had its bad side as well as the good. For someone working the long hours I was working, nightlife was a strain. On the other hand, how could you resist?" (1994a, 107).

Bill and his brother were pretty much left on their own by their parents. In spite of the heavy demands of her nightlife, Kelley attributes this primarily to her work: "The way I've had to work my children had to mature early" (Oakley 1994, 28). Her later statement on the subject in her autobiography seems much more general and accurate: "Bill and Roger were on their own so much of the time that I really had no choice with them. Early on, I had taught them to be self-sufficient because I was gone and big Roger was basically unreliable" (1994a, 155).

THE QUESTION OF ATTUNEMENT

Aside from the issue of Kelley's physical and emotional availability given her other interests, there is also the question of the level of her attunement with her children. Kelley's enthusiastic nightlife raises substantial questions about how attentive and responsive she was to the needs of her children. The most obvious illustration of this is her son Roger's drug problem. The fact that Roger had lots of money and no visible means of earning it, she says, finally made it "through my elaborate defensive system." Bravely, she notes, "I made it easy for Roger to get away with the lie that had become his life. Do you know I never once asked how he made a living? When he was in Little Rock . . . not really seeming to have many engagements, I didn't say, 'Roger, how are you getting your money?' I guess I didn't want to know" (1994a, 245).

Interestingly, she characterizes this approach to Roger's life as reflecting the fact that "I had mothered Roger too much." How is it possible to mother a child too much when one doesn't notice the obvious about him? The answer is found in her observation that "today I even wonder if my decision to stop mothering Roger, *to let him stand or fall on his own,* was just one more way of denying what I knew in my heart, that there was a problem of some sort" (1994a, 245, emphasis mine). Kelley's idea here is that better mothering would have consisted of allowing Roger to stand or fall or his own. "Mothering Roger too much" means allowing gratification by not asking difficult questions. In her view, apparently, if one cannot be gratifying in this way, the alternative is to stop mothering the child and take a sink-or-swim stance. Actually, gratifying a child regardless of his actions or allowing him to stand on his own regardless of his ability are both forms of abandonment. The idea of consistent, nurturing, but firm boundaries as a possible mothering technique seems to have evaded Kelley, since she is, as she herself is quick to admit, "not one for rules" (1994a, 91). This is entirely consistent with her own difficulties with boundaries and her choice of pleasure over responsibility.

Bill Clinton was by no means exempt from this general lack of attentiveness. Kelley's autobiography offers a very striking example of this. She had returned to Hope from her two years in New Orleans and had started to spend a great deal of time with her husband-to-be Roger Clinton. Aside from being a drinker, gambler, bootlegger, bookie, and sometimes violent, he was also a womanizer. Once, before they were married, Kelley was informed by a friend that Roger was "entertaining" a woman at his apartment. "I must have been home along with Bill, who was probably three at the time, because *I decided to take him with me* while I went over to Roger's to investigate. So I packed up the future President of the United States and we drove across town to pursue my own domestic policy" (1994a, 85, emphasis added). After letting herself in with the key he had given her, she found evidence that he had indeed been "entertaining," in the form of a woman's undergarments strewn around. Finding the woman's return airline ticket, she ripped it up into very small pieces and flushed it down the toilet. But Kelley was after some form of *public* humiliation, so "with Bill in tow, I walked around the apartment thinking, 'What's the worst thing I can do to him.' " She hit on the idea of hanging the woman's shredded clothes on the outside clothesline so that all would know what had happened.

Even in its retelling over forty years later, the emphasis is on Kelley herself. She was the woman who was not going to be made a "Hemstead County idiot," who showed her boyfriend the price to be paid for two-timing her, and who searched for a way to humiliate him publicly for his transgression against her.[14] Missing from her thinking when she recounted the incident in her autobiography, as well as when it actually happened, is any appreciation of its effect on her son.

She seems not to have considered—or if she did, not to have been deterred by—the question of what would happen to her child if, in fact, she caught Roger Clinton with another woman. Given her agitated state and the rage she felt when she found evidence of his two-timing, it seems reasonable to believe that there would have been quite a scene. That Kelley was unable to anticipate this strong possibility, or, if she did, was unable to restrain herself from taking Bill with her, thereby allowing him to see her in an agitated, enraged state, is, at best, a failure of attunement. It is a failure, moreover, that reflects the primacy Kelley gave to her own immediate needs and her inability to appreciate those of her son.

RULES AND BOUNDARIES: THE PRECURSORS OF IDEALS AND INTEGRITY

Too many constricting rules inhibit a child's initiative. Too few rules can encourage a child's grandiosity and sense of not being bound by ordinary convention. This can prevent the child from gradually modulating his grandiosity, and thus from developing more realistic and consolidated ambitions and comfort with boundaries.

So, too, the idea that rules must be rigidly adhered to regardless of circumstances, especially when there are many such rules, runs the risk of instilling compliance but stifling the child's initiative and ability to resolve the many complexities that govern rules in the adult world. On the other hand, the lack of rules and the blurring of boundaries deprives the developing child of the opportunity to confront temptation and overcome it in a way consistent with the child's developing ideals and their consolidation in the form of steady values. This is one aspect of what we mean by the phrase "building character." More technically, it means that the person, by confronting and overcoming temptation, by choosing ideals over pleasure, strengthens those internal psychological structures.

Finally, there is the question of how rules and the boundaries they represent are imparted. Many systems of rules and boundaries begin with prohibitions; the best of them then lead to developing principled understanding of the rationales behind them. Principled understanding, however, is related to rule and boundary consistency. It is hard to develop a principled understanding of rules that appear to change at the whim of the parent. The same is true of rules or boundaries that are stated but not observed. The latter is particularly damaging to the development of ethical standards because the lesson learned is that you can say one thing and do another. The important ethical and boundary setting functions of rules can be learned to some degree by admonition or discussion. However, they can only be internalized by making difficult choices and following through in one's actual behavior.

In the Clinton family, rules and boundaries were a problem—indeed, a serious problem. The public has been presented with a glowing picture of Clinton's early experiences in the bosom of a warm, supportive family whose values typified the best of small town America, but the reality was starkly different. Clinton's experiences in Hope, and later in Hot Springs, provided him with no consistent, useful set of ideals and values by which he could have triumphed over the model of pleasure and expediency so prevalent around him, both in his home and in the town of Hot Springs more generally.

Robert Levin, the Clinton biographer who wanted to help out his campaign, writes, "Perhaps the most important influence on his values was his mother Virginia, who often engaged him on the great moral issues of the day" (1992, 17). Virginia Kelley also refers to "philosophical" discussions in her autobiography, although she recalls them as being less about the "great moral issues of the day" than the stories she heard at the hospital (1994a, 153). It is well to keep in mind that these discussions were part of Bill Clinton's late adolescence and not of his childhood, when ideals and values are developing.

Interestingly in this regard, Kelley recalls hiring a local woman, Mrs. Walters, for full-time child care responsibilities for her son: "The things she taught him were priceless. Mrs. Walters was a Christian woman . . . the kind who *lived* her Christianity. . . . [She] taught Bill the Golden Rule and other lessons about how to live and get along and how to treat people in this world" (1994a, 101). Mrs. Kelley notes that her son "is a mighty good man today" and attributes it primarily to Mrs. Walters, acknowledging that it was Mrs. Walters who tried to instill these Christian ideals in young Bill Clinton.

Why Mrs. Walters and not Mrs. Kelley? What of those philosophical discussions? The latter, whatever their content, are best viewed not in the abstract, as some inevitable harbinger of moral stature, but in the context of Kelley's real daily behavior. In that arena it seems clear that her behavior had more to do with her own pleasures than with prevailing community standards. Her drinking, her husband's drinking, and their gambling and nightclubbing could not have failed to make an impression on their young child.

Fidelity to ideals requires both. That is, there must be a sense of what is important (ideals, values) and also an ability to stick with one's understanding. However, the theme that "rules are made to be broken" is consistent in Kelley's autobiography. She remembers that on the night of her first date with Bill Blythe, "We kissed that night, which was something that you just didn't do in those days—kiss on a first date. But I knew the moment I laid eyes on Bill Blythe that all the rules were out the window" (1994a, 42). Those rules included premarital sex with Blythe because "it was wartime . . . we talked fast, played fast, and fell in love fast" (1994a, 43). They also included a consuming interest in partying and nightlife which interfered with her fully carrying through on her role as a mother. When it came to a choice between social convention and Kelley's wishes, the former took a back seat.[15]

Kelley's drinking, gambling, and nightclubbing were consistent with one set of standards, but it was by no means the more home- and community-centered standards of the American South in the mid-fifties, even in a town like Hot Springs. Kelley recalls that Carolyn Yeldell Staley, Clinton's next-door neighbor, told her that her parents (her father was a minister) weren't "a hundred per cent sure how safe it was for Carolyn to be over at our house [because] we drank and went to the track. We gambled at the Vespers" (1994a, 154).

Nor did Kelley draw much inspiration from the institution that traditionally has been a pillar of ideals and values in Southern communities, the church. Kelley and her husband did not attend church very often (1994a, 87, 106), which she attributes to her work schedule. Yet, Kelley apparently arranged her work schedule to be at the track every day it was in session.

Kelley and her husband's immersion in partying and nightlife unquestionably conveyed a great deal of information to their young child about their ideals and values. In this context, she does note one very interesting aspect of her son's behavior regarding religion. Just about the time that the family moved to Hot Springs and her immersion in the party life began in earnest, her son may have tried on his own to find a stable source of ideals and values: "[Bill] decided that he wanted to go to church even when Roger and I didn't. When he got to be about eight years old, he would get himself up and bathed and get himself dressed in a coat and tie on Sunday morning. I would give him his breakfast, and then he would pick up his bible and set out for Sunday school and church" (1994a, 106).

One can understand this behavior in several, not necessarily antithetical, ways. It could represent a wish to "be like the other kids," whose families must have made Sunday church a ritual. But it also may represent an attempt on young Bill Clinton's part to find an alternative to the values and ideals he found at home. After all, Church and Sunday school, are, if nothing else, places where the basic ideals and values associated with religion are taught and extolled. As Clinton himself says, "When I was a kid I walked alone a mile or so every Sunday. It wasn't something my parents did, but *I somehow felt the need*" (Baer, Cooper, and Gergen 1992, 30, emphasis added).

Both adults and children in families play many roles. Parents are financial as well as emotional providers, children may be the vehicles of their parents' ambitions or the "responsible" (or "troubled") child, and so on. What I want to focus on here is not the particular roles Bill Clinton played in the family, but rather their appropriateness. The parent, not the child, is generally required to be the primary guide, the person who shapes the child's developing character structure in directions consistent with his best developmental efforts, and the responsive and responsible adult in the house.

Yet in the Clinton family there is evidence from the start that these boundaries became blurred. Kelley recalls sitting her son down when he was four or five and discussing his father with him. Interestingly, she recalls him at that age as "mature beyond his years," and "that talking to him at that age was like talking with a grown friend" (1994a, 89). He was, however, a child, one who had suffered a substantial psychological blow. Nowhere in her description of what she told her son about his father is there any mention of acknowledging his loss, his possible grief, or his possibly feeling different than other kids with two parents. Nor did she treat her other child, Roger, much differently. She recalls that when he was very young she would often turn to him to lift her spirits by asking him to sing her a song (1994a, 137). He always picked the song that he knew his mother loved.

As Bill got older, his mother continued to treat him as an adult. Staley wrote, "She treated Bill as an adult from the day I met them" (1993, 39). At that time he was just beginning adolescence. Treating him as an adult involved expecting him to be a father to his brother. Commenting that "he was forced into independence early," Staley recalls "that his relations with his brother were almost parental. Because her mother often left for her hospital job before the boys were awake, Bill had to get his younger brother out of bed, dressed, and off to school" (Allen and Portis 1992, 13).

His responsibilities as a surrogate parent to his brother, however, paled in relation to his role as his mother's protector. His mother makes the point directly. Bill, she says, "took care of Roger and me" (1994a, 137). Thinking back over this period in his life, Clinton has said several times, "I was 40 years old by the time I was 16" (e.g., Klein 1992b, 33; see also Baer 1991, 40).[16]

The story of his stepfather's alcoholism is by now well known and will not concern us in detail here. However, it is important to note that as a young adolescent, Clinton was increasingly forced to assume the role of parent to his stepfather and protector to his mother. The apocryphal story of Clinton standing up to his stepfather when he was fourteen is now widely known, although there are reasons to believe that it is not fully accurate (Baer 1991, 40; Maraniss 1995, 39–40; Oakley 1994, 16, 30; Kelley 1994a, 161).[17] According to Clinton, he broke "down the door of their room one night when they were having an encounter and told him that I was bigger than him now, and there would never be any more of this while I was here" (Klein 1992b, 33).

Whether or not the confrontations with his stepfather were as decisive and apocryphal as the family myth suggests is less important than the fact that as an adolescent Clinton had to see what his mother referred to as "unacceptable behavior" (Klein 1992b, 33), due in part no doubt to his parents' heavy partying lifestyle.

Kelley appears to have encouraged her son Bill to succeed. And as long as he did well in school he literally could do almost anything he wanted. His mother recalls how Staley "marveled at how loosely our household was run. Bill and Roger didn't have busywork type duties; big Roger and I always felt that their studying and making good grades and being involved with their school was enough" (1994a, 154). Kelley writes that she "trusted Bill implicitly and so imposed very few rules on him" (1994a, 151).[18] Staley recalls that Clinton's mother entrusted him with "more freedom than most of us had" (1993, 39). There was no curfew for either of her boys because she didn't want them to take any chances with their lives or anybody else's by rushing home to meet some "arbitrary hours of the clock" (1994a, 152). Bill, she recalled, had "a convertible to drive and all the freedom anybody could want" (1994a, 154).

It is very likely that Kelley's decision to impose few rules on her children stemmed as much from her as it did from them. She was, she admits, no disciplinarian (1994a, 155). Moreover, she had grown up filled with hidden anger and rebellion at the rules that her mother had imposed. And, she herself had built a life based on skirting conventional rules.

The effects of these experiences on Clinton were profound. He was a smart, sensitive child who on the one hand was told how special he was, and on the other was not even able to count on those who told him so. Just how little he was able to count on all of the adults in his family is the subject of the next chapter.

CHAPTER 9

★ ───────────────────────────────────

SOME CONSEQUENCES OF HOPE: A TALE OF TWO WOMEN

In the last two chapters I have examined the Clinton family myth and some aspects of the more complex reality of the family's domestic life. One purpose of doing so has been to lay the groundwork for better understanding the experiences that helped to shape Bill Clinton. Another has been to better understand how the psychological echoes of his childhood, along with his later experiences and the circumstances he has faced in office, have shaped his presidency.

In this chapter I will argue that in essence Clinton had two mothers, each with very different temperaments, values, and approaches to raising him. The effects of these two powerful but conflicting influences on Clinton help us to better understand both the dilemmas he faced as he approached adulthood and the experiential resources he had available to draw upon to resolve them.

Virginia Kelley as Mother: A Psychological Perspective

In an interview with Charles Flynn Allen, Clinton has said of his mother,

> She was, I thought, a good role model in three ways. She always worked, did a good job as a parent; and we had plenty of adversity in our lives

when I was growing up and I think she handled it real well, *and I think she . . . gave me a high pain threshold,* which, I think, is a very important thing to have in public life. You have to be able to . . . take a lot of criticism—suffer defeats and get up and fight again. (1991, 20, emphasis mine)

The picture that emerges of Kelley is of a woman who may have adored her children and, in her mind, may have felt she doted on them. However, in many respects the evidence is that her own emotional needs took precedence over those of her children. In choosing to go to New Orleans for two years, she might well have thought the short-term sacrifice for her and her son were worth the long-term benefits, but the same cannot be said for her immersion in partying and nightlife. Her disinclination or inability to moderate her party life calls into question the altruistic justification she provides for having left Hope. More importantly, it was a constant reminder to her son, once she returned, of exactly what her priorities were.

Her partying and nightlife were not necessarily more important than her children, but in terms of her allocation of time and energy, one can reasonably argue that they were certainly strong rivals. Her attachment to partying must also be considered in the context of the loss of Clinton's father. One effect of losing a parent at an early age is a tendency for the child to turn more forcefully to the remaining parent, so Kelley needed to be more, not less, available to her son.

Kelley's narcissism raises the question of what portion of her adoration for her son stemmed from her own needs and how much was a real appreciation of his accomplishments. The children of narcissistic adults are often viewed by the parent as reflecting his or her own sterling qualities. In doing well, the child reflects positively on the specialness of the parent, who, because of biology, socialization, or both, has helped the child to develop into the special person he or she has become. When Kelley notes that "I'm a shameless reveler in my sons' careers and accomplishments," her words suggest something more than just pride (1994a, 14). In using the term "shameless reveler," she implies that his accomplishments have an importance to her beyond a mother's pleasure or satisfaction at the success of her children.

Kelley recalls that her son "never gave any overt indication that he didn't approve of my gambling, or of our social drinking; he just simply moved quietly in the other direction" (1994a, 138). What she doesn't mention is that she apparently tried to imbue her absorption with partying in him. She went to "nightclubs like the Vapors Supper Club, The Southern Club and the Pines, [which] were among the most popular watering holes, and . . . made the rounds whenever possible, *occasionally dragging her son*

Billy on the night's merriment" (Oakley 1994, 27, 96, emphasis mine; see also Sheehy 1992, 214). Kelley said she only took her son "to nightclubs to listen to jazz, [but] he was offended by the smoke and the drinking" (Wills 1992, 63).

Clinton was apparently both attracted and repelled by his mother's favorite watering hole. Clinton told Gail Sheehy in an interview, "It was fascinating. I didn't like to be around dark smoky places where people were drinking too much. . . . I had a real negative association with alcoholism. I think subconsciously I was afraid that it would happen to me" (Sheehy 1992, 214).[1] His mother's attempt to share her partying and nightlife with her son is another example of the frequent emotional mismatches between the two, a lack of empathetic attunement that can be laid directly at the door of Kelley's sometimes faulty judgment. Edith Irons, Clinton's high school counselor, recalled that the principal of the school, Johnnie Mae Mackey, had to limit Bill's tendency to join organizations and also to keep organizations from asking him to take part:

> Miss Mackey had discussed with me that the civics clubs were asking him to do so much that he was missing too much school. At that time the phone rang. It was the chairman of the annual Heart Association drive, asking for Bill to head the health fund drive. She said, "No, Bill's mother said that he was missing too much school." Miss Mackey hung up the phone and said, "Now I have to call Virginia and tell her that I lied," which she did. Of course, Virginia agreed with her—for *no one* disagreed with Miss Mackey. (Levin 1992, 32)

This story is intended to underscore how much Clinton did in high school, and there is no doubt he did a lot. Note, however, that it was the principal, and not Kelley, who observed that Clinton was missing too much school and was perhaps overextending himself. Kelley appears from that story to have been unaware that a potential problem was developing for her son.

THE PRIMACY OF OTHERS: THE QUESTION OF FIDELITY

Both Clinton's and his mother's interpersonal style are characterized by a movement toward people. Virginia Kelley has characterized herself as a person who trusted others, perhaps even too much. She and others have characterized Bill Clinton in the same way.

However, one important lesson of Clinton's early experiences was that it was unwise to invest too much of oneself in individual, specific relationships. This runs counter to the widely held view that Clinton is a person who, like his mother, is very concerned with others and with winning them over. In chapter 5, I argued that underlying his turn toward people was an element of strategic empathy, a method of being in touch with others for the purpose of advancing his own goals. Ultimately, I suggested, this reflected a lack of trust in people.

Many, including Clinton, have attributed his friendly and other-directed style of interpersonal relations to growing up in an alcoholic family. But Clinton's turn toward others began much earlier and for wholly different reasons.

Roger Clinton married Virginia Kelley in 1950, when Bill Clinton was almost four. According to Kelley, problems with her husband's drinking did not become pronounced until well after they had moved to Hot Springs in 1953, at which time Clinton was seven. Yet apparently Clinton had begun to exhibit this turn toward others well before then, as early as kindergarten in Hope. One of his early childhood friends in Hope, Donna Taylor, recalled that Bill would "light up" when he was around other children and that "some people like to be with other children. Billy was like that. He was always right there. Almost obnoxious. He was at the center of everything" (Maraniss 1995, 32).[2] Another childhood friend from Hope recalls that in kindergarten Bill "wanted to be everyone's friend. It would upset him if someone in any group that he went into didn't seem to like him. It would trouble him so much that he seemed to be asking himself, 'What do I have to do to make this person like me?' " (Wright 1993, 28).

If the effects of his stepfather's alcoholism didn't begin to manifest themselves on any regular basis until well after the behavior described above took place, they can hardly be the cause. Clinton's turn toward others is better explained, I believe, by the loss of his biological father and the loss of his mother when she went to New Orleans for two years to study.

Clinton, of course, did not realize at first that he didn't have a father, but it must have become clear soon enough when he started to play with other children. Also critical here was the fact that his mother left him for two years. His traumatic memory of their infrequent visits suggests that her absence was an important early experience for Bill. Recall, too, that a child who loses a parent often longs for him or her and can become "object hungry" (Neubauer 1989, 68)—that is, they search for persons able to provide what is missed in not having the absent parent (in this case *parents*). Clinton's growing realization that he didn't have a father coupled with his mother's absence was a powerful inducement for Clinton to seek out other people.[3]

One other factor crucial to understanding Clinton as a person and a president bears scrutiny, although it has been totally overlooked. It concerns the trustworthiness of others and by extension Clinton's relationship with them. I refer to this as the *fidelity of interpersonal relations* and consider it an important pillar of character integrity. Regardless of the particular style one develops (whether one moves toward or away from people), honest, authentic relationships that reflect what one really thinks and values while at the same time acknowledging others' thoughts and values are a crucial element of developing character integrity.

Clinton's early experiences were not a promising beginning in this respect. His characterization of his father's death as a "fluke" (Baer 1991, 40) that gave him a sense of needing to live life in a hurry expresses the message about life and relationships that: "you never know" and "you can't count on things." This basic message was reinforced by the absence of his mother during his early years.

These early lessons, as powerful as they were, do not in and of themselves fully account for the nature of Clinton's interpersonal relationships and the low levels of trust that underlie them. To do so, we must examine the relationships between Clinton, his mother, and his stepfather. Clinton's stepfather was no more reliable than his mother. He often went out and left his son at home alone in the evening or all night (1994a, 111, 124). So Clinton could count on neither parent, individually or as a couple. Such parental irregularity, unreliability, and concern with pleasures at the expense of a commitment to a firmly rooted family life can be seen by a child as a form of betrayal.

Kelley's earlier experience with her "favorite high school boyfriend," Richard Fenwick, is instructive in this regard. Mr. Fenwick was a solid, hardworking young man who started out selling popcorn after school in a movie theater and worked his way up to a supervisory position (1994a, 31). Kelley's parents approved of Fenwick and Virginia Kelley and he often sat on the front porch discussing their future (1994a, 33). As she recalls, "Most people in town expected us to get married, and I guess we did too" (1994a, 33). Fenwick graduated a year before Kelley and left to work in a shipyard before joining the military. Before he left he gave Kelley a ring, of which she says, "It wasn't an engagement ring exactly—more like an engaged-to-be-engaged ring. . . . I loved it. The ring was the thing, its circle tying the future to the past" (1994a, 34). When Kelley starting her nursing training, Bill Blythe came into the hospital with another woman. He and Kelley were clearly taken with each other, and when the handsome stranger saw her ring and asked her what it meant, she replied "nothing." She goes on to note, "After four years of going with sweet wonderful Richard, I told this total stranger that my ring didn't mean a thing" (1994a, 42).

The most telling component of this tale and its implication for Kelley's way of dealing with others within the Clinton family was her later divorce from Roger Clinton and almost immediate remarriage. In order to appreciate its seriousness for Clinton, one first has to recall how serious it was for his mother. By the mid-1950s, that is, when Bill Clinton was an adolescent, Kelley's husband was drunk "nearly every single day" (1994a, 117). The fights between them escalated, and verbal abuse sometimes turned physical. Kelley secretly began to put away money. The dramatic stories about Clinton standing up to his father to protect his mother and young brother date from this period. Even Clinton's four-year-old brother Roger tried to protect his mother one evening by dragging into the house a large stick he could hardly carry (1994a, 135).

Kelley and her children moved out of the house and she filed for divorce. Once again coming to her aid, Bill Clinton gave a deposition to his mother's attorney to support her case, undoubtedly a difficult experience for him. He has said elsewhere that his stepfather "genuinely did love me, and I genuinely did love him" (Clift and Alter 1992). Kelley reports that through everything "Bill never stopped loving Roger Clinton" (1994a, 169). Given those feelings for his stepfather, taking an open and legal stance against him must have been a very difficult emotional task for Clinton.[4]

The divorce was finalized in May and Kelley began to relent almost immediately. She did so, she says, because her now ex-husband came around, acted so pitiful, and promised that this time he would *really* change. Understandably, Clinton was against his mother's remarriage—she says he told her "that would be a mistake" (1994a, 149). She soon changed her mind, however, and they were remarried three months after the divorce was finalized.

Kelley says of her choice that "I felt sorry for Roger but I didn't love him any more" (1994a, 159). This does not seem like an adequate basis for such a potentially damaging choice. Predictably, his drinking and their arguing at home continued. In keeping with Kelley's tendency not to accept responsibility for behavior that may have caused others, as well as herself, harm, she also says of her decision to remarry Roger Clinton, "I don't regret it" (1994a, 13–14).

Consider what effect these events, and his mother's behavior, must have had on Clinton and his ability to trust. Roger Clinton had struck her on a number of occasions and had threatened her children.[5] Both of her children were concerned for her and no doubt for themselves as well. She had called on them, then aged sixteen and six to cheer her up but mostly to protect her, and they had responded. She had at last separated from this abusive situation, again seeking her son's help to do so, this time by his submitting an affidavit against the only father he had known. Then, she impulsively returned herself and her children to the same dangerous and unpleasant situation. In returning to a set of circumstances in which they all had suffered emotionally (and she physically), she betrayed her own and her family's emotional well-being and sense of physical security (see Kelley 1994a, 134). She specifically betrayed the commitments her son had made to help her and the family, first by repeatedly standing up to his stepfather at some risk to himself, and second by submitting an affidavit against him. Her remarriage subjected them all again to the situation they had escaped and rendered Clinton's stands against his step-father at home and in court null and void. Clinton made an important, sincere, and difficult emotional commitment to his mother, and she responded by first making use of it and then disowning it. The lesson to be learned was that commitments, even those made by a parent, were ultimately unreliable. Things change.[6]

In this context, Clinton's decision to take his stepfather's name, which puzzled his mother (1994a, 149) as well as a number of his biographers, can perhaps be made clearer. By submitting the affidavit, he had chosen his mother over his stepfather in spite of his feelings for him. It is not surprising that Clinton's decision to take his father's name was made in June, when his mother and stepfather were talking about remarrying. He was in essence following his mother's lead and, given the positive feelings he had toward his stepfather, also making restitution of sorts.

A basic lesson of Clinton's early life experiences was that even those on whom you should be able to count are often unreliable. These experiences are consistent with Clinton's adult behavior, specifically his lack of fidelity in his commitments to others—supporters, colleagues, voters—and his admission that he has "caused pain in his marriage." Clinton's early experiences are *consistent* with his willingness to ask others to walk the political plank with (for) him and then reverse himself when it is to his advantage to do so.

CLINTON'S GRANDPARENTS: AN EARLY MODEL OF A SOLID AND LOVING HOME?

One could argue that Clinton's first and formative years, spent with his grandparents, were in fact the key to his later success and may have helped him to surmount the troubles of his subsequent years in Hot Springs.

Clinton has spoken with great affection about his grandfather as the kind-
est man he ever met. Although his financial circumstances while living with
his grandparents were "modest," it was "by all accounts a solid and loving
home" (Klein 1992b, 33). Here again, however, the facts do not quite
measure up to the myth.

Virginia Kelley's mother, Edith Cassidy, and her father, James Eldridge
Cassidy, play important roles in the Clinton family narrative. In understanding them more fully, we are better able to understand their daughter.
More importantly, young Bill Clinton spent early and important years with
them.

Edith Grisham and James Cassidy were both born in Bodcaw, Arkansas, a town with a population of about 100 in the southwestern part of the
state. Both of their families owned farms and neither received much formal
education. Virginia's mother left school after the eleventh grade to help
with the farm work, but, Kelley wrote, "It wasn't because she didn't have
ambition. I've never seen anyone burn with intensity the way she did"
(1994a, 18). Kelley reports that her mother announced from the first that
she wasn't going to raise any child of hers in Bodcaw (1994a, 17).

She and Cassidy were married in January 1922. Her daughter Virginia
was born on June 6, 1923, and five months later the family moved to
Hope. As Virginia remembers it, "Hope was a place where things *happened*" (1994a, 20).[7] It was a junction town on the Cairo and Fulton rail
line, with "elegant strangers," the "plush Capitol Hotel," theaters, and
other entertainment. Kelley says she understood and approved of her mother's desire for excitement and stimulation.[8]

Her mother's psychology, however, was another matter. According to
her daughter, Edith Cassidy's "worst trait was her temper, which was
uncontrollable. She was angry somewhere deep inside of her, and she took
it out on anybody that happened to be around" (1994a, 19). Elsewhere,
she paints a somewhat paradoxical picture of her mother as "one of those
people with a vindictive, manipulative mind. She would go out of her way
to help people—until they crossed her. Then she would stop at nothing to
undermine them, to hurt them in terrible ways" (1994a, 24).

It was Virginia's father with whom she made the most positive emotional connection. She recalls him as "kind and gentle" and says, "I loved
my father as much as it's possible for a daughter to love her dad" (1994a,
19). Her father "loved to be with people" and had an "infectious smile."
His job delivering ice took him into the local community, and Kelley
remembers being told the story of how her father was always kidded
because "he liked to stop off and have coffee with various customers—

usually . . . the prettiest ones. The boys would drive on and keep delivering, and Daddy would catch up with them a few houses down" (1994a, 23).

These stopovers were apparently the cause of increasing friction at home, which escalated into nightly screaming matches in which her mother accused her father of womanizing. Virginia Kelley, as she got older, "began to doubt the jealously was real" and "couldn't believe that my daddy, as devoted as he was to both of us, would do anything with another woman. The fighting went on for years, and Virginia recalls wishing that her father *"would stand up to her, maybe even strike her once"* (1994a, 23, 24).[9]

Virginia herself found it difficult to stand up to her mother. She recalls her mother as being "very strict, very overprotective, which I had grown to think of as her trying to control my life." When she did something wrong as a child her mother would "whip me furiously . . . mostly [with] her hand, but sometimes [with] . . . a special kind of switch she favored—one that inevitably drew blood from my legs" (1994a, 28). In high school, Virginia Kelley recalls, "I . . . decided I wasn't going to cater to my mother's bullying anymore. This wasn't something that I announced with great fanfare, mind you—I was gutsy, not crazy" (1994a, 29). This she accomplished simply by biding her time and leaving at the first opportunity. That opportunity was nursing school.

We are now in a better position to understand why Kelley insisted on focusing on "the good" while persistently overlooking "the bad." She writes that "my mother saw the bad in people," whereas she "dearly wants them to be good, and loyal and trustworthy." This, she admits, got her in trouble, "but better that than negative and cynical and suspicious, like my mother. To the extent that I was like her I compensated by calling attention to my cheerfulness, my flamboyance, my optimism, my upbeat outspokenness. I kept the darker feelings inside deep down and out of sight" (1994a, 29).[10]

In short, Kelley strove to be as unlike her mother as possible. To do so, she embarked on a strongly psychologically motivated quest to become the model of everything she felt her mother was not. This strategy was not completely successful. Early on, as a child, she writes, "I knew I was developing a temper like my mother's. I would sound off at people for no reason, although I tried my best to keep from letting it show. . . . I had also inherited some of my mother's willfulness—which could be good or bad— depending on how I used it—as well as some of her energy and ambition" (1994a, 29). Later, while in nursing school, she lost her temper and threw an electric fan at one of her roommates, while saying to herself, "You are your mother! . . . You are your mother! . . . You will destroy yourself if you don't get hold of this!" (1994a, 37). According to Kelley this was the last temper tantrum she threw, but what she calls her "mean streak" was still around many decades later when she began to see her fourth husband-to-be.[11]

These earlier experiences do not sound like a promising foundation for the time that Clinton spent with his grandparents—and they weren't. When his mother returned to Hope awaiting her husband's return from the war, work was her "salvation (1994a, 52). The second time she returned to Hope, to await the completion of housing arrangements in Chicago, she did so an expectant mother. When her husband died suddenly and tragically, she was stuck in Hope, pregnant and living with a mother she had gone to nursing school to escape.[12]

As they waited for her child to be born tensions mounted. Kelley writes, "Mother couldn't wait to get her hands on it; maybe she hoped to do better with it than she had done with me" (1994a, 66). As soon as young Bill Clinton was brought home from the hospital, her mother began to take over the baby's care: "mother . . . was totally involved in showing me how mothering was done. She meant well, but I felt like a lowly nurse again running around practically taking notes while . . . my mother played God" (1994a, 69).

Given Kelley's later laissez-faire approach to her own life choices and to motherhood, it is important to note how Bill Clinton started out. Edith Cassidy "had Bill on an unrelenting schedule—he ate his breakfast at the same exact hour every day, had his bowel movement on schedule—napped, played, ate, burped, slept, in an unwavering cycle" (1994a, 69). Her child slept a great deal, so much so that Kelley worried about the effect of all the scheduling on him.

Kelley spent time with her new son "when mother wasn't monopolizing him," but at other times she welcomed her mother's attention to her son so that she could go downtown to the movies (1994a, 71). It was at this point that she met Roger Clinton and, feeling that she needed a little fun in her life, began to date him. Edith Cassidy was less taken by Roger than was her daughter (1994a, 77). Kelley says it was because her mother "was very, very protective of Bill, and she probably resented—and maybe even feared—Roger Clinton's attention towards my son. She had two reasons to be glad I was leaving [for New Orleans]; it would remove me from daily contact with Roger, and it would give her total control of Bill" (1994a, 77).

For the next two years of his life, Clinton resided with his grandparents, and his grandmother was the dominant daily force in his life. Not surprisingly, Kelley notes that in her two-year absence her mother "had already grown incredibly attached to Bill" (1994a, 83). When Kelley returned to Hope from New Orleans and began to work, she was often away and her mother "still held sway over [Bill]." She also apparently adored him and doted on him, but in ways that differed from how her daughter came to understand and act on these feelings. At one point Kelley notes that her mother "worshiped Bill" (1994a, 114). Elsewhere she remarks that her mother "would dress him and feed him and buy him things. Nothing was too fine or too expensive for her beloved grandson" (1994a, 83).

Edith Cassidy also spent time teaching young Bill. Kelley attributes this to the fact that her mother had begun to focus her own ambition on the child, and perhaps this is the case. But it is also possible that Cassidy, herself an ambitious woman, wanted to give her grandson the tools to satisfy the ambitions he might develop. At any rate, she drilled her grandson on his numbers with homemade flash cards and played other learning games with him.

During this period, Virginia and Roger began to date exclusively and her partying began in earnest but her mother "continued to be immune to Roger's charms" (1994a, 83). When the couple decided to get married, Cassidy responded by trying to get legal custody of her grandson. Kelley attributes her mother's attempt to gain custody of Bill to the "blackness inside her finally taking over," but she also offers another, more revealing insight: "To her mind, Roger Clinton wasn't fit to be under the same roof with Bill, and she said she was going to stop the possibility of it if she could" (1994a, 86). Edith Cassidy went to an attorney, who conveyed to her the facts of her position. As Kelley puts it, "The laws of the land prevailed" (1994a, 86). Still, it is an extraordinary incident, especially given the time and place. Kelley's mother tried to gain custody of her grandson from her own daughter because she saw and disapproved of the life she was starting to live. She felt it would prove harmful to her grandson, and in retrospect she was right.

Cassidy continued to spend lots of time with her grandson while her daughter pursued her busy work and social life. Clinton has recalled his grandfather with greater fondness than his grandmother (Baer 1991, 40). Still, her intensive attention to him and her concern about him stand in stark contrast to his later family experiences. In a very revealing aside, Kelley notes that when the family moved to Hot Springs (and she and her husband became heavily involved in its nightlife), "Bill frequently went to visit his grandparents in Hope, leaving by bus on Friday and coming back to Hot Springs on Sunday afternoon. He always loved Hope—he once said he felt like he was surrounded by a great big loving family when he was down there" (1994a, 106).

Two other points about Clinton's "second mother" are important to note. It seems clear that Clinton experienced two distinct mothers, experiences radically different in several ways. Both women were themselves ambitious and both encouraged him. His grandmother appears to have tried to teach him, while his mother was content to let him develop more or less on his own. At the level of rules and boundaries, his mother's laissez-faire approach to rules first competed with and then was overlaid on his grandmother's more disciplined approach.[13] What is unusual in Clinton's case is that he experienced these two different approaches alternately in the same childhood from equally determined women.

What Clinton lacked in these early experiences was consistency. He was offered divergent models of how to proceed in life. One, his grandmother's, stressed regularity, discipline, adherence to rules, and maintenance of boundaries. The other, especially as he grew up and watched his mother, stressed freedom, skirting and where one wished ignoring conventional rules, situational commitments and values, and the blurring of boundaries. It would be enormously difficult for any developing child to integrate such diverse character elements, and the evidence from Clinton's adult behavior is that he didn't.

Interestingly, it appears to have been Clinton's grandmother, not his mother, who contributed the most to the development of his character integrity. Clinton's dislike of the clubs his mother took him to apparently extended to her off-color jokes, which she told to his brother but not to him. According to Kelley, "Maybe some of it had to do with Roger's formative years being spent in Hot Springs, while Bill's were in Hope—largely with his grandparents. His Mammaw Cassidy was a stickler for making you keep you nose clean, both figuratively and literally" (1994a, 137–38).

These two poles—represented by his two mothers—provided the boundaries within which Clinton struggled with the choices that helped to define his character. The conventional, responsible, good student—the "perfect child"—is in fact largely a reflection of his grandmother.[14] Yet there is another side to Bill Clinton that has been clearly evident to those who have watched him over the years or more recently in his presidency. This Clinton's words and deeds are frequently at variance, and his commitments (policy, political, and personal) are subject to change, sometimes abruptly so. In this he more clearly resembles his mother.

CLINTON AS THE ADULT CHILD OF AN ALCOHOLIC

Clinton's stepfather's drunken rages and Clinton's confrontations with him are by now enshrined in the Clinton family myth.[15] His stepfather's alcoholism has been linked by Clinton to (1) his tendency to be a workaholic (Clift 1992, 37); (2) his tendency to take on more responsibilities (Baer 1991, 40); (3) his tendency to avoid conflict because of his fear that "expressing conflict would make the world come to an end" (Clift and Alter 1992, 37); (4) the fact that he "grew up with much greater empathy for other people's problems" (Baer, Cooper, and Gergen 1992, 29); (5) his great peacemaking skills;[16] and (6) his "desire to accommodate [which] is probably due in part to the sense that I had from my childhood, that I was the person who had to hold things together at home, to keep peace" (Klein 1992b, 33).

The actual nature of the Clinton family and its relationships is much more complex than these relatively simple extrapolations from the adult child of an alcoholic (ACOA) syndromes suggest. It is crucial to note the wide and sometimes inconsistent range of personal attributes that are supposedly explained by Roger Clinton's alcoholism. If Clinton's "avoidance of conflict" is explained by his stepfather's alcoholism, what then explains his tendency to berate his staff or publicly demonize those groups (e.g., greedy doctors) who oppose his policies? If his stepfather's alcoholism explains Clinton's greater empathy for others, what explains his decision to leave his supporters in Congress out on a limb by themselves?

My point here is that one should be wary about placing too much of an explanatory burden on a very elastic theory. Our knowledge of the adult children of alcoholics and their "dysfunctional families" is a somewhat uneven amalgam of clinical theory and self-help homilies.[17] Addiction is often defined rather broadly as "a pathological relationship to any mood-altering experience that has life damaging consequences" (Bradshaw 1988, 5). Included among the list of "addictions" are drugs, alcohol, food, gambling, rage, work, illness, worry, sex, and even religion. This is quite a broad list and leaves unanswered important questions, such as what the term "life damaging" means and what exactly a "pathological relationship" is.

Among the archetypical roles that ACOA children are said to adopt are: (1) the hero, a role in which the child helps make the family normal by his or her success; (2) the responsible one, who acts as the caretaker for the alcoholic parent; (3) the scapegoat, whose difficulties mask those of other family members; (4) the lost one, a role in which the child disengages from his experiences; (5) the placator, a role of conciliation and reducing family tension; and (6) the clown, a role in which antics are used to draw attention away from the painful realities of family life (see Kritsberg 1988; Gravitz and Bowden 1985; Lansky 1980).

These roles are flexible, and children of alcoholics may take on several or switch roles. This presents a serious theoretical problem. If one may take on any, several, or many of these roles, then they are not particularly useful in explaining psychologically based patterns of adult behavior. Bill Clinton, for example, fits into at least five of the six roles noted above. Yet each role cannot have the same compatibility with Clinton's underlying character structure. The attempt to explain patterns of adult behavior by reference to these roles is based on the assumption that the roles supersede or suppress all other character or personality elements in the developing child. This is an untested and speculative psychological assumption and would, in any case, be difficult to support in Clinton's particular case, since by his mother's account, his stepfather began to become abusive in the mid-1950s (Kelley 1994a, 117). By this time, Bill Clinton was ten years old and had already been significantly shaped by his mother, grandmother, and the loss of his real father.

Turning the focus from Roger Clinton to Virginia Kelley, consider how this description of an alcoholic parent fits Clinton's mother:

> The alcoholic parent is a deeply . . . depriving parent . . . tremendously self-absorbed and unable to give emotionally to his . . . family. Many alcoholics are . . . very inconsistent. When drinking, they are unapproachable . . . when sober they can be willing to give. [As a result] a self-protective barrier is erected . . . by the child to allowing closeness to the object, who while drinking, rejected or attacked. The individual protects himself . . . against this unpredictable and unreliable source. (Ryan 1991, 75–76)

Roger Clinton's alcoholism and Virginia Kelley's avid partying resulted in both being unavailable emotionally to the young Bill Clinton. With the exception of his grandparents, Clinton knew no primary family figures who could impart to him a strong sense of ideals and values.[18] Moreover, he had no primary family figure who could show him the process by which ambitions are reconciled with ideals and ideals reconciled (but *not* abandoned) within the framework of the hard choices that accompany real life.

In an environment with a severely alcoholic parent, a child often idealizes the more stable parent (Ryan 1991, 76)[19] because he cannot afford to lose both parents (in Clinton's case three parents). Political commentators and biographers have focused on Clinton's stepfather because he was a newsworthy subject—it is not often that a president's stepfather is revealed to be an abusive alcoholic. Roger Clinton's drinking, however, deflected attention away from the more complicated and poignant story of Clinton's early experiences, with his mother, grandmother, and the loss of his real father.

In sum, Roger Clinton's abusive alcoholism established itself *well after* a number of very important psychological events had taken place in Clinton's life. Before Roger Clinton's drinking became abusive, Bill had experienced the tragic loss of his father and its emotional consequences, the two-year loss of his mother and its emotional consequences, the parenting of his grandmother and grandfather, the return of his mother, the conflict between his grandmother and mother, and the loss of his mother (for a second time) and his new stepfather to their vigorous nightlife. It is only *after* all these experiences occurred that Roger Clinton's abusive patterns began to assert themselves. Clinton therefore had a lot more to deal with than has commonly been thought. His stepfather's abusive drinking was in fact only the latest complication in an already troubled and extremely difficult childhood. His psychological foundation was undoubtedly *profoundly* affected by *all* these factors.

THE CONSEQUENCES OF CLINTON'S CHILDHOOD DEPRIVATION

How did this childhood affect Clinton, a childhood in which he was left alone and abandoned, in which he lacked reliable, stable emotional relationships, ideals, and guidance on how to mediate between abstract goals and tangible limitations, and, ultimately a firmly established sense of boundaries and self?

Fidelity and consistency in primary family relationships is among the most important means by which we establish a sense of trust in others and the capacity to be trustworthy ourselves. If you cannot count on the emotional availability of your father, your mother, your stepfather, and even (through no fault of their own) your grandparents, it is difficult to derive a sense of trust in the emotional availability of others. Moreover, being emotionally abandoned deprives the developing child of the experience of fidelity, the capacity of parents to put their child's needs *above* their own. The lesson that an emotionally abandoned child learns is that other needs, not his, come first. Thus, later, he feels entitled to put *his* needs first.

When parents are not attuned to a child and require him to submit to their needs, the child has difficulty developing a strong sense of who he is (Winnicott 1975). In learning what his parents need, the child doesn't learn about himself. In acting on what others need, the child loses valuable time and experience in developing and working through his own understandings of himself and balancing his needs and his ideals. In learning and acting on what his parents need, the child is deprived of the guiding experience that his parents might otherwise provide in helping him to develop his needs *in the context of his values*. The child is literally left on his own to navigate complex life circumstances.

Clinton's experience of having been left alone helps to explain his lifelong aversion to being by himself. The capacity to be alone develops as the child becomes comfortable with separation from a parent (Winnicott 1958). The child first tries out, in small steps, being away from a parent and then gradually learns to tolerate not only being on his own in sight of the parent, but being on his own out of a parent's sight. In order for this phase to be successfully consolidated the child must come to believe that the parent will still be there when he chooses to return.

Being left on one's own also turns a child toward others in a search for what he is unable to get at home, namely the sense that he and his needs matter to others. This in turn can damage a child's developing sense of his own worth, setting off an emotional scramble to get others to validate his worth and sense of self.

A lifelong sense of entitlement—that one ought to have what one wishes because one has not had it—is another by-product of emotional unavailability and lack of attunement on the part of parents. An observant critic might ask how it is possible that someone who has been deprived has developed sufficient self-esteem to feel that he is entitled. It is a good question and one that is answered in Clinton's case by emphasizing his status as an adored child. Both his mother and his grandmother, in very different ways, adored him. The fact that both didn't follow through—his grandmother because she was prevented from doing so, his mother because her other pursuits interfered—doesn't negate the development of this sense of being special and entitled. Indeed, in many ways it *facilitates* it.

The exact ways in which this sense of entitlement may manifest itself vary. Some people simply believe that they are entitled to indulge themselves. ACOAs are often "destructively self-feeding" (Ryan 1991, 80)— that is, they may indulge in alcohol, work, food, people, or sex. The experience of childhood deprivation, coupled with the sense that one is special and entitled, can result in an adult with strong appetites. Another likely outcome of this two-pronged experience of deprivation and adoration is the sense that one need not or should not be confined by conventional boundaries. Boundaries, after all, require limits, and limits mean doing without. The deprived but entitled person reasons that he has already been required to give up enough.

In examining President Clinton's approach to the exercise of political power and leadership, we see elements of all these factors in action. While Clinton's presidency cannot be adequately explained solely by these experiences, neither can it be fully understood without them.

★ ───

CHAPTER 10

VIETNAM AND THE DRAFT

The Vietnam War was the litmus test of a generation. The conflict divided America—Left against Right, young against old, children against parents. It provoked a crisis of governmental authority and legitimacy the effects of which remain powerful. Twenty-two years after the end of the war, the published memoirs of one of its chief architects, Robert McNamara (1995), unleashed a storm of anguished and angry debate, as did the earlier decision to extend diplomatic recognition to Vietnam (Mitchell 1995a).

The war resulted in a profound personal crisis for many thousands of Americans and their families. Young men, many barely out of adolescence, faced the prospect of combat and death in a controversial foreign war. Many were torn between their belief that they should serve their country if asked and deepening questions about the war's purpose. Faced with this profound dilemma, most who were called upon to do so served. Many others volunteered to serve. Some could not bring themselves to serve in a war they didn't support and acted on their convictions by leaving or refusing. Whatever path one chose, the war presented a generation with stark choices and equally stark consequences. It was a litmus test not only of a generation's politics, but of individual character, convictions, ideals, and ambitions.

This chapter explores what the draft issue, a source of controversy during Clinton's 1992 presidential campaign, reveals about Clinton as an adult and, importantly, as a smart and ambitious young adult facing perhaps the gravest moral, practical, and physical crisis of his life. Vietnam was for Clinton, as for many others, what Heinz Kohut would call "crucially significant—a point in the life curve . . . at which a final crucial test determines whether the previous development has failed or has succeeded" (1977, 241).

The reconstruction of Clinton's draft history is complicated because it unfolded over a long period of time. Information revealed at one point left one impression, while information revealed later left another.[1] Information that emerged months after the draft story first broke lost some of its impact because it was not immediately picked up or connected to previous information.[2] Moreover, not only did the facts of the unfolding story appear piecemeal, but they emerged in the middle of a furiously contested presidential campaign, with many other issues vying for public attention. Each individual disclosure brought forth a round of new explanations and criticisms but no overall analysis of the story or its implications.

During the campaign Clinton's draft history was framed by one major question: Did Clinton inappropriately avoid the draft? Clinton argued forcefully that he acted honorably. His critics argued that he had not.

The Unfolding Draft Controversy

On February 6, 1992, the *Wall Street Journal* published a long article asserting that Clinton had secured a deferment by promising to enroll in the Reserve Officer Training Corps (ROTC) program at the University of Arkansas and had then reneged on that promise (Birnbaum 1992). In response, Clinton stated that he had felt it would be wrong for him to take advantage of the deferment when other young men he knew were taking their chances with the draft: "I had high school classmates who were already dead, I decided it was an inappropriate thing to do." If he had ever received special treatment from his draft board, he had never asked for it or known about it, and, he said, "I certainly had no leverage to get it" (Ifill 1992c, A16).

The same issue had been raised during Clinton's 1978 campaign for governor in Arkansas. In answer to the charge that he had avoided the draft by securing a deferment on the basis of his assurance that he would enroll in the ROTC program, Clinton claimed he had received a student deferment as an undergraduate and that he had been eligible for induction while a Rhodes Scholar in England but had been fortunate enough never to have received the call. This turned out to be an only partially accurate and extremely limited account.

After the appearance of the *Wall Street Journal* article, journalists and others raised questions about Clinton's candor. Clinton responded with complaints about "the obviously well-planned and well-coordinated negative hits" he was forced to endure (Ifill 1992d). In his view, he had told the truth, and questions to the contrary did not arise from his behavior but from the questionable motives of others. Those who were with him at the time describe Clinton's private reaction as "a sulfurous mixture of anger at the media and pity for himself" and quote him as complaining, "No one has ever been through what I've been through in this thing. *No one.* Nobody's ever had this kind of personal investigation done on them, running for president, by the legitimate media." (Goldman et al. 1994, 118)

On February 12, a letter surfaced that Clinton had written to the head of his local draft board, Colonel Eugene Holmes. The letter was dated December 3, 1969, two days after Clinton had received a high draft number in the lottery, suggesting that he was very unlikely to be called up as a draftee. In it, Clinton thanked him for "saving him from that draft." The letter (written when Clinton was twenty-three years old) is remarkable for the depth of anguish it appears to express over what, for Clinton and others at the time, was a preoccupying personal and political issue.

The issue, as Clinton's letter framed it, was whether he should give up the ROTC slot that had been made available to him and thus make himself liable for the draft, taking the risk of serving in a war that he thought was wrong and perhaps illegal. In the end, he wrote that

> the decision not to become a resister and the related subject decisions were the most difficult of my life. I decided to accept the draft in spite of my beliefs for one reason: to maintain my viability in the political system. For years I have worked to prepare myself for a political life. . . . it is a life I still feel compelled to try to lead. (Clinton 1992)

In addition to its clear reference to Clinton's political ambitions, the letter appears to contradict his statement, made several days before the letter's publication, that he had not asked for or received special treatment. At the very least, it provides additional reasons for his decision to give up his ROTC deferment. The letter suggests a struggle between Clinton's ambition and his values and ideals. In the end, as Clinton saw it, his values and ideals won out and he presented himself for the draft.

Did Clinton Voluntarily Give Up His Deferment?

Did Clinton notify his draft board *before* or after he received a high number in the lottery? Did he make a principled decision to give up his deferment and put himself at risk for his values? Both in public (e.g., Ifill 1992c) and in private to his staff (Goldman et al. 1994, 39), Clinton stressed that the bottom line was that he had made himself available for the draft. The issue, however, was never fully resolved. Some believe he did, but only after it became very clear that it was unlikely he would ever be called (Maraniss 1995, 185–203).

Clinton had been reclassified 1-A (the highest availability for the draft) upon graduating from Georgetown University in the spring of 1968. Given his age, he was highly likely to be drafted because most of the older men eligible for the draft from his district had either satisfied their obligations or been found unqualified. Deferments for students going on to graduate school were no longer allowed. Nonetheless, Clinton received a special deferment from his draft board to go to Oxford in September 1968 as a Rhodes Scholar. According to draft board records, he took and passed a preinduction physical in England on February 3, 1969. In May 1969 Clinton received by letter an Order to Report for Induction (Maraniss 1995, 165). At that point, *he had been drafted* and his options were narrowed. He could report, refuse to serve, flee the country, or try to have his induction notice canceled. He chose the last option.

He returned to Arkansas in the summer of 1969 and at that point met with Colonel Holmes, head of the ROTC unit at the University of Arkansas, and was offered a slot in the program. This removed him from immediate exposure to the draft and allowed him to return to Oxford in September 1969 under circumstances that remain unclear and controversial.

Accepting the ROTC slot also effectively delayed Clinton's availability for the draft at least until the summer of 1970 for two reasons. First, draft calls for the rest of the year, announced in September, were low nationally and particularly low for Clinton's draft district (Hot Springs). Second, and more important, President Nixon announced on October 1, 1969, that even students who were called up could finish their year in graduate school. In September of that year major newspapers had carried the story that the Nixon administration would soon suspend the draft and institute a lottery to which only nineteen-year-olds might be subject. On September 19, 1969, President Nixon announced that the October draft call would be spread out over three months, thus essentially canceling the draft calls for November and December.

Clinton was again reclassified 1-A on October 30, 1969, while in his second year of a two-year program at Oxford. The draft lottery was established on November 26, 1969. In the first lottery drawing on December 1, 1969, Clinton received a high draft number, ensuring that he would not be called in the draft. On December 2, he submitted his application to

Yale Law School. His letter withdrawing from his ROTC promise and thanking Colonel Holmes for "saving him from the draft" is dated December 3, 1969.

In the letter to Holmes, Clinton recalls that he wrote a letter dated September 12, 1969, to the chairman of his local draft board, soon after he and Holmes met (during the summer), asking to be let out of his promise to join the ROTC and to be reclassified 1-A. Clinton wrote to Holmes that he never mailed that letter, "but I did carry it on me every day until I got on the plane to return to England. I didn't mail the letter because I didn't see, in the end, how my going into the army and maybe going to Vietnam would achieve anything except a feeling that I had punished myself and gotten what I deserved" (Clinton 1992, A25). In response to the February 6 *Wall Street Journal* article (before the February 12 release of his 1969 letter to Colonel Holmes), Clinton recalled having informed Holmes of his decision to withdraw from his ROTC promise in September or early October (Kelly 1992g, A23). Given the December 1969 letter in which Clinton relates writing earlier but not mailing a letter of withdrawal and his conviction that being drafted would serve no purpose, it is unclear why he would have so informed Holmes shortly after having concluded that there was no purpose to be served in doing so.

The phrasing of Clinton's response to the February 6 *Wall Street Journal* article implies that he informed his draft board personally in October 1969 of his decision. However, in an interview with Ted Koppel on *Nightline*, Clinton said that he had asked his stepfather, since dead, to pass on to Colonel Holmes Clinton's intention to stand for the draft in late September or October. Again, it is unclear why he would do so, since he had come to the conclusion that his induction would serve no purpose.

Clinton was reclassified 1-A on October 30, 1969, which is consistent with his recollection that his stepfather told the draft board that Clinton wished to be released from his promise. However, Colonel Holmes and his assistant, Colonel Clinton D. Jones, did not recall hearing from Clinton in October but rather after the December lottery in which Clinton received a high number (Kelly 1992g).

Why would Clinton have been reclassified 1-A in October if he (or his stepfather) had not informed his draft board, as Clinton said? One suggestion comes from Colonel Holmes, who told the *Wall Street Journal* (Birnbaum 1992) that he was under the impression that Clinton "was going to finish a month or two in England and then come back to the University of Arkansas" as soon as possible. Just what "as soon as possible" meant is unclear. In the same article, Holmes said he would not have given Clinton another full-year deferment, since to do so "wouldn't have been ethical." Clinton says he did. It is also possible that Clinton had received permission to return to Oxford for a short period with the understanding that he would enroll at the University of Arkansas Law School and ROTC unit later, perhaps in the fall term, which he did not (see also Cliff Jackson's letter in Maraniss 1995, 172).

This is inconsistent with all of Clinton's efforts to avoid the draft and also with his December 1969 letter to Holmes. In that letter Clinton stated, "I am sorry to be so long in writing. I know I promised to let you hear from me at least once a month and from now on you will" (Clinton 1992). That letter was written and sent at least four months after Clinton had met with Holmes in Arkansas in July 1969 and had secured a deferment. Clinton had promised to be in touch with Holmes on a very regular basis and had not done so. It is possible that this failure to contact the Colonel was involved in the decision to reclassify Clinton.[3]

Clinton does not mention in his letter that he or his stepfather had contacted Holmes in October 1969. Before the 1969 letter was released, Clinton insisted that he or his stepfather had been in touch with Holmes in October to convey the information that Clinton wanted to give up his 1-D deferment. Yet his December 3, 1969, letter mentions only the letter Clinton says he wrote but never sent. Clinton's apology for taking so long to write and his acknowledgment that he had not kept his promise to "let you hear from me at least once a month" is inconsistent with the later assertion that he had been in touch with his draft board and with Holmes in late September or early October.

Clinton's letter to Holmes stating that he was not taking up his ROTC slot came as a surprise to the ROTC staff (Maraniss 1995, 204). Ed Howard, the unit's drill instructor, notes that "the letter only intensified the anger that the ROTC staff felt toward Clinton since he had failed to enroll at the Law School." The actual letter regarding his decision not to take up his ROTC appointment was a later, additional source of anger at Clinton.

The issue of whether Clinton notified his draft board before receiving his high number in the lottery, thus making a principled decision to give up his deferment and put himself at risk for his values, is not fully resolved by the public record. Clinton's account, while feasible, is inconsistent in a number of important respects. In the end, "muddled by Clinton's various accounts, which tend to be incomplete or contradictory," the full and accurate story may never be known (Maraniss 1995, 190).

Did Clinton Ask For and Receive Special Treatment?

Did others who saw little or no purpose in serving in the army and perhaps going to Vietnam also have the opportunity to make the choices Clinton made? In other words, did Clinton receive special treatment?

Clinton strongly objected to the *Wall Street Journal* story that accused him of manipulating the draft process to gain a deferment. In response, he emphatically argued that he had never received special treatment (Ifill 1992c). He further claimed that if he had received special treatment, he had never asked for or known about it.

In April 1992, the *Los Angeles Times* printed excerpts from letters written by Clifford Jackson, a Fulbright Scholar at Oxford at the same time that Clinton was there as a Rhodes Scholar in 1969, to friends concerning Bill Clinton. In the excerpts Jackson described efforts by himself and others to help Clinton avoid the draft (a fairly common occurrence at the time). These excerpts described Clinton as "feverishly trying to find a way to avoid entering the army as a drafted private." Jackson's letters further noted that he had "enlisted several . . . friends in influential positions, trying to pull strings on Bill's behalf." *The New York Times* noted when the excerpts were printed that "Mr. Jackson's assertion that Mr. Clinton arranged a campaign of political influence to secure the delay and the R.O.T.C. slot is unproven and has been denied by Mr. Clinton" (Kelly 1992g, A23).

However, seven months later, on September 2, 1992, the *Los Angeles Times* reported that Clinton's late uncle, Raymond Clinton, had led a successful effort to protect his nephew from being inducted during a ten-month period in 1968 when Clinton was reclassified 1-A. This account was important because it focused on Clinton's first year at Oxford in 1968, well before he had approached Holmes for the ROTC deferment. The newspaper reported that Clinton's uncle had used his political connections to have an additional slot created in a Naval Reserve unit at a time when such slots were no longer normally available to young people in the area. Clinton responded that he had no knowledge of any such efforts, saying "It's all news to me" and "This is the first I've ever heard of any of this" (Kelly 1992f).

Two days later, on September 4, Clinton acknowledged that he had been told in March 1992 of his uncle's efforts. He was now responding to an article that appeared in the *Arkansas Democrat-Gazette* the previous day, which quoted Trice Ellis, Jr., a retired Navy commander who had supervised the Naval Reserve program in Hot Springs, Arkansas, at the time in question. Clinton said, "I did not know about any effort to secure a Naval Reserve assignment before Mr. Ellis mentioned it to me in Hot Springs, there was no way to document or confirm what he told me" (Kelly 1992h).

On September 14, Clinton was asked on a talk show whether there was anything about his explanation of the draft that he would do differently now than he had back in 1969 or during the campaign. He replied,

> In terms of whether I could have handled it differently during the campaign, I think there's no question about that. You know, I'd like to explain why I didn't do such a good job of it. I didn't go back through all my letters, notes, to try and put this all back together again . . . and I think I was always kind of playing catch up because I gave a lot of answers to questions off the top of my head, halfway on the run when the press would hit me. And you don't remember everything after twenty-three years, every detail and every specific. (Kelly 1992g)

On September 18, Colonel Holmes released a statement and an affidavit (reprinted in its entirety in Brown 1992)[4] concerning his recollection of the events that took place in 1969. Holmes said that he felt Clinton had deceived him about both his views and intentions. Apart from stating the Colonel's view of the situation, the affidavit contained no new information, with one exception: a recollection of calls received from the office of Senator J. William Fulbright.

On September 19, a story broke revealing that Clinton had asked for help from Senator Fulbright, for whom he had worked while in college, to secure a spot in the ROTC program (Suro 1992). The story, acknowledged by Clinton's aides, was based on a sheet of handwritten notes found in the Fulbright archives. The notes refer to Clinton's wish to get an ROTC slot and deferment and contain Colonel Holmes's phone number and the notation "Holmes to call me Wed. 16th." Clinton's visit to Fulbright's office at this time and its nature were confirmed by an aide to the senator. This story appeared to contradict all of Clinton's early assertions, namely, that he had not asked anyone for help, that he had not received any help, that if he had received help he didn't know anything about it, and that he lacked the leverage to get anyone to give him special help.

When the story that Clinton had received help from the Senator to avoid the draft was first reported back in March in the *Arkansas Democrat*, Clinton campaign spokesperson Max Parker had replied, "Governor Clinton says he never asked anyone for help" (Suro 1992). On September 16, just before the *New York Times* story came out, Clinton aide Betsey Wright said, "Governor Clinton has no specific recollection of any specific actions" (Suro 1992). The September 19 *New York Times* article reports, however, that Lieutenant Colonel Clinton D. Jones, who served as Colonel Holmes's deputy, recalled receiving calls from both Senator Fulbright and Winthrop Rockefeller, then governor of Arkansas, asking if they could do anything to help Clinton. Colonel Homes, in his affidavit, recalled that the day after having spoken with Clinton for two hours at his home, he received calls from the draft board, saying that "it was of interest to Senator's Fulbright's Office that Bill Clinton, a Rhodes scholar, should be admitted to the ROTC program. I received several such calls. The general message conveyed by the draft board to me was that Senator Fulbright's office was putting pressure on them and they needed my help" (Brown 1994, 146).

The day after the *New York Times* story appeared, Clinton acknowledged his visit to the Senator, explaining it as an attempt to get information: "When people ask you about special treatment, they mean did you leverage money or power, or something to get something that other people wouldn't have gotten, and the answer to that is no. But the truth is that the rules themselves wrote in special treatment" (Ifill 1992f). In other words, he did not get special treatment because this term applies only to situations in which money or political power come into play. Moreover, Clinton argued that it was not pressure that got him the deferment, but rather loopholes already built into the system. It was the law's fault, not his.

Finally, on September 26, an article in the *Los Angeles Times* reported that Clinton had been the beneficiary in 1969 of efforts by Arkansas Republicans to arrange a meeting between him and Colonel Willard A. Hawkins, the director of the Arkansas Selective Service System. In response, Clinton acknowledged that he might have met with Hawkins, but that such a meeting, if it did occur, was part of a routine procedure suggested to him by his local draft board—"They told me what procedures to follow, and I followed their procedures" (Kelly 1992g). It strains credulity to believe that meeting with the head of the state's selective service system at the height of the Vietnam War was "normal procedure" for someone seeking a deferment, or that local selective service boards routinely told applicants for such deferments to do so.

Judgments regarding Clinton's candor on the draft issue were, not surprisingly, viewed through the prism of other related issues that also arose during the presidential campaign. The first had to do with a relatively minor issue, namely, whether Clinton had ever in fact received a notice of induction. Clinton, it will be recalled, had stated during his 1978 election campaign for the governorship that he had been eligible for the draft while at Oxford but had "been fortunate enough never to have received the call." This turned out to be untrue.

The Clifford Jackson letter published in April 1992 by the *Los Angeles Times* contained the sentence "Bill Clinton, Friend and Scholar received a draft notice," which, according to the *New York Times* reporter covering the story, resulted in "Mr. Clinton making his third significant amendment to his explanation. Previously, in dozens of interviews about the draft Mr. Clinton had never mentioned the induction notice, and at least twice had denied having ever been called up" (Kelly 1992g).

After acknowledging that he received an induction notice in the spring of 1969, Clinton stated that he had received it after the date he was scheduled to report and therefore was able to obtain a delay until July 28, 1969. By that time Clinton had returned to Arkansas and managed to secure a spot in the University of Arkansas ROTC program through Colonel Holmes and his draft board.

A second issue concerned Clinton's role in organizing demonstrations against the war. Before the December 3, 1969, letter to Colonel Holmes was released, Clinton had always denied that he had done anything other than attend antiwar rallies. Yet in the December 3 letter, he admits that he misled Colonel Holmes about his activities. In that letter, he says that the admiration he felt for Holmes might not have been mutual

> had you know a little more about me, about my political beliefs and activities. . . . You might have thought me more fit for the draft than for R.O.T.C. . . . I have written and spoken and marched against the war. One of the National Organizers of the Vietnam Moratorium is a close friend of mine. After I left Arkansas last summer, I went to Washington to work in the headquarters of the Moratorium, then to England to organize the Americans there for demonstrations Oct. 15 and November 16. (Clinton 1992)

Clinton here overstates his role since "he did not travel to England primarily to organize for the October and November demonstration" and appears not to have been an especially close friend of the Moratorium's organizer, David Mixner (Maraniss 1995, 200). Yet at other times, Clinton took exactly the opposite tack. When confronted with allegations of draft evasion in 1978, while running for governor, he denied "not only that he had been active in the anti-war movement, but that he led protest demonstrations against American involvement in Vietnam. Years later he would claim not to have protested actively within the United States. He lied" (Oakley 1994, 72).

Whether Clinton was being truthful when he took credit for his activities or when he disowned them is important only because both can't be equally true. However, just as importantly, here as elsewhere Clinton tried to have it both ways. If it was to his advantage to claim that he had been active, he did so. If it was to his advantage to claim that he hadn't, he disowned any activity.

AMBITION VERSUS IDEALS

Does the draft controversy reveal Bill Clinton to be an unprincipled opportunist? I think not. But neither does it reveal him to be, as he sees himself, a man of conviction, courage, and principle. A more accurate portrayal reveals Clinton as a young man struggling, not always successfully, to reconcile his ambition and his ideals.

Clinton's ambitions concerning his political career, as expressed in his December 3, 1969, letter, may be unusual for the degree to which they are articulated but are not by themselves suspect. They make clear that Clinton had come to see a goal for himself—a life in public service—that would serve as a vehicle for the realization of his aspirations.

Identity involves a set of ideals and values that can help shape and guide ambition. Clinton's 1969 letter to Colonel Holmes displays evidence of such ideals. He writes that he worked for Senator Fulbright not only for the money and experience, "but for the opportunity . . . of working every day against a war I opposed and despised with a depth of feeling I had reserved solely for racism" (Clinton 1992).

There is little reason to doubt the authenticity of these feelings, although there is a question as to whether he began his work in Fulbright's office with these strong feelings or developed them later (Maraniss 1995, 200). Carolyn Staley, his high school friend, recalls that when she visited him at Georgetown at the time of the riots that erupted after the murder of Dr. Martin Luther King, Jr., she and Clinton drove to the African-American neighborhoods in Washington, D.C. to deliver food (Staley 1993). Clinton's ideals were, at least at this point in his development, authentically felt, if not always realized.

During the campaign, Clinton said he voluntarily gave up his deferment because "he felt a moral obligation to do so," since four of his friends had fought and died in Vietnam (Rosenbaum 1992). This was Clinton's view of himself *as he asked to be seen.* However, this self-idealized view is at variance with the much more complex picture of his motivations that Clinton himself painted at the time. His 1969 letter to Colonel Holmes, in which he speaks of wanting to "maintain viability in the political system" and the "years" he "worked to prepare for a political life," is the starkest example of this discrepancy (Clinton 1992).

After this letter was released to the press, critics focused on Clinton's ambition while his supporters emphasized his principled anguish. While Clinton's strong interest in a political career at this stage of his life is not in itself necessarily questionable, what is striking is the depth of his appreciation, at this relatively early stage in his development, of the possible implications of his choices regarding the draft for his future ambitions. It is not his ambition that gives pause, but the keen calculations that accompany it.

Equally important is how Clinton attempted to resolve this acute dilemma. Opposed to the war, he could have chosen to register his convictions, especially regarding the illegitimacy of the draft, by applying for status as a conscientious objector, as did two friends Clinton mentions in his letter. He chose not to do so. He could also have become a draft resister, but he did not. The first option would arguably have damaged his political prospects irreparably; the second would have doomed them.

Faced with the tension between his desire for a political career (his ambition) for which he had been preparing himself for years and submitting to a draft that he thought illegitimate and a war he thought immoral (his ideals and values), Clinton followed a path that was to become a future pattern in his political behavior, one that would partially define his political identity during the campaign and, later, his presidency: *He tried to do both.* He chose the ROTC deferment. His stated reasons for doing so are instructive. To Colonel Holmes he wrote, "R.O.T.C was the only way left in which I could possibly, but not positively, avoid both Vietnam and resistance" (Clinton 1992).

There is another element to Clinton's letter that has received little attention—that is, Clinton's view of himself as special and entitled. Clinton wrote in his letter to Colonel Holmes that he had decided to agree to join the ROTC unit because he had concluded that he "didn't see, in the end, how my going into the army and maybe going to Vietnam would achieve anything except a feeling that I had punished myself and gotten what I deserved." The guilt expressed in the last part of that sentence seems fairly obvious, as does its probable source.[5] Note, however, Clinton's view that his going into the army (and perhaps to Vietnam) would serve no purpose other than to punish himself. This is an interesting argument.

Clinton decided, on his own, that no purpose was served by his entering the army. Like his mother, he made his own rules and acted in accordance with them. His view was clearly part of his justification (to himself and to Holmes) for avoiding of the draft. There is inherent in this argument a sense of being special, of being different and therefore beyond the rules appropriate for others. He could have chosen to justify his behavior on a number of grounds—self-preservation, the potential usefulness of his abilities to others in the future, and so on. But everyone else who went into the army might also have voiced the same considerations. For Clinton, however, such considerations and the sense of entitlement that accompanies them were, by his own admission, ultimately decisive.

The draft story also throws light on the third area of Clinton's character as it was developing at this time—his relatedness to others. It reveals a less positive aspect of his approach to interpersonal relations—his willingness to tell people what he knows they want to hear in order to get what he wants. Clinton met with Colonel Holmes at his home for two hours during the summer of 1969. He later wrote to thank Holmes for being "so kind and decent to me last summer when I was as low as I have ever been. One thing that made the bond we struck in good faith somewhat palatable was my high regard for you personally" (Clinton 1992). Clinton speaks of his high regard for Colonel Holmes and their good-faith bond, yet Clinton's good faith is not entirely evident. He acknowledges that "*in retrospect* the admiration might not have been mutual, had you known a little more about me and about my activities" (Clinton 1992, emphasis mine). Toward the end of his letter, Clinton relates to Holmes his reasons for feeling upset at having made the compromise with his views that allowed him to accept the deferment. One of the reasons he gives is that "I began to think I had deceived you, not by lies—there were none—but by failing to tell you all the things I'm telling you now" (Clinton 1992).

In using the two phrases "in retrospect" and "I began to think," Clinton seems to suggest that the idea that he may not have been honest with Colonel Holmes only began to occur to him *after* he had received the deferment. This asks Holmes (and us) to believe that a man who was smart, sophisticated, and prescient enough to realize that his ambitions for public office might be damaged by his failure to have served in some capacity in the war would not be aware of the Colonel's likely feelings about Clinton's views and activities.[6] It is difficult to attribute to Clinton such an obvious lapse of understanding and empathy, given that these characteristics were so much in evidence in other parts of his life.

Note too the differentiation between *deception* and *lies*. According to

Clinton, he did not say anything that was directly untruthful. Rather, he began to worry that he had deceived Colonel Holmes by "failing to tell you all the things I'm telling you now." In other words, the deception was passive, consisting of not telling the full story and of keeping major and relevant elements of his beliefs and activities from Holmes. Clinton began to see "in retrospect" that if Holmes had known these things he "*might* have thought me more fit for the draft than for R.O.T.C." (Clinton 1992, emphasis mine).

A pattern of withholding information that is clearly relevant, especially when that information does not present Clinton in the light in which he wishes to be cast, is evident throughout this controversy. It can be seen both in Clinton's behavior toward Colonel Holmes and in his handling of the draft controversy as it evolved during the campaign. For many years as governor, Clinton gave incomplete and therefore inaccurate accounts (Maraniss 1995, 190–91). In 1978, Clinton said he had never received a draft notice, but that turned out to be untrue. In another version Clinton said that he had written to Colonel Holmes saying he wanted to be reclassified 1–A, but that was also inaccurate. In a 1992 interview, Clinton said he gave up his deferment because four of his good friends had died in Vietnam. In that interview he further said that the head of the ROTC unit had tried to talk him out of his decision, but that he was determined to serve. There is no evidence to support this claim.

When the draft story broke in February, Clinton denied that he had deceived Holmes about his intentions. His letter of December 3, 1969, soon came to light, revealing that, by his own admission, he had. Clinton also asserted that he had not asked for or received any special treatment, which also turned out to be inaccurate. He claimed to have been unaware of efforts to secure for him a Naval Reserve slot, and yet he had been told. He never mentioned, and in fact explicitly denied, having received a draft induction notice, but he had.

Clinton's technique here consisted of *selecting* very small parts of a large set of events, parts that gave a very distorted and inaccurate picture. The statements were—sometimes, but not always—accurate, as far as they went, but unrepresentative of the whole. The elements selected for public presentation allowed Clinton to present himself in the best light, or at least to put the best spin on his behavior. Elements of the story that might have contradicted Clinton's idealized view of his behavior were simply omitted or else interpreted in a way that further stretched the bounds of common understanding. For example, when Clinton was forced to admit that powerful others, such as Senator Fulbright, had interceded on his behalf, he responded by offering a new definition of "special treatment" as being exclusively reliant on money or power. His approach here recalls Thomas Eagleton's explanation of what he understood the McGovern campaign to be asking him when they inquired about any skeletons in his closet— Eagleton equated "skeletons" with something awful, arguing that surely his psychiatric hospitalizations and shock treatment could not be considered such (see Renshon 1996, 161.)

By redefining special treatment in a very narrow way (as buying favors with money), Clinton was able to compare himself to the worst possible abstraction and find his behavior acceptable. His definition of special treatment allowed him to place blame on the system for providing loopholes and to imply that they were open for a number of others. This argument might appear to have some merit until one acknowledges the very formidable political power that Clinton was able to bring to bear, through his family, state, and national political connections.

Clinton had many more facts about his behavior at his disposal than did anyone else. That he chose to present only those facts that cast him in a good light reflects the fact that he took some time to think about what he would and would not say. The root of the deception in this issue is not, as Clinton passively framed it, that he "failed to tell." Rather, it is that he consciously *selected* what he would and would not say. His deceptions were more intentional than he has ever admitted to the public, and perhaps to himself as well.

Clinton's wish to avoid the draft is and was understandable on a number of grounds. That is not the issue. However, he seems not to have been willing at the time to pay the price of this decision. Not doing so then only delayed the reckoning and made him have to scramble even harder to cover his original wish to finesse the conflict and preserve his future options. In short, he was unable to muster the courage of his stated convictions or, to put it another way, he was unable to maintain commitment to his ideals under difficult conditions.

Nor has Clinton ever been willing to admit publicly, or even to close aides, the complex motivational mix underlying his behavior. In his eyes he did nothing wrong, was motivated by the highest principles, and acted in accordance with them. Any suggestion by others that questioned his behavior in this situation, thereby also calling into question his idealized view of himself, was met by outbursts of anger and self-pity that he was being singled out (another way of viewing oneself as special).

In 1995, after Robert McNamara's memoirs, in which he wrote that he now came to see Vietnam as a mistake, were published, Clinton was asked if he viewed McNamara's admission as a vindication of his opposition to the war (and presumably his successful attempts to evade the draft). He answered, "Yes, yes, I do. I know it sounds self-serving, but I do" (Purdum 1995b).

Clinton's behavior here calls to mind Harold D. Lasswell's 1930 dictum that the political man pursues power and rationalizes the results in terms of societal interest. Faced with the need to reconcile equally powerful ambitions and ideals, and unable to make a principled choice in favor of his ideals, Clinton tried to bypass the dilemma by choosing a path that appeared (to him and, he hoped, to others) to offer the possibility of accomplishing both without sacrificing either. In short, he tried to have it both ways.

This basic dilemma between Clinton's ambitions and ideals can be seen in his next significant developmental choice, his marriage to Hillary Rodham. Here too, it seems the same dilemma was played out, although in this case no longer solely within himself, but rather between himself and his wife.

★ ───

CHAPTER 11

A LIFE'S CHOICE: HILLARY RODHAM CLINTON

Marriage represents a coming together of two individuals who complement and compensate for each other. Ideally, each partner meets the other's psychological and emotional needs while continuing to pursue his or her own aspirations. How, then, do Hillary Clinton's psychology, ambitions, ideals, and relations with others affect her personal relationship with the president, as well as their political partnership?[1]

Ordinarily, a president's spouse receives only passing attention unless she becomes involved in a directly political way, as did Edith Wilson when she became the guardian of her husband's presidency after he suffered a severe stroke while in office, or she breaks new ground in her public activities, as did Eleanor Roosevelt. The Clintons, however, are unique. They have been true political partners for decades. Bill Clinton said, "If I get elected president, it will be an unprecedented partnership, far more than Franklin Roosevelt and Eleanor. They were two great people but on different tracks. If I get elected, we'll do things together like we always have" (Sheehy 1992, 144).

The accuracy of this prediction is reflected in almost all of the writings about the couple. Hillary is described as "the most influential person in any administration headed by her husband" (Kelly 1993a). The chapter on the couple in one of the Clinton biographies is entitled "Partners in Time" (Oakley 1994, 89–108). A similar chapter in a different book is called

"Rodham and Clinton," conveying the sense of two *independent* people coming together by choice (Maraniss 1995, 246–64). However, the mere fact that the Clintons have been partners does not convey what precisely that partnership has meant for the Clinton presidency. As much of Hillary's role has been ambiguous and controversial, it is important to establish the facts that frame this partnership.

For some, criticisms of Hillary Clinton reflect a backlash against strong, assertive women.[2] Clearly, she has broken new ground for a president's wife—too much ground, according to some (A. M. Rosenthal 1994). She is a very smart, able woman, and some find this fact unsettling. Still, before we dismiss any concerns about her role on the basis of the discomfort of traditionalists, we must assess just what that role is. This is not an easy task.

Hillary Clinton has played many traditional roles as the wife of Governor and President Clinton. She has served as hostess of White House functions, supported traditional "first lady" issues with wide public appeal such as improving the quality of life for children, and has generally served as a protector of her husband's presidency. None of these roles are unprecedented. Most first ladies have served as gracious hostesses in the White House, many have selected and lent their names and voices to safe public causes (e.g., highway beautification, drug education, literacy, mental health), and all have been actively protective of their husbands and their presidencies. The personal and political partnership between Hillary Rodham and Bill Clinton is, by these standards, quite unexceptional.

But Bill and Hillary Clinton have been more than traditional political partners, and Hillary has gone well beyond the traditional roles of the first lady. She has shared in her husband's executive roles throughout his career, and in doing so wielded substantial political and policy power. Her power in the White House seems second only to her husband's (Oakley 1994, 495). Although Al Gore is an unusually influential vice president, Hillary Clinton has eclipsed him in the president's inner circle of advisers (Safire 1993, 26). While it is probably too much to say that Bill and Hillary share the presidency, it is not too far afield to suggest that she is more powerful than any other person in the administration. If one were designing a title for her real role, it might well be Co-President for Domestic Policy.

George Stephanopoulos has said, "One thing was evident: Hillary was his most important advisor and she wanted a senior post in the White House" (Woodward 1994, 103). In reality, her role has been vastly more extensive and important than merely that of heading the health-care task force:

Though it was never announced, she was basically put in charge of domestic policy. Economic policy excluded, she would oversee the agencies and issues she was interested in. Her formal role in health care would be announced later. That would give her a specific project and some protection from the idea that she was corunning the government. . . . On many issues, [Secretary of Health and Human Services] Shalala would report to her. So would Carol Rosco, who was chosen as a chief domestic policy advisor. (Drew 1994, 22)

Evidence for her political and policy importance in the Clinton presidency is everywhere. She was an important principal in the selection of Clinton's cabinet: In Little Rock a small group, consisting of Bill Clinton, Warren Christopher, Bruce Lindsey, Al Gore, and Hillary Clinton, sat around a table and picked the cabinet (Woodward 1994, 59; Drew 1994, 21). Moreover, she interviewed the candidates as a matter of course after her husband had (Drew 1994, 28).

Hillary Clinton also successfully insisted on having her offices located in the West Wing of the White House, where policy is made, rather than the first lady's traditional location in the East Wing. A direct as well as a symbolic reflection of her role, that move was seen as politically risky by some of Clinton's campaign advisers (Drew 1994, 23). In the end, Hillary Clinton's role was publicly affirmed but paradoxically masked by her assignment as head of the president's health-care task force.[3]

Hillary Clinton's chief of staff, Margaret Williams, also served as Assistant to the President, a staffing structure innovation with political implications. Williams was given an office in the West Wing along with Hillary Clinton, limiting the space available for the president's staff (Drew 1994, 23). This marked a dramatic statement of power. Moreover, "she has more senior grade aides assigned to her than Vice-President Al Gore" (Fineman and Miller 1993, 18). In the presidential orbit, proximity to power *is* power.[4] And staff not only organizes information, itself a source of power, but represents power itself.

Hillary Clinton reviewed, along with her husband's political advisers, Clinton's three major campaign speeches "line by line" (Woodward 1994, 29). Before his speech to a joint session of Congress, it was she who, acting like Clinton's chief of staff, insisted that he have a full-dress rehearsal (Woodward 1994, 137). She was an active participant in all the major campaign strategy meetings, a major participant in the transition meetings that determined the future policy directions of the administration, and a critical and central voice at the Camp David retreat (January 30–31, 1992), at which the major direction of the Clinton presidency was charted (Woodward 1994, 33, 49, 87, 109–11, passim). At that meeting, "Hillary Clinton spoke to this group in a way no previous President's wife, however influential through her husband—or even, like Eleanor Roosevelt, in part on her own—would have found imaginable. It made very clear the strong and central role that she would be playing" (Drew 1994, 51).

Hillary Clinton was also a principal and integral part of the budget meetings that preoccupied and shaped the first year of the Clinton administration (Woodward 1994, 254). When Robert Rubin and Robert Reich prepared and delivered five large briefing books and two smaller summary books on the economy, "one set was for the President-elect and one was for Hillary Clinton" (Drew 1994, 58). Hillary Clinton "considered herself a peer of her husband's advisors—not set apart, not omnipresent, but a *full participant*" (Woodward 1994, 254, emphasis mine).

In reality, her status was more powerful than had she been a peer of the president's advisers. For example, she was a key figure at the White House meetings that began in the Solarium on July 3, 1992, around the issue of the energy tax and Clinton's budget. She argued forcefully that "we're not selling the plan," then told Clinton's economic policy people, "You don't think enough about how to explain it." Addressing both the economic policy and political consultants, she voiced the opinion that "you people need a process to talk to each other" (Woodward 1994, 254–55). She strongly urged the organization of a "War Room" in which to plot a strategy for promoting Clinton's economic package.[5] As a result the political consultants prepared a memo dated July 8, 1992 and the War Room became a reality (Woodward 1994, 259). In this and other crucial moments, she functioned more as Clinton's chief of staff than as first lady.

Hillary Clinton plays an unprecedented role in her husband's presidency, particularly with regard to policymaking. Whether the public is (or should be) comfortable with the extent of her involvement is another set of questions entirely, as are the constitutional implications of her role. Certainly, however, the primacy of her role justifies the examination of Hillary as both a person and a political partner.

THE CLINTONS' MARRIAGE

Marriage reflects a commitment to the cultural, social, and legal norms by which people live together and, if they choose, raise children.[6] At a more basic psychological level, it also reflects the attempt to blend together two separate but, ideally, complementary psychologies.

Love, romance, idealization, fantasy, and conscious considerations all play a role in the selection of a marriage partner. For some, romance and fantasy dominate, for others more practical concerns have greater weight. In all marriages, there is some mix of the two. Marriages develop, survive, or prosper with a range of mixes; no one composite model fits all. Similarities and complements in a marriage are evident at many different levels of psychological functioning. Couples can share broad cultural or religious perspectives. They can share social, aesthetic, or political interests and views. They can share personality traits like ambition or intelligence, or particular talents like verbal facility or interpersonal skills.

Under favorable circumstances both partners complement and compensate each other *at the level of basic psychology,* that is, in each person's character domains (ambition, ideals, character integrity, and relatedness). For example, a marriage in which both partners are equally intelligent and determined and each wishes to be dominant and in control would result in substantial conflict. Here, the two basic psychologies are conflictual, not complementary. On the other hand, in a relationship where one partner wishes primacy and the other prefers to be taken care of, there will likely be less conflict.[7]

Development within a marriage is crucial. Individuals do not simply come together with two separate psychologies that remain static and separate. Rather, in any long-term relationship (like the Clintons'), the two psychologies develop *in relation to each other,* as well as in relationship to experiences with the outside world. The idealism that one partner may bring to a marriage can be deepened or damaged by the other's behavior. A partner's ambitions can be dampened or enlarged. And the opportunities to realize one's ambitions in marriage also shape how people come to view themselves, their partner, and their marriage.[8] While the Clintons' marriage has been much scrutinized, no one has examined the ways in which their psychological relationships have evolved over time.[9]

By all accounts, Bill and Hillary Clinton's early marriage was a remarkably good fit, given their basic psychologies, personalities, and larger interests. They were "an evenly matched romance and a fair fight. . . . Two strong willed personalities." Hillary Rodham's "intellect, resilience, and ambition were . . . equal to his."[10] Steve Cohen, a friend of Hillary Rodham's at Yale, has remarked, "Clinton had the charm and sex appeal whereas Hillary didn't so much."[11] Doug Eakeley, a housemate of Clinton's, has described Hillary's "Midwest directness" as "the perfect counterpoint to Bill Clinton's southern charm" (Maraniss 1995, 246–48, 426).

Hillary Clinton's approach to life is "focused, pragmatic, and aggressive" (Oakley 1994, 89). Bill Clinton, on the other hand, remains unfocused, with an aversion to boundaries, and prefers charm to conflict. Bill was sporadic in his attention to his studies, while Hillary was consistent. "Her focused intellect was . . . a perfect counterpoint to his restless diffuse mind" (Maraniss 1995, 247).

Interpersonally, too, both differed and complemented each other. "Hillary required less company than Clinton . . . constant fellowship was not her style" (Oakley 1994, 102). Rudi Moore, who was Clinton's chief of staff during his first term as governor, observed, "Hillary's contribution . . . was the way in which—because her personality is so different than Clinton's—she complimented him. Bill sees the light and sunshine about people, and Hillary sees their darker side. She has much more ability than he does to see who's with you, who's against you, and to make sure they don't take advantage of you. He's not expecting to be jumped, but she always is. So she's on the defensive" (Bruck 1994, 63). John Brummett alludes to Hillary "as clearly more combative, unforgiving and disciplined than her husband . . . [which made her] occasionally valuable as an enforcer" (1994, 54).

Is this a case of "opposites attract"? Not really. In several very important aspects, Hillary and Bill are very similar. Both are "ambitious, socially conscious and political" (Maraniss 1995, 247). Both wanted to make their mark on the world (Warner 1993, 55). Several long-time friends of the couple note another dimension of the fit in their political partnership, and "believe Bill and Hillary were ideally matched to each other because they both wanted the same thing, but for different reasons—for him, it's glory; for her it's power" (Oakley 1994, 496).

Many observers have tried to discern whether Hillary is the more liberal or the more pragmatic of the two. However, in Arkansas, the conventional wisdom "is that both are at heart classic liberals, devoted to societal solutions that rest on taxing and spending and central planning, but also political pragmatists—natural compromisers who will settle at times for victories of symbolism over substance rather than risk losing all" (Kelly 1993b, A1).

Hillary Clinton asserts she has moved beyond the traditional Left-Right categories: "On lots of issues I'm conservative but on other issues I'm liberal. On most issues I'm somewhere in the middle . . . and it's amusing to me that some people are just intent on trying to label me" (Radcliffe 1993, 255). Here she sounds very similar to her husband, both in her views of her own philosophy and of those who see her differently.

However, unlike her husband's, Hillary Clinton's political views have deep family roots. The same is true, of course, of her overall psychology.

THE RODHAM FAMILY

Hillary Rodham was born in Chicago on October 26, 1947, to Dorothy and Hugh Rodham. Her father began as a salesman and built up his own textile business. Her mother was a full-time homemaker and parent.

The family moved to Park Ridge, Illinois, in 1950, a suburban town of "good schools, good churches, and good neighborhoods," and everything about "their life style could have been lifted straight out of an Ozzie and Harriet sitcom" (Radcliffe 1993, 32). By Hillary's account, it was an idyllic childhood and adolescence, defined by a warm, supportive family, friends, and wholesome activities. In short, her childhood was much less difficult than her future husband's.

Education played an important role in the Rodham family. Her father was a first-generation American of Welsh descent, born and raised in the coal-mining region of Scranton, Pennsylvania. During the Depression he worked in the mines, but managed to attend Pennsylvania State University on a football scholarship. He was apparently quite aware of what that opportunity had meant to him in later life, and that recognition found expression in the emphasis in the Rodham house on working hard, doing your best, and making the most of your opportunities.

Dorothy Rodham didn't attend college as a young adult, but she later studied at a local college after her children were older. She apparently felt the lack of a formal education and was determined that her daughter would not be similarly undereducated (Warner 1993, 13). Dorothy Rodham recalls trying to instill a love of learning for its own sake; Hillary recalls her parents telling her that "it was my obligation to use my mind."

Hillary's mother and father focused much energy on their family. Though occasionally absent, Hugh Rodham was a devoted father. Hillary recalls her mother staying up late at night to help her with her homework, making sure she finished what she had to finish and always helping with good ideas. She recalls her father telling her that he would love her no matter what she did, even if he might not approve of specific behavior. Summing up her childhood she says, "You just can't replace that kind of drop-dead stability, it's just the best parents can give" (Radcliffe 1993, 260).

HILLARY RODHAM'S CHARACTER

How did Hillary's ambition, talents, ideals, and relationships evolve as she passed from childhood to adolescence and on into adulthood? Does her character complement her husband's? If so, how?

Ambition

Critical to Hillary's development, the stability of the Rodham family may well have been one of the traits that Bill Clinton was drawn to. This stability, however, was not the exclusive psychological current operating in the Rodham household. Hillary Clinton recalls that neither parent encouraged her any less because she was a girl. One of the strongest messages that her father conveyed to her was that "life is hard out there" (Radcliffe 1993, 259), and he tried to prepare her for it by strongly encouraging her to excel. Hillary Clinton recalls, "My parents set high expectations for me and were rarely satisfied." When she brought home a good grade, her father would respond, "Must have been an easy assignment" (Radcliffe 1993, 16). When she brought home a good report card, her father was not impressed and said, "You must go to an easy school" (Radcliffe 1993, 37). This competitive training extended into other areas as well.

> Hillary's parents, *driven by their desire* that she have the best possible education, urged her to excel in sports as well as in the three R's. If at first she did not succeed in slamming baseballs, her parents insisted that she try again.... After church on Sunday there was *grueling* baseball practice, they subjected her to curveball after curveball until she could finally slam the old horsehide as well as any of the boys." (Radcliffe 1993, 34, emphasis mine).

Hillary responded to her parents' attempts to foster her competitiveness by excelling. Her list of high school accomplishments is as long as her husband's: Junior class vice president, gym leader, and recipient of a science award, she was also involved in the class council, the class newspaper, the girls' athletic association, the National Honor Society, the pep club, speech activities and debate, a spring musical, the cultural values committee, the organizations committee, and a variety show. An A student in the top 5 percent of her class, Hillary was voted most likely to succeed. Her brother Tony recalls that his sister was lots of fun when she wasn't studying, "but she was always studying" (Radcliffe 1993, 39).

In the Rodham family, natural talents, however abundant, were not taken for granted. Hard work, focus, and a determination to excel, even if you were already doing well, were the lessons her family taught; here as elsewhere, Hillary Rodham was an excellent student. Like her husband, Hillary Rodham's talents provided a sturdy vehicle for her ambitions.

What were her ambitions? At Wellesley, Hillary Rodham was as she had been in high school: serious and focused, with a wry sense of humor. She was elected as a representative to student government and, in her junior year, president of the student government. She was involved in many campus and political issues: eliminating irrelevant courses, increasing the number of minority students at the school, relaxing parental restrictions, helping poor students in the community, and organizing and taking part in pro-civil rights and antiwar demonstrations. Like her future husband, she was very involved in the many activities she took part in. However, unlike her future husband's activities, hers seemed not to revolve primarily around *campus* politics. Hillary Rodham's ambitions were to do something important and something good, two aspirations compatible with a career in public service and government.

At Yale Law School a number of classmates recalled that her political ambition was plain and that she did not dissemble about her desire to be an important political figure (Bruck 1994, 60). Another of her classmates recalled, "Most of my friends and I were always agonizing, filled with self-doubt—you know, 'Why are we here? Where are we going?' Hillary had no self-doubt. She knew she wanted to be influential and prominent" (Bruck 1994, 60).

Character Integrity

Her industriousness and ambitions confirmed, what then were the major ideals that shaped Hillary Rodham's aspirations?

The Rodhams were Methodist and the church was a tangible part of their lives. Hillary Rodham was active in her church youth group throughout her adolescence and, through that program, spent time in Chicago with inner-city youth and also was part of an effort to organize baby-sitting brigades to help look after the children of migrant workers. The Methodist church was founded on the idea of individual and social responsibility. Its founder, John Wesley, mixed a gospel of social reform with one stressing individual hard work and personal productivity. Hillary Rodham seemed to fit this dual model so well that one of her ministers called her "a model of Methodism" (Maraniss 1995, 432).

The Rodhams were Republican, as was Hillary until she gradually moved politically left as an undergraduate at Wellesley and as a law student at Yale. Some sense of her political trajectory can be gained by knowing that in 1964 she worked for Barry Goldwater. In 1965, as a freshman at Wellesley, she was president of the Young Republican club. In 1966 she wrote to a friend calling New York a "saved city" because Liberal Republican John Lindsay had been elected mayor and added, "Look how liberal I'm becoming" (Maraniss 1995, 255). By her junior year she was working with poor black children in Roxbury, Massachusetts, taking part in protests against the Vietnam war, and working for the insurgent candidacy of Senator Eugene McCarthy. 1972 found her in Texas helping to organize the McGovern presidential candidacy.

What explains this shift? In part it is a direct heritage of her family and church. The former stressed working hard at what you do; the latter framed that message with a commitment to social responsibility. The times, of course, also played a role. Especially at elite schools like Wellesley, the 1960s were a vibrant time, alive with intellectual, social, and personal ferment. The message of John Wesley, which Hillary Rodham has quoted on many occasions, was to do all the good you can, by all the means you can, in all the ways you can, in all the places you can, at all the times you can, to all the people you can, as long as you can (Radcliffe 1993, 180; Maraniss 1995, 433). It was a message that fit in well with Hillary Rodham's character, talents, ideals, and ambitions. But it also fit in well with the social activism of the school and the period. In short, the 1960s were well-suited for Hillary Rodham, a near perfect fit between the times and the person.

During her college and law school studies, Hillary Rodham's desire to "do good" increasingly steered her toward a career in government and public service. But her ambition went beyond merely doing good in the abstract; she committed herself to following through on her ideals. She chose Yale Law School partly because it would allow her to think about social policy (Bruck 1994, 60). She sought not only to champion children's rights, but to learn about children's development. She worked in the Yale Child Study Center and with lawyer-psychologist Joe Goldstein and psychiatrist Jay Katz—who, with Anna Freud, were involved in writing the seminal study *Beyond the Best Interests of the Child*. Hillary Rodham had strong convictions and she worked hard at translating them into action.

Self-Confidence

Hillary Rodham's straightforward understanding of what she wished to accomplish in her life parallels her husband's clear ambitions. Although this is not in and of itself exceptional for someone so smart and purposeful, and someone trained at an elite school like Yale, one aspect of Hillary Rodham's character does stand out: her confidence in herself, in the positions she developed, and in the work she did.

It is a trait that began to develop early. Her mother recalled that Hillary "always valued herself highly" (Radcliffe 1993, 40). Betsy Johnson Ebling, a childhood friend, recalled, "At a time when all of us were checking a lot of personalities out, she was always very confident about who she was and where she was going" (Radcliffe 1993, 36). Another high school friend, Ellen Press Murdoch, recalled, "She was never subject to peer pressure. . . . She wasn't the type to lie awake nights worrying if anybody liked her" (Radcliffe 1993, 36–37). Her teachers also recall this aspect of her character. Kenneth Reese, who served as student council coordinator, recalls, "She was bright and had strong convictions and she was able to follow through on them" (Warner 1993, 25). Gerald Baker, Hillary Rodham's high school government teacher, recalled that he used to tease her about going to Wellesley and becoming a liberal: "she used to get irritated at me and say things like 'I'm smart' and 'I know where I stand on the issues and that's not going to change' " (Radcliffe 1993, 52). A fellow law school student commented, "Hillary was animated by her sense of what was right . . . she had this religious zeal" (Bruck 1994, 61).

This combination of intelligence, focus, and sustained and serious hard work underlie Hillary Clinton's history of successful accomplishment. Her religious values—the *injunction* to do good—shaped her political and social commitments. Hillary Clinton has said of the difference between herself and her husband that "Bill's desire to be in public life was much more specific than my desire to do good" (Sheehy 1992, 215).

The mix of intelligence, focus, and a strong desire to do good coupled with strong self-confidence has potentially serious consequences for someone who wishes to yield political or policy power. The view that one knows better than others—period—can lead to imperiousness and cause trouble in one's relations with others. It has done so in Hillary Rodham Clinton's case.

In 1969, Hillary Rodham and her friends decided that a student from their group should address their class at the commencement to be held in a few days. The president of the college first refused, but then agreed, to allow Hillary Rodham to address the class after the invited speaker, Republican Senator Edward Brooke. Rodham later characterized Brooke's speech as "a defense of Richard Nixon . . . a pro forma commencement speech"; she was "outraged and insulted" (Radcliffe 1993, 81). According to her friendly biographer Judith Warner, Rodham told the audience that Brooke's remarks "represented just the kind of disconnected irrelevant thinking that had led the country astray for four years" and continued on extemporaneously for a few moments, "rebuking Brooke" (Warner 1993, 38–39; see also Maraniss 1995, 257–58).

Whatever one thinks of the substance of her remarks, they do display a strong sense of certitude regarding the correctness of her views. Her brother Hugh says of her, "Hillary is convinced the way she does things is the right way" (Sheehy 1992, 145). Bev Lindsey, wife of President Clinton's closest personal adviser, has said of her that she "will not revisit a decision . . . she is very sure of herself." This tendency has led one reporter who interviewed many associates for a story about the first lady to say, "In the end, the sureness about her own judgment—at its extreme, a sense that she alone is wise—is probably Hillary's cardinal trait. When one talks to her friends and her husband, one hears it described in various ways, but they are all facets of the same insular unbending characteristic" (Bruck 1994, 91).

Relatedness

How does Hillary Clinton relate to others? Does she move toward or away from them? One clue comes from her parents, who "didn't socialize with the rest of the neighborhood" (Radcliffe 1993, 30). While Hillary lived in a neighborhood with lots of children and spent lots of time with them, her family tended to be insular (Radcliffe 1993, 31).

Hillary was able to maintain her strong sense of self even as her peers worried about being popular. She was a young girl who, according to her childhood friends, "knew what she was about long before other girls her age" (Radcliffe 1993, 36). She was involved with others, but on her own terms.

In high school, her reputation as serious, focused, and hard working extended to her relationships with others. "She was the one who tried to keep everyone on track during group efforts, and when she wasn't successful was visibly frustrated. 'Don't you want to be good?' she might plead in a rehearsal when everybody else was horsing around" (Radcliffe 1993, 38). That lament might easily be read by others as asking, "Don't you want to be more like me?" Her seriousness of purpose was clearly not always infectious and her coolness toward those who did not share it may have caused her to be dubbed by some "Sister Frigidaire" (Bruck 1994, 63). Others recall her as having many friends in this period and being "very hardworking at friendship" (Radcliffe 1993, 39). Though apparently contradictory, these two aspects of her relationships are not necessarily inconsistent.

Hillary Rodham appears to have been able from an early age to work independently to develop herself according to her own views of her interests and purposes. She did not move toward people in the way her husband did, but neither did she move away from them. Her psychology suggests that she is a person who stands apart from others, comfortable with herself. Such a person does not move away from people but finds it troubling always to move toward them and is able and willing, if necessary, to move against them.

This aspect of her personality merits comment. James Carville, a self-described "big Hillary fan," has said, "You could see that this was someone who could be tough if she wanted to. . . . Hillary won't run you down for fun, and she won't run into a ditch to avoid scratching your fender, but if you are blocking something we need to get done you'll get run over in a hurry" (Matalin and Carville 1994, 87–88). While there is some testimony to Hillary Rodham's openness as she began to deepen her understandings of social and political life at Wellesley, once her views had begun to congeal, she held them in characteristically strong fashion (e.g., Warner 1993, 30, 34). She could be "cold, aloof, cuttingly impatient at times—friends knew she didn't suffer fools" (Radcliffe 1993, 65).[12] Ruth Adams, then president of Wellesley, told the *Boston Globe* that "she was not always easy to deal with if you were disagreeing with her . . . she could be very insistent" (Radcliffe 1993, 65–66). One Wellesley classmate recalled, "She wasn't the same as other people, in that everyone was usually more or less of something, and Hillary was quite unique. She had a very strong personality. She wasn't everybody's cup of tea" (Warner 1993, 41). Similar observations were made of her at Yale. Alan Bersin, a fellow student, recalls, "Hillary was intent in her likes and dislikes. She never suffered fools happily. She was direct, she could be sharp, but she also could be very warm to people she liked and trusted" (Warner 1993, 54).

The combination of strong views, strong self-confidence in them, a capacity to stand her ground, and an ability to do what she feels necessary to accomplish her good purposes has buttressed views of her as tough and hard on others. One illustration of this is her temper, which matches that of her husband but often combines scorn with angry outbursts (Brummett 1994, 41, 114–15). Scorn is dismissive of others in the long term, whereas anger leaves room for later reconciliation. A colleague at the Rose law firm where she worked has observed, "She has a temper like you would not believe. It's not so much that she screams—it's more the tone in her voice, the body language, the facial expressions. It's the 'Wrath of Khan.' " (Bruck 1994, 66).

This style has continued in the White House. At a meeting called to discuss health care,

> Some of those who attended found her intimidating—hard to argue with and uninterested in the points they made. Mrs. Clinton's style was very direct. She told people straight out what she thought. She'd say, "You're right," "You're wrong," "That's the way to proceed," "No, that's not right." . . . Mrs. Clinton displayed a certain impatience. And her humor was biting. (Drew 1994, 194–95)

Some have seen in these traits a tendency to assign people credit or importance based on their capacity to further what she sees as the right thing to do. When troubles began to mount for the nomination of the Clintons' good friend Lani Guinier, Guinier writes,

> It languished without either emotional or logistical support from my friends in the White House. I saw Hillary Rodham Clinton in the West Wing. . . . She breezed by me with a causal "Hi, Kiddo." When someone tried to tell her that we were in the White House to strategize on my nomination, she turned slightly and said, "Oh" . . . and, to no one in particular, announced, "I'm thirty minutes late for lunch." [Since that time] I have not had any communication with the President or First Lady, although I did get two identical, machine signed White House Christmas cards in December. (Guinier 1994, 43–44)

Jan Piercy, an old friend of Hillary's from Wellesley, nominated by the Clinton administration to a position at the World Bank, sees the same trait somewhat differently, "Hillary uses different people for different purposes" (Bruck 1994, 66).

The picture that emerges of Hillary Clinton's interpersonal worldview is one divided into two camps: those who hold the right view and those who don't. Coupled with her own sense of virtue—which, like her husband's, is the foundation of her idealized self-image—this has led to the tendency to experience herself as besieged by enemies. She doubtless has many enemies because of her political efforts, but her own psychology and perceptions play an important role as well.[13] She "has long been inclined toward bunker mentality. She tolerates critics much less graciously than her husband. . . . She defines morality on the legacy of the issues of her youth . . . and assigns partisan evil to most detraction" (Brummett 1994, 244). Ellen Brantley, whose husband is the editor of the *Arkansas Times* and who was appointed by Clinton to be a judge, said of her, "She always disliked the press. Her attitude is 'We're the ones who are trying to accomplish some good, we're doing the best we can, we're on the *right* side—so stop taking potshots at us. And, especially, don't raise anything during a campaign' " (Bruck 1994, 67).

Like her husband, Hillary Clinton has arrived at the view that it is others who are primarily responsible for her misfortunes. She seems to believe that no matter what she does she can't win. When a reporter was working on a story on her and the "politics of meaning,"

> It was suggested that for Hillary Rodham Clinton, a career liberal activist and former seeker of ecstatic living, to sound the call for a return to traditional ethics will strike some people as a bit much. . . . The First Lady jumps hard on the point. "That's irrelevant to me," she snapped back. "I know that no matter what I did—if I did nothing, if I spent my entire day totally disengaged from what was going on around me—I'd be criticized for that. I mean it's a no-win deal, no matter what I do, or try to do. (Kelly 1993e, 65)

THE CLINTONS AS POLITICAL PARTNERS

The Clintons are two highly intelligent people who want to make their mark and who share some definite ideas about how to do so. Each has a distinctive psychology: Bill Clinton is smart, unfocused, and charming; Hillary Rodham Clinton is smart, very focused, but less able and willing than her husband to move toward others.[14] In these ways, each provides some more of what the other might benefit from having.

Intelligence aside, both share certain characteristics. Both are very ambitious and confident in themselves and the policies and approaches they propose. How, then, do these similarities and differences affect the Clinton presidency?

Two Psychologies, One Presidency

One of the major characteristics of the Clinton presidency has been its substantial policy ambitions. A question naturally arises as to Hillary Clinton's role. Is she, as has often been alleged, the more pragmatic of the two? Or is she, as has also been alleged, the "real" liberal?

This question cannot be answered adequately at the level of political ideology, but rather is better addressed at the level of ambition. Here the data are quite consistent: Hillary Clinton's ambition trumps her husband's.

Together, two people with strong ambition and high self-confidence will multiply each partner's ambition, not moderate it.

Senior presidential advisers suggest that it was Hillary Clinton who came to Washington with a very ambitious view of what the administration should try to accomplish (Drew 1994). At a meeting of the entire cabinet and senior White House staff at Camp David on January 30–31, 1992, the discussion turned to what items should be in the president's agenda. Some cabinet officials suggested limiting the large agenda because many of the items were difficult. However, Hillary Clinton "gave a ringing speech in favor of just the opposite—doing everything. 'Why are we here if we don't go for it?' she asked at the end" (Woodward 1994, 110–11).

It was Hillary Clinton who championed the large, mismanaged, and, many believed, unnecessary government program to purchase vaccines for children (see chapter 14). She was also the chief architect and strategist for the administration's complex health-care proposal, which went down in defeat. Early in its development, a debate on a "bare-bones" plan (labeled "A") and a comprehensive health-care package (labeled "B") was held. After the presentation, an open discussion took place in which everyone was supposed to have the chance to raise objections. Earlier the Clintons had both raised numerous questions about the bare-bones plan, which indicated that Clinton "was not thinking small" (Woodward 1994, 199). Many at the meeting wondered whether such a plan could ever meet Clinton's goals. Perhaps not surprisingly, in these circumstances, "None of Clinton's senior economic advisors endorsed the bare-bones, Plan A, nor did they directly challenge the arguments for the comprehensive Plan B. Instead, the skeptics praised Plan B, qualified with escape hatches, such as 'if the numbers work out,' or, 'so long as it doesn't divert resources from other things we want to do' " (Woodward 1994, 199). Many Treasury and National Economic Council members were aware that the numbers of the health-care plan didn't add up. They warned that the plan contained "fatal flaws" that could cause "real-world havoc and potential disasters" in the nation's health care system (Pear 1994f). However, "because it was Hillary's project, everyone was nervous about criticizing it" (Drew 1994, 195; see also 287).

The problem of who will say no to the president if he errs is here compounded by the problem of who will say no to his wife. Given her capacity to be withering to those who disagree with her, her tendency to hold on to her anger, and her obvious power in the administration, Hillary Clinton's psychology and views are pretty much unchecked. A congressional aide who has dealt with her has said her staff is "terrified of her . . .

232 ★ GROWING UP, COMING OF AGE

they are very loyal . . . but they are scared to death . . . she will fire them if
they tell her the truth" (Bruck 1994, 88). This problem is apparently not
confined to her staff. Her decision to lead the U.S. delegation to the United
Nations Conference on Women in Beijing in September 1995 "promoted
much hand-wringing among administration officials who are worried about
the political risks posed by her wish. . . . [Because] of all the powerful
people in the White House, there is probably no one—not even the President—to whom aides like less to say no" (Purdum 1995d).

Hillary Clinton's Pragmatism

A 1993 article in the *Wall Street Journal* entitled "Beyond Feminism and
French Fries: Portrait of First Family Debunks the Accepted Stereotypes"
argued against the accepted view of Hillary Clinton as the "Dragon Lady
of the Liberal Left" and pushed the argument that she is the more "pragmatic" of the two. As an illustration it offered the fact that she "was the
one responsible for keeping the word abortion out of the health care
package" (Birnbaum and Perry 1993). While this is technically true, the
words that were in the plan—"pregnancy related services"—did, according to Hillary Clinton, cover abortion (Bruck 1994, 89). Would she
have jeopardized passage of the whole plan for that one point? This seems
unlikely.

Hillary Clinton's pragmatism must be viewed in the context of her
policy ambitions and goals. An early report on the developing health-care
plan noted, "Mrs. Clinton and Ira G. Magaziner . . . have been moving
steadily toward bolder, more complex and more sweeping proposals . . .
even as some members of Congress urge them to simplify and scale down
their plan" (Pear 1993f).[15] The resulting health-care plan was "breathtak-
ing in its sweep, its complexity, and its ambition" (Pear 1993c). Paul
Elwood, the "father" of the managed-care concept on which the Clinton
plan was based, said "even those of us who have spent our careers pursuing
health care reform cannot fully comprehend it" (1993). The administration
health-care plan was a vehicle for an unprecedented government role in a
wide array of health-care choices, including the types of plans offered, the
services provided, the financing of the plan, the regulation of medical
training (including caps on the number of specialists trained), and mandated targets for the number of medical training slots on the basis of
ethnic, gender, and racial categories. Viewed against this backdrop, Hillary
Clinton's pragmatism was essentially a pragmatism of small compromises
in the service of very large ends. An assessment of pragmatism, even in
connection with this one bill, requires more than a look at one provision.

Becoming More Alike

Over time, a couple's individual psychologies develop in relation to each other. Couples learn from each other. Each partner's behavior can affect the other's psychology. Romantic or other fantasies can be realized or frustrated, ambitions developed or thwarted, or trust deepened or betrayed. Couples can come to resemble each other in certain basic ways.

That is precisely what has happened with the Clintons. Surprisingly, given the strength of Hillary Clinton's psychology, the direction of the change has been that she has become more like her husband than the reverse. To be sure, although she has learned to soften publicly what others have viewed as hard edges, Hillary Clinton remains a fiercely independent person (Bruck 1994, 66, 79). She is focused and steadfastedly committed to the basic values and interests that have informed her ambitions. She has spoken out on the importance of finding meaning in life that goes beyond success (Kelly 1993e). Her push for a government program to buy vaccines, for example, is consistent with her longstanding interests.

Yet in other ways she has come to resemble her husband—in their shared sense of the basic purity of their motivations and idealized view of their behavior, in their conviction that, because their intentions are good, they ultimately know what is right and best; and in their belief that others who don't share their views are driven by base motives or, at best, misguided. They have also come to share a view that they can't win; that no matter how good their motives, no matter how competent their policies, others—special interests, Republicans, the far Right, journalists, commentators, some segments of the public—are all, at one time or another, out to get them.

And there is some truth in this belief. The Clintons have opponents, and even enemies. But the Clintons' own behavior has substantially contributed to their problems. This can be seen clearly in what is perhaps the most surprising way that the Clintons have come to resemble each other: their belief that they can, *and should,* have it both ways and the erosion of ideals and values that maintaining that view represents.

Blurring the Boundaries

Hillary Clinton has over the years made use of her role as an independent lawyer to further the Clintons' personal and political interests. As a Rose law firm partner, she worked on several very sensitive issues that were extremely important to her husband as governor. One of these was a desegregation case brought against the Little Rock school system. The judge, Henry Woods, appointed a three-person committee to try to resolve the suit, naming Hillary Clinton as counsel to that committee. By all accounts she was instrumental in fashioning an agreement that allowed the schools to remain segregated but allocated increased funds for minority schools, on the theory that this would make them more attractive to white students, thus ending the segregation. The cost of this settlement was $73 million, a figure significantly lower than the amount the court might have ordered had the parties not reached agreement. The judge rejected this agreement, however, arguing that it would only serve to increase segregation. He was also upset that several million dollars were to be allocated for legal fees. His order was appealed and the appellate court upheld the agreement (Bruck 1994, 70; Oakley 1994, 349–51).

What is extremely odd in this incident is that Hillary Clinton apparently asked the judge who had appointed her to the committee to let her argue *his* side of the appeal, *against the very agreement she had been instrumental in fashioning.* The judge, a close friend of Hillary Clinton's, demurred because he felt she could not argue it adequately, having been so instrumental in forging the agreement. Put another way,

> As counsel to the committee (and advisor to the judge), Hillary was arguably in a position of conflict, since she had a political interest (her husband's) in achieving a settlement . . . she then assumed a role far beyond her appointed one and became a critical facilitator in achieving agreement. . . . To have then sought to argue against (ostensibly) the very agreement she had helped mediate was almost breathtakingly audacious. (Bruck 1994, 70)

Hillary Clinton played a similar dual, protective role in working on a case representing the state's Public Service Commission in a financial dispute over Arkansas's disengagement from the construction of a costly nuclear power generating station in 1985–86. Here again her husband had a strong interest in getting this matter settled. The potential conflict of interest in this case "provoked questions even from Clinton's allies" (Maraniss 1995, 429). Clinton said he needed his wife on the case because "anyone else would mangle it," thus sidestepping the propriety of Hillary Clinton, a private lawyer, watching out for her husband's political interests (Maraniss 1995, 429).

In another instance of blurred boundaries, Hillary Clinton wrote to a top state regulator, Beverly Bassett Schaffer, a personal friend of the Clintons who had been appointed by Governor Clinton, on behalf of her client, Madison Guaranty, asking state regulators appointed by her husband to make a favorable ruling for her client, James McDougal, with whom she and her husband were business partners in the Whitewater Development Corporation (Engelberg and Gerth 1994). Just a few weeks before that letter was written, McDougal had raised money for Governor Clinton, "to help relieve the Clinton family of a $50,000 personal debt that the Clintons would have otherwise had trouble paying" (Gerth and Engelberg 1993). Moreover, Schaffer had before her appointment as the top state regulator worked as an attorney for Madison Guaranty "and had approved the stock sale in the face of her own prior knowledge that Madison had failed to comply with Federal land-sale laws" (Gerth and Engelberg 1993).

During his years as governor, Clinton personally set up four funds and borrowed hundreds of thousands of dollars from a small Arkansas bank run by Maurice Smith, a close aid of his, to finance his legislative proposals. Clinton's aides solicited funds to pay off these debts from some of the state's most wealthy and powerful political interests, including Tyson Foods, utility companies, and savings and loan associations. Frank Hickingbotham, owner of TCBY Yogurt, where Hillary Clinton served on the board of directors, contributed the single largest donation, $25,000, to retire these debts. At the time the Clintons were personally liable for mortgages on the Whitewater development of over $200,000. Betsey Wright, Clinton's chief of staff at the time, said, "These were not slush funds . . . these people contributed to specific programs that they believed in and that they had a stake in. It may look clumsy to you now, and it may look sticky to you now, but we really did try to find ways to disclose it and make it comply with the laws that were on the books" (Labaton 1994c).

In these and similar situations, Hillary Clinton viewed her own motives as

> practical—she was looking for solutions—but there was also a sanctimo-
> nious aspect to it that tended to blind her and her husband to the appear-
> ance of what they were doing. . . . Hillary dismissed those who questioned
> her as quibblers who did not appreciate that what she was doing was for
> the greater good. She framed her actions in moral terms. Beyond all the
> particulars, in the grand scheme of right and wrong, she felt with almost
> religious conviction that she was on the side of right. (Maraniss 1995,
> 431)

Hillary Clinton, paralleling her husband, appears to have developed her own boundary problems. His seem largely a result of his failure to develop strong internal boundaries, coupled with a sense of entitlement. Hers appears to stem from her strong self-confidence in the correctness of whatever she does. In both cases, the results are the same: a tendency to not want to be bound by limits that apply to others.

Ideals versus Politics

Like her husband, Hillary Clinton has often faced the dilemma of having to choose between her (and her husband's) political interests and ideals. Sometimes the Clintons' political interests have been in direct conflict with Hillary Clinton's longstanding personal commitments. While she has long been associated with children's causes, Arkansas was sued in 1991 for underfunding the state's child welfare system. The problem had been studied repeatedly during Clinton's terms as governor; more funding was promised but never realized. Once the lawsuit was filed, while Clinton was considering whether to run for the presidency, Governor Clinton lobbied the legislature extensively to fund a settlement for the lawsuit, which it did. Five days later, in a move reminiscent of his wife's attempt to argue against the desegregation agreement she had forged, Clinton's administration appealed the lawsuit which, had he been successful, would also have nullified the settlement he had forged (Bruck 1994, 78; see also Brummett 1994, 50).

While Bill Clinton has developed a reputation for telling people on both sides of an issue that he agrees with them, Hillary Clinton is widely seen as extremely direct about her opinions. On occasion, however, she appears to have adopted a form of her husband's approach. When Martin Lancaster, a Democratic Congressman from North Carolina who had been friends with the Clintons for many years, learned of the possible tax on tobacco to support the health-care plan, he argued that other health-risk items like alcohol should also be taxed so that the burden would not fall solely on tobacco growers. As the vote approached, representatives of the tobacco-growing states had not publicly voiced their position but were privately holding out for more widely shared taxes. At that point Hillary Clinton called Lancaster to indicate that she understood and agreed with his position that one item should not bear the full weight of the plan's taxes. Lancaster asked for and received a guarantee from her (and later from the president), and he in turn produced the votes of all the tobacco state representatives. However, when the health-care plan was unveiled, it recommended a seventy-five-cent-per-pack tax on tobacco and a 1 percent tax on large companies that didn't join the health-care collectives, leaving tobacco as the major source of tax revenues. When Lancaster complained to Hillary Clinton that she had double crossed him, "she replied that the administration had lived up to its pledge. 'Tobacco has not been singled out,' she said. The conversation was on the phone and Lancaster wondered whether she had made her assertion with a straight face. Hillary [said] she had not been specific, and she believed people often heard what they wanted to hear" (Woodward 1994, 294).

The problems of means and ends arise continuously in politics and are especially relevant for those who truly believe themselves to be acting in the best interests of others. In chairing the health care task force, Hillary Clinton chose to conduct its deliberations in private. Yet she organized a number of public health-care forums that were ostensibly to collect ideas. Whether this purpose was realized is open to question. At one such public function entitled "Conversation on Health: A Dialogue with the American People,"

> there was a near unanimity that illustrated the limits of public involvement in the White House health care project. The hearings . . . appear as public events but are actually by invitation only, with panelists and audience members selected from a list put together by the foundation [which had proposed the idea of the hearings to the White House] with at least some guidance from the White House. (Kelly 1993d).

Ira Magaziner wrote a memo to then-candidate Bill Clinton about health care in January 1992, which he said was "very similar to where the Clinton plan is today [before its public unveiling]. . . . Some of the explicit mechanisms didn't come until later but it was very close" (Bruck 1994, 85). Alan Enthoven, a consultant to the health-care group, said, "I think what they were doing was creating the illusion of participation. Yes, there were five hundred [participants], but there was really a core group who wrote the thing and there's little evidence that anything changed. I guess the more they heard the more sure they were right they became" (Bruck 1994, 85).

The tactic of public consultation on an already developed policy had its roots in Hillary Clinton's public meetings on education in Arkansas, her first public statewide role. The Educational Standards Committee she chaired held seventy-five public meetings taking testimony "at the same time that it prepared the public for a *largely predesigned* set of reforms, from mandatory kindergarten to smaller class sizes in elementary school to competence tests for teacher and students" (Maraniss 1995, 411, emphasis mine). One Clinton biographer has described this process as going "through the pretense of listening to people" (Oakley 1994, 282). Kai Erickson, then head of the Arkansas Education Association (which opposed the teacher competency tests), thought the meetings were designed to look like an exhaustive fact-finding process, but in fact were political—"basically getting people to agree there was a problem, so that the solutions already devised would be accepted" (Bruck 1994, 68). One might agree with all or most of the committee's policy proposals, while still questioning why the process had to be presented as something it apparently wasn't.

Against Greed, For Their Own Wealth

During the 1992 campaign Hillary Clinton criticized the Reagan years as the decade of greed. She has said of herself, "I'm not interested in corporate law . . . my life is too short to spend it making money at some anonymous firm" (Radcliffe 1993, 79). Yet there have been a number of inconsistencies between her stated position and behavior, beginning with the fact that when Hillary Clinton went to Little Rock, she "seemed to have no trouble embracing the acquisitive and competitive corporate life that she had once repudiated" (Maraniss 1995, 369).

During the health-care debate, Hillary Clinton made a number of strong attacks on "people who make their money out of the current status quo" (Clymer 1993d). Yet during her years in the Rose law firm, she made a substantial amount of money doing just that in the health-care field. In 1989, Beverly Enterprises, the nation's largest nursing home company, was in serious financial trouble. The Rose law firm helped to put together a leveraged buyout that took advantage of a 1986 tax reform loophole by using government-issued bonds to finance the sale of Beverly's nursing homes to a nonprofit shell company fronting for profit-making companies. The shell company put up no money, while Beverly came away with over $20 million in profit, all financed by the government. As one reporter who broke the story said, "The deal . . . was precisely the sort of arrangement that the future First Lady would have called a health-care rip off . . . and a district judge who scrutinized the transaction called the profits unconscionable" (Kelly 1994, 31). Legal and financial experts have estimated that the Rose Law firm netted up to $500,000 on this complex deal, "resulting in hefty bonuses for the law firm partners, including Hillary Clinton" (Oakley 1994, 411). The deal might never have come to light had several local school districts not successfully sued over the loss of tax revenues involved in selling all the assets to a "not-for-profit" company.[16]

In response to questions raised about this possible conflict of interest in 1986 by Clinton's Republican opponent in the gubernatorial race, Frank White, the Clinton campaign ridiculed him for picking on the governor's wife.[17] The Rose law firm issued a memo stating that fees from the case had been segregated and were distributed to members other than Hillary Clinton, so that she in fact received no direct or indirect benefit from them (Maraniss 1995, 429). Actually, this was not wholly accurate. As a partner at the law firm she had been part of a move to oust its onetime chairman C. Joseph Giroir, Jr.—"a move that coincided with changes in the compensation system at Rose that particularly benefited her (intangibles such as 'civic involvement' and 'reputation' would carry much more weight than before" (Bruck 1994, 70). Moreover, the segregation of funds that Hillary Clinton helped earn doing the state's business was apparently a response after the fact. During the 1992 primaries, a memo emerged that Hillary Clinton had written to her law firm partners in 1986—the same year that Frank White was making his allegations. The memo said that

> she hadn't technically violated her rule against profiting from public funds; a private company was paying the bills, not the Arkansas treasury. Still, she added in the memo, she planned to return the money she had received in the past for the bond business—it totaled $10,000 or so—and she wouldn't be accepting her cut in the future. (Goldman et al. 1994, 197–98)

At first the campaign consultants thought the memo exculpatory, showing how far Hillary Clinton was willing to go to be above reproach. However,

> the problem was that neither she nor anyone else had told the campaign that it existed. The distinction between the two kinds of money wasn't clear to the handlers, not at first. The potential damage was. Out in public Hillary was saying she had "never, ever" taken money from state business—and here, in her own words, that maybe once upon a time she had accepted just a teensy bit.[18] (Goldman et al. 1994, 198)

Explanations

Hillary Clinton's responses to questions raised about her behavior, at times, resemble those of her husband. This seems particularly the case when she is called upon to give a straightforward explanation of what appears to be self-interested activities or conduct. The most glaring inconsistency between Hillary Clinton's criticisms against the decade of greed and her own behavior was reflected in the stories of her $100,000 profit in the very risky cattle futures market (Gerth 1994b). Her response to that unfolding story and to aspects of the Whitewater investigation parallel her husband's response to the draft controversy: tell some, but not all of the relevant facts; put those facts in the best light; plead for understanding in recalling events that transpired long ago and are in any event irrelevant to the important and good work she is doing; and, finally, when all else fails, passively acknowledge some errors.

The man who helped engineer the $100,000 profit three weeks before Clinton took office in 1978 was a Clinton friend, James B. Blair, then outside counsel to Tyson Foods, the enormous poultry company that was regulated in a number of domains by the state. During Clinton's tenure in Arkansas, Tyson Foods benefited from a variety of state actions, including a $9 million government loan, the placement of company executives on important state boards, and favorable decisions on environmental issues. The cattle future trades were placed through an office (Refco) run by Robert L. (Red) Bone, who had a history of regulatory and legal difficulties stemming in part from his alleged allocation of profits to favored customers while sticking other, less-favored clients with losses (Labaton 1994d). While Hillary Clinton was making a $100,000 profit in her Refco account, another smaller account she had opened with another firm experienced minor losses.

The trades first became an issue during the campaign, when reporters asked about the source of the Clintons' $60,000 down payment on a house. The campaign initially traced the source of the funds to an investment, later releasing a statement in Hillary Clinton's name that said the money had come from "our savings and a gift from my parents." When the story of the trades broke on March 17, the same spokespeople amended their statement to say the money had come from savings and the commodity investments.

At first the Clintons described Blair only as an adviser and claimed that Hillary had learned to trade by reading the *Wall Street Journal,* but on April 10, they amended that to acknowledge that most of the trades were in fact placed by Blair to Bone, who was his good friend (Hershey 1994). Since Hillary Clinton's was a "non-discretionary" account, the placing of trades by anyone other than her was technically a violation of Security and Exchange Commission rules. Records also show that she received preferential treatment in the form of not having to put down deposit money to cover her trades (Engelberg 1994c). Others were not given this option (Maraniss 1995, 372).

At first the White House would not disclose the amount of the initial investment, saying they had been searching for the old check stubs. However, the White House had these records well before they were released;

they had been shown to a reporter who was not given permission to copy them (Dowd 1994b). Questions also arose regarding the closing of the account. At first White House officials indicated that Hillary Clinton closed the account because she was pregnant and found the high-risk trading too nerve-racking during the final stages of her pregnancy. Yet in mid-April it was revealed that she kept another commodities account in which she invested $5,000 shortly before her daughter was born in February. A senior White House official described the first account as "inoperative" now (Ifill 1994b). That account produced a $6,498 profit that the Clintons said they had mistakenly failed to report to the IRS.

During the presidential campaign, questions were raised about the Whitewater development deal. The Clintons argued that it was ridiculous to question the propriety of an investment in which they had lost substantial sums. To buttress this view, they released a report prepared by a Denver accounting firm concluding that the Clintons had lost $68,000 on their investment (Engelberg 1994a). The loss incurred by their investment partner, the McDougals, was estimated at $92,000. The lawyer who prepared that report, James Lyons, subsequently revised it to show that the Clintons' total loss was actually $46,635, an error he attributed in a publicly released letter to "interviews and statements made by the Clintons" (Gerth 1994a). The White House never provided a revised figure for the McDougals' actual losses in the venture.

When asked at a news conference about the differing accounts of how much they lost in their Whitewater investment, Hillary Clinton insisted that she and her husband were equally liable for any losses the venture incurred, "and there was no gift in that" (H. Clinton 1994, A12). When she was asked why the Clintons had contributed less than the McDougals she responded that she and her husband gave "whatever money we were requested to give by Jim McDougal" (H. Clinton 1994, A12). However, in July, the first independent accounting of the Whitewater records revealed that the McDougals steadily reduced their partner's indebtedness. Overall the Clintons contributed $42,000, the McDougals $158,000. The Clintons had received far more benefit than they had revealed.

When questioned as to why she had not given the correct information about the nature of her commodity trades, Hillary Clinton blamed the difficulty of recalling things that had happened many years ago and the fact that she didn't have all of the records immediately needed to reconstruct events accurately (H. Clinton 1994, A11). Moreover, she said, "I don't think we gave enough time or focused enough. I have been traveling, and I'm more committed to health care than anything else I do" (H. Clinton 1994, A12).

CONCLUSION

While the question of whether Hillary Clinton and her husband did anything illegal is debatable, these incidents clearly suggest a pattern of behavior that, even if technically legal, raises questions of appropriateness and propriety.

All these circumstances—her work as a private attorney in cases where her position could further her husband's political interests; her involvement in the complex web of professional, public, and private interests that characterize the Beverly nursing home leveraged buyouts, Whitewater, and Madison Guaranty; her incredible "beginner's luck" while trading in futures—create a strong general impression. The *New York Times,* in perhaps its most psychologically insightful editorial on the Clintons, notes,

> The inescapable conclusion is that this couple, early and late, suffered from a thematic insensitivity to the normal rules of conflict of interest. At every turn of their financial life, the then-Governor and First Lady of Arkansas were receiving financial favors from individuals who had something to gain from having friends in high places.... [They] *seemed to have extraordinary indifference to, or difficulty in understanding, the normal division between government and personal interests.* (1994a, emphasis mine)

Once again, boundaries are for others.

Psychologically, the Clintons appear to have come to resemble each other in profound ways. The pioneering psychiatrist Harry Stack Sullivan once said that we are all more alike than otherwise. This theorem appears especially true when applied to two immensely talented, ambitious people, united in purpose, assured of the essential personal, moral, and political correctness of their views, and convinced that they are entitled, for these reasons, to enjoy the fruits of their labors.

IV

THE POLITICAL
CONSEQUENCES OF
CHARACTER

★ ────────────────────────────────────

CHAPTER 12

JUDGMENT AND LEADERSHIP: THE CORE
OF PRESIDENTIAL PERFORMANCE

Why are there such conflicting views of Bill Clinton as a political leader? Surely one reason is that political leaders in general, and Clinton in particular, are controversial figures.[1] Given this, how can we agree on a basis by which leaders can or should be evaluated?

At first glance it would seem obvious that political leaders should be evaluated on their concrete accomplishments. On that basis, no critic could claim that the Clinton presidency is anything other than a rousing success. His direct student loan program, NAFTA, the crime bill, the family leave bill, and others all make up a substantial list of achievements. What then is the problem?

One problem is that all modern presidents have generated a long list of accomplishments. For precisely this reason, we should hesitate before applying "the length of these lists as a yardstick of [a president's] relative success" (Skowronek 1993, 17). Moreover, we can reasonably ask whether Clinton's programs are what the public had in mind regarding its needs when it voted in 1992.

Measuring Clinton's performance solely by the number of his legislative victories tells us very little about how well he has actually accomplished his or the public's purposes. It is too soon to make judgments about the effects of the legislative programs that were passed during Clinton's first three years, and the passage of time may ultimately not prove of much help.

Even today, there is substantial disagreement about how much Clinton accomplished as governor and its value.[2] In education, for example, where Clinton and his wife made substantial and well-publicized efforts to change the system, evaluations of his performance are decidedly mixed. Diane Blair (1988, 252) cautions that in considering Clinton's record, "Any attempt to assess public policy 'improvements' is highly hazardous and dangerously prone to subjectivity." Others believe that, despite Clinton's image as the "education governor," he "did not solve all of Arkansas' educational problems, or even most of them" (Allen and Portis 1992, 274–75).[3]

THE SEARCH FOR GREATNESS

Evaluating presidents has been complicated by the search for "greatness." The major problem of greatness as the chief criterion for assessing presidents is that not many are, nor are likely to be, great. Using greatness as the standard runs the risk of making the best the enemy of the good.

What constitutes greatness is far from clear. Broad intellectual brilliance correlates positively with rankings of presidential greatness (Simonton 1993, 541; see also Simonton 1986), but so does getting assassinated. Historians' ratings of greatness are sensitive to changing fashions and views. Some presidents look better, or worse, in retrospect to biographers and the general public. As one writer put it, "The reputation of past presidents are endlessly bid up or down on a vast historical stock exchange" (Beschloss 1995, 43).

Some believe that greatness comes from resolving a dramatic problem. Thus, Abraham Lincoln often tops lists of presidential greatness because he was called upon to save the union. Likewise, Franklin Delano Roosevelt is often rated as great (or at least near great) because of the enormous economic problems he faced upon entering office. Yet, it is not clear that even the so-called "great" presidents have actually resolved the problems for which they are accorded greatness:

> The commanding authority that presidents wield at these moments does not automatically translate into more effective solutions to the substantive problems that gave rise to the nation-wide crisis of legitimacy in the first place. Jefferson's response to the international problems that had plagued the nation over the 1790s proved to be a national disaster itself. . . . Lincoln's response to the sectional crisis of the 1850s plunged the nation

into the Civil War, and Roosevelt's New Deal failed to pull the nation out of the Great Depression. The fact that these presidents were not especially adept at solving the nation's problems only accents the rather sobering point that presidents freed from any connection to the politics of the past *have not needed to solve these problems.* (Skowronek 1993, 37, emphasis mine)

If presidents don't actually resolve large public problems, just what standards should be used? One possibility is to evaluate presidents according to their levels of activity and legislative success. On the basis of Clinton's first year in office and the legislation he passed, some have dubbed him a "great American President" (Weissberg 1994). Maybe. But the legislative scorecard is the presidential analogue of the primary victory/delegate count that frequently occupies press and public attention during campaigns, and it shares some of the same virtues and drawbacks. It is an assessment that lends itself to evaluations by addition.[4]

While pundits and presidents keep track of the "numbers," the success of particular programs ultimately may not be the issue. It has been argued that "while Roosevelt's symbolic leadership was related to definite, concrete acts of government, his interpretation of the situation, in the broadest sense, was more important than any specific program" (Burns 1956, 144). Clinton's most valuable accomplishment as the "education governor," for instance, according to many is that he "instilled in Arkansans an awareness of the importance of education" (Allen and Portis 1992, 274–75).

Measuring presidential success primarily as *winning* often neglects the *means* by which a president accomplishes his purposes. A president may get legislation passed by a number of methods. He may stand on principle and marshal his forces on the side of his strong policy beliefs. He may compromise and settle for less in order to accomplish some of what he feels is important. He may be anxious to get public credit for his efforts or care more about policy progress than credit. He may dispense large amounts of government programs or funds. He may mobilize the public to support him by candor or deceit. How a president gains legislative victories reveals important information about him.

The "greatness" and legislative success of a president may be less important than the qualities he brings to bear on the problems he faces and its effects on public confidence and psychology. In the next section, I suggest a different approach to evaluating presidential performance, focusing on the two major tasks that *every* president, *regardless of character or party,* faces: decision making and leadership.

THE CORE OF PRESIDENTIAL PERFORMANCE

The modern presidency is accumulating a growing number of expectations (Rose 1988). The office's complex responsibilities defy efforts to accomplish or even to categorize them. And yet, there is a basic and irreducible core of presidential performance. This core does not pertain to specific policy debates but rather to a president's general approach to policy. It involves analyzing methods, not counting victories. In short, the core of presidential performance is *quality:* the quality of a president's thinking about policy and the quality of the character elements he brings to bear on the political process.

Two fundamental facts stand out when considering the core responsibilities of any president. First, a president holds the ultimate responsibility to decide. Second, a president must be able to mobilize support to carry out his plans. The first leads us to focus on the quality of a president's understanding and decision-making. It points toward the qualities of analysis, temperament, and appraisal that underlie all the president's decisions. In short, it leads to a consideration of his personal, policy, and political *judgment.* The second points to a president's need to build public and institutional support and the methods by which he does so. In short, it leads us to consider the quality of his *political leadership.* Emphasizing judgment and leadership as the basic pillars of presidential performance allows us to ask more precise questions about how character affects them and how President's Clinton's character, in particular, is related to his performance.

The President's Judgment

At the heart of leadership lies choice. At the heart of choice lies judgment. It is here that character, experience, and vision intersect with political realities to produce results that are central to assessing presidential performance. Presidents are called upon to make a wide variety of decisions. Some function to set the political agenda. Some structure the process of policy debate and resolution. Some serve as the final word on a policy issue.[5] Underlying all of these decisions is the elusive but crucial domain of presidential perception, inference, and preference.

The Nature of Judgment

Judgment is the quality of analysis, reflection, and insight that informs the making of consequential decisions.[6] Only decisions that pose significant questions and therefore have significant consequences for presidential responsibility raise the issue of judgment in any fundamental way. The chief framing decision that faces most (but not all) presidents is *the basic public dilemma*. For Clinton, as noted in chapter 1, this issue concerns the public's trust and confidence in its leaders and their policies. Next to the other decisions that face him, this one is the most basic. Many of the decisions that Clinton makes across a wide number of areas, whether ultimately right or wrong, may be less important than how he handles this basic issue.

Assessing a president's judgment requires a focus on four related considerations: the problem itself, the domain(s) within which decisions are made, the basis of the decisions, and their results. In analyzing the problem, we must know what fundamental issues it raises. In analyzing the domain, we can distinguish between domestic and foreign policy spheres and then further categorize the problem within those spheres (e.g., economic interdependence). In analyzing the basis of the decisions, we need to understand what factors were weighed (for example, the relative weight given to policy and political concerns)[7] and with what results. And lastly, in analyzing results we need to appreciate the specific consequences, intended and unintended, of the decisions.

Good judgment is to some degree situational. A president's judgment is related to his experience with (and understanding of) problems in a particular sphere.[8] A president could have very good judgment on domestic issues and politics but lack the experiential frame to have equally good judgment on national security or foreign policy issues, and vice versa. Even within one domain, say international relations, a president may respond to different problems with different levels of judgment. He might be very well positioned to exercise good judgment in the areas of international political competition and conflict, but not so if the major international challenge was, say, economic.[9] This is not to contend that good judgments cannot be reached in unfamiliar areas, only that judgment is facilitated by understanding that has been refined by experience.[10]

Does Intelligence Equal Good Judgment?

Does a good judgment framework require a complex mind? On first glance it appears that it does. Clinton's obvious intelligence would here be a great asset. After all, the ability to hold and synthesize alternative frameworks is partially a reflection of cognitive capacity, and Clinton has certainly demonstrated that.

However, it is not clear that cognitive complexity is necessary for high-quality decisions (Suedfeld 1994; see also Tetlock 1992) or that complex thinking necessarily leads to better policy judgment. Obsessive thinkers, for example, usually exhibit highly complex and differentiated thinking. However, they do not as a rule have good judgment. While their thinking may be complex, it often lacks depth, flexibility, and sophistication. It is the latter three qualities, and not complexity, that help to define the quality of good judgment.

We usually think of obsessive thinkers as people who ruminate, but it can take other forms, such as an inability to reach closure. Observers of Clinton's approach to decision-making have characterized it as follows: "Clinton never stops thinking"; "There were lots of last-minute decisions and changes. That's Clinton's way"; "His decision making style is not . . . toting up the costs and benefits. He makes a decision when he absolutely has to"; and "You couldn't really tell when he was making a decision and when he wasn't" (Drew 1994, 67).

It is understanding, not complexity per se, that is crucial to good judgment. The amount of reflective insight that a president brings to bear on a problem may prove more important than the degree of complexity in his thinking. Reflective insight, a crucial element of good judgment, is not directly related to intelligence or complexity. This is especially true as a president tries to distinguish his own personal motives from those connected with advocacy for the public. Many intelligent people, including presidents, have difficulty seeing themselves in any perspective, especially as regards their personal motives. They can easily use their complex thinking to distance themselves from their own real motives.

Character and Good Judgment

A president's judgment is not primarily a result of intelligence, but of character. Character, in favorable circumstances, reflects a president's realistic sense of himself as an able, honest, and related person. It includes the methods (style) that he has developed to engage the world. His feelings of capacity and worth, and the psychological structures that support them, are linked to skilled judgment in a number of ways. So, too, feelings of inadequacy (or hyperadequacy) and low (or high) self-regard, and the psychological structures in which these are embedded, are linked with poor judgment.

It is important to know the extent to which a president's character structure has evolved, integrated, and consolidated the diverse demands with which it must deal.[11] A president must be able to modulate but still satisfy basic (developmentally normal and appropriate) wishes for accomplishment and recognition. He must have satisfactorily resolved sometimes conflicting needs and their resulting dilemmas: for interpersonal connectedness versus personal autonomy, approval versus independence, or for self-interest versus a concern for others. Finally, in the process of resolving these dilemmas, he must have developed and consolidated a set of ideals and values. Presidents with more consolidated characters have also developed a personal and professional identity—an internal compass of sorts—which serves as a vehicle for the expression of themselves in the world, and which is in turn voluntarily recognized and validated by others.

Why is the president's character integrity critical to good judgment? Good judgment requires serious reflection, not merely extended musing. Reflection requires the capacity to weigh information from a series of perspectives that make intellectual, experiential, emotional, and ethical sense not only to the president, but to those whom the decisions affect. Does the president give more or less weight to his own policy ambitions, the policy concerns of others, his standing with the public, or his calculations for reelection? No president can keep from making political calculations; the question for assessing any president is how often and how much weight he gives his own political prospects and how he resolves the tensions between good politics (for him) and good policy.

Character, and in particular the president's basic identity, ideals, and values, are a critical judgment lens. They provide the president with an anchor, a frame though which myriad facts can be evaluated and pressures withstood. A president without a coherent personal or political identity, and the strong ideals and values that underlie it, is like a ship without a rudder. Subjected to strong currents, he runs the danger of drift, or worse.

Finally, character reflects a president's relative success in another crucial developmental and functional task—developing interpersonal relationships. The capacity to make emotional commitments and maintain fidelity to them reflects, among other important psychological accomplishments, the capacity to go beyond self-interest. This is crucial to real empathetic attunement to others, a fundamental element of political empathy as well as good policy and political judgment.

Presidents must also find the means to implement their judgments, and those choices enter into any evaluation. Are the means adequate and appropriate to the task? Are they honest and straightforward or do they attempt to obscure or otherwise mask what the president wants to accomplish? Does a president choose to educate, to mislead, to threaten, to fight, or a mix of the four? Are there other less costly means that could accomplish the same ends? The means a president chooses reflect not only on his judgment, but on his character.

Character and Policy Analysis

Good judgment begins with understanding a problem. To do so, a president must first recognize there is one. Not all presidents are equally able to do so. Some cannot discern the facts, others cannot accept them, while others find reasons to ignore them.

At the level of character, the reasons for these responses are varied. They can originate from a meager or from an inflated sense of capacity, self-confidence, or self-regard. Presidents who suffer from low self-regard will be too inhibited to respond boldly or directly to an issue and will prefer optimism to realism. Similarly, wishful thinking, a dislike of conflict, a strong sensitivity to criticism, or a strong need to be liked can inhibit good judgment. So can an inflated sense of capacity and self-regard. The belief that "it can't happen here" can inhibit a realistic appraisal of a problem. A president's feeling that he possesses unusual competence, or is beyond the reach of ordinary circumstances, is also damaging to good judgment because he may discern the facts but discount their consequences.[12]

When a president's confidence or ambition exceeds his reach, poor judgment results. In such cases, a president may realize the risks but, because of overconfidence, feel he will be able to overcome them. Certainly this has been a problem for President Clinton on occasion. One example is Clinton's ambitious, complex health-care program. Many of his aides expressed concern, but he went ahead. Why? One answer perhaps lies in his sense that he is "smarter than anyone else," that he, like many of his staff, "considered themselves masterly politicians with a fine feel for the public" (Drew 1994, 305).

Diagnosing a problem is related to a president's experiences and his ability to learn from them. Learning requires that making mistakes be tolerable and not indictments of competence and respect. On the other hand, presidents with an inflated sense of their own virtue coupled with strong intellectual ability often learn the wrong things from their experiences. Rather than integrating real lessons about themselves from their setbacks, they can be prone to focusing on avoiding their past mistakes without changing the patterns of behavior that led to them. This is a primary reason that Bill Clinton's first two years as president are so similar to his first two years as governor, and that both ended with stinging defeats.

Empathy and Good Judgment

The president acts in a world of others, many of whom do not share his values or views, yet he is expected to represent all the people. He, more than any other leader, therefore must be able to take on the role of other. This is a virtue that Clinton has been much praised for.

Empathy in general, and Clinton's in particular, has been touted as an all-purpose cure for misunderstanding and conflict, yet there are limits to what empathy can accomplish. And, while presidential empathy with the position of others is an important aspect of good judgment, it may not be what it seems and should not always be taken at face value.[13] The relentless pursuit of empathy by a president, like the relentless pursuit of activity or even virtue, can mask less altruistic feelings such as personal ambition and subtle dishonesties. Empathy does not require that a president be devoid of self-interest, only that he be able to suppress it temporarily. Feelings of competition are part of ordinary life, and certainly of political life, and a president who feels he must always suppress these feelings in favor of attunement is not being fully candid with himself or others.

Why is empathetic attunement important in making policy judgments? National interest is rarely simple, and self-interest is ultimately a poor criterion for adequate policy. Realistic empathy with the concerns of citizens is an important aspect of legitimate authority in democracies.[14] Citizens cede power to a president with the expectation that it will be used for their good rather than his. At the more psychological level, the capacity for authentic interpersonal connectedness that undergirds empathic attunement has implications not only for good judgment, but for effective presidential leadership as well. Since every policy decision a president makes affects others, the real ability to consider how others might feel and maintain fidelity to that understanding helps distinguish effective presidents from their counterparts.

Presidents whose ambitions and sense of entitlement lead them to view their actions as inherently justified don't worry much about the real effects of their acts on others. To do so might require them to reconsider their sense of entitlement or moderate their ambitions. However, it is clearly politically inexpedient to reveal any such feelings. Besides, leaders often want to calculate the effects of what they do for their own political purposes. The result is *strategic empathy*.

Strategic empathy is clearly distinguishable from empathetic attunement. Its basic purpose is *advantage* rather than *understanding*. There are several motivational variations of this strategy, each of which reflects a different level of interpersonal connectedness (see chapter 5). One source of strategic empathy is the attempt to please others so that one can be liked or appreciated in return. This form of strategic empathy can adversely affect judgment—the president may not do what is necessary because others who provide emotional support or validation for him won't like it. This appears to be a particular danger for President Clinton.

The President's Political Leadership

Good judgment facilitates good policies but does not guarantee them. A president's judgment is the start, not the conclusion, of a complex political process. Presidents must still put their judgments into action.

While the search for leadership has become increasingly important in presidential politics, it remains an ambiguous concept (see Hermann 1986; Tucker 1981; Greenstein 1982). Some associate leadership with charisma—that vaguely defined term that includes the ability to generate political excitement. Others view it as a personal quality, akin to *gravitas,* that allows the leader to command respect and, above all, compliance. Still others see leadership as the act of faithfully representing constituent views and goals.

Political leadership may involve all of these elements, but in a democracy it is to be found in the capacity to mobilize support and exercise power for public purposes. Presidential leadership therefore can be defined as the capacity to act effectively on political and policy judgments to achieve results. In that respect, leadership and power share a definition that includes the ability to accomplish purposes. However, political leadership in a democracy requires, where power does not, that a president's judgments not only lead to fitting solutions, but be publicly understandable and defensible.

Political leadership requires skills to translate judgment into effective policy. It is important to emphasize the means a president selects to exercise leadership. Even good judgments can be frustrated if the means of their implementation are not productive and appropriate. We learn something of psychological importance when focusing on whether or not a president can get along with, bargain with, and influence others and *how* he does so. Some presidents bargain to avoid hard conflict. Others depend on influence because they are particularly able to charm. Some are sly in their presentations and lack fidelity to their commitments. A few get along because they are honest, sincere, and principled. A very few are honest, sincere, principled, and tough.

Much has been made of the *consensual* nature of presidential power. Presidents bargain, they persuade, but they rarely command (Neustadt 1990).[15] There are, however, several major drawbacks to this focus, one of which is that it neglects the president's important role of educating the public on his view of its needs. Public education is not merely a "textbook" virtue for a president. It has direct and practical consequences on his ability to lead. This is especially true for the Clinton administration, given the basic public dilemma that frames his presidency.

Education is part of how the public comes to understand its predicaments. It is how they begin to understand what can (and cannot) be done about public problems and the consequences of different actions (and inaction). Establishing credibility in these areas is central to establishing trust between the president and the public, a crucial element in presidential leadership and effective performance.

All presidents must sell their policies to some degree. But there are important differences between selling and *educating*. One striking characteristic of the Clinton presidency is the extensive role of political consultants, which is without precedent. "Previous Presidents had pollsters and other outside political advisors, but never before had a group of political consultants played such an integral part in a Presidency" (Drew 1994, 124).

The president's economic stimulus package, his health-care proposals (Kelly 1993d), and even the inauguration (Berke 1993b) were carefully scripted public events designed and carried through for political purposes. This strategy has worked in some cases. But can it be successful as an overall approach to policy, given Clinton's promise to reinvent government and the lingering problems of trust with which he began his presidency?

The Tasks of Presidential Leadership

Presidential leadership involves three distinct tasks: mobilization, orchestration, and consolidation. Although they are related, each requires different skills of a president. A skilled president will be adept at all three or know enough to authorize others to carry them out. Most effective presidents have strong skills in at least one of the first two areas; it is very rare for a president to be an effective leader otherwise.

The first task, *mobilization,* refers to the president's ability to rouse the public. To do so, he must clearly identify a problem in need of solution and convey that need to the public. In arousing the public, education is ultimately more productive than anxiety. Creating a sense of crisis or danger does arouse people, but at a price. Anxiety can be the basis of quick, but not necessarily deliberate, political action.

Mobilization requires that the president be invested in solving the problem. We can distinguish here between ritualistic public announcements and intensively felt and acted upon commitments to particular policy goals. A president who takes on too many commitments runs the risk of dissipating the public's sense that he is invested. After all, if the president is equally invested in so many things, how can the public tell which are truly central? Ultimately, the president's ability to sustain mobilized support depends on how clearly and honestly he conveys what is at stake, as well as how much consistent effort he invests in getting results.

Once the public has been aroused, presidential leadership requires that this arousal be applied to the achievement of goals. This involves *orchestration*, a president's ability to shape mobilization in specific, policy-relevant ways. It requires the ability not only to enlist people to one's goals, but also to coordinate their activities. George Bush proved very adept at making use of the international community's arousal after the invasion of Kuwait to craft specific policies and U.N. resolutions to further his policy objectives.

The third aspect, *consolidation*, refers to the skills and tasks necessary to preserving a set of supportive relationships and institutionalizing the results of a president's policy judgments. It may entail the creation of new agencies, working groups, or other institutional mechanisms. Or it might combine these with refocusing the functions or direction of existing policy structures. It may involve continuing public education as a policy dilemma develops or recognizing and responding to changes in circumstances among the various parties involved as the problem unfolds. All of these methods of consolidation represent ways in which a president's policy decisions can have an enduring effect. They are, in essence, a legacy of a president's judgment and leadership.

TRUST AND THE CRISIS OF POLITICAL LEADERSHIP

If presidential leadership is essentially a relationship, then at its heart lie trust and trustworthiness. Trust and trustworthiness are the psychological foundation of the citizen-leader relationship. In giving their trust, citizens bestow legitimacy. In being trustworthy, leaders earn it. Why do I place so much emphasis on trust and trustworthiness? Because policy problems are pervasive, and proven answers are in short supply. Realistically, presidents can promise only to address problems thoughtfully and skillfully, not necessarily to solve them fully.

The expectation that policy can truly solve very difficult, longstanding problems, which may develop in new and complicating ways, has resulted in a large measure of cynicism about our government and our presidents. Part of the responsibility for this lies with the public, which understandably wishes that these claims were true. But a good deal of the responsibility lies with presidents themselves, who persist in claiming that they will accomplish what they can't. Either because they truly believe in their promises or because they think these promises will further their election chances—or both—presidents continue to promise rather than educate. Paralleling this trend is the blurring of political identities and the construction of personas for political advantage.

In the end, these trends damage everyone. Presidents gain office but cannot govern. Citizens become less trusting and, as a result, it is harder for future candidates and presidents to convince citizens that their worst suspicions are untrue. Ultimately, the fabric of democracy is in danger as the psychological adhesive that holds it together loosens.

The president must have ambition, even substantial ambition. He must believe he can make things better and want to try. However, some uncertainty that he has all the right answers is preferable to its opposite. A president must be willing—indeed, anxious—to explain to the public honestly and straightforwardly what his plans entail. He must share with citizens the range of possibilities for success and what they would actually mean in concrete terms. He also must candidly explain the risks involved in his efforts, as well as the limits of what can be accomplished. To do this, a president has to be enough at ease with himself to acknowledge the *real* concerns of those who oppose him. It requires of him the psychological ability to do without artificially created enemies and to distinguish himself from those who oppose some or all of his views without demeaning them or grossly misrepresenting their concerns. Most of all, in order to exercise effective presidential leadership, a president must have fidelity to his commitments, to his word, to his ideals, and to those in whose name he governs. If he has the psychological capacities to do so, he will be able to maintain his commitments even if they prove unpopular. Such a president would ultimately subscribe to the view that gaining public trust by candor is more important than gaining legislative victories by deceit.

Does this sound too good to be true? It shouldn't. I have simply described a president whose character development allows him to express his aspirations for accomplishment in a context of well-realized ideals, tempered by a sense of his responsibilities to himself and others. It is perhaps a measure of our current state that this character, drawn from sound analytic theory and not from some idealistic fantasy, seems so far removed from our realistic expectations.

CHAPTER **13**

★ ───

CLINTON'S PRESIDENCY

Every president has two responsibilities: to make decisions and to translate them into policy. A focus on the first requires us to ask whether a president has the requisite intellectual and emotional capacities to reach sound judgments, and whether he makes good use of them. What is his decision style? Does he generally go directly to a problem's core? Or does he prefer to think about a problem from varied perspectives? How does he organize the process by which options are considered and selected? How does he make use of those who are available to help him in this process? And finally, standard rhetoric about bipartisanship aside, do his policy decisions really integrate disparate policy views?

CLINTON'S JUDGMENT AND DECISION-MAKING

President Clinton has the intellectual tools to be an excellent decision-maker. He is smart and able to handle large amounts of information. His campaign promise to focus like a laser conjured up the vision of a president with an ability to pinpoint important issues and then resolve them. It promised a president able to distinguish the important from the peripheral and what was truly needed from what might be merely preferable. Clinton's promise, however, has floundered on the shoals of his character.

259

Clinton's inability to recognize and accept limits has often hampered his judgment. For instance, he has immersed himself in the minutiae of many policy issues, which has not always helped him. His attention to policy detail is almost legendary. Discussions about policy details can be productive in working through to a better understanding of a policy and its possible implications. The drawback to a deep immersion in detailed policy debates is that there are many of them and their significance varies. If there are many policies under consideration, as is the case in the Clinton White House, such debates can be a lethal drain on a president's time. President Clinton has said he is acutely aware of the fleeting nature of time; the many hours spent debating minor policy points seem an inconsistent indulgence.

Further, facts are no substitute for a president's policy vision. Deeply informed, Clinton sometimes gets lost in the facts (Drew 1994, 79). Clinton has sought to emulate Franklin Roosevelt's decision style of sitting back and letting his advisers argue different positions (Drew 1994, 69). However, this approach works best when the president removes himself from the debate, which Clinton by all accounts rarely does. It also works better when the president has a strong idea of where he wants to go and wants to make certain he hasn't overlooked something important. A president participating in a basic debate about the overall direction of an administration is a different situation entirely from more focused policy debates.

Moreover, Clinton's problems stem not only from his oft-reported love of detail, but also from his desire to reach down into his administration to make minor decisions best left to others. Consider the delays in filling important jobs in the administration. Clinton demanded that he be involved in "signing off on the appointment of every assistant secretary, and sometimes deputy assistant secretaries" (Drew 1994, 99).

The desire to be involved in every level of administration and in the many detailed debates of his policies reflects more than a quest for excellence; it suggests a need for control. The element of control has been little noticed in Clinton's psychology but is evident in his presidency. By setting up a freewheeling staff system without clear lines of authority, by allowing lines of authority to be blurred, and by attempting to act as his own chief of staff, Clinton not only retains a large measure of control but remains the focus and the center. By appointing a cabinet that reflects both strong left-of-center leanings (Donna Shalala, Henry Cisneros, Robert Reich) and strong moderate leanings (Lloyd Bentsen, Janet Reno), Clinton has done more than ensure he will get conflicting views; he has set himself as the center, as the person to be convinced, the person toward whom all debate is addressed.[1]

Clinton is not the first president to centralize power in this fashion. Lyndon Johnson and Richard Nixon did so as well. But unlike Nixon and Johnson, Clinton combines a desire to make himself the center of his presidency with an inability to orchestrate the power he accumulates. Former chief of staff Thomas "Mac" McLarty has said of Clinton, "What I'll never understand is how someone with such a genius for organizing his thoughts and articulating them could be so disorganized in managing himself" (Brummett 1994, 44). Clinton's tendency to centralize power in his own hands, coupled with his lack of focus and his personal, disorganized leadership style, magnifies the disadvantages of each without capitalizing on their benefits. A president who is personally disorganized but has a strong staff system will benefit from the latter. A more fluid staff organization coupled with a well-organized president can also work well. But a president with a very fluid staff system, who is himself disorganized because of his many, varied interests, results in the worst of both worlds.

Even Clinton's tendency to immerse himself in policy is inconsistent and episodic. A matter as important to his administration as his first budget suffered because he "didn't bring a sharp focus to the issue. He was soon onto new subjects, and he only sporadically argued the budget case" (Drew 1994, 83). What accounts for this episodic attention? One factor is clearly that Clinton is not interested in one thing, a few things, or even many things. Rather he seems interested in *everything*. One cabinet member has said of him, "He's like a kid—he wants to do everything at once" (Page 1993, 70). Given how much he wants to accomplish, the amount of attention he could realistically allocate to one or a few items is limited. Clinton's expansive view of his presidency resulted in his administration taking on a wide range of complicated issues, *all at the same time*. Bruce Lindsey, a senior presidential aide, pinpointed the problem:

> There are only twenty-four hours in the day, and you should sleep a few of them. You can't be meeting with Boris Yeltsin, reforming health care, and working on campaign reform, lobbying restrictions, education reform, and welfare reform. If you try that you can't be effective on anything. What he's starting to do is to figure out the best use of his time. He would say [the problem] is the way he's been scheduled, *because he never thinks he has taken on too much.* (Drew 1994, 134–35; emphasis mine)

This appears to be a clear manifestation of expansive (grandiose) thinking. Good policy and political judgment requires time, as well as information and perspective. Even for a very smart president, the more he undertakes the less time he will have to focus on any particular issue. To regret this fact is one thing, to ignore its implications another.

Clinton's Decision-Making Style

Clinton's style of decision-making has sometimes adversely affected the quality of his decisions. One participant in the meetings during which the first Clinton budget was hammered out has said, "Clinton is not sequential. When you put a list in front of some people—setting forth what is most important and what is least important—they go down the list. Clinton goes around the problem. He circles it and circles it" (Drew 1994, 67).

Discomfort with closure is a hallmark of Clinton's decision-making style. In his policy debates there are "lots of last-minute decisions and changes . . . [he] makes a decision when he absolutely has to" (Drew 1994, 67). Why would someone who has taken steps to preserve his final say find making a decision so difficult? A final decision closes off options. It involves drawing a line, effectively stating, "Here is where I stand." For a president as averse to limits as Clinton, the drawing of lines and the closing off of options may leave him with a commitment that he may later regret.

Clinton's endurance, which in someone else, or in other circumstances, might be identified as a virtue, has also had a negative impact on his decision-making style. Early on in the administration, budget meetings sometimes started in the morning and stretched until 8:00 or 9:00 p.m., at which time someone would ask the president if he had time to continue, "hoping, along with others who were also exhausted, that he would call it quits. And Clinton would respond, 'Sure, let's continue.' One participant said, 'there'd be almost audible groans in the room, and he'd go on for another couple of hours' " (Drew 1994, 67–68). These sessions were long and grueling and clearly took a toll on Clinton's advisers, as well as on Clinton himself (Berke 1993b). McLarty concluded that the president was spending too much time in meetings and that they were distracting him from other important matters. Further, these meetings, according to McLarty, "took a lot out of him and took away time for reflection and rest" (Drew 1994, 68).

In the White House, a president's psychology is magnified, as Clinton's presidency to date confirms. He apparently believed that he and his staff could attend meetings from morning to night and remain unaffected by them. In the Clinton White House one can do everything without adverse consequences, as long as one works relentlessly.

Chemistry and Advice

The Clinton presidency is in many ways a remarkably personal one. People are crucially important to Clinton. According to Elizabeth Drew, Clinton is "recharged by contact with the public" and has "almost a mystical sense of his relationship with 'the people,' " (1994, 95). There is no question that Clinton has dropped many of the protective walls surrounding the presidency in an effort to establish a close personal relationship with the public. As a result, he has often revealed more of himself than the public necessarily wanted to know (such as his revelation, during an appearance on MTV, that he wore boxers, not briefs).

Similarly, Clinton feels the need to provide a running commentary on his own presidency. This stems in part from his belief that he has to bypass the press because he cannot count on their good will. It also reflects his strong personal belief that he can convince anyone of his good intentions and the advantages of his positions, if he can just speak with them directly. Prior to his first meeting with Alan Greenspan, chairman of the Federal Reserve, Clinton informed Al Gore that he wanted to meet Greenspan alone, to establish "one-to-one chemistry" (Woodward 1994, 68).

Chemistry, of course, weighs very heavily in Clinton's calculation; he must feel *personally* comfortable with others in his administration and those he appoints to other important positions.[2]

When Clinton interviewed Alice Rivlin for the budget director post, he "made it clear to his aides that he found her prickly and lacking the easy warmth and humor that he liked" (Woodward 1994, 114). Both Bill and Hillary "have a greater need than is good for them to have people around them whose loyalty—and lack of independence—wasn't in question" (Drew 1994, 235).[3] When it came to selecting his first chief of staff, "Friend after friend of Clinton said Clinton didn't want a Jim Baker (Reagan's strong, and cunning Chief of Staff). He wanted someone with whom he was utterly comfortable, whom he could completely trust, who had no agenda of his own, and who wouldn't get in his way" because, "to his own great detriment, Clinton wanted to be his own Chief of Staff" (Drew 1994, 130).[4]

Clinton's selection of advisers on the basis of "chemistry" (which can be translated as "they get along with me and I with them") runs the risk of giving too much weight to concurrence, in the decision process. By all accounts, President Clinton dominates his domestic policy staff meetings. He has "surrounded himself with deferential advisers who are either without national experience or much younger" (Blumenthal 1993b, 37).[5] Drew observes that, "with the exception of Anthony Lake, who was on the foreign policy side, not a single Clinton White House aide had ever worked in the White House before. The lack of maturity on the part of a high percentage of the Clinton White House staff was costly" (1994, 130). Similarly, among the administration's foreign policy advisers, there was no one with the stature, breadth of geopolitical thinking, or confidence in his own strategic vision to provide leadership to the group.[6] They got along so well that, "instead of flying sparks, they sometimes seemed to produce no chemical reaction" (Sciolino 1993). Reflecting on Clinton's foreign policy advisers, Anthony Lake noted, "There is a danger when people work well together; you can take the edge off the options [and] he [Lake] was increasingly on guard that 'groupthink' was not settling in" (Friedman 1993b).

Is anyone among this group likely to feel knowledgeable enough, strong enough, and secure enough in his or her position to tell Bill Clinton when they think he's wrong? Senior advisers with independent stature like Gore and Bentsen fulfill this role to some degree, but one or two such persons is not enough, and even Gore is limited in pressing his views and Bentsen has returned to private life (Berke 1994a).[7]

Resolving Policy Dilemmas

Central to Clinton's political identity has been his view of himself as a president who can go beyond the traditional liberal-conservative debates to resolve policy dilemmas. Yet his approach to resolving these dilemmas clearly reflects his wish to have it both ways (see chapter 6). Examples abound.[8] In favor of a strong defense, Clinton also wants to cut defense spending dramatically. Having stated that it was possible to cut defense spending by over a third in 1997 by cutting unnecessary weapons systems, Clinton, on the eve of the Connecticut primary, supported construction of a $2 billion Sea-Wolf submarine, built in that state (an item President Bush had deleted from the defense budget as unnecessary and too expensive). He is both for and against a law requiring the parents of pregnant teen-agers to be notified when their daughters seek an abortion (Church 1992, 44). He is for keeping abortion legal, but "making it as rare as possible" (Kelly 1992e). Yet one of the first acts of his administration was to lift restrictions on abortion counseling at federally financed clinics (Toner 1993). Later, in September 1993, he expanded abortion coverage for poor Medicaid patients. He is for the free trade agreement, but only if there are a number of side agreements acceptable to labor and environmentalists (Drew 1994,

288). More generally, he is for free trade but feels we must protect vital industries (Bradsher 1993). At the same time that he was pressuring Japan to open up its markets, he was also concluding an agreement with China that put stringent quotas on its silk exports to this country to protect American jobs (Tyler 1994). He was against the dilution of the U.N. resolution authorizing the use of force in the Persian Gulf in 1991, but two days before U.N. forces attacked, asked whether sanctions should be given more time. Clinton is for affirmative action but against quotas—yet his administration has supported setting aside specific voting districts for minorities (Greenhouse 1993), has endorsed race-based scholarships (Chartrand 1993), has argued for continuing court controls on the Kansas City school system to aid minorities (Greenhouse 1994), has provided minorities with special preferences in bidding for FCC licenses (Andrews 1994), and, in his health-care plan, proposed numerical "targets" for the numbers of minority candidates accepted into specialist training (Pear 1993d, A22).

Is Clinton's approach a function of intellectual sophistication, political opportunism, a dislike of being bound by the inevitable limits of decisions, or a combination of all three? One way to approach this question is to examine Clinton's *integrative complexity,* his ability to distinguish various positions from each other (differentiation) and then find the interconnections among them (integration) (Suedfeld 1985; Suedfeld and Wallace 1995). Integrative complexity is independent of content—there are no necessary variations in complexity or levels of integration between prochoice and prolife positions, or between liberal and conservative policies. Presidents can be located on a continuum with little policy differentiation or integration at one end and high differentiation and integration on the other.

Where would we locate Clinton on this continuum? Given his intelligence, verbal facility, and his own views of his policy thinking, we might be tempted to place Clinton at the high differentiation-high integration end. However, while intelligence and verbal facility reflect a capacity for integrative complexity, they do not ordain it. In fact, a president who has on occasion been unable to clearly separate his convictions about what is good for the public from what the public itself wants, reveals a lack of differentiation. Alternatively, a president who realizes the two may differ but decides to do what he wants anyway indicates how ambition can interfere with integration. A strong wish to have it all would reflect a lack of differentiation. A president who pursues too many policies simultaneously would be reflecting high differentiation but low integration.[9] A president who selects his advisers on the basis of "chemistry" and loyalty might risk less differentiation in policy thinking and therefore less possibility of real integration. And a president who imposes time pressures on himself generally reduces his ability both to differentiate and to integrate policy alternatives.

Clinton's dislike of limits is consistent with his stated disinclination to be bound by traditional Left-Right dichotomies. However, whether his policies truly synthesize alternative policy ideals in a constructive way is another matter (to be discussed in the next chapter).

CLINTON'S POLITICAL LEADERSHIP

Once decisions have been reached, the second major presidential responsibility is to translate them into policy. This task focuses our attention on Clinton's presidential leadership—his skill in mobilizing, orchestrating, and consolidating public support for his policy decisions, and the methods he chooses to do so. What are Clinton's strategies for achieving what he wishes to accomplish? What skills have facilitated his presidential leadership? Most importantly, what methods has he chosen to realize his aspirations in office?

A Politics of Ambition

While President Clinton has been criticized for his lack of conviction, he has on occasion been quite clear about his intentions. Looking back on his first three years in office and a disastrous 1994 midterm election, Clinton said, "I think in the first two years, I knew exactly what I wanted to do and I was obsessed with doing it" (Purdum 1995c). Clinton's psychology—especially his ambition, his confidence that he knows what the public needs, and his determination to give it to them—is clearly in evidence here. A large ambition that produces moderate, even good, results does not appear to be what Clinton has in mind for himself or his presidency.[10] This ambition results in a very large agenda. Clinton is disinclined to focus for long periods of time on a few things; his orientation is toward getting many things done. His leadership style is thus distinctly framed by a politics of ambition.

The first two years of the Clinton administration saw a large number of major policy initiatives, a number of which were successfully enacted into law. An obvious and tangible reflection of Clinton's ambitions are the numerous domestic legislative initiatives undertaken by his administration in its first year alone. A partial list would include his economic stimulus package, reform of the banking system, his "reinventing government" initiative, the family-leave policy, a new student-loan program, a major health-care reform initiative, NAFTA, a major crime bill, a change in policy regarding homosexuals serving in the military, a national service program, an immunization and vaccination program, a retraining and jobs bill, a deficit reduction plan, and so on.

Even after the Republicans swept the House and Senate in the 1994 midterm elections, the Clinton presidency was soon proposing, among other things, welfare reform, an initiative to add $5 billion to the military budget, and a ban on some forms of embryo research with live fetuses. The impulse of the administration remains activist, even if it cannot dominate the political agenda.

Based on its energy and ambition, Clinton's presidency should have been a resounding public success. But it wasn't. The question is why. One argument is that, given the scale of Clinton's policy ambitions, he frequently falls short of them. Clinton, this argument goes, promised so much and raised such high hopes that his performance was bound to be disappointing. While partially explaining Clinton's difficulties, this argument assumes, without demonstrating, that Clinton's performance as president has been much better than he is given credit for. It also leaves unanswered the question of why so many people have turned away from Clinton instead of demanding that he do more.

For an answer to the paradox of Clinton's performance, we must look elsewhere. One place to begin is with the inside views of those working to deliver on Clinton's promises. Clinton's advisers were worried about the number of initiatives and their effect on one other and on Clinton's ability to deliver on them. Books by Bob Woodward and especially Elizabeth Drew are replete with quotes from high-ranking Clinton officials who worried about President Clinton taking on too much and more than occasionally advised him that he was doing so:

> While the President was fighting for his economic program, he was also trying to get his national service program and his empowerment zone program and a number of other things through Congress. Bentsen was so troubled by the overload that in mid-May he told Clinton in a private meeting in the Oval Office, "You have too many issues out there, and the public is losing focus on what you're trying to do." . . . But nothing much changed. (Drew 1994, 166)

Some of Clinton's large agenda in his first two years is attributable to the political climate and the expectation that his power would diminish as time passed (Drew 1994, 94). But even when Clinton had ample time, as governor of Arkansas from 1982 on, his agenda was still crowded every term. In 1983 Clinton gave the Arkansas legislature a 312-page booklet containing eighty bills that he was proposing in the areas of economic development, education, crime, and utility regulation (Moore 1992, 96). Recall that this was in Clinton's first year back in office after his 1980 reelection loss. In 1987 Clinton presented the legislature with a 214-page report on his proposals (Moore 1992, 123), and in 1989 his report to the legislature contained proposals for over ninety new bills (Moore 1992, 148). In addition, Clinton called special sessions of the legislature in June 1987 (to find more sources of revenue), in the fall of 1987 (to deal with taxes on trucks), in January 1988 (to deal with ethics issues), in early 1989 (to deal with the Little Rock segregation lawsuit), and later in 1989 (to deal with additional funds for education and drug programs).[11] President Clinton's large policy agenda may spring from a combination of factors, but high among them would have to be his (and his wife's) ambitions.

A Presidency of Persistence

Clinton's large agenda, great self-confidence in its correctness, and obsession with accomplishing it are the basis of his determination. Clinton accurately views his determination as a political asset (Blumenthal 1994, 33, 43). He has experienced many setbacks, but experience suggests (and he believes) that through planning, intelligence, and sheer determination he will eventually accomplish his goals. Clinton is not used to losing or to permanent setbacks; there is always another way to be tried and another day to succeed. His level of energy, coupled with his self-confidence and determination, results in a strategy of persisting until his opponents either tire or despair. Clinton acknowledged this political strategy in an interview with political scientist and historian James McGregor Burns. Burns asked Clinton what he would do if Congress really resisted him and all the usual attempts to get them to pass his agenda didn't work, and Clinton replied, "Just keep going at 'em till they tire." [12]

Persistence and determination in the service of a large agenda can function to wear down opposition. A president's persistence, however, can turn from a leadership asset to a public liability. While Clinton himself has enormous energy, *he often exhausts public understanding*. This strategy may be effective in the short term to get policies passed, but it does not provide a firm foundation for public acceptance. Thus, while Clinton has been successful in getting a number of his policies enacted, it is much less clear that he has made progress in resolving the basic public dilemma his presidency faces.

A president must be able to educate the public if he wishes to gain its trust. An ambitious agenda may not leave much time for public education because citizens are struggling to keep up with all the implications of what they are asked to judge. To an ambitious president, assured of his own intentions and the virtue and necessity of his plans, having the public raise too many questions may seem unnecessary or undesirable since it might interfere with the pace he has in mind.

Institutionally, such a strategy can easily lead to overload. As new proposals are introduced, then modified, then put forward in different versions to be reconciled, both the public and their elected representatives have difficulty keeping track of which bill says what. The president's health-care proposal provides a perfect illustration of this danger. At one point in the health-care debate, several Senate committees released their own versions of a major health-care bill. Keeping track of the provisions, much less of their implications, was difficult at best. Many Americans quickly lost interest.

A Presidency on the Brink

The Clinton presidency has a discontinuous, episodic quality to it and has often seemed on the brink of disaster, only to be saved at the last moment. For instance, Clinton's budget passed by a narrow one-vote victory in the Senate, and his Haiti policy succeeded in part due to the last-minute diplomatic mission of Jimmy Carter. The titles of two books about the Clinton presidency—*Highwire* (Brummett 1994) and *On the Edge* (Drew 1994)—highlight this trait.

The roller-coaster nature of Clinton's approval ratings in his first year in office offers dramatic evidence of this discontinuity. In early January 1993 his approval rating stood at 58 percent. By the end of January it dropped to 50 percent, then rebounded to 60 percent by mid-February. However, by the end of February it had dropped again to 55 percent and by mid-March hovered at 52 percent. By the end of March it was back up a little to 55 percent, but by the end of April had plunged to 45 percent. By the end of May Clinton's approval ratings hit 36 percent.[13] With the 1994 midterm election debacle, the Clinton presidency went right over the brink.

For each legislative victory[14]—the expansion of the Head Start and Earned Income Credit program, the passage of NAFTA, a pilot program of national service, a program for National Educational Goals, and so on[15]—there has been a serious setback, many of the administration's own making. The setbacks include difficulties with the appointment process (Kimba Wood, Zoe Baird, Lani Guinier, Bobby Ray Inman, Henry Foster); the controversial nature of the people nominated, confirmed, and forced to resign (Dr. Joycelyn Elders [surgeon general], Webster Hubbell [associate attorney general], Michael Espy [former secretary of agriculture], David Watkins [director of administration]); policy reversals; and ethical investigations by Justice Department special counsels of lapses on the part of Clinton administration officials (Henry G. Cisneros [secretary of housing and urban development], Michael Espy, Ronald Brown [secretary of commerce], as well as the Clintons themselves).

One reason for the episodic nature of the Clinton presidency is clearly the scope of his ambition and the sheer number of initiatives. Mark Gearan, Clinton's deputy chief of staff, has said,

> Every day we are throwing a ball in the air to get through the day. There's been a growing sense here in the last couple of weeks that we can't do this every day. We thought all we had to do was throw that particular ball in the air. Now, as we approach April and May, they're all in the air. We have to juggle. That's what terrifies me. (Drew 1994, 113)

All things being equal, even a focused and determined president who tries to accomplish many things will not be fully successful. President Clinton is determined, but with so many policy initiatives he has found it hard to focus.[16] For example, Clinton was deeply involved in his first budget, often at a level of extraordinary detail, but soon moved on to new subjects (Drew 1994, 83). As governor, Clinton "tended to lose interest in programs after he'd managed to get them enacted" (Brummett 1994, 8). Others note "a pattern discernable earlier in his life, of long dilatory periods followed by frenetic last-minute spectacles of personal diplomacy and showmanship" (Wills 1993).

Another, less-noticed consequence of Clinton's tendency to devote intense energy to an issue for a brief period is that other issues get neglected.[17] In the three weeks leading up to the NAFTA vote, Clinton did little else but work on and lobby for its passage (Drew 1994, 340; Ifill 1993e). As a result, foreign policy was set aside, health-care was further delayed, and welfare reform slipped farther from view. The sense that the administration is always having to scramble is directly related to Clinton's large agenda and lack of sustained focus.

Some of Clinton's difficulties originate in the fact that he is an activist president in an age of public distrust of large-scale government programs (Drew 1994, 127). However, the fundamental contradiction between Clinton's policy ambitions and the basic mood of the country is only the beginning of an explanation. Part of the episodic nature of the Clinton presidency has to do not only with this basic dilemma, but with Clinton's *response* to it. In choosing how to realize his policy ambitions, Clinton has focused on selling the public what he thinks is best. However, he has done so in a way that has left him constantly scrambling to explain his last set of explanations, as was the case with the administration's different sets of figures regarding health-care costs. At one point, three different sets of figures succeeded each other. In trying to mediate between public education and his own ambitions, Clinton often emphasizes expediency, not substance. Many of the administration's scrambles and much of the time spent teetering on the brink might well have been avoided if he had adopted an approach emphasizing candor.

Struggles with Trust and Mobilization

At the root of the Democrats' dismal showing in the 1994 midterm elections is a basic paradox. No recent modern president has been so successful in having his policy translated into legislative action and yet been so thoroughly repudiated by the electorate. What accounts for this? The answer is to be found in the explosive mix of short-term policy successes whose pace, subject matter, and methods call into question the larger enterprise. The 1994 election results were a clear message, less about Clinton's general goals than the means he employed to try to achieve them.

Effective presidential leadership involves the ability to mobilize others. The president must not only have a view of where he wishes to go, but a reason for going there and an appreciation, honestly conveyed to those he wishes to lead, of the realistic costs and opportunities involved in doing so. This was part of the promise Clinton made as a New Democrat. The specific policy positions of the administration were meant to reflect not only that they had a plan, but that they would be direct and forthright regarding their intentions. The ability to sustain public mobilization depends on trust, and trust in turn requires candor.

Clinton began his presidency with a "trust deficit" left over from accusations about him during the presidential campaign, and this deficit was magnified by his own handling of the issues. Under those circumstances, and given the suspiciousness of the electorate in general about government activity, a more useful approach would have been to do less and explain more.

For example, Clinton's regional health alliances were ultimately shown to be government entities and not, as Clinton had argued, an example of private enterprise in action. The report by the Government Accounting

Office (GAO), "put its finger on something the Administration was loath to acknowledge: Mr. Clinton's health plan depends heavily on the power of the government to compel behavior." This was inconsistent with Clinton's attempt "to minimize the government's role and to insist that his plan represents merely an expansion of the existing system of private health insurance . . . not a vast new Federal enterprise" (Pear 1994d). Clinton derided the GAO report as technical and trivial. However, as one reporter noted,

> the dismissal of the issue verges on the disingenuous from an administration that went through considerable contortions, in a hopeless effort to . . . create the complicated purchasing alliances in such a way that spending could be counted as private, not governmental. They didn't consider it a trivial Beltway issue back then. (Clymer 1994c)

Selling the Clinton Presidency

With his great communications skills, Clinton is a president very adept at selling. He believes, with good reason, that he can convince most people of almost anything.[18] Not surprisingly, selling plays a large role in his approach to presidential leadership. James Carville, one of his closest campaign advisers, has said, "We've got to get this guy something to sell. This ain't him, sittin' here waitin' for someone to drop something in his 'in' basket" (Brummett 1994, 66).

As a result of his approach to presidential leadership, Clinton's presidency has been a very political one. The combination of a large and controversial policy agenda, an early decision against a bipartisan approach (see chapter 6),[19] and a persistent style that emphasizes relentless efforts to win people over contributed to a "permanent campaign" presidency in which the public is consistently lobbied to support a continuous series of Clinton initiatives. Bob Woodward has written of Clinton, "He had essentially extended the campaign through the first nine months of the presidency taking up the battle with all the urgency of FDR during the Depression or a president in war" (1994, 329).

The roots of the permanent campaign can be traced to Clinton's reelection as governor after his 1980 defeat. At that time, Clinton devised a political strategy based on three central axioms: (1) means and ends had to be "completely interwoven"; (2) the press was to be bypassed or at least outflanked in getting out Clinton's message; and (3) "voter surveys would be used in similarly perpetual fashion, taking poll results to shape the substance and rhetoric of policy debates" (Maraniss 1995, 407–8). The third axiom in particular holds an important key in understanding Clinton's approach to presidential leadership. The goal of Clinton's strategy was "to discover more than whether voters supported or opposed an initiative. . . . Word by word, line by line, phrase by phrase, paragraph by paragraph, rhetorical options would be tested to see which ones were most effective in moving the public in a certain direction" (Maraniss 1995, 408). The strategies selected by Clinton for his permanent campaign led some to question whether Clinton's will to get his way would overwhelm his convictions (Maraniss 1995, 418).

Clinton has made extensive use of an extremely wide-ranging, not always effective, public lobbying apparatus. Other presidents, of course, have made use of polls and political consultants, but their role in the Clinton presidency has been, as noted, "without precedent. . . . [Everyone] made a point of saying that they weren't involved in foreign policy matters, but at various times, in various ways, they were." (Drew 1994, 124) By means of this apparatus, policy issues and positions are fully pretested with multiple focus groups, while words and phrases are honed or deleted. The results are marketed through sophisticated public relations strategies, which include the systematic convening of selected members of the "ordinary public" to whom the president presents the most effective, but not necessarily the most representative, aspects of the policies that are to be "sold."

Clinton's political consultants Stan Greenberg, Mandy Grunwald, Paul Begala, and James Carville attended most key strategy meetings and were constantly probing and polling the public for clues about what Clinton needed to do to sell his programs and presidency. They also had direct and independent access to the president and Hillary Clinton, a fact that was upsetting to other White House aides like Howard Paster, who was in charge of congressional relations. Paster felt that the consultants tended to remake policy because poll numbers were down, whereas he and others thought that "sound policy would be followed by good poll numbers in the long run" (Woodward 1994, 247).[20]

Not surprisingly, Clinton's emphasis on perception and marketing carried over to foreign as well as domestic affairs. In May 1994, as Clinton's approval ratings in foreign policy deteriorated and he left for an eight-day trip to Europe, he quadrupled the size of his foreign policy press office. He transformed that office "into as large an operation as any White House in modern history," so that he could win back public confidence "by doing a better job of communicating our foreign policy" (Jehl 1994f).

In May 1993, Clinton sent Secretary of State Warren Christopher to Europe to convince the allies to rally around his "lift and strike" plan for bombing the Serbs. The French and British, however, had already made it clear to the administration that they needed to be consulted *before* a plan was formulated, not after. Clinton sent Christopher anyway, in the belief that he might turn the Europeans around. This trip, taken in the face of clear and stiff resistance by U.S. allies, is directly attributable to "Clinton's unbounded faith in salesmanship, and a naiveté about other nations' interests" (Drew 1994, 156).

Presidents must never lose sight of the distinctions between selling and *educating*, especially in an era of public distrust of government. The Clinton administration, however, has opted to market itself rather than to educate the public on the merits *and limitations* of its plans and the rationale for its choices. This policy development by focus group does not augur well for President Clinton's attempt to resolve the basic public dilemma of public trust in public policies.

Clinton appears to have recognized this, at least in passing. In a September 1995 interview, he acknowledged that it would have been better had he "done just slightly less, [and] people had understood more of the big picture" (Purdhum 1995c). However, two days later, clarifying his comments to reporters, this insight seemed to have again eluded him: "I may have a marketing problem, I do not have a substantive one" (Rosenthal 1995).

Numbers, Policy, and Candor

President Clinton has shown a willingness to shade meaning and be less than forthright. This first arose during the presidential campaign in his evasive answers to questions about controversies surrounding the draft, his purported affair with Gennifer Flowers, and his use of marijuana. It has resurfaced repeatedly in his presidency.

One fundamental problem is the administration's tendency to play loose with budget figures and estimates. Given that trust in government policies is the major public dilemma facing Clinton, his recurring suggestion that major savings would help finance his new programs was bound to generate some skepticism. In announcing his welfare reforms in 1994, for example, unspecified large savings were put forward as the method of funding. In announcing his health-care proposals, Clinton also suggested savings as the means of funding them. Speaking for the administration, Vice President Gore insisted that the Clinton health-care proposal could be paid for largely by eliminating "unnecessary paperwork and bureaucracy" (Clymer 1993c). Many experts, among them economists, consultants, and members of Congress "both Democratic and Republican used terms like 'not credible,' 'difficult,' 'wildly optimistic' and 'illusionary' to describe the President's plans" (Greenhouse 1993b). A study by the Congressional Budget Office (CBO) found,

> In its budget for the fiscal year 1995, the administration estimates that its health proposals would *reduce* the deficit by $38 billion in 2000 and by a cumulative total of $59 billion over the 1995–2000 period. In contrast, the CBO estimates that the proposal would *increase* the deficit by $10 billion in 2000 and by a total of $74 billion over the six year period. (Reischauer 1994, 35–36, emphases mine)

New and dramatic savings were also said to be one result of the administration's "reinventing government" initiative. That initiative developed diffuse meanings, but was originally intended to convey a commitment to efficiency and an entrepreneurial approach to government services "which put customers first" (Wilson 1994, 671). Gore claimed the savings would be over $100 billion, a figure that senior aide George Stephanopoulos thought unrealistic (Drew 1994, 295; see also Woodward 1994, 329). Leon E. Panetta, then director of the White House Office of Management and Budget, found the figures so questionable that he refused to sign off on them. In the end, however, the questionable $100 billion figure was presented to the public as accurate (Drew 1994, 295). Clinton introduced the report on the White House lawn on September 7, 1993, by remarking in part, "We have to revolutionize government so that the American people trust the decisions that are made and trust us to do the work government has to do." Shortly thereafter, a study by the nonpartisan CBO suggested that the real savings from the program would be substantially less than those projected by the Clinton administration (Reischauer 1993).

This practice has continued throughout the administration's first term. Clinton's 1995 plan to balance the budget in ten years would, according to a study released by the CBO, actually generate a deficit of $200 million for each of the ten years, resulting in a $209 billion deficit by the year 2005.[21] Or consider the student loan program. According to the administration's estimates, direct low-cost loans to college students would save the Treasury Department $5.3 billion over five years. The CBO estimated that the savings would be $4.27 billion, but that figure did not include an estimated $2.19 billion in administrative costs (Krauss 1993). The administration and the then-Democratic Congress inserted a provision in the 1993 Budget

Reconciliation bill that *required* the CBO and the Office of Management and the Budget to exclude federal administrative expenses when calculating the effects of loan programs on the federal budget. Both supporters and critics of the loan program agree that this tactic "gave direct loans an unfair advantage in any budget making comparison" (Clymer 1995). The point here is not that Clinton's direct loan program was wrong-headed; many supported it as sound policy. Rather, by mandating an accounting practice that masked the true costs to the government, Clinton provided a very misleading picture of the program's efficacy.

While previous administrations may also have supplied misleading cost and savings projections, candidate Clinton actively campaigned against "politics as usual." He promised to inform the public more fully and carefully. Clinton has publicly praised his own administration for being more candid with budget figures, and pointed to the use of more conservative figures from the CBO for his first budget as an example. Yet, as is clear in the health-care budget, welfare reform budget (Woodward 1994, 86), "reinventing government" budget, and other instances,[22] the administration has fallen into a pattern of supporting its program initiatives with questionable numbers.

The Importance of Appearance

The Clinton administration tends to concentrate too much on *appearances*, even when an appeal to *substance* would reflect well on its plans. It attempts to sell its policies through clever packaging and slogans rather than through frank education. Clinton has frequently chosen to manage the public's perceptions instead of stating clearly, explaining, and standing behind what he really was attempting to do.

This tone was set very early in the Clinton administration. In the memo entitled "Hallelujah: Change is Coming," members of the administration were told, "Anytime you're asked about a specific in the economic plan, look for ways to bring it back to the general points that this is good for the country and this is real change" (Woodward 1994, 261). In other words, *don't explain, market.*

The economic conference held shortly before Clinton took office was presented as analogous to a free-ranging university seminar, with no question too difficult to ask. In reality, it was more of a showcase for President Clinton than a real, no-holds-barred debate about the usefulness of alternative economic approaches. The economic views given the most prominence were those already in substantial agreement with Clinton's views or those designed to make his appear more moderate.[23] The conference simply affirmed publicly that President Clinton knew what he wanted and what he thought was needed. To present the conference as a wide-ranging education for the American public was largely misleading.

This concern with appearances is evident in many of the administration's dealings. Sometimes it competes with substantive considerations, other times it takes precedence. At the beginning of his administration, Clinton promised a cabinet that "looks like America." That pledge set off a frantic scramble to "get the right combination before the cameras" (Drew 1994, 24). In fact, the words "look like" should be underscored, because while the cabinet looked like America, its substantive dimensions were quite traditional. A close analysis of Clinton's cabinet choices suggests that "if the Clinton administration 'looks like America,' then we have become a nation of lawyers and lobbyists" (Dye 1993, 694; see also Safire 1993).[24] There is nothing wrong with ensuring that talented individuals from many communities are recruited for an administration.[25] But when Clinton said that his cabinet would look like America he was clearly referring to their *appearance* as members of racial, ethnic, and gender groups, and not their substance as representatives of the American people.

The same concern was evident in the inauguration. One reporter noted that "never before has an inauguration week been so carefully prepared for camera" (Berke 1993b).[26] Another reporter described the group of fifty "average Americans" flown to Washington for the inaugural week at a cost of $500,000, paid for by the inauguration committee:

> Hardly a random committee of Americans, the guest list appears to be as calculated as the diverse group invited to Mr. Clinton's last event where he mingled with the people, the economic conference in Little Rock, Ark. The guests, from veterans and teachers to preachers and people whose children have mental disorders, were painstakingly picked to make political points. The guest list was arrived at after an initial list of more than 300 people was culled to those with the most compelling stories. (Berke 1992c)

Another example of this emphasis on appearances is Clinton's tendency to claim more for the results of his policies than is warranted. This is a trait with some history,[27] and ordinarily it would be puzzling given that Clinton has so many real accomplishments to point to. It does make sense, however, in view of Clinton's strong desire to be appreciated and his confidence in the power of appearances. Clinton is not the first president to exaggerate the results of his policies. However, given the current public distrust of government that he and his administration face and his personal problems with issues of honesty and trust, this disingenuousness is most unfortunate.

The July 1993 economic summit in Tokyo provides a public case in point. The ambiguously worded agreement reached by Clinton and Japanese prime minister Kiichi Miyazawa at the G-7 summit was hailed by the administration as a "major breakthrough" (Apple 1993). In fact, it was an agreement to hold future talks about trade, and it appears to have been brought about by the administration's retreat from its publicly stated position of requiring Japan to agree to specific levels of reduction in its trade surplus (Sanger 1993; Pollack 1993). By February 1994 the "breakthrough" based on "mutual understanding" had, in fact, resulted in a total impasse and renewed threats of a trade war (Ifill 1994d). A subsequent analysis concluded that "the Clinton's administration's assault on the barriers in Japan's automotive market has . . . [been] notable for the bellicose U.S. threats—but not for the significance of its results" (Blustein 1995, 22).

A Presidency of Fluid Ethical Boundaries

The president sets the ethical and moral tone of his administration. If the president demands probity and the avoidance of even the appearance of questionable practices, and if he adheres to that demand for himself, the members of his administration will get that message. If he doesn't pay attention or is seen as holding somewhat flexible boundaries of what is permissible, it is quite likely that his aides will get that message, too. Clinton's difficulties in setting and maintaining boundaries for himself appear closely related to issues of integrity and appropriateness in his administration.

From the start, the Clinton administration has been on unsteady ground in these areas. After his election, Clinton began his administration's transition by announcing it would be guided by a stringent set of conflict-of-interest guidelines. Yet almost immediately they were relaxed to allow the president's close friend Vernon Jordan to join the transition team as an adviser (Berke 1992b). Clinton's wish to have it both ways by skirting the laws regulating campaign contributions (see chapter 6) and the many promises he has made and abandoned (see chapter 4) have no doubt contributed to the perception that he is a president for whom no boundaries, including those ethical boundaries he espouses, are necessarily fixed.

In matters large and small, serious and trivial, the Clintons themselves and members of their administration have behaved in ways that raise serious concerns. Other administrations have had their share of criminal and ethical lapses.[28] However, the Clinton administration appears riddled with impropriety, both real and perceived.

A partial list must begin with the president and his wife. The series of public/private transactions that have been lumped together under the name "Whitewater" have raised a number of questions about the propriety of their involvement in this venture. Then there is Clinton's solicitation of "soft" money and his wife's reliance on a well-connected friend to help her make $100,000 in the commodities market under circumstances that are still not fully resolved. Clinton himself is currently being sued by a former Arkansas employee for sexual abuse.

Three years into the Clinton administration, a number of officials, some at the most senior levels of the administration, have been forced to resign. Walter Hubbell, associate attorney general and a longtime friend and associate of the Clintons, was forced to resign amid criminal and ethics charges. He later pleaded guilty to stealing more than $394,000 from his law firm and from his clients, resulting in charges of mail fraud and tax evasion (Labaton 1994b).

David Watkins, director of White House administration, who was also reprimanded for his role in the White House travel office problems, was forced to resign for using presidential helicopters for golf trips (Ifill 1994c). Shortly thereafter, it was revealed that a number of White House aides used the presidential helicopter on at least eleven other occasions. The White House said that all the uses were legitimate, including one marked "classified" that included Secretary of Housing and Urban Development Henry G. Cisneros and Budget Director Alice M. Rivlin. The White House would not describe the purpose of that journey or why these two officials were involved in a "classified" mission (Jehl 1994a).

William H. Kennedy III, a senior White House aide, was stripped of his job overseeing background checks of administration appointees after it was learned that he had used his position to conceal embarrassing information about himself (Jehl 1994e). Bernard W. Nussbaum, the White House counsel and a close friend of Hillary Clinton's, resigned "amid criticism that he may have bent ethical standards to protect the Clintons on Whitewater" (Dowd 1994a). Deputy Secretary of the Treasury Roger C. Altman and Treasury Department Counsel Jean E. Hanson[29] both resigned after being harshly criticized by members of the Senate Banking Committee conducting Whitewater investigations for misleading them in their testimony about the extent of contacts between the White House and Treasury Department regarding sensitive Whitewater-related investigations (Bradsher 1994a).

Altman, who at the time was also acting head of the Resolution Trust Corporation (which made him the nation's top savings and loan regulator), admitted to having briefed senior White House officials, who were themselves being investigated by his agency, of the progress of the Whitewater investigation (Labaton 1994g). The *New York Times* (1994f) noted that Altman was "supposed to be politically independent at the same time that he was advising Mrs. Clinton about how to avoid further investigations." The newspaper further noted that while independent counsel Robert Fiske found that Altman's actions didn't constitute obstruction of justice as defined by the relevant criminal statues, "there could hardly be a clearer example of an unethical conflict of interest." Sound ethics requires more than the lack of criminal behavior.

Three years into President Clinton's administration, an unprecedented number of his senior cabinet officials are under investigation by independent prosecutors. Henry Cisneros, secretary of housing and urban development, is being investigated by a special prosecutor over payments made to his former mistress, allegedly the result of his having approached a wealthy Texas businessman, Morris Jaffe, for financial help for her, and for allegedly giving false statements to the FBI during his background check (DeParle 1994b). It was later revealed that the Clinton administration had known of these payments as far back as the postelection transition, but had concluded, based on advice from Hubbell, that they should not be an obstacle to a cabinet position (Devroy and Thomas 1995, 14). One official noted that the fact that the Democrats controlled both houses of Congress and would run the nomination process "gave us confidence that we could surmount a lot of problems if they ever came out" (Devroy and Thomas 1995, 14).

An independent counsel has been appointed to investigate the business dealings of Secretary of Commerce Ronald H. Brown, the second such investigation into his affairs. He is accused of failing to disclose a series of substantial transactions in the sale of his stake in a company that made no profits and in which he had invested no money (Bradsher 1995). Clinton's secretary of agriculture, Mike Espy, forced to resign, is under investigation for accepting gifts from companies he regulated (including Tyson Foods of Arkansas), including Super Bowl tickets and a college scholarship for his girlfriend (Johnson 1994c).

In addition to those Clinton administration members who have resigned or are currently under investigation by special prosecutors, the administration has engaged in behavior that, while not illegal, skirts appropriate boundaries for high government officials. For example, in order to defray costs connected with their legal difficulties regarding Whitewater and the sexual harassment suit filed against the president, the Clintons created a legal defense fund. White House spokeswoman Dee Dee Myers justified the fund, the first ever established for a president, by the "unprecedented circumstances" of a president being faced with such large and ongoing legal bills, arguing that "it is in the best interests of the country and the Presidency to have these bills paid" (Johnson 1994b). The White House noted that their self-imposed restrictions were more stringent than those governing Congressional rules on such funds. However, in an editorial entitled "The Tainted Defense Fund," the normally supportive *New York Times* (1994d) questioned

> the decision to allow contributions by lobbyists and people who do business with the administration. . . . Is there no one in this White House who understands the erosive impact of the administration's habit of demanding full credit for half measures? . . . The Clintons choose not to deny themselves the guaranteed income stream from those who will contribute to a President because he is President . . . in other words, the Clintons once again have chosen dollars over the principles of ethical government.

When criticism arose about granting operation of White House airline business to a Clinton relative and close friend, William Kennedy of the White House Council's office held a White House meeting with the FBI on May 12, 1993, in which he sought to enlist the FBI to conduct a criminal investigation to buttress the charges of "financial mismanagement" at the travel office. In response to criticism about politicizing the FBI, Nussbaum issued a directive forbidding any further contact with the FBI on this matter, except through the attorney general. Shortly thereafter, on May 21, 1995, another White House meeting with the FBI took place, attended by George Stephanopoulos, Vincent Foster, Kennedy, and Nussbaum, who asked the FBI agent to "strengthen" its statement regarding the travel office. Janet Reno publicly criticized the White House Council's office for calling in the FBI without informing her (Drew 1994, 180–81).

The list goes on. A Federal District Judge has accused Ira Magaziner, the administration's chief architect, of giving "misleading testimony" to the court as it tried to determine whether the administration's health-care panel of experts should or should not be considered government employees. The judge characterized Magaziner's comments as "misleading at best" and directed the Justice Department to determine if there was sufficient grounds for a charge of perjury or criminal contempt (Pear 1994a). The Justice Department decided not to file charges.

The White House confirmed that Stephanopoulos called an official in the Treasury Department to complain angrily about its decision to hire a former Republican prosecutor to investigate the collapse of the Madison Guaranty Savings and Loan Association. During the conversation, Stephanopoulos asked "whether the hiring was final or whether Mr. Stephens could be replaced" (Labaton 1994h). When Altman decided to excuse himself from the Whitewater investigations, he was subject to "enormous pressure" from the White House to stay in that role (Labaton 1994e), pressure first denied by the White House but later confirmed by White House Counsel Lloyd N. Cutler (Labaton 1994f).

The skirting and sometimes crossing of ethical boundaries is not confined to members of the Clinton administration; is also evidenced in Clinton's own behavior. When two Arkansas state troopers alleged that they had acted as intermediaries with several women with whom Clinton was involved, the president repeatedly called them. It was later revealed that others had placed similar calls, including Bruce Lindsey, a senior aide and longtime friend of the Clintons', Clinton's chief of staff Thomas "Mac" McLarty, and former Arkansas state trooper Buddy Young, who had been given a high-paying federal job as FEMA regional manager by the administration (Drew 1994, 382–83).

Clinton also involved himself regularly in the ongoing Whitewater investigations. He was made aware of the progress of the investigation by members of his staff who had talked with Altman. Clinton approached Eugene A. Ludwig, a friend and administration appointee who holds the position of comptroller of the currency (the country's top bank regulator), and asked for legal advice regarding his and his wife's ties to the failed savings and loan being investigated. Ludwig declined, writing in a memorandum covering the contact that "it would be impermissible for me to discuss the matter with the President or First Lady" (Bradsher 1994b).

The *New York Times* (1994c) summed up this contact and other examples of President Clinton's behavior when it noted,

> His overture springs from the same insensitivity that allowed his subordinates to order up White House-Treasury debriefings and earlier, to misuse the powers of the Federal Bureau of Investigation to build a case against the White House travel department. The governing assumption seems to be that government agencies exist mainly for the convenience of the President and his staff.

In short, the normal boundaries that govern others don't apply to President Clinton and his administration.

V

CONCLUSION

★ ——

CHAPTER 14

LOST OPPORTUNITIES: PRESIDENT CLINTON'S FIRST TERM

Bill Clinton began his administration with the capabilities, skills, and experience to be counted among our best presidents. Intelligent, informed, exceptionally articulate, and clearly capable of communicating a vision, he seems to possess all that is needed to find a common ground among Americans and, in so doing, reduce public anxiety and conflict by serving as a common point of reference for diverse views. In a political system in which legislative and political accomplishments often turn on the capacity to develop and maintain relationships, Clinton is an acknowledged extrovert and master of personal charm. An experienced political leader, he has been training for a political life since his first try for office as a high school student many years ago. On the way to the presidency he has accumulated as much political experience as it is possible to acquire given his age, and has done so systematically with a view toward his future.

Yet the first term of his presidency stands in danger of being remembered more for its volatility and controversy than for its accomplishments. His reelection is in doubt. His party, in disarray, was forcefully repudiated in the midterm elections. Even if he is reelected, he is likely to face vastly different and more difficult political circumstances than when he entered office in 1992. And yet, paradoxically, the sweeping Republican midterm victories may prove to be a source of Clinton's salvation should he gain a second term.

The puzzle of the Clinton presidency is not only to be found in the discrepancies between his enormous capabilities and his tenuous political standing, but in the fact that, if success is measured by legislative accomplishment, Clinton should be on much firmer political ground than he is. Why has Clinton, as he has often complained, not received sufficient credit for all that he has done?

Clinton has offered a number of explanations for this gap. He has attributed it to the fact that he has accomplished too much for people to fully appreciate it all. Speaking to reporters, Clinton noted, "I was doing all these things that 70% of the American people really agreed with, when they heard about it, but . . . a lot of them couldn't receive it . . . [they] couldn't absorb it" (Clinton 1995a, 1680). He has attributed it to the fact that "there's a big gap between what we've done and what I've been able to tell the people about [and] I've got to do a better job [of telling them]" (Clinton 1993h, 24). He has criticized the media for not fairly or fully reporting his administration's efforts. He has said that there is simply too much information out there and that, as a result, the public has difficulty focusing on what he has done: "It's almost impossible for people to know what's going on out there given the nature of communications today. There's a lot of information, but it's always on something new day-in and day-out. And it tends to emphasize conflict over achievement" (Clinton 1995c, 1391). Many Americans, he also believes, cannot yet see the direct result of his efforts in specific improvements in their daily lives: "A lot of people haven't felt the positive effects of the things we've done. There's a time lag between when you do something in Government and when people feel it" (Clinton 1995g, 1518).

While these arguments are not without foundation, they do not tell the entire story.

WHAT WENT WRONG?

While Clinton's precarious political standing is not the result of a single factor, the fundamental mismatch between the scope of his ambitions and the public's hopes and fears has certainly played a central role. To understand this more clearly, we must return to the basic public dilemma that framed Clinton's election. What did Americans want from President Clinton? They wanted a president who addressed their problems in a fair, honest, consensual, and effective way. A president whose policies would be equitable to groups across the political spectrum. A president who would be clear in telling them what was at stake in the policies he proposed: what the dangers were, what the potential gains were, and how he would address and manage the risks. A president who was able to work with others—even those who did not share his views—to develop a bipartisan consensus that would help redefine America's political center. Finally, they wanted a president who would effectively address some of the country's most urgent problems without resorting to large government programs, which they increasingly viewed with suspicion.

Clinton understood all of this. His self-identification as a "New Democrat" was an explicit response to the public's hopes. Yet Clinton failed to fulfill his promises because they proved to be incompatible with his ambition and his psychology. His personal, political, and policy ambitions, and those of his administration, have unsettled the public. Compounding this problem is Clinton's view that he knows best. This was perhaps most evident in the Clintons' complex, vastly ambitious, and highly regulatory health-care plan.[1] The administration felt it was giving the public a policy of biblical importance. When asked about the delays in introducing the plan, Mark D. Gearan, White House Communications Director, replied, "We have no interest in rushing this . . . *we are coming down from the mountain with stone tablets* (Ifill 1993c, B10, emphasis mine). The public felt differently—Clinton was no Moses, his wife's health-care plan no Ten Commandments. Two years later Clinton was still attributing its defeat to a well-financed campaign of distortion (Clinton 1995i, 957).

The first two years of the Clinton presidency represent its views and assumptions in their most pristine form. The post-1994 Clinton presidency reflects modifications in response to the Republican midterm landslide. These two years have been marked by a series of mismatches between Clinton's aspirations and the public's, differences already in evidence during the campaign.

Some have linked Clinton's early troubles to his support for allowing homosexuals to serve in the military. But a different policy initiative frames the sources of his troubles much more instructively. Well before health care, there was the troubled government vaccine program. The first major administration policy initiative, it clearly reflected Clinton's combination of abundant ambition and self-confidence.

THE VACCINE DEBACLE

Immunizing children is, by any measure, a laudable and politically safe goal. It reflects a government's responsibility for the basic physical health of its citizens and saves lives, money, and suffering. However, the Clinton vaccine program serves as an emblematic and cautionary tale, made all the more troubling because of how unassailable it should have been.[2]

Clinton's program, championed by Hillary Clinton, to buy up and distribute all childhood vaccines had its roots early in the administration. In a series of meetings on the first Clinton budget, Clinton insisted on a government program guaranteeing immunization of every child for diphtheria, polio, and tetanus (DPT) (Drew 1994, 72). Along with full funding of Head Start, this program had been at the top of the agenda of the Children's Defense Fund, an advocacy group headed by Marian Wright Edelman, a close friend of Hillary Clinton.

The campaign was viewed by the Clintons as the kick-off for their health-care plan, and was based on two premises: (1) rates of immunizations were too low, and (2) the high cost of vaccines was the reason. The first premise had come to federal attention because of major outbreaks of measles between 1989 and 1991. The General Accounting Office (1994a, 6) noted that statistical studies of immunization rates in 1985, the last year for which data were available, suggested that only 55 percent of preschoolers had received three or more polio vaccines and only 65 percent were fully vaccinated against DPT. Half of the measles cases in 1990 occurred in preschool children; of these, only 20 percent of those eligible were thought to have been vaccinated.

The view that high costs were responsible for the low immunization rates first surfaced in a February 1993 speech given by Hillary Clinton in which she noted that in the public sector it cost $6.69 to immunize a child in 1981 and $90.43 in 1991 (the comparable figures for the private sector were $23.29 and $243.90). "Unless you're willing to take on those who profited from that kind of increase and are continuing to do so," she noted, "you cannot provide the kind of universal immunization system that this country needs to have" (Pear 1993h). The next day, President Clinton criticized drug companies for pursuing "profits at the expense of our children," announced plans to spend $300 million to increase the number of vaccinations, and said he was considering a program to purchase the entire supply of children's vaccines and distribute them free of charge (Berke 1993d). In subsequent public talks, he was even harsher, presenting a simple moral story with drug companies as the identifiable villains.[3]

The drug companies fired back by citing a number of factors that contributed to increased costs: more shots are recommended now than in 1982; costs of production have gone up; the federal government imposed an excise tax on vaccinations from 1988 to 1992; and companies had to absorb the cost of litigation associated with the small percentage of people who experience adverse physical effects after being vaccinated (Berke 1993d; Freudenheim 1993). Most importantly, they argued, enough free vaccine *was* available for those who needed but could not afford it, but children were often not brought to get the free shots. The problem was not price but lack of parental responsibility (Marks 1993, A1).[4]

In April 1993 Clinton submitted a proposal to Congress (The Comprehensive Child Immunization Act of 1993) that called for the federal government to buy up all the childhood vaccines produced and distribute them free of charge to all children, rich and poor, at an estimated cost of $1.1 billion a year, plus a $200 million outreach program and a $275 million tracking system (DeParle 1993a). No mechanism was suggested to pay for this new entitlement. The bill would have abolished the private market in vaccines, a move that drug companies warned would "kill industrial vaccine research and development" (Vagelos 1993). Critics also pointed out that providing immunization for all children, even those whose parents could well afford it, was a poor use of government resources.

The creation of a vast new entitlement program for rich and poor, without asking anything in return, appeared inconsistent with Clinton's campaign emphasis on being a New Democrat, one who would focus on responsibilities as well as rights. At congressional hearings on the bill, Donna Shalala, secretary of Health, Education, and Welfare, defended the administration's proposal by arguing that cost was the main impediment to immunization and that it favored the distribution of free vaccines *as a matter of principle.*

At the same congressional hearings, newer, post-1986 data on immunization was made public, suggesting that immunization rates were much higher than had previously been thought. More than 95 percent of American children were fully immunized by the time they entered school, although only 55 percent were fully vaccinated by the age of two, which health-care professionals thought preferable (DeParle 1993a).[5] There were real problem areas, but the problems appeared to be of a different kind and magnitude than those that had prompted Clinton's comprehensive initiative. One problem was clearly the low rate of early immunization. The other problem was that rates of immunization were substantially lower for poorer children, especially in inner-city neighborhoods. But the real question was, what accounted for this?

Donna Shalala argued that the culprit was the unconscionable cost of vaccines. Others pointed out that the government already bought twice the amount of free vaccine needed to immunize all poor children. Moreover, in the eleven states that already bought and distributed free vaccine to all who needed it, immunization rates were not much better than in the other forty-one states. The problem was not cost, but rather the infrastructure of delivery and "disorganized or even neglectful parents," a phrase that came from doctors who devoted themselves to working with high-risk inner-city children (DeParle 1993a). When the question of linking welfare payments, food stamps, or refundable tax credits to proof of immunization was raised, "that proposal drew no enthusiasm from Ms. Shalala" (DeParle 1993a). Early in the Clinton administration, a focus on personal responsibility and a targeted attempt to improve delivery took a back seat to a vast new entitlement program, albeit one that appeared sound and laudable.

By May, facing likely defeat in Congress, the administration modified its proposal. It agreed to preserve a private market for vaccines and to buy vaccine only for those who could not afford it or whose insurance did not cover it. Under the agreement, however, there was no mechanism to determine whether parents could afford the vaccine, or whether or not they had health insurance that helped to cover the cost. The revised proposal called for increasing clinic hours and hiring health-care professionals to conduct outreach programs. A proposal by Republicans to allow states to offer seventy-five dollars a month more to families on welfare whose children were fully vaccinated, and lower payments to those whose children weren't, was voted down on a straight party-line vote (DeParle 1993d). On August 14, 1993, the president signed the revised bill into law, which called for the program to become operational by October 1, 1994, under the auspices of the Center for Disease Control (CDC).

In July 1994, the General Accounting Office (GAO) released the first of the two comprehensive reports it made on the Clinton vaccine program, calling it "very ambitious." Eight months after the law had been signed, and two months before the program was to be fully operational, the GAO found severe problems in its design and implementation.[6] Worse, the report noted, some implementation decisions ran counter to the CDC's stated program goals. For example, there was no attempt to institute an individual-child tracking system, without which it was impossible to keep track of who had or had not gotten the required shots. However, the most damaging finding of the report was that although the program

> aims to increase vaccination coverage rates by removing vaccine cost as a barrier to vaccine . . . most recent studies, including those of four inner-city areas where the undervaccination tend to be concentrated, indicate that vaccine cost is not an important barrier. . . . Although lower socioeconomic status is definitely associated with undervaccination, this rela-

tionship does not appear to function through cost, but rather through other factors associated with poverty. (GAO 1994a, 19).

In short, the program as conceived was unnecessary. Based on laudable goals but an erroneous premise, the program, defined by an ambitious implementation schedule, was poorly designed, with no built-in accountability or program evaluation. The GAO study called attention to numerous difficulties in the seven areas it examined (see note 6) and also suggested more targeted strategies to address these problems.

In his inaugural address Clinton had promised that he would make the government "a place for what Franklin Roosevelt called bold, persistent experimentation" (Clinton 1993g). Implicit in his promise, and in his self-identification as a New Democrat, was a commitment not only to be bold, but to be smart and flexible, to implement policies on a provisional basis, to see if they worked, and to scrap them if they didn't.

How, then, did the administration respond to this new information? Did Clinton revise the program in light of the GAO's findings and recommendations? Did he scale back its ambitions or reallocate resources, as a New Democrat might have done? On the contrary, while the GAO was conducting its investigation and was in touch with the administration and CDC on an ongoing basis regarding its concerns, the Clinton administration plunged ahead, expanding the program's ambitions. That spring, members of Congress, Democrats and Republicans alike, complained that "the Clinton administration has gone far beyond what Congress intended when it passed legislation last year to insure that all children would be vaccinated" (Pear 1994c). It had placed orders for far more vaccine than needed for its purposes.[7] Senator Dale Bumpers (D-Arkansas), a long-time champion of child immunization, charged that the administration was trying to bypass the agreement it had reached to scale down the original program by buying enough vaccine for middle- and upper-middle-class children whose insurance might well cover most of the recommended shots.

The administration had also begun to set up its own distribution system by purchasing a large warehouse, thereby bypassing an already functioning private enterprise distribution system with years of successful experience. Senator William Danforth, a moderate Republican who had supported the Clinton plan, described this as "crazy." Senator Bumpers called it "dangerous" and noted that the plan, as implemented, "took us dangerously close to nationalizing the pediatric vaccine market, a result . . . Congress never intended. A fairly simple law, designed to benefit a relatively small group of uninsured children, was transformed into a bureaucratic nightmare that put the safety and availability of a third of our nation's vaccine supply at risk" (Pear 1994c). In the words of a *New York Times* editorial, "the administration, having predicated part of its free vaccine program on the 'greed' of the pharmaceutical companies, proceeded *to demonize an established, largely private delivery system that was working just fine*" (1994e, emphasis mine). On August 22, in response to severe public criticism of the plan from Democrats, Republicans, drug company executives, federal auditors, state officials, and doctors, the administration reversed itself and abandoned its plan to operate a national vaccine distribution system (Pear 1994e).

The final chapter in this story began to unfold when the GAO released a second study of the Clinton vaccine program in June 1995, one year after its first report and ten months after the program had been scheduled to become fully operational. In a second, independent assessment the GAO (1995b, 14–21) found once again that cost was not a barrier to immunization. Another GAO report on the price of prescription drugs released in May 1994 found that "the Labor Department overstated inflation rates in prescription drugs in some parts of the market by 23 percent to 36 percent," a mistake that led government statistics to show "drug prices rising, on average, at triple the rate of general inflation during the 1980's and early 1990's" (Freudenheim 1995). The GAO study of the vaccine program noted that an independent analysis conducted for the U.S. Department of Health and Human Services found that 54 percent of the cost increase for immunizing children was attributable to the addition of new vaccines to the immunization schedule, and 15 percent to the government-imposed excise tax (GAO 1995b, 19). While costs did rise rapidly in the early 1980s, this growth "flattened out considerably after the National Vaccine Compensation Program began in 1988 . . . [and] since 1988, per dose revenues *have not grown faster than inflation*" (GAO 1995b, 19, emphasis mine). In short, the basic assumptions underlying the Clinton's program were again shown to be fundamentally flawed.

The second GAO study also undertook a more thorough analysis of the rates of child immunization for the two quarters (six months) prior to implementation of Clinton's program, and compared these to the administration's 1996 goals of 90 percent immunization for DPT, Measles, Polio, and Influenza and 70 percent for Hepatitis B (the most recently introduced vaccine). The study found that before the Clinton program was even implemented, goals "had already been met for two of the five, and they had nearly been met in two others" (GAO 1995b, 14–15). The point made in the 1993 congressional hearings was correct: There was no real "crisis," but rather pockets of undervaccination.

Clinton had committed the government to a major new entitlement that required it to take over and essentially close down the private childhood vaccine development and distribution market, thus endangering childhood vaccine research and development. Moreover, it did so on the basis of erroneous data and assumptions about immunization rates and costs, and by attributing the most base of motives to companies in a highly competitive market, whose purpose was to develop useful products while profiting from doing so.

Undervaccination was and is a real issue, but it is extremely questionable whether this problem necessitated a vast entitlement program. Furthermore, it remains unclear if Clinton's program really helped. The GAO found that although there had been improvements in the program since its last audit, "six of the [seven] VFC's critical tasks remained incomplete" (GAO 1995b, 4, 22–31). No change had been made in the program's implementation to ensure accountability, and thus there was no way to "detect fraud and waste . . . and no way to ensure that VFC is reaching the target population, let alone pockets of undervaccination" (GAO 1995b, 29). As of May 1995, there were still no plans for evaluating the program, and thus it was and would not be possible to assess its effect (GAO 1995b, 30). In spite of this fact, and in spite of the GAO finding that immunization levels were already at or close to the program's targeted 1996 goals six months before the program was implemented, the administration's 1995 budget report claimed credit for having "made substantial progress toward its goal of immunizing 90% of children up to age two by 1996" (Goldberg 1995).

Just how little progress Clinton's program actually made in addressing what had emerged as the one major problem in this area—the pockets of undervaccination in poorer urban and rural neighborhoods—Clinton himself revealed in remarks made during a 1995 speech at the National Governor's Association Meeting. Touting AmeriCorps, another major Clinton initiative that had become controversial because the GAO had found that the program required over $30,000 to support each participant, he noted that "Texas was the first state to use national service workers, AmeriCorps volunteers, in the summer of '93 to immunize over 100,000 children and since then they've immunized 50,000 more" (Clinton 1995j, 1348). One can applaud that result while still noting that outreach programs were part of the mandate and costs of the vaccination program. Either the latter was not accomplishing its purposes, or the government now had two separate programs requiring two separate and substantial revenue costs doing the same thing, or both.

The vaccine program is a virtual catalogue of all the issues that have made Clinton's first term so problematic. Another crucial factor, however, is the mismatch between Clinton's desire for change and the electorate's yearning for stability.

COMMITMENT TO CHANGE VERSUS A YEARNING FOR STABILITY

Is Clinton a pragmatist, a liberal, a moderate, an amalgam of those three, or something else entirely? With his commitment to substantial government programs to solve a wide range of social problems, Clinton is certainly solidly within the traditional liberal Democratic party tradition, his calls for traditional values such as responsibility notwithstanding. But Clinton's commitment to government intervention masks a more radical element in his leadership psychology: his commitment to sweeping, and continuous change.

Consider his words to the National Governor's Association in 1993: "I am convinced that what this nation really needs is a vital center, one committed to *fundamental* and *profound* and *relentless* and *continuing* change" (Clinton 1993a, 1631, emphasis mine). In a *Meet the Press* interview on his first year in office, Clinton said, "I was absolutely certain a year ago that I could pursue this aggressive agenda of change . . . and convince them [the American people] that we were going right" (Clinton 1993h, 24). In a 1995 interview defending his record, he continued in the same vein: "I think the most important thing I've done is to try to *force the government, and hopefully the American people,* to keep looking toward the future and say, 'Okay, there are these problems. Let's take them on. Let's move into the future'" (Clinton 1995f, 1498, emphasis mine). In remarks at a September 1995 fundraiser, Clinton noted that "a lot of the decisions that come to me are hard ones and because we [the administration] *are always pushing the envelope of possible change*" (1995h, 1639, emphasis mine).

So what's wrong with change? Precisely this: change is psychologically unsettling. Decades of research document that even positive change, such as a promotion, brings with it anxiety as well as opportunity. Many people approach change cautiously and prefer what they know, even when it entails substantial costs. When change results in too large a gap between a person's ability to cope and the demands to do so, the results can be traumatic. Change may be a friend to Clinton, but it is decidedly less so for many citizens worried about the present as well as the future.

Clinton has recognized this fact, but he has not yet connected the contribution that his own commitment to be a driving force for relentless change makes to public anxieties. At one fundraiser he said, "There is a lot of unease and uncertainty in our country because we're going though a period of change as profound as the change that we went through when we became an industrial society. . . . The period we're living through is the most profound period of change since roughly the time between 1895 and 1916" (Clinton 1995g, 1518). When asked during an interview with Larry King why Americans are so upset, Clinton responded, "Because it's an unsettling time. . . . The bad news is that there's all this pressure unsettling people's lives, whether it's people being less secure in their jobs, or working harder for less, or being subject to smaller fanatic groups who practice destruction . . . so it's a time of great ferment and upheaval" (Clinton 1995d, 1642). Clinton has correctly diagnosed the traumatic consequences of change, but he has failed to appreciate that his own persistent drive to be "always pushing the envelope of possible change" is part of the problem rather than a solution. It is another example of how empathy can flounder on the treacherous shoals of ambition and certainty.

This problem has been exacerbated in several instances by the administration's tendency to foster a sense of public urgency in order to bolster support for programs it wants to implement. The most dramatic example of this was the Clintons' oft-stated view that the whole health-care system was in crisis, when in fact the United States has one of the finest health-care systems in the world and most Americans are very satisfied with the quality of their care and their physicians. To be sure the system has flaws, but whether these problems constitute a real profound crisis, or whether the idea of a crisis is more politically useful than factually correct is a matter of some debate. A similar tactic can be seen in the administration's public alarm at the "immunization crisis," which on closer inspection turned out to be much less critical than the administration insisted it was.

Proclaiming a crisis can spur short-term public support for an administration's initiatives. But it does so at a price. Crises increase public anxiety. Declaring a crisis may also result in a sense of public malaise, as more and more of the country's basic institutions are said to be in or near crisis circumstances, and the public adds to that its own concerns about issues like crime, welfare, and race relations. Finally, by stressing those figures that support the idea of crisis and downplaying or ignoring data that don't, as it did in the immunization debate, the administration deceived the public. Unable to believe that the public would support the needed measures, or unwilling to put forward a modest incremental program for reasons of personal or other policy ambitions, the administration resorted to mobilization by misdirection.

The relentless push toward change is understandable in the context of Clinton's psychology and his dislike of limits. Change, after all, runs counter to structure. And Clinton is accustomed, because of his own early experiences, to the lack of structure and the stability that accompanies it. Left on his own as a child and adolescent, Clinton had to be his own parent—literally to develop himself. Clinton's empathetic lapse is to be found in his assumption that because he was forced to confront instability *and did*, others can as well.

Managing Change

Clinton's enthusiasm for "fundamental and profound and relentless and continuing change" and his assumption that citizens will, like him, embrace such change points to two rather profound mismatches between him and the public. The first entails the process by which the political center is defined; the second is the critical question of how change, even if deemed good, is managed. The first requires us to focus on how Clinton, as a self-professed "New Democrat," locates the political center. The second requires us to focus, with Clinton's commitment to change in mind, on how well he has managing the educational functions of his presidency.

Clinton's ambition and high self-confidence lead him to embrace a "top down" theory of change—change that is mandated by himself and his administration for what they define as the common good. Both Clintons see themselves as transcending the "brain dead" politics of Left and Right and believe they have developed policies that are not bound by traditional categories of ideology. By moving beyond such categories, they promised to find the vibrant, moderate, smart, and effective center of American politics. But what exactly is this center and how is it to be reached? The answer to both questions is: *through the medium of President Clinton himself.* Throughout his candidacy and presidency the "central myth of the Clinton administration [has been] that conflicting ideas could be brought rather easily *through the agency of himself* into something that would pass for agreement" (Kelly 1993a, emphasis mine). In the case of Lani Guinier, for example, Clinton argued that, although her ideas were very controversial and she would have immense power to interpret and enforce civil rights law, it didn't matter because the president is the ultimate source of any discretionary power.

The problem with this view is that it makes the public highly dependent on Clinton as *the* arbiter of the political center. But the message he conveys about the location of this center is confusing to many. He is pro-business *and* pro-labor; he is for economic growth but also for environmental protection; he is against quotas but for affirmative action. Clinton himself will locate the center somewhere within the range of his diverse—some think incompatible—views. The process leading to this end is located in *his* unique ability to transcend the "brain-dead" politics of the past.

Such an approach places a heavy responsibility on Clinton to take the public into his confidence and share with them how he arrives at his policy conclusions. It requires him to give strong emphasis not to selling his policies but to explaining them. Because what he is proposing is new to American politics, which has for many years been locked in the struggle of Left and Right, because his agenda involves substantial political and social change, and because a climate of mistrust frames his presidency, Clinton not only has a presidential responsibility to educate the public regarding the changes he desires, he also has substantial self-interested political reasons to do so. Yet, the administration has preferred to finesse the issues rather than address them.

DEFINING THE POLITICAL CENTER

The fundamental, and ultimately irreconcilable, policy inconsistency of the Clinton presidency was his promise to "reinvent government"—to make it smaller, more efficient, and smarter—while at the same racing to introduce dramatic expansions of government programs and responsibilities. Clinton has occasionally kept his word. The administration's family leave bill, allowing parents to take time off from work to be with ailing family members or new babies without fear of losing their jobs, is a model of a modest, needed, and successful initiative. It remains, however, the exception to the rule.

Was it possible for Clinton to reduce government, while at the same time developing a health-care plan that created 105 new governmental entities, expanded the responsibilities of 47 others, and committed the federal government to vast new regulation of a sector that accounts for one-seventh of the gross national product (Specter 1993)?

Was it possible to reduce the scope of government while endorsing a Housing and Urban Development (HUD) draft report that argued, erroneously according to Jenks's (1994) analysis, that 600,000 people were homeless on any night and "seven million have experienced homelessness

... at some point in the latter half of the 1980's" (HUD 1994, 2)? That report was the pretext for justifying a request for billions of dollars in new "homeless prevention" programs for an agency that Clinton had been warned during his transition period was riddled with waste and inefficiency (DeParle 1993b).[8]

Is it possible to be serious about cutting the deficit while at the same time implementing a National Service Program that, in its first year, cost $31,017 to support each participant (GAO 1995a 23)? Early nonadministration estimates suggested that to fully fund the program would cost at least $13 billion a year (Samuelson 1993a). It seems quite likely that such a program would in reality cost many billions a year more than the early estimates. Assuming laudable purposes, is this program the best or most cost-effective way to accomplish them?

Is it really sound policy, as Clinton proposed in his original welfare plan, to invest new billions (artfully hidden)[9] in retraining programs that have had mixed results,[10] and child care subsidies for the poor that are not available to the working and lower middle classes, and then guarantee that the government will be the life-time employer of last resort for those who are still unable to obtain or keep jobs?

Is it really possible to be against quotas, as President Clinton has said he is, but try to mandate targets for the numbers of minorities candidates placed in specialty medical training, as the Clinton health-care plan tried to do?

Is it consistent to insist, as President Clinton has done, that abortion "should be safe, legal and rare," and that "there are too many abortions performed in America," while at the same time extending federal financing of abortion to poor women who already without such help have three times more abortions than better-off women (Clinton 1995e, 1429)?[11]

Who knows what would have happened had President Clinton impressed upon Americans how important it is to balance compassion for the needy with a realistic sense of what government can accomplish when people don't take much responsibility for their lives, and even when they do? Who knows what would have happened had President Clinton led the public in a national discussion of how it might be possible to reconcile affirmative action programs and the value of rewarding people for their performance and not their group membership? Who knows what would have happened if President Clinton had led Americans in a national discussion about how one might be both pro-choice and pro-life? Who knows what would have happened if President Clinton made clear the real responsibilities and limits of the government's role and the benefits and limitations of its doing more or less?

Debates about whether President Clinton is really a "New Democrat" and what exactly that means are now largely beside the point. Clinton badly fumbled a historic opportunity to lead the public discussion he promised. By not doing so, he failed the country and himself. His failure is all the more poignant because it is clear that he understood this opportunity and made effective use of it during his campaign. However, in the end his ambition proved far stronger than his ideals.

Because the president didn't initiate these discussions, the country now faces a ruthless and divisive presidential campaign sure to be fought with harsh accusations, misleading statistics, and delegitimizing characterizations. The president has already hired reelection strategists "with reputations for shrewdness and ruthless tactics," one of whom readily boasts, "I subscribe to terror" (Frisby 1995). Bob Dole was quoted in the same article as saying he expected a "scorched earth" campaign. Presumably that expectation would then justify his or some other Republican candidate's view that he must respond in kind. The building of a new, broad, bipartisan set of domestic understandings is the most tragic victim of this process. As a result, all Americans are losers.

It is possible that President Clinton and his allies can make the labels "callous," "extremist," and so on stick, and maybe even win reelection. That process is already in full swing. Clinton has accused the Republicans of attempting to "destroy" Medicare, although under their plan monthly premiums would rise to $53.50 from the present $46.10. He has accused Republicans of targeting "deep" cuts in education which would "undermine our schools," when the reality is that the federal government provided only 6.9 percent of all state educational funds and the relative small decrease in federal funding could hardly have this draconian effect when it accounts for so little of what the states actually spend. As Samuelson notes of Clinton's reelection strategy,

> We have witnessed a spectacle . . . that, although not quite unique in American history, is certainly rare and remarkable. It is the spectacle of the president actively striving to poison public opinion against a policy that seems best for the country to bolster his own political stock. There is no other way to describe President Clinton's behavior on the budget. Clinton routinely exaggerates and misstates [and] repeatedly vilifies the Republican budget. The purpose is to destroy and not debate. (1995, 5)

However, even if he should succeed, the first term of his presidency will be no less failed. The basic public dilemma will remain, and Clinton, even though reelected, will have exacerbated rather than resolved it. It is a sad conclusion to such a hopeful beginning.

Why a Second Clinton Term Might Be Better Than the First

As contradictory as it might seem, Clinton could prove to be a better president during a second term than he was during his first. Should he gain reelection, his second term might help to redeem his first. If this happens, however, it will not be because Clinton has learned new crucial lessons. Neither will his character abruptly change during his second term.

The most basic truism of social theory is that behavior is a joint function of the person and the environment. But this maxim is almost always framed as if an emphasis on the person must be at the expense of the contribution of the environment and vice versa. The view that a president's response to circumstances negates the importance of his psychology is one illustration of this assumption. Yet we often fail to appreciate just how closely linked external circumstances and a president's interior psychology are.

Consider President Clinton. A highly ambitious and self-confident person, he has repeatedly demonstrated difficulty in setting limits and clearly defining his political identity. Clinton entered office with a Democratic majority in both houses. The 1994 midterm election wiped out this majority and the 1996 election appears unlikely to restore it. What implications do these facts have for possibly improving Clinton's performance should he gain a second term?

Nowhere to Go: Ambition Finally Realized?

Clinton's mother dates her son's interest in politics to the moment when he was sixteen and met President Kennedy as an Arkansas delegate to the American Legion Boy's Nation Program. Over one hundred delegates attended and it was expected that the president would not be able to shake each boy's hand. But young Bill Clinton, then sixteen, determined that his hands would be among those so favored:

> I remember the day it occurred. I didn't know if the president was going to shake hands with all of the 100 boys, but because I was from Arkansas, I was at the top of the alphabet—and because I was above average in size, I would sort of elbow my way up to the front of the line. So I made sure I got to shake his hand. (Clinton 1995f, 1497)

Clinton has been successfully pushing his way to the front ever since.

Should he win reelection, however, it will mark the first time in his life since his mid-adolescence that Clinton is where he has always wanted to be and can aspire to no higher office and no further time in that office. Clinton's second term as president, if he gains it, will in a profound way mark the fullest realization of his life-long ambition. What then?

For a man who all his life has asked "What else? What else?" the question "What now?" will most likely be very disorienting. However, once this realization has set in, Clinton may feel liberated. No longer forced to struggle to a higher plane or fight for political survival, he will have an opportunity to separate more easily his personal, political, and policy ambitions. Clinton has always emphasized the last and defined it solely in terms of his commitment to the public good. He has bristled at suggestions that the first two played any role. His critics have emphasized the importance of the first two. A second term might provide decisive evidence on this matter.

Yet beyond the question of the relative weight of personal, political and policy ambition, it seems clear that personal and especially political ambition may play a reduced role in a second Clinton term. The constellation of internal forces will have changed. What will Clinton do with the opportunity?

The Imposition of Boundaries

President Clinton is a person who has not developed a substantially consolidated set of internal constraints. During his first term his personal psychology was exacerbated by three additional circumstances. First, while his wife tried to help him focus, her purpose was to help him more fully realize their own joint, ambitious agenda. Her attempt at imposing limits or structure on her husband was in the service of breaking through other limits and expanding vast new structures of government action. It is difficult to develop internal boundaries by offering the opportunity to expand external ones.

Second, Clinton's staff essentially exists to serve, not constrain, him. They serve at his pleasure, for his purposes. Therefore, there are severe limits to the degree to which they can compensate for his interior psychology, even if they worry about its effects.

Finally, and most importantly for the argument I wish to make here, *Clinton came into power with his party controlling both houses of Congress.* The importance of this fact for Clinton's psychology is obvious. Not only did Clinton lack a substantial set of internal constraints, but in Congress there was no countervailing center of power.

The first two years of the Clinton presidency provide the most accurate readings of his administration's primary impulses, and these impulses reflected Clinton's fundamental belief that he could solve a great many if not most problems by government programs. Clinton's vast agenda reflected this belief, and neither Hillary Clinton, his staff, or the Congress did much to modify it.[12]

With the 1994 midterm elections, a new external set of constraints has been imposed on Clinton—one might argue in response to his demonstration that he lacked and needed them. *The Republicans may well prove to be the most important basis of Clinton's rehabilitation as a second-term president.*

Arthur Schlesinger, Jr., (1974) once argued that alternative centers of political power are the best reality principle available to check the personal excesses of a presumptuous presidency. The Republican gains in the 1994 election appear to validate that point. If given a second term, Clinton will have to be modest in his policy aspirations, not because his character or ambition has changed, but rather because he *must.* If Republicans maintain, or further solidify, their hold on Congress, Clinton will be unable to propose large-scale social programs. Those programs he does propose will be much more closely scrutinized.

Clinton will be forced to settle for more modest programs, and he may find some public success in doing so. A substantial number of smart, modest, targeted, cost-effective programs may be the kind of activism that the public will support and reward. Clinton may even find satisfaction in their support and the prospects that his presidency will be remembered, if not for any "historic" accomplishments, at least for its many substantial ones.

Redefining the Political, and Clinton's, Center

The 1994 Republican sweep may also provide another great service to Clinton. It may help him to truly define himself. Clinton's pre-1994 political identity can be described as a "yes and" identity. Clinton was for many things: labor, business, environmentalists, growth and development, and so on. Except at the polar extremes, it was hard to find something Clinton was really against.

The Republicans have provided Clinton with an enormous personal and political opportunity in this regard. Freed from the need to scramble constantly to make sense to the public of how he can endorse so many seemingly incompatible positions, he can now directly, honestly, and more clearly find where he really stands. He no longer has to be for many things; he can now be for and against specific things. Clinton's new public stance of opposition may well resonate with the part of himself that he has only infrequently allowed the public to see, but which his staff and advisers are very familiar with—his anger. When Clinton's larger ambitions have failed him, his anger may help to mobilize and sustain him.

In defining himself in the context of a real opposition, Clinton (as well as the Republicans) may be performing a valuable public educational service that was missing in his first term: a real debate on where the political center is located. This would not be the somewhat artificial political center manufactured by Clinton, but rather the concrete center that is located through real debate and compromise on specific policy issues. It may well mean that conservative Democrats and moderate Republicans directly address the views of their more liberal and conservative peers, while trying to find the range of accommodation possible to solve important public problems. Through this process, which is possible only when there are real alternative centers of power, we might begin to learn how it is possible to be pro-choice and pro-life, compassionate and realistic, and for policies of inclusion that don't result in new forms of discrimination.

WHY CLINTON MIGHT FALTER AGAIN

That a second Clinton term will benefit from the dramatic change in political circumstances is by no means assured. This hopeful prediction depends on a continuation or further strengthening of the changes brought about by the 1994 midterm elections. While it does not seems likely, any substantial loss of Republican power in the Congress would probably buttress Clinton's original psychological and political impetus in his presidency. Clinton has argued that reelecting him is one way to guard against Republican policy excesses; the Republicans, however, might as justifiably argue the same in asking the public to maintain their hold on Congress.

Assuming that Republican congressional power remains intact, several other dangers lie ahead for Clinton should he get a second term. One potential serious problem is the frustration he and his wife might well feel at being unable to do what they have done all of their political lives. The Clintons have never had modest accomplishments in mind when they think of their presidency.

The Clintons may turn to other avenues to fulfill their ambitions in these circumstances, one of which might be to govern more directly by executive order and veto. A second Clinton term, if it goes in this direction, may be one of persistent stalemate, with the president unable to propose and Congress unable to override. The result is still likely to be more modest policies, but also a more substantial deterioration in public confidence in both institutions. In that case the basic public dilemma that framed Clinton's first term will remain unresolved in his second.

Even if the Clintons do not attempt these tactics, there is still a substantial risk that conflict will spiral in a second Clinton term. The Clintons, and especially Hillary Clinton, might find it hard to be pragmatic when pragmatism entails reaching agreements with those who hold very different views, and who in the past have served as villains in many of the Clintons' policy stories. Hillary Clinton, with her strong sense of occupying the moral high ground, may find such compromise beyond her abilities.

Bill Clinton has also burned many bridges during his first term. He left members of his own party on a limb during the stimulus bill debate and, more dramatically, on the budget debate, when he got members of the House to back his call for a large tax increase and then quickly reversed himself when opposition surfaced in the Senate. Clinton again called into question his fidelity to the commitments that he had asked others to make, at great personal and political risk, in an October 1995 speech in which he said, "Probably in this room there are people who are still mad at me because you think I raised your taxes too much. It might surprise you to know that I think that I raised them too much, too" (Purdum 1995a). The administration tried to withdraw the remark and argued that it had raised taxes only because the Republicans would not give him any support for his budget, a position

> dramatically at odds with the statements he made when he presented his budget plan. On February 15, 1993 Clinton told the nation in a speech from the oval office that "after working harder than I've ever worked in my life" in studying budget alternatives, he decided the tax increases were necessary to pay for increased spending "to invest in your future by creating jobs, expanding education, reforming health care" as well as for deficit reduction. . . . Clinton's budget pronouncements came two weeks before he had his first meetings with them [Republicans] in early March. (Harris 1995)

Predictably, Republicans expressed bemusement and incredulity at Clinton's reversal and explanation. Democrats expressed outrage at what they felt was Clinton's latest betrayal in the service of his own self-interest. And herein lies the risk in Clinton's reelection strategy of "triangulation." [13] Even if Clinton is reelected, he may find it difficult to govern. Presidential prerogatives and his own ambitions will ensure Clinton a continuing role, but of what kind? Clinton has few friends or admirers among the Republicans and, increasingly, among the Democrats as well. No modern president is likely to be irrelevant to the policy process, but contempt and anger from one's own party colleagues as well as one's opponents complicate governing and are a poor recipe for influence.

Clinton's strategy also threatens to decrease his already tenuous informal authority. Reputation is a key ingredient of a president's informal authority, and character—competence, integrity, and fidelity—is the foundation of his reputation. According to Clinton's chief campaign adviser, Dick Morris,

> The President's midterm correction, which began in earnest last June, with his embrace of the balanced budget plan, and intensified this fall, with his acquiescence in drastic cuts in welfare, currently accounts to nothing less than a Second Clinton Administration. . . . By January's State of the Union message, the President will have so utterly coopted the more popular parts of the G.O.P. agenda that he will be ready to unveil a Third Clinton Administration: a return to traditional Democratic issues of a kind that have strong middle-class appeal, such as education and the environment. (Mayer 1995, 59)

The attempt to turn Clinton back into the "third party centrist" that he promised to be in the 1992 election is a clever and necessary strategy. It may even prove successful. But at its core is a potentially fatal flaw. Arguing that a liberal Democratic Congress was responsible for pulling Clinton off track to the left raises the question of why Clinton allowed it to happen. Did he lack the courage or conviction to resist? Did he allow himself to be pushed because he was really secretly in agreement with them?

This strategy may well increase, rather than diminish, questions about where Clinton really stands and what he really stands for beyond clever, self-interested politics. In electing a second Roosevelt, Truman, Eisenhower, or Reagan administration, the public voted for and received a single, coherent presidency. Is the public ready for three different presidencies, all from the same president? Will this not add to the public's confusion and disaffection? Can the basic public dilemma regarding trust in government be successfully addressed and resolved by this strategy, even if Clinton is successful?

Conclusion

Gearing up for his reelection campaign, President Clinton was asked what the most important thing was he had learned about leadership since he had been elected. He replied,

> The most significant thing I've learned . . . is that . . . being an effective president . . . is about more than what you actually accomplish. It's about more than the bills you pass in Congress or the executive actions you take. It's also about the words you say and how you say them. . . . The President must be much more careful, much more clear, much more unambiguous . . . in discussing an issue . . . and I am much more . . . sensitive to . . . giving the American people the understanding that we're making the decisions based on my convictions. (Clinton 1995d, 1651)

Whether President Clinton will be reelected to a second term is one major question. Whether Clinton's new-found awareness expressed above is real or part of his reelection strategy is another. And, finally, if he is reelected, whether he will be seen as having fidelity to any convictions beyond his own self-interest is perhaps the most basic question for the Clinton presidency.

★ ──

BILL CLINTON'S CHARACTER AND
PRESIDENCY: A NOTE ON METHOD

What is the best way to understand a president's interior psychology? The most common approach is to focus on particular aspects of a president's personality that are deemed important. Many have, for example, focused on what they see as Clinton's need to be liked. However, that trait has been made to carry too heavy an explanatory burden. The problem with using a single trait to explain Clinton is not only that of trying to explain too much with too little, but also that such an approach tends to oversimplify his psychology. Clinton's psychology is robust, complex, powerful, and expansive. It is not easily or accurately captured by any single trait, and certainly not simply by a need to be liked.

Examining more than one presidential trait is an improvement, but does not necessarily resolve this issue. We need to know not only if traits are related to each other, but why. Trait studies can tell us something about the former, but not much about the latter. David G. Winter, for example, recently profiled the 1992 presidential candidates on their affiliation, power, and achievement scores. He found that President Clinton scored high on achievement, above average on affiliation, and moderate to high on power motivation (1995, 126). Leaving aside questions of measurement and validity (Clinton has been characterized by many as having a high need for affiliation), such a study cannot tell us why these three traits adhere like this for Clinton, and why Perot and Bush have very different configurations.[1]

Finally, a focus on traits, however many and however central, omits a critical element of psychological information for assessing presidential performance—*how* the president translates the trait from internal psychology to the arena of political action. The trait of power motivation, for example, can take many forms. It can take the form of blatantly exerting power over someone. It can take the form of secrecy, or of ordering rather than listening. It can take the form of accumulating rather than sharing decision-making, and so on. Power motivation in a president can even take the form of trying to accomplish laudable public purposes. Clearly, it is critical to know what a trait means, how it is connected with other parts of the president's psychology, and how it is manifested in the concrete world of presidential performance.

There are four basic questions regarding any president's psychology. First, what are the basic elements of a president's psychology that most accurately characterize him.[2] Second, how are those elements related to each other? Third, how did the president's psychology develop? Fourth, how is his psychology manifested in his performance?

The elements that make up a president's psychology do not exist in a vacuum. A president's pattern of behavior in the external world of presidential performance reflects a parallel internal pattern of psychology. Put another way, a president's psychology represents a generally integrated, consolidated, and at least somewhat successful effort to use his talents and overcome his weaknesses in pursuing his personal and political goals.

Which theory provides the best chance to answer the four basic questions of any president's psychology? In my view, the answer is comparative psychoanalytic theory. It is the only theory of psychological functioning that addresses the basic functional elements in an individual's psychology and accounts for their relationships to each other. Moreover, it is the only theoretical perspective that attempts to account for the development of a president's character, as well as locating its effect in the real world of action and behavior.

I use the adjective "comparative" to describe the psychoanalytic theory I recommend. The reason is quite simple. Psychoanalytic theory no longer means only Freudian psychology. To be sure, the basic elements of the topographical and structure models that Freud outlined remain relevant in varying degrees to most, if not all, psychoanalytically framed theories. But to equate psychoanalytic theory solely with the work of Freud at this point in time would be analogous to equating classical music solely with Mozart. A knowledgeable student of psychoanalytic theories today must be conversant with the developments of ego psychology, object relations theories, interpersonal and relational theories, and the various forms of self psychology.

This does not mean that psychoanalytic theory is a modern Tower of Babel. There is broad and basic agreement about what I would term *first principles*. What are they? First, that the most basic building block of a person's psychology is his character structure. It follows that a president's personality is an outgrowth of his character and not an unrelated assembly of various traits. Second, that character and its associated psychological parts contain both conscious and unconscious elements—experiences that have helped to shape them and remain "in storage," so to speak. Third, that character develops but also imposes limits on a person's behavior.

An analyst developing a psychologically framed biographical analysis of a president operates at three different levels.[3] First, he operates at the level of historical fact. What are the key events? What evidence is there that they took place, and as described? Second, he operates at the level of interpretation and meaning. What did it mean psychologically for Clinton that he grew up in Hope and Hot Springs, or that his mother, stepfather, or grandmother had certain psychological characteristics? Third, he operates at the level of theory. How shall we understand and explain the facts that we find? Do we use, as many have, the theory of the psychological dynamics of the adult children of alcoholics to explain major elements of Clinton's character? Or, focusing on Virginia Kelley's early and prolonged absence from her young child, would the theory of attachment (and its darker side, abandonment) be more appropriate?

When all of these levels operate in constant interplay, they can provide a full, rich, credible analysis consistent with both biographical elements and psychological theory.[4] What makes data or formulations at each level more (or less) useful? At the level of factual information, the analyst relies on the density of information, the authority of the source(s), and its accord with other known facts. Some facts on Clinton are easily ascertained and validated by the density of recollections of him by family, friends, and associates now available (e.g., Allen 1991; Levin 1992; Dumas 1993).[5] Other solid traditional biographies of Clinton (e.g., Maraniss 1995; Oakley 1994) have been published that provide important basic factual data for more theoretically focused and psychologically framed analyses.

The psychoanalyst studying public figures must examine various understandings of the person he is analyzing, and compare and reconcile them with the facts as he can establish them and the theories that best frame and support them. However, facts alone, even facts that are consistent with theories, do not automatically confer a meaning or psychological significance. How is the analyst to determine these matters?

Unlike the clinician working in a psychotherapeutic context,[6] the analyst of a public figure cannot rely on the rich, diverse, and patterned data available there.[7] In this sense he is more limited. However, in some respects he has more latitude. Whereas the psychoanalyst is confined to what the patient says and does in his office, the psychoanalytically oriented analyst of a president's psychology and performance can look to a wide range of public behavior, inside accounts, commentary by presidents and others on their choices and behavior, and so on. These data provide a very large array of information from which the analyst can plausibly develop a good understanding of a president's psychology and the patterns that underlie it.

What of a president's formative years, about which much less information is ordinarily available? Generally, the psychoanalytically oriented analyst trying to construct an understanding of a president's early years must rely on several sources, none of which is likely to be wholly satisfactory. The analyst can gain *some* information from what the now grown child says of his parent(s), but this is limited by emotional attachments, discretion, and even political needs. Clinton has given a number of interviews in which he has discussed his childhood (Baer 1991; Baer, Cooper, and Gergen 1992; Clift and Alter 1992; Blumenthal 1994). These reflections are useful when compared and used in conjunction with other data.

The analyst would also, ideally, like to draw on the parents' for their views. However, here too it would be foolish to believe that such recollections would not be colored by the wish of parents, like other people, to put themselves and their son in the best light. In Clinton's case, the most significant parental figure in his life was undoubtedly his mother, Virginia Kelley, and, to an important degree, his stepfather, Roger Clinton, and his grandmother, Edith Cassidy. Kelley has given a number of interviews (1992, 1994b; Purdum 1992). However, these are for the most part campaign interviews that are not very revealing and, in any event, are meant to help bolster her son's candidacy. Garry Wills (1994, 6) notes that anyone who met Virginia Kelley would attest to the fact that she was a vivacious and outgoing woman and that she definitely reveled in being a "character." However, the analyst cannot depend on interpreting persona alone, as revealing as the choice or enactment of a persona might be. More importantly, the interviews don't reveal much of the psychology that lies behind the persona she has adopted. It is an appreciation of the parents' psychology, not necessarily their recollections of their children's early years, that may be of most use to the analyst.

Fortunately, in this respect the analyst is enormously helped by Virginia Kelley's autobiography (1994a), published after her death. The book was written with James Morgan, a freelance magazine writer who interviewed Kelley, her husband, family friends, and President Clinton. These parties "often provided facts and reminiscences that Mrs. Kelley, with an admittedly weak memory for details, had forgotten" (James 1994). Caryn James (1994) noted that Kelley had seen "two thirds of the manuscript and an outline of the rest before she died." President Clinton, among others, reviewed the completed manuscript for accuracy before publication, a fact that has some bearing on the ethics of using this material.

Joyce Carol Oates (1994) in reviewing the book notes that it is "a celebration of the life of feeling. . . . It is not self-reflective, except in the most modest terms." Still, a lack of self-reflection is not the same as a lack of self-disclosure. In Kelley's case the former appears to have facilitated the latter. Kelley's assisted autobiography is the best, most useful record available of her psychology and experience in raising the future president. It is an invaluable resource that allows the analyst to appreciate the psychology of the person behind the persona. It is, in many respects, a troubling document. Kelley's autobiography reveals far more than she intended, much of which does not reflect well on her.[8] It also raises troubling questions regarding her son. This creates certain issues for the psychoanalyst. It is obvious from her autobiography that her behavior, as a parent, had a decisive influence on her son's psychology, not always for the best. Her impact is not the salutary one that both she and her son describe. What should an analyst do in such circumstances?

Her autobiography is, of course, a public document, made so by Kelley and her son, who reviewed the manuscript before publication (Kelley 1994a, 285). In doing so, he and she presumably stand by her account as presented. Still, the material that emerges from the autobiography is damaging to the image that both held publicly of each other. The only path an analyst can follow under these circumstances is to frame the material as carefully as possible, noting its limitations and, where plausible, alternative explanations. Above all, the material merits respect and tact since anyone's adaptation to his circumstances can too easily be second-guessed.

By revealing herself, she also allowed others access to the heretofore very private and carefully presented world of Clinton's developmental experiences. They often do not coincide with what Clinton has said about them. In many ways Kelley's book reveals more problems than her son has either been aware of or chosen to reveal. His mother's book, therefore, has the effect of helping to undercut the Clinton family myth. In doing so, it reveals much about the gravity of the emotional issues Clinton faced, which has not been fully in front of us before.

An analyst, gaining some appreciation of the severity and emotional costs of these issues, can only empathize with what Clinton faced growing up. In doing so he must acknowledge, and may also admire, Clinton's courage and resilience in trying to and to some degree succeeding in not being debilitated by them. At the same time, the analyst of presidential performance has another responsibility, which is to trace the public consequences of what he uncovers. The emphasis in assessing a president's performance cannot lie solely in appreciating the distance he has traveled to become president, but what he actually did once he got there.

BEHIND-THE-SCENES ACCOUNTS

This book makes use of behind-the-scenes accounts of the Clinton presidency that have recently become available (Drew 1994; Woodward 1994), and a special word about them seems in order. Both books are based on extensive interviews with both high-ranking and more modest ranking members of the White House staff, including those with daily and direct access to the president. Both books have been characterized in a number of reviews as "descriptive." That is, they have no theoretical framework anchoring their work. Nor, in the interest of being fair and objective about a controversial president, do they argue a point of view. For example, in characterizing her book, Elizabeth Drew, says, "This is a genre of middle-distance journalism, intended to catch events and people's involvement in them or reactions to them while they are still fresh and before they have been fuzzed over, and retouched, in recollection. *It is intended to offer the analysis and perspective of someone close to the events, seeing them unfiltered*" (1994, 438, emphasis mine).

Andrew Sullivan (1994), reviewing Bob Woodward's book, faults it for "showing little sense of history and [being] unable to relate a narrative to a larger argument" and for reflecting the "journalism of mere process." Yet what bothers Sullivan is precisely what makes the book useful for those who are interested in theory. Another kind of critique comes from Frank Rich (1994a), who faults the book because "Woodward provides no new reportage about Gennifer Flowers or any other scandal." According to Rich, "So prosaic is most of what Mr. Woodward's sources have to say that their . . . anonymity seems superfluous." Worst of all, according to Rich, is that the book's characterization of the Clintons "is familiar—he can't make decisions; she (Hillary) can't stop making them."

These points are accurate but completely miss the importance of these books, which is to provide a detailed, day-by-day, or issue-by-issue, account of a process. As Christopher Lehmann-Haupt (1994) points out in his review of the Woodward book, "Readers with a solid background in Presidential politics will probably find Mr. Woodward's book invaluable." The same is true, it might be added, for psychologically minded analysts of the Clinton administration, for whom the specific details provided by Woodward's (and Drew's) informants are literally a psychological treasure trove. Rich and others could not be more correct in their statements or more mistaken in the critical implications they draw from them.

Woodward and Drew asked many members in the higher (and lower) levels of the Clinton administration to describe their experiences and views. The material is, of course, subject to all the cautions already discussed, but even so such narrative and descriptive material provide the theoretically inclined researcher with a wealth of important data describing the inside workings of the Clinton presidency as they were unfolding.

These inside accounts provide a crucial complimentary set of data to supplement and deepen our understanding of the public record and cross-check against it. I have used their books exactly in that way, as one more evidentiary strand.

ANECDOTAL EVIDENCE

Biography and other forms of history, like behind-the-scenes accounts, often rely on the accumulation of narrative incidents. The subject himself may tell of the incident, or a friend may do so, or someone who was present at the time, or a person may even report what others say they have seen or heard. The weight of these accumulated narrative stories is often used to draw a portrait that either contributes to or supports an analysis. Such materials have played an important, but controversial, role in the analysis of presidents and their presidencies. Some object to such narratives as being merely or only "anecdotal," the implication being that such data are inherently suspect.

This implication is not necessarily fair or accurate. In attempting to answer the question of what happened and why, a presidential researcher might depend on many types of data, including presidential news conferences and interviews, interviews with major actors, documentary evidence, and so on—none of which, as I have shown elsewhere (1996, 405–8), are without flaws. Each can be viewed as a form of commentary designed to influence the framing and understanding of particular narrative lines or incidents. Thus, a presidential press conference can be viewed as the president's narrative of his behavior and the reasons for it. Likewise, interviews with other actors provide their own narrative perspective. Even what seems to be less subjective data, such as a report released by the White House (or its opponents) on the number of welfare mothers helped to find employment, is part of a narrative based on a particular sample with a particular program, operating with a particular definition of work and of success.

The presidential analyst who makes use of anecdotal case material must, like his statistical data oriented counterparts, address the issue of the quality of the data.[9] There are essentially four areas of concern raised by the use of such material: validity, degree of representation, consequence, and meaning.

An anecdote is a story, and anecdotal evidence is a story put forward to support a characterization. The first question that must be addressed is whether the story is true. Who is telling the story? Were they there, or are they repeating what they have heard elsewhere? What is the relationship of the person telling the story to the person about whom it is told? What is his or her motivation for telling the story? What independent evidence is there that the event took place? Does that confirmation differ in any particular respects? Obviously, independent evidence that any event took place as portrayed, buttresses confidence in its narrative utility. But establishing that a particular event did take place is only the first step.

The next question is how representative is the incident, and of what? Consider in this regard the various stories about President's Clinton's anger. Woodward reports a number of instances of Clinton's anger (1994, 33, 54, 133, 255, 278), as does Drew (1994, 96, 218). When one totals up these incidents and adds to them other public displays of temper toward reporters during and after the campaign, including the outburst of rage and indignation during the *Rolling Stone* interview (Wenner and Greider 1993), it seems clear this *is* an element in Clinton's psychology that warrants attention and explanation.[10]

The question then arises as to whether the element is consequential, and if so, what does it mean. Importance is not necessarily established solely by frequency. A point often lost is that the ordinary sampling of behaviors by presidential scholars, although limited, can be very consequential. Alexander and Juliette Georges' (1956) study of Woodrow Wilson focused on a self-defeating pattern in his behavior that resulted in unnecessary political losses three times in a long and otherwise successful political career. Yet it would be difficult to argue, certainly, in the case of the defeat of his League of Nations Treaty, that the results were inconsequential.

Establishing the *meaning* of the psychological elements revealed in anecdotes is critical to the analyst. The analyst must investigate how a particular characteristic functions, what psychological purposes it serves, and what role it plays in a person's overall psychology. To answer these questions, the analyst cannot rely on anecdotes, as plentiful, accurate, and consequential as they may be, but on dynamic formulations. Consider John Brummett's (1994, 14–16) anecdote regarding then Governor Clinton's indecisiveness in connection with a bill to give tax credits to those contributing to public colleges, which he first signed and then "unsigned." Brummett refers to this as the "unveto story."

In 1985, at a time of slow economic growth and tight budgets, the public and private state college presidents proposed legislation that would grant tax credits to persons making financial contributions to these institutions. According to Brummett, Clinton worried about the possible effects of the bill on tax revenues but told the college presidents who favored it that he would take no stand on it before the legislature. The bill then passed and Governor Clinton had five days in which to either sign it, veto it, or let it become law without his signature. According to Brummett, Clinton "pondered . . . fretted . . . agonized . . . [and] stalled." The idea of having citizens contribute directly to colleges, thus bypassing the need for the government to provide more, was attractive. However, his budget advisers could not estimate the potential drain on the state's treasury.

On the fifth and final day, after business hours, Clinton made the decision (which Brummett characterizes as the right decision) to veto the bill. He stamped the word "disapproval" on the bill, affixed his signature below the stamp, and sent an aide to deliver it to the House Clerk. The aide, finding everyone done for the day and the clerk's door locked, slipped the bill under the door.

That evening Clinton called some college presidents to say what he had done. After talking with them for a while, he called in a state trooper and sent him to the capitol to retrieve the bill. The trooper, who had to use a coat hanger to retrieve the bill from under the door, returned it to Governor Clinton, who then crossed out the prefix "dis" leaving only the word "approved," and had the revised approved bill returned to spot from which it was retrieved. Some months later Clinton had to call a special legislative session to repeal what had turned out to be an overly generous tax credit.

Is there enough independent evidence to suggest the incident took place as generally described? It would appear so.[11] Does the characteristic revealed in the anecdote have real political consequences, or is it merely a cautionary story? In this case, the consequences were that Clinton's inability to stick to his original decision cost the state so much money that a special session of the legislature had to be called to repair the damage.

Granted it took place, granted it had consequences, what does it show? Is it representative, and if so, of what? An anecdote draws its meaning by its relationship to other similar instances of the same characteristic and the extent to which it reflects a pattern that is consistent with other known elements of a person's psychology. For Brummett, the unveto story is about Clinton's indecisiveness. Brummett believes (1994, 16) that the same trait is reflected in a number of Clinton's actions as president, including his nomination and subsequent withdrawal of Kimba Wood and Lani Guinier, his changing positions on Bosnia, the zigs and zags of his Supreme Court nominations, and other policies such as the middle-class tax cut. What is similar in all these cases is a change in position and an apparent lack of the strong convictions that would lead to bold, direct, and committed action.

In making use of anecdotal material, as with any other data, the researcher must be aware of its possible pitfalls and protect his analysis by not being too dependent on one data source. In the end, the level of confidence that an analysis allows depends on the extent to which many avenues of inquiry and data analysis converge. And finally, it depends on the ability of the various theoretical lenses used to make sense of the data and further our understanding.

THE PROBLEM OF OBJECTIVITY

Evaluating Clinton's leadership is complicated by his style, which reflects a very strong interpersonal emphasis. In Arkansas, he was known to travel many hours and more miles to meet small groups of voters. He has made a three-decade long point of meeting the people of his state in his quest for political office, and has been especially sensitive to meeting elites and opinion makers.[12] The fact that he knows and is known by, and in many cases has developed close personal relationships with, many of these individuals has complicated assessments of his tenure in office. It is probably an exaggeration to say that everyone in Arkansas has met Clinton, but he's done his best.

Clinton was particularly attuned to the role of the press long before the 1992 presidential campaign. Brummett notes in his recent biography that he would have preferred to write the book without contacting Clinton (but in the end spoke to him on the phone) because "Clinton prefers contact: he believes he can persuade intellectually and seduce interpersonally, and often he can" (1994, 23). Ernest Dumas (1993, xvii), a reporter who also covered Clinton as governor, recalled, in his introduction to a recent collection of reflections on Clinton by his friends and associates, a call to his wife by Hillary Clinton asking her why her husband wrote stories critical of the governor. Bruck (1994, 67–68) details how Hillary Clinton and her husband made a concerted (and successful) effort to neutralize one of Clinton's more persistent press critics by having Hillary cozy up to him.[13] Meredith Oakley, an Arkansas reporter who covered Clinton as governor and who recently published a detailed and useful political biography of Clinton covering those years, also notes the many calls just "to pass the time of day," which she understood to be Clinton's attempt to keep the lines of communication open after they had a falling out over her assessment of his performance. Unlike others, she was able to keep her professional distance, dryly noting that "expediency, like opinion, is a two-way street" (1994, xv).

The fact that Clinton knows, is known by, and in many cases has attempted (and often succeeded) in establishing close personal relationships with many of the same individuals who might evaluate his performance has complicated assessments of him.[14] Not everyone has been willing or able to separate their personal and professional associations with Clinton. Many of the people who have written about Clinton have been connected to him politically[15] or else have begun with a positive view of him and gone on to gather evidence supporting their original view.[16]

The two best forthright and balanced biographies to date are by David Maraniss (1995) and Oakley (1994). They both provide valuable basic evidence. Other biographies are best approached and used with care. The same caution applies to biographical analyses of Clinton like the Levin biography or Johnson's study of his governorship, noted in footnotes 15 and 16 above.

THE ANALYST'S STANCE TOWARD HIS SUBJECT

At least since Freud's analysis of Woodrow Wilson, it has been clear that the analyst's own views can play a role in any analysis of a public figure, if care is not taken. Does the analyst favor activist presidents, liberal or conservative values? Does a particular president anger, excite, or puzzle the analyst?

The analyst, especially one who makes use of and is trained in psychoanalytic psychology, has a particular obligation to be clear in these matters. No analyst can avoid personal responses to the materials with which he or she constructs an analysis, but one can try to be as explicit as possible. In that explicitness lies at least a partial solution to unintended, or worse, systematic bias.

I therefore want to frame my analysis by clearly stating my stance toward Clinton. I voted for Bill Clinton in 1992, but did so on balance. His expressed political philosophy of balanced, smart, and focused government initiatives to address public needs and inequalities, coupled with an emphasis on individual responsibility came closest to my own personal views. Nonetheless, as I observed the presidential campaign, transition, and first months of the administration, I could not help being struck by his inconsistent mix of enormous political skills and puzzling missteps. It became clear that this mix, and its implications, would frame the most important questions about Clinton's presidency. This book addresses the puzzle of this unusual mix and offers an explanation of their nature and origin.

In the end, of course, the analyst's stance toward his subject, examined or not, must stand the scrutiny of others. Do the frames of analysis reveal important aspects of Clinton's psychology? Are its manifestations found in the real world of his performance as president? Is the evidence put forward in support of the analysis persuasive? These questions, and not the analyst's personal views, are what must ultimately be primary.

★ ──

NOTES

NOTES TO THE INTRODUCTION

1. I use the masculine pronoun here and throughout this book for two reasons. First, the primary focus of the book is President Clinton. Second, to date all presidents have been men. This should not be taken to indicate that the possibility of a female president is unlikely or to be avoided.

2. The relationship is, of course, to some degree reciprocal. The Clinton presidency is part of the continuing development of the institution itself. Clinton's tenure in the office will no doubt affect him and the public, but it will also have effects on the institution.

3. See Greenstein (1969, 42–46) for a list of the circumstances in which leaders and, by analogy, presidential psychology will have freer reign.

4. So-called "great man" theories of leadership argued that such persons set in motion sweeping causal tides. Others, most notably scholars influenced by Marxist theory, see leaders as hemmed in by large social, economic, and political forces.

In an attempt to refine this overly broad debate, Hook (1943, 154) distinguished the eventful from the event-making man. The former was anyone who because they were at a particular place at a particular time influenced subsequent developments. Hook gives as an illustration the Dutch boy who stuck his finger in the dike and remarks that anyone could have done it (ignoring the important question of whether everyone would have). The event-making man is the eventful man whose impact is the result of outstanding personal attributes like intelligence, will, or character, and not dependent on accidents of position. While not denying that the eventful man's actions have causal consequences, Hook's focus is on "greatness," that combination of characteristics that lifts the event-making man above circumstances as he finds them.

Hook's analysis points to a distinction that later theorists of political psychology have utilized (cf. Greenstein's [1969, 40–57] distinction between action and actor dispensibility), between those who affect events because of where they happen to be, and those who affect events because of who they are. The argument for causal impact that I am advancing relies on both.

The president's location in the political system and the power and resources that flow from that fact are clearly important elements in magnifying his causal importance in the chain of effects. However, his own particular personal disposition, including his character, judgment, vision, and skill, also plays a large role in determining not only how much effect he will have, but what kind.

5. I use the term "psychology" (and elsewhere "presidential psychology") in the general sense to include both characterological and personality elements. I will further differentiate between the two classes of psychological elements in chapter 6.

6. The psychological constellation that consists of character and personality elements may also provide compensatory capacities that can serve political ambitions and functions. Determination, a trait whose origins lie in an individual's psychology, can compensate (to some degree) for a lack of political skills, for example, interpersonal skills so important for campaigning.

7. The Foster nomination became imperiled when the number of abortions performed by Dr. Foster during his career was misstated by the White House and Dr. Foster. Democratic critics faulted the White House not only for not checking the accuracy of the numbers they first gave out, but also for failing to realize that the number of abortions was likely to be an issue, because abortion itself was controversial. Dr. Foster was the first surgeon general nominee in his specialty, obstetrics and gynecology, which was likely to raise this abortion issue directly. Dr. Foster's nomination was eventually killed in the Senate.

8. Brown's exclusive focus on what he sees as Clinton's negative behavior is not typical, even if the complaints he raises are.

9. The use of anecdotes is central to many biographical enterprises. However, they are viewed with suspicion and often disdain by many. I take up the use of anecdotes in general and more specifically in this book in the Appendix.

10. Clinton's so-called "need to be liked" is presumed by some to be causally connected to this fact. Clinton himself has suggested that his talents as a mediator are related to these experiences. However, a closer examination of the timing of the emergence of Clinton's turn toward others and the sequence that resulted in his stepfather's abusive drinking suggest that the former preceded the latter. (This does not deny the possibility that the latter reinforced the former).

Clinton's attribution of his ability to mediate to his stepfather's alcoholism is certainly possible, if one believes, after examining the record more carefully, that

Clinton does in fact have strong mediation abilities. Still, a closer look at the literature on the effects of alcoholism on children suggests that heightened abilities in mediation are not the only, or even necessarily the most likely, outcomes of these experiences (Ryan 1991). Maraniss (1995, 38) has offered a more complex version of the possible effects of Roger Clinton's alcoholism on Bill Clinton.

I take up this issue in chapter 9 and other issues of the impact of Clinton's childhood in chapters 7 and 8.

11. Wills (1994) reviews several books on Clinton, including an autobiography by Virginia Kelley. Wills, whose essays do not ordinarily reveal such a strong appreciation of the psychology of life-histories, nonetheless sees some of the important implications of Kelley's book for understanding her son. Kelley (1994a) and Maraniss (1995, 38–39) present some of the import facts surrounding Bill Clinton's childhood, but do not develop their psychological implications.

NOTES TO CHAPTER 1

1. Among these other concerns are such important matters as relationships with the former Soviet Union and its allies, the problems of countries attempting the transition to democracy, the problem of "rogue" states, inchoate states, low-intensity violence and terrorism, and of course a host of economic and social development problems.

2. The success of Ross Perot's candidacy cannot be measured in the percentage of his popular vote alone. Both major party candidates were looking over their shoulders at Perot voters, hoping to win them over, or at least to keep them from voting for their major party opponents. Moreover, both major party candidates made direct personal and policy overtures to Perot and his constituents when he withdrew from the race in the middle of the campaign and even after he resumed campaigning.

3. I use the word "leader" here to refer to those in positions with large amounts of discretionary power. Hereafter, I will refer specifically to the president, although my analysis in this section is meant to apply more broadly.

4. For the intricacies of measuring "trust in government," see Miller (1974) and Citrin (1974).

5. While not all of the decline in public trust can be directly attributed to Johnson himself or his Vietnam policy in particular, there is evidence that his behavior in office did play an important role. For example, in 1968, 56 percent of those who rated Johnson's presidential performance as "poor" had low levels of trust in government (Citrin 1974, 977, Table 2).

6. A president, of course, upon taking office, is tested by many problems for which the public expects at least some partially successful response. In addition, presidents come to office with their own views of what they wish to do, as well as what they were elected to accomplish. The basic public dilemma to which I refer may be, but is not necessarily, related to either of these.

7. Understanding the inner workings of an administration is part of the attempt to explain its policy intentions and effects (intended or otherwise). These, of course, must be gauged in part by the administration's actual policies and their consequences. The two domains—the public and the internal—and their relationship to each other are central to the analyst's task of explaining and appraising presidential administrations.

As is the case with learning more of the inner workings of an administration, analyses of its actual policies and their impact is often not immediately possible. A policy's full impact is not always evident during an administration's time in office or even immediately afterwards. Moreover, impact itself is complex and must be assessed along a number of different lines. For example, a policy may increase military strength but cause social or economic dislocations. Policy decisions may also combine with other unfolding (or future) events in ways that produce a range of unexpected and *unforeseeable* outcomes.

NOTES TO CHAPTER 2

1. The importance of the president's psychology is recognized by most presidential scholars, even those who choose to focus their intellectual energies elsewhere. Skowronek, for example, who focuses on the political context within which a president must work, notes that "the fact that the political system does not take a more exact measure of the capacities of the individuals we elect—of their individual talents, their political skills, their personal characteristics—has led to all sorts of distortions in our politics" (1993, 29).

2. The concept of consolidation is an important but sometimes overlooked aspect of self-esteem. It refers to the level of regard that is both *stable* and *resilient*. The lack of consolidation is reflected in either wide swings of esteem or the tendency for esteem to diminish in the face of modest setbacks.

3. One mistake often made in analyzing the character of presidents is to assume that because character develops early in a person's life history and lies "deeper" in the personality structure, its operation in adulthood will be primitive too. It is true that by the time a person reaches mid-adulthood, basic character elements have been established, elaborated, and, in most cases, consolidated. Therefore, by the time a president is ready to enter office, he does so either with a stable, consolidated sense of self-regard and identity or without such a sense.

However, it would be a mistake to look for simple repetitions of childhood patterns in presidential behavior. By the time individuals reach adulthood, they have had ample opportunity to develop more fully a range of skills that in turn will affect their capacity for accomplishment. Most political leadership positions involve a large number of opportunities to specialize; indeed, they require it. It is quite possible for most people to find some areas within complex role structures to express their skills as well as satisfy their needs.

4. The following discussion draws on a more extensive discussion found in

Renshon (1996). On the question of the development of character and its potential for change over the course of life, see Renshon (1989).

5. More than fifty years later, Baudry reaffirmed that character refers to "the broadest grouping of stable, typical traits by which we recognize a particular person. Our concept of character is made necessary by the fact that we find in individuals reoccurring clusters of traits with a degree of consistency suggesting that some underlying principles govern the selection, ordering and relations of these traits to one another" (1989, 656).

6. Character elements need not be equally present in all circumstances. Situations may either elicit or inhibit them, according to how they resonate with a person's history or needs.

Moreover, as individuals get older and the circumstances they face change, the ways in which character elements manifest themselves can also change. Competition in a child and an adult may share similarities but be expressed in different ways. Whether, how, and under what circumstances a particular character element will appear cannot be an a priori matter. It must be settled by observing behavior over time and across circumstances.

7. There appear to have been two real chances for Clinton as an adult to ask these kinds of questions of himself; both occurred around defeats or troubles. The first was after he lost his bid for reelection as governor in 1980. That opportunity was apparently lost in the high activity levels of the campaign to rehabilitate Clinton politically for reelection. These efforts began very soon after his defeat and included Clinton spending "several months in 1981 traveling the state, running as long and as hard as a non-candidate could run" (Maraniss 1995, 391, 395).

The other opportunity took place around the issue of his brother's arrest and conviction on a drug charge. At this time, Clinton and his family entered family therapy, where he recalls he learned a lot about himself and his family. Clinton said that he learned that "we were two prototypical kids of an alcoholic family. . . . Like most families of alcoholics, you do things by not confronting problems early. . . . I think the house in which we grew up, because there was violence and trouble, and because my mother put the best face on it that she could in later years a lot of stuff was dealt with by silence" (Wills 1992, 63; see also Maraniss 1995, 421).

As I document and analyze in chapters 7, 8, and 9, Clinton's formative experiences were more complicated than being the child of one alcoholic parent. However, the therapeutic experience did provide an opening and there is some evidence that it did raise questions for Clinton beyond the somewhat elementary and fashionable ACOA (adult children of alcoholics) theory of effects and consequences. Betsey Wright, a long-time aide to the governor, recalls that at the time Clinton was "coming to grips with the fact that he had places of real weakness. He was trying to sort all that out in his life. . . . He did a lot of introspection that I had never seen him do like that before" (Maraniss 1995, 422). Wright recalls conversations about how Clinton's experiences had made him prone to avoid conflict, a staple (but not always true) understanding of the ACOA literature. There is some evidence that

Clinton was considering other, perhaps more difficult, issues. Clinton's next-door neighbor and old friend Carolyn Yeldell Staley recalled that Clinton indicated he was struggling with his own psychology and not only that of his family. Staley recalls Clinton as saying, "I think we're all addicted to something. . . . Some people are addicted to drugs. Some to power. Some to food. Some to sex. We're all addicted to something" (Maraniss 1995, 422).

For whatever reasons, the process of introspection begun after his brother's arrest, did not continue. According to Wright, Clinton's introspection did not lead to any change in his behavior, it only meant that "he could see what he was doing far better" (Maraniss 1995, 422). An analyst can only view this lost opportunity with regret.

8. I have reviewed elsewhere (Renshon 1974, 43–58) the relevant theoretical foundations for this assertion as it is found in the psychoanalytic clinical literature, as well as in personality theory and developmental psychology.

9. Early ideals are primitive in the respect that the child, operating within the framework of as yet unmodulated naive grandiosity, is likely to absorb them in fairly undifferentiated form. Being good means *always* being good. Transgressing rules means being punished, period. Gradually, the child comes to appreciate that ideals and values, like the world in which they operate, are complex and differenti-ated. The child can still be basically good even if he or she throws a temper tantrum and gets punished. A child can still feel jealous that an older sibling has more freedom and not come to believe that these feelings represent some irredeemable flaw.

10. Ideals represent the more abstract, affect-laden elements of identity; values are closer to experience. Ideals incorporate identifications and associations that are unlikely to be fully accessible to the individual. They may be made of "part-objects," that is, aspects of oneself or others whose views were important when the ideals were developing. Values represent the more specific, conscious manifestations of ideals. A person's character integrity incorporates both.

11. While a president's political identity has its roots in personal identity and values, it develops as he engages the public issues that are part of his political coming of age and those issues that help to define his political maturity. For Clinton a defining ethical moment of his identity was the Vietnam War and his response to the draft, which I discuss in chapter 10.

12. Sullivan (1953) viewed the self as the "sum of reflected appraisals." His point was that how others see us has much to do with how we experience ourselves. Our view of ourselves is unlikely to be a simple sum of what others think, since some views are clearly more important than others. However, the basic point is well taken. Making interpersonal connections, sustaining them, and being nurtured by them are basic building blocks of character. Character and its intrapsychic elements have an interpersonal, relational dimension.

13. The term that covers all these relationships is *object relations* (Greenberg and Mitchell 1983). Kohut's (1971, 3–6) concept of a "selfobject" and the clinical

work that has followed it (Goldberg 1988; Wolf 1988) have confirmed the importance of the role of others in developing an individual's character structure and operation.

NOTES TO CHAPTER 3

1. Achieving the presidency requires an enormous investment of time, energy, and oneself. Even Reagan, who approached his presidency in a more detached manner *after* he reached office, made substantial personal and professional investments to gain it. How do we account for this? An answer must surely include an account of the role of substantial levels of ambition.

2. The data I use to make these observations are drawn from diverse but publicly available sources. One reason for doing so is that I wish to demonstrate that it is the density of data (especially when they lead in similar directions), not their psychological "deepness," that is important. Character, I argue, is reflected in the everyday world of observable behavior, and is not limited to a psychotherapeutic context.

The data are drawn from the 1992 presidential campaign, Clinton's first three years in the White House, and, where appropriate, the information that has emerged regarding Clinton's developmental experiences. For each of the three major character elements, I distinguish between what was learned about them during the campaign and what was learned during his first three years in office. This comparative perspective allows us to assess the extent to which character elements do in fact carry over from one quite distinct context (campaigning) to another (governing). Further information on the methodological issues connected with this approach may be found in the Appendix and in Renshon 1996.

3. I use the term "virtue" here and throughout to refer simply to a characteristic that is considered positive and desirable.

4. These included the Beta Club (for outstanding achievers), the Calculus Club, the Mu Alpha Theta Club (for advanced math students), Junior Classical League Club (for advanced Latin students), the Bio-Chem-Phy Club, Key Club, DeMolay (a civic organization whose purpose is to develop leadership in young students), and many activities surrounding the school band (Levin 1992, 29; Maraniss 1995, 42, 45; Allen and Portis 1992, 11). He played in the marching band, concert band, stage band, pep band, and band key club, and became first chair tenor saxophone in the First All State Band. He was also a band officer and worked as assistant band director.

In addition to these activities, he was junior class president, a member of the National Honor Society, and a National Merit Scholarship semifinalist. He was chosen to attend Boy's Nation in Washington (which produced the famous picture of Clinton shaking hands with President Kennedy), and was frequently asked to speak about his experiences in Washington at local civic clubs such as the Elks, Optimists, and Heart Association.

5. At Georgetown he ran for freshman class president (and won), sophomore class president (and was reelected), joined Alpha Phi Omega (the fraternity responsible for organizing and running student elections), worked in his first full-fledged political campaign (Frank Holt's campaign for Governor of Arkansas), ran for president of student council (and lost), and also joined the Student Athletic Commission, a move Maraniss (1995, 101) links with Clinton's preparing for the Rhodes Scholarship competition, which, it was widely but erroneously believed, required successful candidates to have some demonstrated connection to athletics.

6. Here is how Kelly (1992a) describes a typical vacation day taken to relax from "a grueling year of 16–hour workdays":

Day 2. Took his daughter Chelsea horseback riding. Ran on the Beach. Played Volleyball. Posed for snapshots. Shook hands. Signed autographs. Put on a tuxedo, flew to Pasadena with his begowned wife, Hillary, and the similarly attired Thomasons to attend a starry (Robert Wagner, Jill St. John, Dionne Warwick, John Ritter) black tie birthday party for Mr. Thomason. Partied until early in the morning ("I think he was the last one to leave," said Mr. Clinton's mother, Virginia Kelley, who was also a guest). Ordered Pizza from room service at 3 a.m.

Day 3. Awoke at 9:00 a.m.

7. There are, however, by-products of an emphasis on activity that run counter to effective presidential performance. An emphasis on activity or "getting things done" can easily result in policies or programs whose implications have not been fully thought through or whose consequences have not been fully explained to the public. Activity, including the obsessive grasping of details, can lead to a faulty decision process in which reflective thought regarding the forest may be lost in the intense attempt to bring into focus more trees.

8. Woodward (1994, 70) also says Greenspan thought that "Clinton was very close to being an intellectual. He was at home with ideas and knowledgeable about history. [Greenspan] was quite surprised at the level of abstraction of their conversation."

9. There is evidence that the budget caps were discussed with Clinton. Drew (1994, 166) writes, "Aides said he had been told—on at least two occasions. Leon Panetta, the OMB director [at the time], had plainly told him. The political advisors, always looking for ways to lay blame on the economic advisors, said that the problem hadn't been emphasized enough to the President."

Clinton's angry question, "Why didn't anyone tell me?," may really mean, Why didn't anyone make me more aware of the implications of the caps. However, this incident raises questions about Clinton's approach to issues of personal responsibility, and raises even more directly why, if Clinton was told, he did not himself realize the significance of the facts. Clinton's strong desire to accomplish his purposes, or alternatively his strong confidence that he could do so, may have caused him to underestimate or otherwise downplay the information he was given.

10. Drew (1994, 85), in reviewing Clinton's first year in office, offers this

tempered assessment: "He had to learn to discipline himself in many ways once he gained the Presidency. Clinton was a learner, usually a fast one, but in certain particulars of the Presidency, learning took him some time."

11. I am not in full agreement with Greenstein's formulations regarding Clinton's pragmatism, nor with his characterization of Clinton's willingness to acknowledge his own contributions to his difficulties. I will take each of these issues up in subsequent chapters.

12. Among the questions that might be legitimately asked here are: Why has it been necessary for Clinton to change direction so often? What accounts for the large number of political and policy shifts from left of center to moderate views that have characterized the Clinton presidency? These questions are addressed in more detail in chapters 4, 13, and 14.

NOTES TO CHAPTER 4

1. See Renshon (1995; 1996, chaps. 10 and 11). Additional evidence is presented throughout this book. Oakley, who covered Clinton in Arkansas and has provided the most detailed examination of his time as governor, writes,

> During the many years I covered his political activities in Arkansas, first as a reporter and chief of the *Arkansas Democrat*'s Capitol bureau, and later as a political columnist, I documented numerous falsehoods, broken promises, and ruses, some of which never saw their way into print because of the personal nature of the exchanges. Fairly early in our professional relationship, I learned not to go "off the record" with Clinton; he had a clever way of saving his strongest and most colorful reactions to my criticism for those private exchanges, which he knew I was honor-bound not to publish. (1994, xiv)

2. Overall judgments in which one attempts to weigh the good that presidents do against the harm they cause are a difficult, tricky undertaking. In some cases it appears easy, as when a president fails the basic tests of noncriminal behavior. However, how much weight, and what kind of weight, do we assign to President Johnson's "Great Society" programs as opposed to his stance toward the Vietnam War?

The analyst gains firmer ground by giving up definitive, overarching judgments and confining himself to documenting and explaining patterns of behavior that have an important impact on the president's performance that he can demonstrate on theoretical and empirical grounds.

3. Some of these presidents had these issues raised in connection with their actions. Eisenhower misled the public at first about the U-2 flights over Russia; questions have been raised about Kennedy's womanizing in the White House; Ford was criticized for the appropriateness of pardoning Nixon; and questions have been raised about the extent of Reagan and Bush's knowledge of and participation in the Iran-Contra affair. The point is that none of these presidents is broadly considered

by scholars to be widely and generally dishonest in his public life, even though questions in specific areas have been raised.

4. In favorable circumstances, identities are not simply selected from among the roles available in a particular social setting, but rather are chosen and enacted in a way that does justice to one's aspirations, ideals, and psychology. The presidency is, of course, a flexible vehicle for the expression of identity. It provides, within the context of its constitutional mandates, varied opportunities for presidents to express their ideals and particular values and exercise their specific skills and capacities and, of course, their personal, professional and political aspirations.

5. The ability to commit oneself to an identity, even one that feels appropriate from an earlier time, still requires a recognition of what one has lost as well as what one will gain in so choosing.

6. I have added specific citations for all those examples not mentioned in either Woodward (1994), Drew (1994), or Stencel (1993).

7. The three different positions are documented in Clymer (1994a, 1994b) and Jehl (1994d).

8. The three different positions are documented in Greenhouse (1993a), Purdum (1995f), and Jehl (1995).

9. How much of Clinton's response was a part of his strategy, and how much reflected his real conviction that he was not really the person depicted by press stories? There seems little doubt that Clinton's portrayal of himself as a victim was one of a number of tactics used by his campaign to manage a substantial credibility problem. In this strategy, he clearly recalls Gary Hart's efforts along the same lines. However, the evidence indicates that the strategy accords with Clinton's own views of himself.

10. Elsewhere (Renshon 1996, chaps. 3 and 15) I have examined in some detail the nature and importance of temperament for presidential performance.

11. A separate issue arises here in connection with Clinton's early experiences, which were obviously difficult (see chaps. 7, 8, and 9). Must we assume that Clinton's self-confidence is solely a compensation for his childhood?

Certainly Clinton's childhood experiences were real enough, as were their effects. However, Clinton also was and is a person of substantial capacities—intellectual, interpersonal, and in some ways psychological. Did his difficult early experiences affect his psychology? Of course. Is his self confidence an attempt to compensate for this? I would argue that it is not. Substantial talents and skills, such as Clinton manifests, have an independent existence and their own line of development. They are real, as are the successes that accompany them.

However, what is true of his talents is also true of the other, more problematic areas of his character and experience. They too have developed and become woven into his character structure. They have influenced the uses to which his talents are put and the methods he has developed to realize his ambitions. In short, they too have become part of who he is.

12. It can have other results too. Oakley notes, "At times Clinton's arrogance

. . . overwhelmed his pragmatism" (1994, 4). Arrogance is fueled both by a sense of one's certainty (self-confidence) about one's views and by one's capacities to accomplish them.

13. The next day Clinton denied having said this (Brummett 1994, 25) but then backtracked somewhat, given that the quote was taken from a tape of his remarks, and said that his comments had been misinterpreted.

NOTES TO CHAPTER 5

1. *Object* is the technical term for representations of the external world, including events, things, and persons, that find a place in an individual's intrapsychic life. The term itself denotes that the object begins as an externally separate entity. However, there are a number of more technical arguments about the development of the capacity to experience and internalize objects, as well as their various functions once they have been internalized, which will not concern us here. The interested reader is referred to Goldberg (1988) and Mahler (1968) for two representative but very distinctive views.

2. The rough preponderance of each object type in the individual's internal representational life is significant, but so are the primary objects, which had a disproportionate impact because of their role in the individual's development.

3. In Kohut's term these internal representations are "selfobjects," or objects in which the self and the former external object have been fused. This type of object relationship can be distinguished from "true objects," which remain separate and identifiable as such to the person. For a discussion of the distinction see Goldberg (1988, 206).

4. Clinton achieved substantial popularity in high school because he was smart, talented, and friendly. There is a danger here, however, that idealization by others may reinforce, rather than modify, the individual's self-idealization. This in turn may reinforce rather than moderate the individual's sense of being special.

5. See, e.g., Clift (1993) and Klein (1993a).

6. Clinton has invited public anger at groups he ordinarily supports. In his pitch for universal coverage in his health-care proposal, he argued that everyone but the middle class has coverage: "The politicians have it. The wealthy have it, The poor have it. If you go to jail you have it. Only the middle class doesn't have it" (Wines 1994). In this speech Clinton appears to be inviting middle class anger at the poor because the latter (along with the wealthy and the criminal) have something that they don't but ought to.

7. The variable that comes closest to validation is respect. However, they are not synonymous. Respect reflects an acknowledgment and appreciation of accomplishment (including how something was done). Respect makes no necessary connection between the acknowledgment of others and what is central to the person's own self-definition. That connection is central, however, to the concept of validation.

Validation is a more comprehensive concept than respect, affection, or, more generally, an individual's need for external assurances of his own positive self-image. Validation is an acknowledgment by others of those things the person views as most important about himself. It differs from affection in that one need not be liked to be validated, although for some people being liked is an important source of validation. When the need to be liked develops as a primary source of personal validation, it leaves the person dependent on doing what others want, rather than what he feels is central to do.

It is also important to identify validation that is connected to the acquisition and imposition of power. There, the psychological equation is "I'm acknowledged because I am powerful." This, of course, leaves open the question of whether one could be so acknowledged for accomplishment rather than power (beauty, wealth, etc.).

8. Actually Clinton's proposed tax increases were to fall mainly on the wealthy, to a far greater degree—by as much as one-third over existing law—than Clinton had proposed in his campaign. The top rate was moved from 31 to 36 percent (on couples earning 140,000 and above), and a "millionaires surtax"—a 10 percent surtax on people earning a million dollars a year—that Clinton talked about in the campaign became a surtax on couples earning over 250,000. To the campaign veterans . . . these people were millionaires. Further tax revenues would be brought about by removing the limit on the income against which Medicare taxes would be applied. The actual top rate, as a result of the various changes, was over 42 percent. (Drew 1994, 72)

9. Clinton later backed away from the middle-class tax cut he had promised.

10. Barber (1992) has written that the best presidents are those who invest a lot of energy in their work and enjoy doing so. He terms them "active-positive" character type and suggests this particular character type is most congruent with the role of president.

However, there is more to both these elements than his theory suggests. High levels of activity may be a problem as well as a virtue, and there is more to enjoying one's work than being able to feel good about accomplishments. Barber's typology has been criticized, accurately in my view, on a number of grounds by George (1974). The problems of placing Clinton in the "active-positive" category, as Barber has done, seem substantial in view of Clinton's behavior in each of the three character domains we have examined.

11. Charm played a very important role in Clinton's early developmental experiences. His mother, Virginia Kelley, was very outgoing and charming. Equally important, she was attracted throughout her life to men who turned out to have more charm than substance. I take up the issue of charm in Kelley's life and relationships in chapter 7.

In drawing attention to this (and other) connections between Clinton's character and his mother's, I am not arguing that the latter caused the former. For example, in noting Kelley's charm, I am not implying that Clinton is charming *because* his mother was, or that because his stepfather appears to have had more charm than substance this flaw was automatically transmitted to his stepson. What it does mean is that Clinton had a number of early and powerful experiences around the power of charm and his mother's attraction to it, including ample opportunity to see and practice it.

12. The example given of Clinton's speech regarding Saddam Hussein in the previous chapter is, of course, an example not only of Clinton's high level of self-confidence, but of his self-confidence in relation to a particular skill—convincing others.

13. For an example of strategic empathy in the context of the "rational actor" model of international conflict management see Allison (1971, 256). White (1983) has examined the impact of empathetic identifications with the Soviet Union and their implications for American foreign policy.

14. Real empathy begins with the capacity to make real interpersonal connections. This is not, it should be stressed, a matter of appreciating what "I would do or feel if I were in this situation." That approach presupposes that the other is fundamentally similar to oneself. Rather, realistic empathy involves an attempt to enter into a different frame, one that starts from different assumptions and may lead to different conclusions.

15. A person who lacked the capacity for empathetic attunement would have difficulty making any strategic calculations in this area. Similarly, a president who was too empathetically attuned to others might be inhibited from taking action. Acts of leadership may require the temporary suppression of empathetic attunement.

Effective presidents must have some capacities of empathetic attunement, but also find ways to make some use of these insights in pursuit of their personal or political goals. This is not by itself suspect.

16. The strongly held belief that one embodies a nation, which, after all, consists of a very large, highly varied group of individuals, is in some respects grandiose. It also appears to reflect a substantial degree of self-idealization.

17. Oakley argues that "at times, his self-absorption has undermined the greater public good" (1994, 4).

18. For a representative but not complete list see Woodward (1994, 33, 54, 84, 133, 165, 172, 174, 224, 255, 278, 280, 287) and Drew (1994, 96, 218).

19. Clinton's high expectations are more difficult to explain on the basis of his political circumstances. He was a elected with only 43 percent of the vote and faced an ideologically situated Congress that was somewhat cautious regarding Clinton's substantial plans for new government programs. Indeed, it appears safe to say that a strong expectation of success would have to work hard psychologically to overcome these political facts.

20. After three days, the aide found the low-level employee who was responsible and had made an innocent mistake. By that time, Clinton's temper had cooled.

21. Readers familiar with clinical or psychoanalytic theory will immediately recognize these factors as belonging to a pattern of narcissism or being part of a narcissistic character structure. That reading is correct, but I have sought to eschew labels in favor of describing Clinton's behavior and exploring some of its implications.

22. The Clinton administration's response to the Whitewater investigation has, in some respects, echoed the Watergate investigation. Consider the improper briefings given to the president and his staff by supposedly independent investigators (see chap. 13), and the questions raised about the handling of Vince Foster's files by Clinton staff and allies, and the Clintons' refusal to provide certain documents to Whitewater special counsel Kenneth W. Starr, thereby setting the stage for a legal battle over "executive privilege" (Labaton 1995).

NOTES TO CHAPTER 6

1. Clinton appears unwilling or unable to acknowledge his ambition even though his life history supports the view that it is substantial. Clinton's insistence that he is in politics only for what he can do for others recalls Lasswell's (1930, 75) famous dictum that the political man is one who displaces private motives onto public life and rationalizes the process in terms of public interest.

2. In fact, Drew subtitles her third chapter with a quote from a friendly Clinton observer: "They hit the ground barely standing (1994, 36)." Drew documents the difficulties of the administration during the transition and the astounding fact that Clinton had no plan prepared as he began his presidency in January.

3. More details on the sequence may be found in Pear (1993d, 1993f); Friedman (1993c); and Kelly (1993c).

4. The Supreme Court during Franklin Roosevelt's first term was another institution whose members' views of their role was inconsistent with the president's aspirations at the time.

5. Winter uses a content analysis method in which words or phases that convey any of his three main variables—power, achievement and affiliation—are plotted as a function of their appearance in each thousand words. This technique helps to control for the length of the speech.

6. Clinton is not the only president who wishes to be appreciated for his efforts. What sets Clinton apart in this area is primarily the force of his need for public validation.

7. This feeling is also related to aspects of Clinton's childhood experiences, which I take up in chapters 7, 8, and 9. Chapter 9 in particular bears directly on the experiences surrounding Clinton's sense of being special.

8. There are many reasons why presidents may choose to try to have it both ways. One reason is that it gives them political flexibility in dealing with problems of mobilizing the public. Another is that it also may give them policy flexibility as they attempt to orchestrate their initiatives. It may also be used as a gauge to

ascertain responses to one side of an issue or another; alternately, it may be used to reassure every side that the president is considering all points of view. As noted, Clinton used this approach to political decision-making as governor of Arkansas.

9. Brummett puts his finger directly on Clinton's dilemma, "A 'new Democrat,' remember, is a Democrat with novel ideas for government programs, which cost money" (1994, 178).

10. As Fred Greenstein has emphasized to me (personal communication, November 22, 1993), the Clintons may feel there is good reason to send their daughter to a school where her privacy may be better protected or where she will feel more comfortable. His point is fair and well-taken. However, it doesn't fully address two other related issues. First, Clinton does not support choice outside of the public school system. In doing so, he denies to other parents the choice that his economic circumstances allow. Other parents might want such a choice for equally compelling (in their view) personal reasons. Second, the private school issue is only one of a very large number of documented discrepancies between Clinton's words and deeds. When the analyst is confronted with numerous examples of discrepant behavior, he or she is theoretically bound to attempt to account for the pattern.

11. The full text of that memo is reprinted in Goldman et al. (1994, 657–64). See also their discussion of the "Manhattan Project" (244–68).

12. The debate on the effects of NAFTA has continued. It was used by the administration to justify its controversial bailout of Mexico in 1995, and debates over the loss of American jobs caused by the pact have yet to subside.

13. The issue of Clinton's extramarital relationships came up several times during the presidential campaign and again after Clinton was in office. Extramarital relationships occur for many reasons and take many forms. The issues involved in such behavior ordinarily go well beyond the simple question of whether or not a president or candidate had a sexual relationship outside of his marriage (Renshon 1996, 246–48).

Did Clinton have extramarital relationships? A substantial body of evidence suggests he did. In 1988, before Clinton was set to announce his plan to run that year for president, Betsey Wright, a long-time aide, recalls having felt

> the time had come to get past what she considered his self-denying tendencies and face the issue squarely. For years, she told friends later, she had been covering up for him. She was convinced that some state troopers were soliciting women for him . . . "Okay," she said to him . . . then started listing the names of women he had allegedly had affairs with and the places where they were said to have occurred. "Now, I want you to tell me the truth about each one." She went over the list twice with Clinton, according to her later account, the second time trying to determine whether any of the women might tell their stories to the press. At the end . . . she suggested that he should not get into the race. (Maraniss 1995, 440–41)

Roger Starr, managing editor of the *Arkansas Democrat* for most of Clinton's tenure as governor, recalls, "We were talking about the Gary Hart factor in politics, and I asked him something to the effect of 'well, you haven't done anything like that have you?' You know (I was) expecting a negative answer, be it a lie or the truth. And he said, 'Yes' " (Oakley 1994, 150).

Woodward (1994, 22) reports a similar discussion between Clinton and another friend in 1987, when Clinton was considering running for president. Clinton asked the friend if he knew why he had chosen not to run. The friend guessed it had something to do with the infidelity issue that forced Gary Hart to withdraw from the race. In response, Clinton agreed and acknowledged he had strayed. And, of course, on *Sixty Minutes* Clinton admitted in response to a question about his marital fidelity that he had "caused pain in his marriage."

Assuming there is sufficient evidence to make this case, what does it reveal? In the case of Clinton not much more than we could learn by examining his fidelity in other areas. For that reason, I do not deal at any length with these matters. Whatever useful information they might reveal about Clinton is more than adequately found in behavior that is more publicly accessible.

14. Clinton's inattention to Somalia provides one illustration in which "inattention turned a secondary problem into a front-page crisis" (Page 1993, 70; see also Drew 1994, 319).

15. In a major departure from previous practice, Clinton did not bring high-level foreign policy or national security agency personnel with him on most of his domestic trips. At one point, facing a key decision in Bosnia, Clinton was in Texas and the most senior expert in the president's traveling group was a respected, but second-level, official whose expertise was in Russian and East Asian politics. White House officials defended Clinton by saying that he could be in touch with his advisers, if needed, by phone. However, other administration officials noted that these staffing decisions reflected the fact "that unlike Mr. Bush, who reveled in discussions of foreign policy, Mr. Clinton has still shown little interest in holding even regularly scheduled foreign policy meetings" (Jehl 1994c).

16. Clinton was able to acknowledge in retrospect that he probably shouldn't have given himself a Christmas eve deadline for naming his cabinet and "should have delayed the thing for a few days" (Drew 1994, 41).

17. That problem started when the White House summarily dismissed seven members of the Travel Office staff amid allegations of criminal conduct. A distant cousin of President Clinton from Little Rock, Catherine Cornelius, was put in charge of the office. Originally, the White House said that changes were brought about as a result of Vice President Gore's national performance review. This turned out not to have been true. The original charges of mismanagement had been brought by Clinton's cousin Cornelius and helped along by Harry Thomason, a very close Clinton friend, whose company World Wide Travel stood to benefit. His company was selected by the White House to make all travel arrangements. Before the firings and subsequent controversy, Thomason had raised the issue with both Clintons, and then later with Hillary Clinton, who instructed both Mac McLarty and Vincent Foster to look into it (Drew, 1994, 175–82). Only one employee, Billy

R. Dale, was eventually accused of specific wrongdoing, and he was acquitted of charges that he misused Travel Office money. Dale insisted throughout that he had done nothing wrong and that his legal troubles were a result of the Clinton administration's attempt to justify its behavior. President Clinton expressed sorrow for what Dale "had to go through," but an editorial in the *Washington Post* pointed out that a more accurate phrasing by the president would have been to say "he was sorry for what Mr. Dale had been 'put through' by the White House" (1995, 25). A detailed chronology and analysis of the White House travel operations accusations and their consequences can be found in the General Accounting Office's report to Congress (1994b).

18. This itself was part of a policy straddle. Clinton had received strong support from the homosexual community but unlike other Democratic party nominees had declined to support a civil rights bill for homosexuals.

NOTES TO CHAPTER 7

1. I would like to thank Miss Dara Monahan of Mozark Productions for providing me with a copy of the tape originally shown at the Democratic National Convention. For a brilliant deconstruction and analysis of the implications of the images evoked by the text and narrative of this film see Rosteck (1994).

2. In this and the following two chapters I rely on Virginia Kelley's own views of the events as contained in her autobiography (Kelley 1994a). Throughout these chapters, quotes, unless otherwise noted, are drawn from Kelley's autobiography.

3. Ifill says that Blythe was killed six months before Bill Clinton was born (1992b). Levin puts the time four months before Clinton's birth (1992, 4). However, Virginia Kelley puts the date of her husband's death at May 17, 1946, three months before Clinton's birth (1994a, 60).

In this and other matters concerning when events actually occurred, there is often some ambiguity. There are several possible causes for this, including imperfect or selective memories. Another possible explanation is that the Clinton family had no "family historian." Clinton's mother, as will become clearer, was too busy living her life to pay close attention to family history, and Clinton too had his reasons for not wishing to record his family history, much of which was difficult for him.

4. See Levin (1992, xxii), Oakley (1994, 24), Allen (1991, 8), and Maraniss (1995, 30). There is some ambiguity about these dates. Levin's chronology reports that Virginia Kelley left Hope in 1948 when Bill Clinton was two and was away until he was four (1992, xxii). Allen reports that Kelley was away two years but doesn't give the dates. Oakley reports only that she completed her training when Bill Clinton was four, and Maraniss reports that she left in the fall of 1947 and was away two years. This latter view is at least somewhat consistent with that of Kelley herself, who recalls that she called Charity Hospital in New Orleans to see about their program within a week of the time she and her new son returned from the hospital in August 1946 and was told there was an eight-month back-

log in admissions (1994a, 70–71). Assuming that the nursing program started in either August or September, the first possible date for her to go would have been August-September 1947, at which time Bill would have been a little over one year old.

There is less ambiguity regarding the length of time she was away. Levin, Allen, and Maraniss all report her as being away for two years. However, Kelley recalls of her plan to leave Hope that "I hated the idea of not seeing my baby for a whole year" and elsewhere notes that she couldn't take her baby with her for "the year of additional training" in New Orleans (1994a, 70, 77). Yet the evidence is that she was away for two years, not one year. The implications of this are explored more fully in the following chapters.

5. This is not simply a matter of working backwards from the present in a post hoc, proper hoc analysis. The more technical methodological concerns in constructing a developmental analysis are contained in the Appendix and Renshon (1996, 62–65), and the reader is referred there for the details of how this analysis was undertaken.

6. There were other important family members in young Bill's life too.

7. There are a number of examples of Kelley's roller-coaster life experiences. One somewhat prosaic example occurs when she describes her decision to open up her own office. She notes, "I'm making it sound as though I just decided to open my own office and went out one day and did it. By now you ought to know that my life doesn't work that way. I had to have an ordeal first" (1994a, 214). She then goes on to describe her problems with the agency that did her billing for her.

8. Technically, denial is an unconscious screening out of discomforting information that takes place outside of the person's awareness. It is among the most primitive of psychological defense mechanisms, and is ordinarily distinguished from more mature mechanisms such as suppression (Vaillant 1977, 75–90, 393–95). Suppression—which, on first glance, seems to be what Kelley is describing (but isn't)—consists of deferring confronting a problem for a strategic reason. A person may choose, for example, not to confront a spouse when he or she has a major work assignment to complete. However, to use the latter as an ongoing reason not to confront an issue would be a different matter.

The strategy Kelley describes can easily become a habit and thus slide over into a not fully conscious, but too readily used response. In short, it can become part of one's character style. Moreover, this practice also leads to the atrophy of the judgment skills that come from working through hard facts toward more mature solutions.

9. Kelley spends several pages giving her husband's version of the events that led to his arrest and conviction (1994a, 186–88).

10. Speaking of the doctor against whom she struggled for decades over her professional practice as a nurse-anesthetist, she notes, "The irony is, Buddy Klugh is a charming man—tall, handsome, smart. He is someone I could've been friends

with" (1994a, 121). As with the other men she was drawn to, charming, tall, and handsome lead the list, and more substantive attributes follow.

11. In describing her brief time in Chicago with her first husband, Bill Blythe, she says, "There were times that holiday season when I felt like life had become a movie, and I was the star" (1994a, 58).

12. This remark is apparently a reference to her father's tendency to be too trusting of people and too quick to extend credit (1994a, 51). Her identification with his goodness is the other side of her decision *not* to identify with what she saw as her mother's meanness.

13. This leaves unresolved the question of why she was so determined to be independent and self-sufficient. Basically the answer to that question is contained in understanding her relationship with her mother.

14. Kelley mentions that she may have gotten the idea from a movie, which would help to account of her description of her choice as being an "exciting, romantic idea." She makes no mention that her mother's being a nurse had any influence on her decision, which is consistent with her consciously stated intention of being as unlike her mother as possible. Nonetheless, one cannot help but note the parallel, as well as Kelley's wish to become something *more* than a nurse, a nurse-anesthetist.

15. Kelley does not mention having any of the traditional "idealism" associated with that profession, such as helping people. What she does mention is her vision of how she would look in that crisp, white uniform.

Another possible reason her work became (or continued to be) instrumental rather than a source of pleasure was that there were too many conflicts associated with it. One large conflict had to do with having her skills accepted by the local medical profession, a conflict she was over time able to overcome. Another, however, concerned questions of her professional competence, an issue that arose with the filing of two separate lawsuits against her in connection with patients under her care. Another was her enjoyment of drinking, gambling, and partying.

16. It seems unlikely that this was an official part of the class trip.

17. Since Hempsted County, in which Hope is located, is dry, Roger's whiskey-making was illegal (1994a, 80). He also apparently ran a bookie joint in Hope (1994a, 76).

18. By high school Kelley was already plotting her escape from her mother's rules and control. The picture she draws is of an adolescent rebelling against what she considers to be the rigid and inflexible rules of her mother. It is possible, of course, that her mother's rule-conscious practices made Kelley's subsequent choices against convention more attractive. However, it is also possible that there were things about the unconventional paths Kelley chose that appealed to her. Two suggestions along these lines are contained in my discussion below of narcissism and boundary issues.

19. The worry about the diminution of looks, and the need for constant reassur-

ance in early middle age, is a typical pattern in narcissistic men (Masterson 1988, 88).

20. Kelley notes that the church was "located a few blocks away from the racetrack in Hot Springs," and goes on to say, "most likely we selected it for convenience" (1994a, 87).

21. Baer (1991, 40), in his portrait of Bill Clinton drawn from interviews with him, makes a reference to his "his grandfather's drinking problem." Oakley (1994, 22) refers to the fact that "he often drank too much." Maraniss (1995, 23), in his biography of Clinton, notes that by the time Virginia Kelley was twelve, her father was offering her a swig or two of his whiskey. Kelley herself mentions that when Bill Blythe died in the car crash on the way to Hope, he was carrying a case of bourbon for her father (1994a, 60).

22. The references to her drinking are found on the following pages: 15, 37, 38, 48, 58, 72, 74, 76, 79, 80, 84, 90, 91, 107, 108, 127, 154, 173, 181, 226, 235, 242, 257, 259, 260, and 274.

23. This is another parallel to her early family experience, in which her mother was always accusing her father of having relationships with other women. These accusations caused her mother to engage in all-night tirades against her father. Interestingly, Kelley's husband Roger made the same accusations against her, and they too were the cause of all night tirades (1994a, 94, 111, 116).

NOTES TO CHAPTER 8

1. In psychoanalytic theory the somewhat awkward sounding term "object" denotes a person, a part of a person, or an inanimate object (e.g., a doll, money) that is invested with psychological significance. "Object relations" refers to a person's relationships with important objects and may be either conscious, unconscious, or, as happens in many cases, both.

2. On this literature see, generally, Lamb 1975, 1976a, 1976b; Abelin 1975; Cath, Gurwitt, and Ross 1982; Blos 1985; Cath, Gurwitt, and Gunsburg 1989; and Lamb and Oppenheim 1989.

3. In fact, Freud's views on the phallic and oedipal phases of development changed considerably over time. See Mächtlinger (1976, 279–87) for an overview of these changes as well as a useful and comprehensive review of psychoanalytic research in this area, including the intensive observation and analysis of the mother-father-child dyad.

4. More recent psychoanalytic theory has explored the important developmental experiences that occur in the first few years of a child's life (Mahler, Pine, and Bergman 1975; Neubauer 1989). The purpose of examining so-called "pre-oedipal" development is not to argue that everything important psychologically now is thought to happen between the ages of one and half and four and a half, as opposed to the period of five to six. Rather, it is an attempt to conceptualize and document empirically a psychological theory of development as a process. It is

a process that does not begin at five (or even one and a half) and end at four (or six).

The fact that psychological development begins early does not require a commitment to the view that early psychological experience is determinative. There is enough evidence in the adult development literature to suggest otherwise. On the other hand, a recognition of development that can and does take place in adulthood does not require a commitment to the "life-long openness" model—or its postmodern variant—the "postmodern identity," in which adulthood is a matter of open choice not shaped or influenced by previous psychological development or the lack thereof.

5. Love and hate refer here to both the primary and undifferentiated feelings associated with these states that children (and adults) can feel, and the more nuanced, mature versions that also develop over time.

6. I will return to the issue of Bill Clinton as a premature adult later in this chapter. The tendency to treat a young child as a confidant or as an adult is another indication of the lack of empathy.

7. The wish to "accentuate the positive" is understandable. It is an attempt to put the best face on a difficult situation. A child might welcome such an approach, but it is also clearly consistent with Kelley's psychology.

It is, however, in some important ways a breach of empathy. Certainly the child in such circumstances needs reassurance, but the child also needs to be able to acknowledge the profound loss involved with the death of a parent. I think this is one illustration of the more general lack of empathetic attunement that one can discern in aspects of Kelley's relationship with her son.

8. In psychoanalytic self psychology, a person who serves the needs of another so that there is strong psychological connection between the two is termed a "selfobject."

9. For a child, the failures of parental empathy are difficult, even harmful psychological experiences. The child whose parents are not in touch with his needs can easily experience a sense of loss, anger, entitlement to compensation for his suffering, and many other feelings. However, a child whose special talents and/or interpersonal skills make him the center of attention also runs the risk through adulthood of burying the original feelings of hurt, anger, and so on, that he or she might have felt and substituting for them ever expanding feelings of gratification (deserved both in the sense of earned and entitled to) related to success.

10. More technically, the "gleam in the parent's eye" communicates back to the child his first sense of being loved, wanted, and entirely focused upon. It is a crucial beginning to the development of an internal sense of oneself as a good-enough person, one who has been and is an important emotional pillar in the lives of those most important primary selfobjects, one's parents.

11. Fick (1995) is an example of this tendency.

12. Kelley is referring to the first year of Bill's life. It is quite possible that she was depressed after the tragic loss of her husband, for whom she had waited

through the war years and with whom she was to have left Hope for a new life in Chicago.

13. The dramatic scene described by Clinton has a number of aspects to it that merit some comment. First, it is clearly a powerful memory for him. Second, it is an emotionally charged memory. His mother is literally on her knees crying with regret and his grandmother is essentially telling him (according to Clinton) that this is happening because of him. Clinton's feelings, whatever they might have been of missing his mother, appear to be downplayed in favor of the focus on his mother's pain and his responsibility for it.

14. Kelley recalls three other episodes with her husband Roger that focus on her publicly humiliating him (1994a, 111, 117, 125–26). The desire to humiliate another publicly is a reflection of several factors. It is certainly a reflection of substantial rage, perhaps made all the more powerful by continued attempts to "look on the good side." Kelley's rage and attempt to publicly humiliate her husband recall the parallel episode that she recounts of her own mother's acting out of her rage at her husband in front of his favored child Virginia (1994a, 25).

15. Her favorite song, which she mentions twice (1994a, 31, 221), was entitled "Don't Fence Me In," about which she says, "I liked that song, and I liked the ideas it conveyed." The song itself is about land and space ("Give me land, lots of land and the starry sky above, but don't fence me in"), which Kelley brings up in connection with her desire during high school not to be tied down to one boy. However, the song can also be viewed as a more general reflection of a desire not to be limited by boundaries.

16. In another interview (Clift 1992, 36) published about two months after his interview with Klein, Clinton had another take on this quote. Clift asked Clinton about acting 40 at 16, but then added to it that "when you were 40 you acted 16." Clinton replied, "I didn't quite say that. I said that I was always warned that—or I always wondered if I'd want to be 16 when I was 40 because I never felt like I got to complete my childhood."

17. There is with this incident, as with many other events in the Clinton family story, ambiguity about which events took place when. His mother relates *two* different, but extremely similar episodes (1994a, 134–35, 161) in her autobiography, one of which took place when Bill was fourteen, the other when he was sixteen. Both stories involve her husband threatening her and her son Bill coming to her rescue and saying to his father that he would not stand for him to ever touch his mother again.

In May 1962 Clinton and his mother filed depositions in her divorce proceedings against his stepfather. In his deposition, part of which he reprinted in his mother's autobiography (1994a, 146), Clinton refers to the continuing physical abuse directed against his mother by his stepfather.

A question then arises as to whether Clinton's memory of standing up to his stepfather and "stopping the violence" are accurate. If his deposition is accurate, the pattern of his stepfather's abuse, both verbal and physical, continued unabated up to the separation and divorce. If his deposition is accurate, the decisive apocryphal confrontation when he was fourteen may not have taken place as described. If it happened, it did not succeed in stopping the violence.

18. Somewhat ironically in view of Clinton's later difficulties in the presidency, the only rule that Kelley remembers imposing on her children was to tell the truth (1994a, 151).

NOTES TO CHAPTER 9

1. The fear to some degree reflects the power of the wish, if not the temptation, hence the use of the term "fascinated" by Clinton. The "fascination" with the less conventional and riskier side of life is also found in Clinton's relationships with women, and in his association with Hollywood figures during his first two years in the presidency (e.g., Drew 1994, 182–83, 188).

2. The tendency to want to be in the center of things reappears throughout Clinton's developmental history. During high school, "Group activities seemed to hold special appeal for Bill; friends say he rarely dated, preferring instead the company of many, against whom he would invariably emerge as the center of attention. None of his friends recall begrudging him the spotlight because he worked hard at including them in the fun" (Oakley 1994, 32).

This desire to be in the spotlight is a strong psychological echo of Clinton's childhood. This is precisely what Kelley strove for in her development as a "character," and also in her alcohol-aided forays onto the stage at the Vesper and other Hot Springs nightclubs. There are also strong echoes of this tendency in Clinton's very public approach to his presidency.

Having noted the similarities, however, one must also note the different psychological mechanisms involved. For Kelley, the wish to be the center of attention is related to the psychological lift provided to her by being noticed. For Clinton, this tendency appears to have more to do with validation of his strong sense of his own self-worth, as well as an element of obtaining and maintain control.

The other side of wanting to be the center of attention is that Clinton did not like being alone. Oakley described this aspect of his behavior as a student at Georgetown. She characterized Clinton as "the ultimate social animal—unless engrossed in a good book, he becomes very restless when left alone and seeks out conversation, however mundane or inconsequential—Clinton made a point of meeting as many people as possible, and his insatiable curiosity about everyone he encountered served him well in striking up new and useful acquaintances" (1994, 41).

3. There also may be some biologically based aspect to Clinton's early sociability; however, the only (inconclusive) data his mother presents that is relevant to this possibility is that he slept a lot in the first year or so of his life and thus was not very "sociable" as an infant (1994a, 70).

4. There are obviously oedipal overtones to this situation. One could view this as Clinton's unconscious attempt to replace his father and win his oedipal victory. Several aspects of the situation, however, weigh against such an interpretation. First, these events occurred when Clinton was sixteen, not four or five. At best, these circumstances might retain some *echo* of an oedipal situation. Second, Clinton had already done something much more directly relevant to the oedipal issue when he physically (and emotionally) stood up to his father. To the extent that his behavior represented some aspect of an oedipal situation, however, his victory was short-lived. Clinton's real rival during the oedipal period (roughly four through six) was not only his stepfather, but his mother's immersion in Hot Springs night life.

5. In Clinton's court affidavit he wrote that his stepfather threatened "to mash my face in if I took her [his mother's] part" (1994a, 147).

6. When Kelley called her son in England to tell him that she planned to marry Jeff Dwire, a convicted felon, his response was, "Whatever, Mother" (1994a, 180). That response conveys a sense of futility in saying what might be said in such circumstances. Clinton clearly felt some ambivalence about the marriage. His mother says he was "apprehensive" about the relationship. As was her style, however, she interpreted his response as "supportive."

7. Here again we see the importance of stimulation to Kelley and of being in places that fostered it.

8. Kelley's approval of her mother's wish to leave Bodcaw for the larger town of Hope is paralleled by Kelley's preference for the bright lights of Hot Springs and New Orleans (1994a, 21). There are a number of parallels between Kelley's life and her mother's, just as there are between Kelley's life and Bill Clinton's. Parallels are not necessarily causally significant and so I will note them where appropriate, without necessarily making a claim to their causative importance.

9. There is an obvious parallel between the issues that arose between Virginia Kelley's parents and those that arose between her and her first two husbands.

10. Kelley says that "some people call this trait naiveté, but I prefer to think of it as hopefulness" (1994a, 29). Or, to put it another way, the need to relentlessly trust in others, to the exclusion of finding out whether it is justified, is the opposite of cynicism.

11. She and Dick Kelley would go to the racetrack every day and make a final bet on the last race between the two of them. After he won the bet several times in a row, she put his winnings in the toilet for him to retrieve. Why? "The money wasn't the point; my pride was" (1994a, 236). When their mutual friend offered Mr. Kelley some rolls of pennies so that he could get her back by putting them in the toilet, he declined.

12. As noted, it is possible that she was depressed as a result of her extreme and sudden loss. However, she does not give any indication in her autobiography that this was the case.

13. Which is preferable? The answer is that within broad limits either approach is all right so long as the parent is responsive to the child's needs both generally and specifically.

14. Some (e.g., Klein 1992a, 33) have attributed this aspect of Clinton's character to the experience of growing up as a child of an alcoholic parent, a view which I believe mistaken.

15. A *strong* caution is in order for the many observers who have too quickly attributed Clinton's political style to his experiences as the son of an alcoholic (e.g., Klein 1992b, 33; Wills 1992; Clift and Alter 1992, 37; Baer 1991, 42; Clift 1992, 36; Kelley 1994a; Levin 1992). Ifill suggests that the "balancing act with his stepfather seems a blueprint for Clinton's drive to blend opposites [in politics] and find common ground" (1992b). Clinton's campaign worker and biographer Robert Levin notes, "There is *no doubt* that facing up to violence, alcoholism and drug abuse in his own family have strengthened his character, contributed to his moral development, and fostered an ambition to help people themselves" (1992, xv, emphasis added).

Some of this may be true, but many adult children of alcoholics (ACOA) "overemphasize their ACOA background" (Ryan 1991, 75). Clinton himself has contributed to the focus on his stepfather's alcoholism, as has his mother. There are several reasons why both would do so. The experiences were certainly blatant and highly charged. They may have also, paradoxically, been easier for Clinton to deal with than the more pervasive, subtle, but no less difficult psychological circumstances he faced, for example, with his mother.

It has also become more acceptable socially and politically to publicly acknowledge such experiences. There are advantages to doing so. The stories create sympathy for the young victim (and his mother). They help to explain and justify aspects of Clinton's behavior that might be troubling, and at the same provide a basis for attributing character virtues to him. These take the form of dramatic stories of courage, "character," and ultimately (in the case of Clinton's relationship with his dying stepfather) forgiveness.

16. According to Clinton, "I had to be very careful as I grew older, not to overuse the peacemaking skills that I developed as a child" (Baer, Cooper, and Gergen 1992, 29).

17. See, e.g., Brown and Beletsis (1986); Wood (1987); Bradshaw (1988); Kritsberg (1988); and Gravitz and Bowden (1985).

18. In more technical language, Kohut notes of one his patients (Mr. M), "A successful, phrase-appropriate, chip-off-the-old-block-type merger with (or twinship relationship to) the idealized father, and the subsequent gradual or phase appropriate disappointment in him, might yet have enhanced Mr. M's self-esteem via the temporary participation in the omnipotence of the idealized self-object, and might yet have provided him ultimately with appropriate buffering structures and discharge patterns in the sector of his greatness-fantasies and in his exhibitionism, *undoing the damage that had resulted from the earlier psychological interplay*

with an insufficiently mirroring mother" (1977, 13, emphasis mine; see also 212, 218).

19. This is true even though the nonalcoholic parent often "is an emotionally underdeveloped person with significant interpersonal limitations," who as a result of their own limitations and the difficulties of dealing with their spouse's alcoholism, "gives the child much less than he needs" (Ryan 1991, 76).

NOTES TO CHAPTER 10

1. This analysis of the draft issue draws on Renshon (1996, 263–78). Kelly (1992) contains a good overview of the draft story up to December 15, 1992. Goldman et al. (1994, 39, 112–25) present a view of the controversy from the standpoint of an inside observer of the Clinton campaign, which, however, appears to accept at face value Clinton's explanation of it.

2. For example, a chronology of Clinton's draft status from March 20, 1968, when he graduated Georgetown, until he received a high number in the draft lottery on December 1, 1969, which appeared in the *New York Times* in February 1992 (Rosenbaum 1992), did not contain the important fact (see below) that Clinton actually did receive an induction notice in April 1969. That fact only emerged in April 1992 and was not widely reported (Maraniss 1995, 165).

Another example is the news story that broke in the *New York Times* on September 19, 1992, that Clinton (contrary to his earlier assertions) asked for and received help from the office of Senator J. William Fulbright in securing an ROTC slot (Suro 1992). The story was first reported in March of that year by the *Arkansas Democrat* and was followed the same month by the *New York Post*. However, the significance of the story was not appreciated at the time it first came to the public's attention.

3. Maraniss believes that the fact that Clinton promised to be in touch at least "once a month" suggests that Holmes expected Clinton to be at Oxford for a second year before taking up his ROTC slot at the University of Arkansas Law School (1995, 180). However, if that is true he never told his subordinates or other ROTC staff members, since they were all expecting Clinton to show up in September. On the other hand, Maraniss also presents evidence in the form of a letter Clinton sent to his friend Denise Hyland that suggests he would be going to the University of Arkansas in the fall and not back to Oxford (1995, 174).

4. Brown's book is polemically anti-Clinton, but it contains some useful material, such as the Holmes affidavit, which is not easily obtained elsewhere.

5. One possible source of guilt is Clinton's two-year battle to escape the draft by means that were in some cases based on misleading others as to his views and intentions. The fact that several of his friends died in Vietnam while he avoided serving may also have been an important factor.

6. One other possibility is that Clinton is actually accurate in his choice of words and did not begin to appreciate how his views would have be seen by the

Colonel Holmes until after he had successfully obtained his deferment. The failure to see this obvious point, given the circumstances of the strong feelings in the military about war-objectors and draft resisters, is striking. If accurate, it means that Clinton most likely had to work very hard psychologically to keep himself from recognizing the obvious.

NOTES TO CHAPTER 11

1. The analysis of Hillary Clinton that follows is based, as is the analysis of Bill Clinton, on composite sources, including events analysis, interviews, press conferences, analyses of Hillary Clinton and her public role, and several biographies. In using those sources it seems useful to draw a distinction between *documentation* and *interpretation*. A source that proves questionable with regard to its viewpoint or interpretation may still be useful to establish occurrences or patterns of occurrences. The analyst may then use them, along with other sources, to confirm occurrences, as the basis of other more appropriate interpretations, or both.

The Hillary Clinton biographies merit some further observations in light of the above. Judith Warner's (1993) biography is written from an advocate's perspective. The book cover introduces its subject with the following breathless accolades, "Lawyer, Activist, Mother, Political Wife, Feminist — and now First Lady." The book gives some biographical information, but supplements this primarily by pulling together only positive memories of her development and views. Even so, a discerning reader can, with the help of other materials, find much here that is interesting and useful.

More serious and useful is Donnie Radcliffe's (1993) biography. She covers some of the same ground as Warner and is thus useful in confirming some basic data, but she at least considers some of the controversies that have surrounded Hillary Clinton. Her perspective is basically supportive of her subject. However, here too the discerning reader will find useful information that provides insights into aspects of Hillary Clinton that are not covered in any depth by either book.

Another lengthy analysis of Hillary Clinton is the *New Yorker* article by Connie Bruck (1994). Bruck's article covers some of the same ground as the Warner and Radcliffe biographies, but specifically attempts to assess the extent to which Hillary Clinton's public persona fits the heretofore private but slowly emerging picture of her. As is appropriate for such an analysis, Bruck does not assume that the public persona gives a complete picture of the private person, and in focusing on the latter as well as the former, she inevitably invites a revision of our understanding.

All three sources are best used comparatively and in conjunction with other data, and, most importantly, within a framework for analysis and a set of specific questions to be addressed. How is a reader to tell which materials to weigh more heavily? One useful exercise is to compare such materials on a particular subject— say, in this case, the questions of whether the amount of influence exercised by Hillary Clinton crosses some boundary, and exactly what that boundary is and represents. This is obviously a controversial issue regarding Hillary Clinton, and one can gain some insight from seeing how various authors treat it. For many of the Bill Clinton biographies, one might compare what is known about Clinton's handling of the draft issue with how each of his biographers treat it. Levin's (1992) FOB biography barely skims the surface of this complex issue, while Maraniss (1995) presents a balanced account of the issues raised by it. Clearly one can make some use of the former, but better use of the latter.

In addition, one other caution must be observed. In making use of one person's observations about another, it is essential that the analyst have some idea of the relationship between the two people involved, and if possible something about the person making the observations. The failure to be do so can lead the analyst astray.

2. Warner, an extremely sympathetic biographer, takes this somewhat simple advocate's view (1993, 205). More useful is Radcliffe's analysis, which while generally supportive of Hillary Clinton's political role, does recognize that some might feel legitimate qualms about its nature and extent (1993, 228–29). She notes, "Even among those supportive of women playing a bigger role in policymaking, Hillary would be a discomfiting presence as she put herself forward to speak, admittedly authoritatively, on issues like health care and children, sometimes saying 'my husband' but more often than not using the more ominous-sounding 'we' " (1993, 228).

3. A fierce debate took place in Little Rock regarding Hillary's Clinton's role and title (Drew 1994, 23–24). The term "Domestic Policy Advisor" was apparently considered and dropped as being too controversial. The health-care role seemed to solve several problems. It gave her an important job with visibility, yet it also appeared to be a limited task. One friend of hers said that in taking this public role, "she decided not to be clandestine," and that going public in this way "was a risk she was willing to take" (Drew 1994, 23).

This is true as far as it goes, but it is not fully accurate. First, it underemphasizes her role as second in command. Second, it tends to obscure the extent to which decisions to emphasize her traditional roles functioned to mask her more powerful real position.

Mrs. Clinton's abandonment of the pretense of her role in the latter part of the campaign—as the adulatory and largely silent wife—was complete once she reached Washington. . . . There were transparent efforts to keep things in balance. The first press interview she gave was with the food correspondent of the *New York Times,* whose front page displayed an evening gowned Hillary checking the place settings for the Clinton's first large, formal dinner. . . . The story was about how much Mrs. Clinton liked going over menus for dinners. . . . One morning in early February, Mrs. Clinton's social secretary, Ann Stock, was on all three networks' morning shows, talking about how much Mrs. Clinton loved her role as hostess. *But Hillary Clinton remained involved in most major decisions made by her husband—and some minor ones as well."* (Drew 1994, 101, emphasis mine)

At the Camp David retreat early in Clinton's presidency, when major themes of his administration were discussed and decided upon, Hillary Clinton took a major role. She was the one who raised the importance of developing a "story" that would shape the public's understanding of the president's message and then took charge of working with the political consultants to develop it. Woodward reports that Mandy Grunwald, a key participant and political consultant,

> was delighted to see the First Lady moving things. She was a great planner. In the first days of the administration, with attention focused on Hillary as potential dragon lady, Hillary had posed in a great dress, the attentive hostess overseeing the [White House] kitchen and dining rooms. The photos were intended to soften her image. Now Grunwald could see some of that familiar planning would finally be directed where it was needed most, at the economic plan. (1994, 111)

A similar strategy had been used by the Clintons in Arkansas:

> Hillary may have been bored by the tea-and-cookies role assigned by the public to the state's first ladies, but it served her personal interests well. . . . She was able to ply her lawyer's trade and manage the couple's investment portfolio without public scrutiny of any sort. Indeed no one was more surprised than the Arkansas news media when revelations about Hillary's involvement in Whitewater-Madison began to surfacing late in 1993. (Oakley 1994, 520)

4. The access-equals-power equation is clear to those who have exercised it. That is why Woodward (1994, 61) reports that direct, unfettered access to the president was one condition that Lloyd Bentsen laid down when discussing the secretary of the treasury position with Clinton.

5. The concept of a "War Room" to coordinate the marketing of the president's economic package is interesting. It reflects the assumption that the administration was engaged in a war, just as the Clintons had been in the campaign. The metaphor is appropriate to some degree, but not fully. In a campaign, the winner does take all (e.g. the office). However, once in office, the president must enter a process of bargaining, which makes the metaphor of winning all or losing all less fitting.

6. This analysis will not examine or attempt to determine the exact state of the Clintons' marriage. That is a subject on which others, far closer to the couple, have different views, and which, at any rate, is not relevant to the questions I raise and the analysis I pursue.

Clinton himself, responding to a question during an interview with Steve Kroft on CBS's *60 Minutes* about whether he and his wife had "reached an understanding" or had an "arrangement," replied, "You're looking at two people who love each other. This is not an arrangement or an understanding; this is a marriage. That's a very different thing" (Kroft 1992, 5). Others have been less certain. George Stephanopoulos has concluded "there was no way to know their real relationship" (Woodward 1994, 103). Bev Lindsey, wife of President Clinton's close confidant and constant traveling companion Bruce Lindsey, has said that she "didn't know what Hillary's relationship with Bill Clinton really was" (Bruck 1994, 75). Drew notes that "the real state of the Clinton's marriage was something known to a very few people, most of whom didn't talk about it" (1994, 103).

7. I take no position on the appropriateness of the psychological fit these illustrations represent. In analytic work, the judgment of whether a particular psychological fit between two individuals is appropriate rests on a larger array of information about the actual functions and consequences of such a relationship for both. For example, the relationship described in the text could be abusive, but it could also be nonabusive and fulfilling. No a priori judgment can be made in the absence of more specific information.

8. Many discussions of their marriage have focused on Hillary Clinton's investment in it. Some think it is she who has given up a great deal (her own identity, which has been to some degree modified for political purposes; her own independent ambitions, etc.). Others (e.g. Oakley 1994, 495) believe the opposite and focus on what Hillary has gained through her marriage. Both are clearly part of the Clintons' relationship. It would be naive to believe that the extraordinary opportunities afforded to her ambitions to do good by her relationship with her husband have no impact on her overall feelings about the relationship. However, it is one matter to see it as part of their relationship, quite another to see it as its primary or only basis.

The view that their marriage is an arrangement is premised on the assumption that their relationship is devoid of affection and warm feelings and continues primarily on the basis of self-interest. If accurate, it would reflect a deeply cynical "I'll take what I can get (or deserve)" calculation, which would be inconsistent with Hillary Clinton's character and developmental history. Perhaps the most nuanced treatment of the interrelationships between her aspirations and his political role is found in Bruck (1994, 88–89).

9. Clinton's character and subsequent behavior might have diminished the early idealism and her captivation by his charm that played an important role in the early relationship. Perhaps for Bill Clinton, too, early idealized views of what his marriage would be like have been dealt a blow by reality. For both partners time and experience has provided a more realistic appraisal of the other's character and a fuller appreciation of the implications of that character on their hopes for the relationship.

This does not mean that there are not continuing strong emotional ties between them, although the nature of the ties may have changed. At this point they may reflect mutual interests, shared experience, common fate, respect, and perhaps even admiration of each for the other's talents and skills.

10. Exactly which partner is smarter has been debated (Brummett 1994, 245), but such debates miss the more essential point that both are extremely intellectually able while having somewhat different skills. Hillary Clinton's capacity to focus clearly allows her to master complex information and her logical skills facilitate analysis. Clinton's intellectual capacities appear more geared to drawing

larger interconnections, although he, too, is quite able in some areas (for example, voting statistics) to master large amounts of information when motivated to do so.

11. One indication of Hillary Rodham's sense of herself is found in her general disinterest in those aspects of personal appearance (e.g., clothes, make-up, glasses, etc.) that were the focus of many of her contemporaries. For documentation of this see Oakley (1994, 97–98) and Bruck (1994, 62).

12. There is a presumption and a conceit in this phrase, since a person who doesn't necessarily share your views is not necessarily a fool.

13. Speaking of her attacks about critics of the administration's health-care proposal, Max Baucus, Democratic Senator from Montana, and a strong supporter of Hillary, said, "I know that there is a tendency in the White House to develop a siege mentality. I think there is, first, that tendency institutionally, and I think there is that in her personality. I was surprised ... at some of her comments: *how* partisan, *how* negative, *how* quick to judge.... She's a very smart person, of course, so she forms judgments very quickly" (Bruck 1994, 88).

14. This is one primary trait that creates an interpersonal mismatch in the Clinton relationship. He wants validation and the emotional support of others, she is not easily able to give it to him. There are, throughout the materials analyzed in conjunction with this book, a number of instances that reflect this basic psychological mismatch (Brummett 1994, 37, 50; see also Bruck 1994, 72). One long-time friend said, "Clinton needs reinforcement all the time ... [and] looks for affirmation in even the smallest things. Sometimes you can see that Clinton needs this affirmation and Hillary doesn't give it to him. During the campaign you could see her be aloof when he needed ... just a little warmth. She can be very cold. He's alone a lot. Hillary isn't the one to provide approval" (Drew 1994, 233).

The other side of the issue is that joining together two very smart, very ambitious people who are also highly self-confident about the virtues of their particular views, one of whom tends to be very disorganized and one of whom isn't, can also create strains. In Arkansas, to protect her husband, Hillary along with Clinton aides Betsey Wright and Joan Roberts, put up a protective cordon around him, which had the effect of not only protecting Clinton, but also limiting him. For a person who dislikes boundaries the result was predictable. When Wright insisted that a policeman accompany the governor on his early morning jogs, Clinton shouted, "I won't have it! I won't have it!" (Maraniss 1995, 427).

Over the years, Hillary Clinton has had to take on many roles in their life, some no doubt less congenial to her than others. Before Leon Panetta became chief of staff, she had been in charge of organizing her husband's time and staff (Drew 1994, 49, 137, 254). Since their time in the governor's mansion, she had become his gatekeeper, especially after his 1980 reelection defeat, and she increasingly took on the role in the Clinton family of earning money.

15. The Hillary Clinton-Ira Magaziner work on the administration's health-care plan provides another illustration of what can happen when two smart, ambitious

people with strong ideas about what they know is needed collaborate: "Each had long evidenced an extraordinary self-confidence (coupled with a tendency to be dismissive of others), and a conviction that no social problem, however complex and seemingly intractable, could resist his or her applied power to solve it. . . . [They] not only possessed these qualities but were vivified by them; and this project provided the greatest opportunity either one had ever had to give full expression to them" (Bruck 1994, 82).

16. The use of the loophole was technically legal, and the Rose law firm put together a second sale, this time depending almost entirely on $81 million in bonds issued by the Arkansas State Development Finance Authority. This time the Whitehead shell company, the underwriters, and the lawyers stood to make $8.3 million in profits. That deal had received preliminary approval from the Clinton administration but was withdrawn when allegations of bribery and corruption to secure the approval were made public by Steve Clark, the State's attorney general and a possible challenger to Clinton in the primary. Clark's public allegations and the resulting bad publicity "compelled Clinton to kill the second bond proposal" (Oakley 1994, 409).

17. The ability to affect policy behind the scenes while not being accountable was one of the ways in which Hillary Clinton's dual roles allowed her the latitude to have it both ways. It also afforded her protection, since she was not only the governor's (president's) wife, but also an independent professional person in her own right. In 1990, when her husband's primary opponent called a news conference to ask whether Clinton had been in office too long, Clinton strategists decided that Hillary would confront him because "it would put him in an impossible position— he couldn't answer back . . . also Bill didn't want the negatives that might come with his doing it" (Bruck 1994, 76).

18. In his news conference on the Whitewater affair, Clinton repeated his view that "when my wife did business for the state, when her law firm represented some state agency itself . . . if she did any work for the state she never took any pay for it" (1994b, A19).

NOTES TO CHAPTER 12

1. As Clinton himself (1994b, 278) notes, "I've always had fanatic supporters and strong opponents, always—even when I started out." This has made it difficult to assess Clinton's performance as a political leader. One observer has concluded, "What one thinks of Bill Clinton depends on what version [of his contradictory aspects] one finds most defining, most endearing, most distressing, or most disgusting" (Brummett 1994, 268).

2. Kelly (1994; see also Ayres 1992; Holmes 1992; Brinkley 1992), for example, in examining Clinton's record as governor lists a number of improvements in various policy areas that he characterizes as "moderate reforms." Dale Bumpers and David Pryor (1994), senators from Arkansas responding to the Kelly article,

saw the same list as reflecting a somewhat more substantial contribution, given the circumstances in which he had to work.

3. The starting point for any assessment of Governor Clinton's role in this policy area is the Alexander Report commissioned by the state legislature in 1978, which found that, "by almost any standard, Arkansas' system of education must be considered inadequate. Overall, and in many if not most areas, Arkansas lagged behind almost every other state" (Blair 1988, 253). A partial listing of the areas in need of help included levels of school funding, the quality of curriculum, school attendance, inadequate teacher's salaries, graduation and promotion rates, and the number of students going on to college.

From this starting point, there was nowhere to go but up. Johnson (1983, 27), in her review of the programs that Governor Clinton introduced during his first term, concluded that "his policies can be assessed as . . . [having] resulted in substantial positive improvements." Blair (1988, 262–63) agrees, citing the institutionalization of increased functioning for the educational system. Brummett (1994, 74–75) sees Clinton's reputation as the "education governor" as resting on a complex amalgam of commitment to school improvement, self-promotion, trickery, and a dose of demagoguery. Brummett argues that Clinton's focus on testing teachers "accomplished precisely nothing, except to disparage the teaching profession." Allen (1991), whose dissertation on Clinton's role in educational policy provides a more mixed evaluation, reported views ranging from outright praise to severe criticism.

4. I do not mean to imply that a president's legislative efforts and success are irrelevant to assessing his political skill and other characteristics. A president's ability to translate his policies successfully into legislation does reflect, at least indirectly, his political skills. Furthermore, a president's ability to accomplish his legislative purpose in one instance also increases his chances of doing so the next time (Neustadt 1990). Finally, a president's ability to enact his programs also means that he has been able to put forward *his* solutions to the problems that he feels he was elected to address. However, an emphasis on winning, without looking further at how it is done and what it accomplishes, is likely to be misleading.

5. There are numerous variations in the types of decisions presidents face and the ways in which they organize their information resources. Decisions also vary in their time frames. Some decisions, like where to base the United States ICBMs, were debated for years. Others, like how to rid Cuba of offensive missiles in 1962, had to be decided in a matter of days. Finally, decisions vary in their location along a public-private continuum. Some presidential decisions are made in the context of public debate. More often they are the product of small decision groups, and occasionally decisions are made by the president acting alone.

6. This discussion builds on an analysis of judgment and decision-making in the 1991 Gulf War (see Renshon 1993a).

7. George (1980, 1–3) has discussed the tradeoff that often occurs between the quality of a decision and its acceptability. A decision might be sound but not

feasible or, alternatively, feasible but not sound. Reconciling these two is a critical task of any president or decision maker. A similar tradeoff may take place between judgment and politics. During the 1992 check-cashing scandal in Congress, some Congressmen faulted the House Speaker "for being thoughtful and judicious but not political enough" (Clymer 1992).

8. There is an anonymous aphorism that is relevant here: "Good judgment comes from experience. Experience comes from bad judgment." The thrust of this aphorism is that mistaken but corrected judgment is the basis of better judgment. So, too, the concept of skillful judgment suggests that skills in making judgment, like other skills, can be developed and refined.

9. This possibility is raised by Gelb's (1992) analysis of George Bush's mishandling of his trip to Japan in January 1992 with executives of the major automobile manufacturers.

10. The extent to which good judgment is possible in the absence of accumulated experience in a major area (e.g., domestic politics or foreign policy) is an open question. When experience is lacking, sophisticated judgment frameworks are difficult to develop. Certainly experience, even highly successfully experience, in another area is no guarantee of good judgment or of successful presidential performance. In the 1992 presidential election Ross Perot argued that his experience running large corporations and "getting things done" were sufficient qualifications for him to be seriously considered for president.

Perhaps. But what experience provides are judgment frameworks developed and refined in the same contexts in which they will be applied. Perot's business experience, however successful, would not necessarily prepare him for the political and military complexities of possible military intervention in Bosnia. Or, to approach the issue from another perspective, owning one's own business often involves making "command decisions." One may solicit advice, but ultimately what one says, goes. As many presidents have learned, politics, especially presidential politics, is rarely a command experience. Congress, the courts, public opinion, bureaucracies, and special interest advocacy groups also expect to have their views taken seriously.

11. Describing persons as having some degree of psychological maturity does not mean such persons are conflict free. Psychologically developed persons have areas of conflict and emotional and interpersonal difficulties like everyone else. However, their difficulties take place in the more general context of psychological accomplishment, rather than vice versa.

12. A president's grandiosity and accompanying sense of invulnerability and entitlement can often reflect an underlying masked anxiety and/or an insufficiently consolidated sense of self-esteem. This anxiety may arise from the direct personal and political implications of events themselves or may be related to the steps that may need to be taken if events are viewed clearly and seriously.

13. Empathy is related but not synonymous with good judgment. Empathy, like other psychological characteristics, is not without its dangers. Strong empathetic attunement with others can combine with other characterological elements to pro-

duce effects that run counter to good judgment. A president can become pulled too much by the emotional weight of an empathetic experience. President Carter was extremely preoccupied and distracted by his concerns for the fate of the hostages taken from the American embassy in Iran. While this concern was personally laudable, such a preoccupation can have troubling consequences to presidential performance.

14. Empathy is a difficult psychological task. It requires a president to "suspend self" and self-interest, if possible, if only for a short period. It also requires that the president enter into a perspective that can frequently be approached by analogy and extrapolation, not by directly similar past experience. Realistic empathy does not require that a president be bound by the concerns, expectations, experiences, and perspectives of others, only that he really consider them. Ultimately a president must be guided by his personal and political identity. His ideals, values, policy aspirations, and feelings regarding a given policy issue are appropriate and legitimate tools of policy choice. The ability to follow an analysis to some conclusion requires a coherent political and personal view, if not vision. These come primarily from a strong sense of purpose, direction, and identity.

15. I focus on Neustadt primarily because his classic work is still the best, clearest formulation of these issues. Neustadt's model suggests that presidents, and those who observe them, look to the short term rather than the long term. Power, after all, is to be found in the daily, almost hourly calculations of the president and those who watch him (Sperlich 1975). Both the press and President Clinton have apparently accepted the idea of short-term benchmarks. How many cabinet officials named by the transition? How many appointments made? How many policies proposed and passed during the first hundred days? The model is not responsible for, but appears to reinforce, recent presidential tendencies to be concerned with how things look rather than how they are and what to do about them.

NOTES TO CHAPTER 13

1. In doing so, he seems to be drawing on his high school and early political experiences, when he was the center of attention among a group of mostly admiring FOBs. What is wrong with a president wanting to be at the center and in charge of his own administration? In the abstract, nothing. Realistically, however, there are limits to what a president, even a very smart one, can accomplish by himself. There are also questions about how much of an administration must turn on the president's every view or thought in order to be effective. A president who reserves for himself the prerogative of resolving every issue raises the question of why he doesn't have more confidence in his cabinet or staff to reflect his views. All these debates may help Clinton to see where he stands, but a good argument can be made that a great deal of this preliminary work might best be undertaken before entering the presidency.

2. Perhaps the clearest case of this concerned Clinton's decision-making process

in selecting his two nominees to the Supreme Court. In both instances, chemistry played a key role. When making his decision on whom to nominate, Clinton spoke with Judge Stephen Breyer, but "just didn't feel right about him" (Drew 1994, 215). Later, when he meet Ruth Bader Ginsburg, aides said that Clinton "fell in love" with her and liked her "story" (Drew 1994, 217). Later, of course, Clinton nominated Judge Breyer to the court to fill a second vacancy. Their second meeting apparently went much better than their first.

What is wrong with picking Supreme Court nominees on the basis of "chemistry"? Ordinarily, a president's sense of the chemistry between the nominee and himself would seem a perfectly reasonable aspect of the decision process. It's importance lies in its decisive influence (in first knocking out then bringing back Breyer and in ensuring the nomination of Ginsburg). It is also of note because it is part of a pattern in Clinton's selection of administrative staff and aides of giving strong weight to "chemistry."

3. The selection of Gore as vice president does not on first examination appear to fit with this view. As Drew notes, "It was fairly impressive that Clinton had chosen someone who was probably as smart as he was" (1994, 227). However, she also notes that "Gore was utterly loyal . . . [and] chose carefully the times he stood up to Clinton" (1994, 228; see also Woodward 1994, 53).

4. In 1994, Clinton appointed Leon E. Panetta as chief of staff. Panetta has imposed some discipline on the freewheeling decision structure he inherited, by controlling and limiting access to the president and by reducing the size of some planning meetings. Panetta said of the daily morning meeting of principals, "There was no structure to the meeting. There was no presentation. There was no recommendation, and it became just a kind of talking session that never led anywhere" (Mitchell 1995b). The account goes on to note that Panetta's ability to impose some order is a measure of his success. However, Mitchell also notes, "Just how much he has failed is demonstrated by months of renewed turmoil inside the White House this spring when the president once again began favoring the advice of political consultant Dick Morris, leaving aides complaining that the White House Staff was competing with a shadow government."

5. Blumenthal notes that Clinton's "imperiousness can be seen in the design of a White House that would not challenge him when he chooses indecision" (1993b, 37). Of "Mac" McLarty, Clinton's childhood friend and former chief of staff, Blumenthal notes that "he is not . . . a peer as other presidents have had peers; he would be the old (self-protective) friend as manager." Blumenthal suggests that "Clinton is acting as his own chief of staff," and that a number of Clinton's friends have speculated that "he put McLarty in the slot in order to retain control."

6. The lack of a such a person, given the complexities of the changing international system, and Clinton's more focused interest in domestic policy are also matters worth thinking about.

7. Drew noted in connection with the discussion over Clinton's Supreme Court nominee Stephen Breyer, "It was Gore's style to argue hard for a position and then,

if he thought the president was somewhere else, to say, Of course, if you're not comfortable with this . . ." (1994, 216).

8. The following list, unless otherwise noted, is drawn from Church (1992, 44).

9. In September 1993, Clinton tried to argue that all of his various policy initiatives should be understood to have a common theme, that of building a stronger economy (Rosenbaum 1993d). A month later, he tried out a new broad integrative theme to unite his disparate program initiatives—that of providing "security" (Ifill 1993e, 1993f). That attempt at integration soon faded when the public failed to respond positively.

10. It is not enough to note that a president has a high or low level of achievement motivation, although that is a beginning. It is important to clearly specify the nature this motivation. Is the number of initiatives important, or is their content? How does the person actually define accomplishment and why? By anchoring these major character-based traits in the person's actual character configurations, answers to these questions may emerge with greater clarity.

11. Some details of these sessions can be found in Moore (1992, 133, 136, 138, 159, 164).

12. The quote is taken from my notes of an excerpt played at a panel at the Annual Meeting of the International Society of Political Psychology, 1993.

13. These data are drawn from Klein (1993d, 16).

14. I use the term "legislative victory" because it is not clear that the passage of legislation itself necessarily reflects on its quality. Some have raised the issue, for example, of whether it is government's proper role to fund a national service program. Others have questioned whether the "crime bill" was a large amalgam of packages whose title was more important than its substance.

15. I draw from a six-page list entitled "Clinton Administrative Accomplishments," produced by the White House and obtained through the Office of Media Affairs. I would like to express my appreciation to Miss Barbara Nevins-Taylor of WOR-TV for helping me to obtain this list.

16. Some have blamed Clinton's staff for his troubles. A *New York Times* editorial (January 25, 1994, A18) refers to his staff as sloppy and self-serving. By his behavior, however, a president also sets an example of expectations and helps shape the administration in this respect because of his aides' need to respond to his psychology. I am not arguing that the president's level of personal organization directly accounts in a one-to-one way for the overall nature of his administration. However, I think in these two specific ways his behavior does help to account for it. A president unable to be disciplined himself is less likely to have a disciplined administration.

17. Clinton's capacity for intense, if only short-lived, personal involvement has impressed a number of people, but this has raised another question: "What if the President had been faced with a foreign crisis? It seemed that the Clinton White House couldn't do more than one big thing at a time" (Drew 1994, 340).

18. Jim Moore, an "FOB" who wrote a short political biography of Clinton,

mentions having some doubts about Clinton's truthfulness regarding his relation-ship with Gennifer Flowers before sitting down to interview him; however, "these few moments along with the candidate are enough to banish all doubt" (1992, 15).

19. Well into his presidency, Clinton was still claiming that he had gone to Washington determined to work with Democrats and Republicans, "but had been shocked to find out people say 'Well, I'm not going to work with you because you're in the other party . . . we have to oppose you . . . it's the political thing to do' " (Clinton 1995f, 1499). This view discounts Clinton's own contribution to the Republican's concerns with his budget priorities and his decision not to modify them.

20. An example arose in connection with administration debates on keeping or abandoning the energy tax in their economic plan. All four consultants were key figures at the White House meetings that began in the Solarium on July 3, 1992, around the issue of the energy tax and Clinton's budget. During the campaign, when all four consultants agreed, "they would virtually dictate the decision" (Woodward 1994, 251). However, in this debate the consultants were split. Some argued for retaining the energy tax, others argued it was too politically costly (Woodward 1994, 245–57). In the face of disagreements among his consultants Clinton had difficulty adhering to a position, first supporting, then abandoning any form of energy tax.

21. The differences between the Clinton estimates and the CBO estimate, though large, are the result of small differences in estimating costs and savings, which because of the large numbers involved become magnified over time (Rosen-baum 1995). Yet both sets of figures make the assumption that there will be no economic slowdowns or recessions in the next ten years, a fairly optimistic assump-tion. Therefore, both sets of figures are likely to underestimate the amount of the deficit, the Clinton budget by more than the CBO estimates.

Former CBO director Robert Reichauer said much of the progress claimed by the administration comes from "defining a problem that's much smaller than the one Congress is addressing" (Allen 1995). He further notes that the administrations projections are "on the optimistic side, and if achieving balance is an important objective, Congress's assumptions are certainly more prudent."

22. During the campaign Clinton promised to cut the federal deficit, at the time estimated at $194 billion, in half in four years. However, by late July 1992 it had climbed to $254 billion. Drew notes in this regard that although "the Clinton people were perfectly aware of this new number they had not revised their cam-paign pledge, or even acknowledged the change" (1994, 59; see also Woodward 1994, 76–77). One Clinton economic adviser told Drew, "The campaign knew about it, but didn't want to talk about it." After the election, the worsening budget picture was one rationale that Clinton gave for having to go back on his campaign promise of a middle-class tax cut.

23. For example, the conference organizers put liberal economist James Tobin on the program to present his argument for a $60 billion stimulus program, "so

that Clinton's forthcoming proposal, whatever it was, would look more middle of the road" (Drew 1994, 114–15). Blumenthal characterized it as "one last campaign stop, a sterile event conducted in the absence of conflict" (1994, 34).

24. Dye found that Clinton, like every president since Harry Truman, has drawn his appointees overwhelmingly "from among the most-privileged, best educated, well connected, upper and upper middle-class segments of America" (1993, 693). However, Dye found more lawyers than in the Carter, Reagan, and Bush administrations, as well as more of those who had never practiced their profession but "had devoted their careers principally to elected and appointed government office" (1993, 693). Dye summarizes his finding by noting that "overall, the Clinton administration is clearly distinguishable from previous administrations in its top heavy reliance on politicians and bureaucrats, its over supply of lawyers and its absence of experience in business and the military."

25. The Clinton administration was determined to better George Bush's record on diversity. This sometimes led to bending the administration's own standards. For example, Clinton's policy was that no one who served as a policy "cluster leader" during the transition be given a cabinet post in the area he or she examined. Yet, in naming his cabinet Clinton found himself one Hispanic short (Bush had named two to cabinet positions). With time running out, and the self-imposed need to beat Bush's record, Clinton named Federico Peña as secretary of transportation, in spite of the fact that he had been the cluster leader studying that policy area.

The Clinton's administration's concerns with diversity sometimes led to making it the most important, or even the only, criterion for employment. Clinton was under heavy pressure from women's groups to break the so-called "glass ceiling" for the "big four" cabinet posts (State, Treasury, Defense, Justice) and name a woman. He wanted a woman for the job so badly, according a group of *Newsweek* reporters who were allowed behind the scenes during the first hundred days of the administration, that "at first he interviewed no men for the job" (Mathews 1993, 36). When George Stephanopoulos gave Robert Shapiro, an economist and close adviser to the Clinton campaign, the go-ahead to hire a full-time staff person to coordinate economic issues and options for the president, "He gave Shapiro one specification: find a black" (Woodward 1994, 36).

At the Department of Defense, Les Aspin's slates of appointees were held up repeatedly because they were thought insufficiently diverse. The emphasis on EGG—ethnicity, gender, and geography—as it came to be known, "led to a certain amount of tokenism, of putting people in jobs they weren't ready for, and was leading to some highly controversial appointments" (Drew 1994, 100).

26. When the president visited Tokyo, his "impromptu" walk was in fact choreographed in advance in minute detail by Hollywood producer Mort Engleberg, who also planned the Clinton-Gore campaign bus trips (Kranish 1993).

27. This tendency has been observed at other times in Clinton's career. As one biographer notes, "Even in the 1970's Bill Clinton was not adverse to assigning himself whatever title would enhance his standing before people of influence"

(Oakley 1994, 117). In June 1972 he boasted to the *Arkansas Gazette* that he had been a member of George McGovern's national campaign staff since the start of the campaign. However, he was later named in a news article as a "staff person" for McGovern in South Carolina and Arkansas. By 1977, he was claiming he had been McGovern's campaign coordinator for the whole state of Texas, a claim contradicted by Clinton's long-time aide Betsey Wright.

28. The Reagan administration had a number of its members plead guilty to criminal charges, including Paul Thayer, Richard Lavelle, Michael Deaver, and, of course, Oliver North (Kurtz 1995). In addition, several members of that administration were investigated for possible ethical lapses, including Ed Meese, William French, William Casey (who resigned), Thomas Reed (acquitted), and Raymond Donovan (also acquitted).

29. Hanson was in trouble with Treasury Department officials because she told congressional investigators that Altman had order her to brief the White House on Whitewater developments and that she had told Secretary Bentsen of this order (Bradsher 1994a). Both officials denied this.

NOTES TO CHAPTER 14

1. It is also evident in Clinton's attempt to extend government involvement into highly risky areas never before considered to be a primary responsibility of government. Clinton first planned for the government to be the chief architect of the "information superhighway," apparently believing that the government was or could be more entrepreneurial than businesses whose existence depended upon it. The administration also began to take steps to develop an industrial policy in which the government would decide which technological innovations the country should invest in. One can see here the arrogance of presumed competence—the belief that he can do better what government has never successfully done, what companies and their leaders devote their lives and full energies to accomplishing, and what they attempt to accomplish without the distortions introduced by the political process.

2. The title is borrowed from a *New York Times* editorial dated August 24, 1994.

3. At the Camp David retreat for all senior administration officials just after Clinton assumed office, Hillary Clinton took the floor after her husband spoke. She emphasized that the administration would have to communicate with people by describing a vision and a journey. She said that her husband had lost his reelection bid in 1980 because of a lack of a coherent story. In 1983, when he had come back, "they had devised a simple story, with characters, with an objective, with a beginning, middle, and end. And it had all come from a moral point of view. . . . They had taken on educational reform. . . . They realized the need for a story, *complete with enemies and villains.* They even villainized the teacher's union, which had been their ally" (Woodward 1994, 110, emphasis mine).

Examining the working papers of the health-care task force, one reporter noted, "The mindset of some administration officials can be inferred from work papers that say the drug industry must pay for its sins of the past" (Pear 1994b).

4. A study by the Congressional Office of Technological Assessment commissioned by Representatives Henry Waxman (D-Cal.) and John Dingell (D-Mich.), two critics of the drug companies, found that the companies enjoyed "excess profits." The profits were excess, the report said, in the sense that compared with other high-technology, high-risk industries that are also dependent on scientific research, like electronics, the returns to drug companies were two to three percentage points higher, in the range of 13 percent to 14 percent (Hilts 1993).

The study did not effectively deal with major differences between drug and other high-tech companies like electronics on the issue of legal liability, which for the period used in the study and up to 1988 was a major factor. It also does not address the issue of why investors would want to invest in a high-risk venture without getting a better rate of return. In the so-called "decade of greed," capital could find many other, safer opportunities for substantial returns.

Some of the complexities involved in assessing claims and counterclaims regarding pricing can be found in Elizabeth Rosenthal (1993) and the General Accounting Office report of June 1995 (GAO 1995b). It is also relevant that in 1983 there were eleven companies in the United States making vaccines but by 1992 there were only four, two of which were American-owned (Vagelos 1993). This fact helps to account for some distortions in the market, but also underscores the high-risk nature of the business.

5. Just what was meant by "full immunization" is an issue that was often passed over. For some this meant the full array of all vaccines including those for diphtheria, tetanus, whooping cough, polio, measles, mumps, rubella, hepatitis B, and Haemophilus influenza. Some immunizations require more than one shot (dose) to become effective, others require boosters to retain effectiveness. Using this robust list, the administration estimated that only 40 to 60 percent of the nation's children got the recommended shots. However, the GAO (1995b, 15–16) study found several problems with these figures, among them that it misrepresented the extent of problems by treating one missed shot the same as a total lack of any immunization. More to the point, the extent of immunization says nothing by itself regarding the cause of the high (or low) figures. In July 1995, one year after the first GAO report (1994a) and while the GAO was circulating a draft of its more comprehensive examination of immunization levels and the administration's questionable measurements, Donna Shalala was still misleadingly arguing that before Clinton took office, "about 50 percent of America's two year olds were not properly vaccinated" (Shalala 1995).

6. Among them were the following: four of fifteen contracts had been awarded, while eleven remained in negotiation; only five immunization projects had mailed enrollment forms to potential vaccine providers; training for staff who would use vaccine-ordering software had not yet begun; CDC had chosen the Government

Services Administration (GSA) to manage the distribution function without any review of other options, although the GSA had no experience in the storing and timely delivery of such temperature-sensitive materials and the CDC did not require any validation of their procedures or ability; and there were no accountability mechanisms developed, nor were there any evaluation plans to assess the cost and effectiveness of the program (GAO 1994a, 10–18).

7. For example, it was attempting to purchase 23 million doses of oral polio (41 percent more than would be needed to immunize all eligible children in that age group) and 13 million doses of the combined vaccine against measles, mumps, and rubella (60 percent more than would be required for children who needed it) (Pear 1994c).

8. The report noted that if the HUD budget had kept pace with inflation since 1980, it would be spending $40 billion a year more than the $25 billion it currently spends (HUD 1994, 85). That figure is apparently given as a baseline for the report's assumptions about what its new initiatives should be measured against, although no cost estimate is given for the programs it recommends, outside of a doubling of assistance to $2.1 billion (HUD 1994, 4). The report suggests, for example, that housing costs be considered when figuring the tax credits due low-income workers, a potentially very expensive addition to a program already criticized because of problems with fraud and the structure of its incentives. As maximum benefits are approached, the motivation to work more lessens.

9. The costs of the original Clinton proposal might easily reach $6 billion a year. However, the plan phases in its costs during the first five years and thus "significantly underestimates the eventual costs of the plan which will begin escalating in the sixth year and beyond. . . . Because Congressional rules have a fixed five-year accounting period, the administration is not forced to explain how later costs will be borne" (DeParle 1994a).

10. Clinton wanted to quadruple this program to over $4 billion a year. However, past programs in this area have had very mixed results. As governor, Clinton instituted worker retraining programs in Arkansas (Project Success), and after three years "participants were still earning an average of only $1,422 a year in addition to whatever welfare payments they collected. That was an average of $337 dollars a year more than women who had not joined the program, but hardly the making of a revolution" (DeParle 1993a).

Another indication of the problems involved in this area is contained in a review of a jobless program for the homeless, which was described as being in danger of "being a casualty of its own success" (Kilborn 1994). The report says that 34 percent of those who asked for help got jobs (66 percent didn't). Of those who got jobs, 53 percent were still employed after thirteen weeks (47 percent were not). That means the overall success rate for all those who started the program and remained in their jobs for two months was 18 percent. In other words, the program failed to help over 80 percent of those who began it.

My point here is not that such programs are useless (they do help some) or should not be tried. It is that such programs, with a history of such high percentages of poor outcomes, should not, without careful review and experimentation, be given vast sums for new initiatives.

11. This figure is drawn from Wolf (1995, 32). Even if one assumes that her figure is too high, allowing the government to pay for more abortions would result in a dramatic increase in the number of abortions performed. However, this same result might serve to limit the number of children born out of wedlock and thus reduce welfare expenses and poverty. This is a difficult dilemma, one of many in the abortion debate. Wolf's straight-thinking analysis of the debate represents just the kind of issue leadership that might help bridge different policy views.

12. With Democratic majorities in Congress anxious for him to succeed, Clinton faced an unusual alignment of opportunity. He could have chosen to focus sequentially on a few large issues—the budget, welfare, health care—or he could have chosen to focus on a limited number of large issues and supplement these efforts with developing smaller demonstration projects in other areas. Instead, he tackled an enormous number of issues, large and small, with programs of varying size, scope, complexity, and cost.

13. "Triangulation" is the term given to Clinton's emerging reelection strategy of (1) appropriating by presidential support the most publicly appealing aspects of the Republican "contract"; (2) distancing himself from what he considers to be the more "extreme" positions of the Republicans, about which the public has doubts; and (3) distancing himself from his former Democratic allies in Congress (Mayer 1995).

NOTES TO THE APPENDIX

1. Beyond the question of how traits are connected to each other lie problems with the assumption of equivalence. This assumption is found in the logic of inquiry that underlies trait analysis, and especially comparative trait analysis. Basically, it assumes that a high power motivation score for, say, Richard Nixon is the same as a high power score for Bill Clinton. I would not agree that Clinton has a high need for power in the conventional understanding of that term in political psychology research (Lasswell 1948). But even if the two had similar power motivation scores, the nature of that "need," its connection with other interior psychological elements, and therefore its implications for presidential performance, would differ dramatically and consequentially.

Consider also the trait of achievement motivation. By Winter's (1995, 126) measure, Clinton scores high on this need, and I believe this score accurately reflects his psychology. However, what exactly does it mean that Clinton, or any president, scores high on achievement motivation? One problem here is that given the length and intensive nature of seeking the office, any person who campaigns and gains the presidency has already demonstrated substantial personal and political ambition.

What, then, does a high (or low) score on achievement motivation mean in this context? It makes some sense to distinguish personal political ambition from policy ambition, though in many presidents they become intertwined.

2. The analyst gets some assistance in answering this question by examining available psychological theory. However, this assistance is somewhat limited. General theories can provide a starting point for understanding patterns of a president's interior psychology, but as Hall and Lindzey (1978, 9) point out, "no substantive definition of personality can be applied with any generality." What they mean is that even a theory that aspires to universality must address the issue of a particular person's unique psychology growing out of his or her particular strengths, limitations, life experiences, and so on.

3. A comprehensive treatment of the methodological issues that arise in connection with such analyses may be found in Renshon (1996, Appendix I).

4. Kaplan's (1964, 12–18) distinction between the contexts of discovery and validation are relevant here. My analyses try both to discover and partially validate, keeping in mind limitations of data and of theory. Biographical data are sometimes limited, and they are often filtered though the emotional lens of those who report them. Moreover, a set of even well-established facts can often be viewed profitably through more than one theoretical lens.

5. Other facts are less easily validated. When Wills (1994, 6) interviewed Virginia Kelley, she did not remember that she had filed a deposition against her husband Roger, did not recognize the name of her lawyer, and did not recall when or where her remarriage took place. Fortunately, from the standpoint of validating these facts (as opposed to their meaning), local courthouse records Wills had tracked down (Wills 1992) helped to supplement Kelley's memory. Finally, at this level of analysis one must recognize that many possibly important facts are simply lost, so that historical narratives of any kind must be acknowledged as based on partial, not fully comprehensive, data.

6. There are a number of "psychoanalytic psychotherapies," and the term now ordinarily covers much more than was traditionally covered by the term *psychoanalysis,* as it first evolved from Freud. I use the term to cover all those analyses based on psychoanalytic theory (broadly defined) that make use of transference, genetic, and dynamic interpretations, and which aim at uncovering, clarifying, and modifying unproductive and often unconsciously anchored patterns of behavior. This may occur within psychoanalytic or psychotherapeutic work, which takes place once, twice, or more times a week and is conducted face-to-face or "on the couch."

7. What allows the analyst (and the patient) to have confidence in the historical and narrative constructions? And in what respects is this confidence more or less warranted when comparing psychotherapeutic and more public reconstructions of a president's biography?

The patient brings to the analyst the historical facts of his or her biography. Ordinarily, the analyst is confined to these facts and cannot verify them in the ways that are available to scholars and to other analysts of public figures. A psychoanalyst treating Virginia Kelley, for example, would not ordinarily go down to the courthouse to see whether she did or did not file a deposition against her husband.

While the analyst must work with a patient's presentation and understanding of biographical data, he or she is not wholly dependent on them. A patient can recall, as one of mine did, sitting on her father's knee while he explained things to her at a level she could not hope to understand, the point of which was to require her to acknowledge his erudition. An analyst, on hearing this, can reasonably hypothesize a self-involved, narcissistic parent. This one data element is not decisive, but because character comes in patterns, other evidence of self-absorption, lack of empathy, and unresponsiveness can be reasonably expected to emerge. If they don't, the analyst must account for their absence. Moreover, the various elements that emerge must ultimately make theoretical and psychological sense. A patient who insists that his parents were emotionally distant and unavailable but, on another occasion, also remembers playing long Sunday afternoon games of Monopoly with them clearly raises a discrepancy that needs to be addressed and resolved.

The understanding that develops in analytic work (and with presidents) is not "the whole truth," or "the only truth." Some historical elements are not remembered, others are remembered in a particular way that may or may not fully accord with what an outside observer might have recorded at the time. Yet, while there is variability in the narratives that can be developed to successfully account for developmental experiences and their meanings, it is not infinite. Explanatory narratives, whether of patients or presidents, are bound by the density, coherence, and consistency of the information. Psychological understandings, whether of patients or presidents, must make sense in terms of biographical facts, be consistent with relevant clinical theory, and must make interpretive sense. Ultimately, the purpose of analytic work, and of the psychologically framed analysis of presidents, is not to present *the* objective truth of historical elements, but rather to accurately render their psychological and, in the case of presidents, political significance.

8. This is true in spite of the fact that the book is, of course, a narrative of Virginia Kelley and her life as she saw herself living it, and as she wanted others to see it. Kelley said she wrote the book to "let people see beneath the surface" (1994a, 16). James calls it "a shrewd exercise in image making" (1994). A close friend of the president and his mother, Carolyn Staley, said, "Before there were spin doctors, there was Virginia Kelley. . . . She just puts on a very positive spin. . . . It's not that she even has to work at it" (Purdum 1992, C6). If anything, the book presents Clinton's mother in what she felt was a positive light.

9. In statistical analysis, data validity and reliability are affected by sampling, indicator construction, and using appropriate statistical tests. The difficulties that attend these elements of numerical validity and reliability are well known. These difficulties, like their counterparts in more case-analytic approaches, do not invalidate their use, but rather require that researchers be aware of the advantages and limitations of the method(s) they select.

10. A related but somewhat different question is whether a particular incident reflects something about this president, or presidents more generally. In order to answer this question, the researcher must develop instances of this behavior across presidencies, being careful to ensure that the behaviors presented as belonging to a particular category do in fact belong, even though they might differ in some surface respects.

11. One bit of evidence is that Clinton appeared on a weekly news commentary program on the Arkansas Television Network with Brummett (1994, 13), who raised the story with him. Clinton first criticized Brummett for having brought up the same story "hundreds of times," but then admitted that he had made a mistake with the bill. The televised exchange between the two is also reported by another Clinton biographer (Allen 1991, 111). Clinton, in an interview with another Arkansas reporter (Laningham 1987) essentially confirmed the story, but added as an explanation for his behavior that he had changed his mind only because he had promised to support the bill.

12. In the political culture of Arkansas government, media, business, and other elites are very well known to each other and often have close personal and professional ties. For a detailed documentation of the strong personal connections among the elites in various sectors of Arkansas, see Boyer's (1994) analysis of the interrelationships of the various actors involved in what has come to be known as the "Whitewater Case." Also relevant to this point is a summary by Engelberg and Gerth (1994).

13. Ernest Dumas, a "Friend of Bill," told Bruck (1994, 67) that "Hillary and Betsey Wright decided that they had to neutralize the *Democrat*. They knew that John Robert Starr had a tremendous ego, that he was weak, that they could pander to him. Before long, you'd see Hillary and Starr at lunch over in a corner. We found it nauseating. And for eight years he wrote very little bad about Bill."

14. For example, this difficulty complicates the evaluation of Clinton's educational policies as governor by Diane Blair, a political scientist at the University of Arkansas. The account and evaluation of Clinton's educational policies is contained in her otherwise very solid work on Arkansas politics (1988, 252–63). Blair's evaluation of Clinton's educational policies focuses on measurable financial outcomes, like teacher's salaries and state budget allocations. In these, she finds much to applaud, and she reports little of the controversy that has surrounded some of his initiatives.

Blair does not note in the book that she and her husband have a very close personal relationship to Bill Clinton. Yet, in the Dumas book (Blair 1993, 62) she writes that she and her husband have been close personal friends of the Clintons for two decades. She says she first met Clinton at the National Democratic Convention, where she and her husband had been elected delegates, and that when he later dropped by her office to chat she "was instantly taken with this friendly and interesting young man" (1993, 63). Clinton performed the marriage ceremony for her and her husband, and the Clintons were often houseguests of theirs and visited the Blairs many times at their lake house (1993, 65, 69). Moreover, Engelberg (1995a) notes that Blair took a leave from the University of Arkansas during the presidential campaign to work in a Little Rock office that fielded questions about Clinton's draft history, record as governor, and extramarital relationships.

It is obvious that there is a very close personal friendship between them and that Blair took on the role of Clinton's advocate during the presidential campaign. The question then becomes whether this close personal relationship has had any spill-over effects. Friendship need not bias someone in favor of a friend's effort, but a close personal relationship over a long period of time raises an issue that should have been addressed.

15. As an example, consider one of the few analyses of Clinton's policy making and leadership, Johnson (1983), which covers Clinton's first two years in the governor's office. Johnson's study relies heavily on news accounts from two local newspapers (the *Arkansas Gazette* and the *Arkansas Democrat*) but supplements these with interviews of Clinton and other actors in his administration, as well as some material from Clinton's gubernatorial and personal papers, to which she was given access.

In her 1983 book she mentions that Clinton had agreed to provide her with access to his gubernatorial and (to a more limited degree) personal papers and also to be interviewed. She then notes, "I appreciate Bill Clinton's respect for my insistence that this book contain my interpretations and analysis as a historian who was not a member of the Clinton administration" (1983, 10).

However, ten years later, in the book of recollections on Clinton by his friends and associates noted above (Dumas 1993), Phyllis Johnson (using her married name Anderson) writes (1993, 132): "I spent *ten* years working in various capacities for Bill Clinton." She notes that she had intended to stay on Clinton's staff "only long enough to satisfy my curiosity about how state government functions from the perspective of the office of the chief executive," and then goes on to note the two years she spent interviewing Clinton and writing a book about his first term. Her recollection makes it somewhat unclear whether she was working on Clinton's staff at the time she was interviewing him and writing a book on his first term, or whether her position on Clinton's staff began after the book was published, or whether the two overlapped in some way.

Anderson's admiration of Clinton is clearly and directly stated—she calls him the "complex and brilliant man for whom I would continue to work for many years" (1993, 132). The reasons for her own intense investment in Clinton's administration are also directly stated. She writes that she stayed because "it became clear that Clinton was committed to making the lives of Arkansans better, and that by helping him, I, too, was doing something worthwhile" (1993, 132).

The theme that Anderson touches on is one that can be found throughout the recollections of those who knew and helped Clinton along the way (Dumas 1993). It is a theme that begins with the view that Arkansas was in many respects a backward state, which had a long way to go before it would be in the rank of states with progressive, effective, and focused governmental policies. For many of his admirers, Clinton's attempts to address the state's backwardness made him a person who deserved support and some latitude. This theme has surfaced again on a national level in connection with Clinton's presidency.

16. Robert E. Levin volunteered his services to the Clinton campaign, and the result was an authorized biography, which, however, does not reveal that fact. Levin said in a telephone interview conducted by the author on December 29, 1993, that he worked for the Clinton presidential campaign, and that his book is a result of his asking the campaign "what he could do to help." A reader can gain an appreciation of the issues of independence and reliability by examining the author's introduction: "This book contains the evidence and the story of a man with a restless spirit of can-do idealism which is rare in American politics today. The sources here go beyond the media filter to reveal the *real* Bill Clinton, a man of integrity and compassion who believes in the values that make America great. Bill Clinton, I have come to believe, has what it takes. This book tells us why" (1992, xvi).

Another Clinton biography notes in its preface that "to say that I have been impressed by Bill Clinton would be a vast under-statement. . . . That sense of awe— there is no other word for it . . . propelled me to seek out this project and write this book. . . . It is to be sure not an overly sensational or critical look at Bill Clinton. I freely admit my admiration, respect and affection for the candidate" (Moore 1992, xii, xiii).

Another example is found in Dumas, who notes that his collection "is largely the recollections of friends and associates of Bill and Hillary Clinton" (1993, xvii). The editor himself says, "I began to wonder about the potential value of essays written by people most of whom were close to or who served a politician, essays which would surely largely be a testimonial to his goodness." While the tone and substance of the recollections are overwhelmingly admiring and friendly, the discerning reader will be able to make use of these observations for purposes beyond the intentions of the authors.

★ ————————————————————————————————————

REFERENCES

Abelin, E. 1975. "Some Further Observations and Comments on the Earliest Role of the Father," *International Journal of Psycho-Analysis* 56:293–302.

Allen, Charles Flynn. 1991. "Governor William Jefferson Clinton: A Biography with a Special Focus on His Education Contributions. Ph.D. diss., University of Missouri.

Allen, Charles Flynn, and Jonathan Portis. 1992. *The Comeback Kid: The Life and Career of Bill Clinton.* New York: Birch Lane Press.

Allen, Jodie T. 1995. "Clinton's Budget Plan At Second Glance," *Washington Post National Weekly Edition,* 26 June-2 July, 21.

Allison, G. T. 1971. *Essence of Decision: Explaining the Cuban Missile Crisis.* Boston: Little, Brown.

Allport, Gordon. 1937. *Patterns and Growth in Personality.* New York: Holt, Rinehart and Winston.

Alter, Jonathan. 1994. "The Record Nobody Knows." *Newsweek,* 3 October, 49.

————. 1993. "Less Profile, More Courage," *Newsweek,* 1 November, 33.

Anderson, Phyllis. 1993. "Just Tell Your Story to Me," 131–36 in *The Clintons of Arkansas: An Introduction by Those Who Know Them Best,* edited by Ernest Dumas. Fayetteville: University of Arkansas Press.

Andrews, Edmund. 1994. "Minorities and Women Win Airwave Rights," *New York Times,* 9 November, D2.

Apple, R. W., Jr. 1994a. "Many Democrats Accuse Bill Clinton of Incompetence," *New York Times,* 16 February, D21.

———. 1994b. "Bring Another Presidency and Inquiry to Mind," *New York Times,* 7 March, A1.

———. 1993. "A High Stakes Gamble That Paid Off," *New York Times,* 18 November, A1.

Ayres, B. Drummond. 1992. "Despite Improvements, the Schools in Arkansas Are Still among the Worst," *New York Times,* 1 April, A22.

Baer, Donald. 1991. "Man-Child in Politics Land: An Interview with Bill Clinton," *U.S. News and World Report,* 14 October, 40–42.

Baer, Donald, Matthew Cooper, and David Gergen. 1992. " 'Bill Clinton's Hidden Life': An Interview Conducted with Bill Clinton," *U.S. News and World Report,* 20 July, 29–36.

Baker, Russell. 1993. "Make It Bill and Lyndon," *New York Times,* 9 October, A23.

Balint, Michael. 1979. *The Basic Fault.* New York: Brunner/Mazel.

Barber, James David. 1992 [1972]. *Presidential Character: Predicting Performance in the White House.* 4th ed. Englewood Cliffs, N.J.: Prentice-Hall.

Bassett, Woody. 1993. "The Clinton Factor," 71–76 in *The Clintons of Arkansas: An Introduction by Those Who Know Them Best,* edited by Ernest Dumas. Fayetteville: University of Arkansas Press.

Baudry, Francis. 1989. "Character, Character Type, and Character Organization," *Journal of the American Psychoanalytic Association* 37:655–85.

Bennett, W. Lance. 1995. "The Clueless Public: Bill Clinton Meets the New American Voter in Campaign '92," 91–112 in *The Clinton Presidency: Campaigning, Governing and the Psychology of Leadership,* edited by Stanley A. Renshon. Boulder, Colo.: Westview.

Berdal, Mats R. 1994. "Fateful Encounter: The United States and UN Peacekeeping," *Survival* 36:30–50.

Berke, Richard. 1994a. "The Good Son," *New York Times Magazine,* 20 February, 29–35, 54, 57, 62.

———. 1994b. "Survey Finds Voters in U.S. Rootless and Self-Absorbed," *New York Times,* 21 September, A21.

———. 1993a. "Hatch Assails Idea of Justice Babbitt," *New York Times,* 9 June, A17.

———. 1993b. "An Inauguration Designed to Play to the Cameras," *New York Times,* 18 January, A11.

———. 1993c. "Inside White House: Long Days, Late Nights," *New York Times,* 21 March, A1.

———. 1993d. "President Assails 'Shocking' Prices of Drug Industry," *New York Times,* 13 February, A1.

———. 1993e. "Advisors Looking Askance at Pledge for 25% Staff Cut," *New York Times,* 7 January, 18.

———. 1992a. "Easing Friction, Clinton Meets with Jackson," *New York Times,* 23 November, A14.

———. 1992b. "Many Will Escape Ethics Restriction," *New York Times,* 9 December, A1.

———. 1992c. " 'Let's Do Lunch,' Clinton Says, Calculatingly," *New York Times,* 29 December, A1.

Beschloss, Michael R. 1995. "Seven Ways to Win Friends," *New Yorker,* 30 January, 43–46, 51.

Biller, Henry B. 1976. "The Father and Personality Development: Paternal Deprivation and Sex Role Development," 89–156 in *The Role of the Father in Child Development,* edited by Michael Lamb. New York: Wiley.

Binder, David. 1994–95. "Anatomy of a Massacre," *Foreign Policy* 97:70–78.

Birnbaum, Jeffrey H. 1992. "Clinton Received a Vietnam Draft Deferment for an ROTC Program That He Never Joined," *Wall Street Journal,* 6 February, A16.

Birnbaum, Jeffrey H., and James M. Perry. 1993. "Beyond Feminism and French Fries: Portrait of First Family Debunks the Accepted Stereotypes," *Wall Street Journal,* 1 December, A21.

Blair, Diane D. 1993. "Of Darkness and Light," 62–70 in *The Clintons of Arkansas: An Introduction by Those Who Know Them Best,* edited by Ernest Dumas. Fayetteville: University of Arkansas Press.

———. 1988. *Arkansas Politics and Government: Do the People Rule?* Lincoln: University of Nebraska Press.

Blos, Peter. 1985. *Son and Father.* New York: Free Press.

Blumenthal, Sidney. 1994. "Letter from Washington: The Education of a President," *New Yorker,* 24 January, 31–43.

———. 1993a. "Letter from Washington: Rendezvousing with Destiny," *New Yorker,* 8 March, 38–44.

———. 1993b. "Letter from Washington: Dave," *New Yorker,* 28 June, 31–43.

Blustein, Paul. 1995. "An Auto Market Left Undented," *Washington Post National Weekly Edition,* 3–9 July, 22.

Bolton, John R. 1994. "Wrong Turn in Somalia," *Foreign Affairs* 73:56–66.

Boyer, Peter J. 1994. "The Bridges of Madison Guaranty," *New Yorker,* 17 January, 32–38.

Bradshaw, John. 1988. *Bradshaw On: The Family.* Deerfield Beach, Fla.: Health Communications.

Bradsher, Keith. 1995. "Special Prosecutor Is Sought for Commerce Chief Inquiry," *New York Times,* 18 May, A1.

———. 1994a. "Altman Resigns His Post Amid Whitewater Clamor," *New York Times,* 18 August, B10.

———. 1994b. "Bank Regulator Says Clinton Sought Advice on S. & L.," *New York Times,* 19 July, A15.

———. 1994c. "Treasury Department Counsel Resigns," *New York Times,* 19 August, A16.

———. 1993. "Clinton's Shopping List for Votes Has Ring of Grocery Buyer's List," *New York Times,* 17 November, A21.

Brinkley, Joel. 1992. "Clinton Remakes Home State in Own Image," *New York Times,* 31 March, A1.

Brown, Floyd D. 1994. *"Slick Willie": Why America Cannot Trust Bill Clinton.* Annapolis, Md.: Annapolis Publishing.

Brown, S., and S. Beletsis. 1986. "The Development of Family Transference in Groups for the Adult Children of Alcoholics," *International Journal of Group Psychotherapy* 36:97–114.

Bruck, Connie. 1994. "Hillary the Pol," *New Yorker,* 30 May, 58–96.

Brummett, John. 1994. *Highwire: From the Back Roads to the Beltway—The Education of Bill Clinton.* New York: Hyperion.

Buchanan, Bruce. 1987. *The Citizen's Presidency.* Washington, D.C.: Congressional Quarterly Press.

Bumpers, Dale, and David Pryor. 1994. "Mr. Clinton Moved the State Forward," *New York Times,* 3 September, A16.

Burkhalter, Holly J. 1993. "The 'Costs' of Human Rights," *World Policy Journal* 10:39–49.

Burnham, Walter Dean. 1995. "Critical Realignment Lives: The 1994 Earthquake," 363–94 in *The Clinton Presidency: First Appraisals,* edited by Colin Campbell and Bert A. Rockman. Chatham, N.J.: Chatham House.

Burns, James McGregor. 1956. *Roosevelt: The Lion and the Fox.* New York: Harcourt, Brace.

Campbell, Angus, Philip E. Converse, Warren E. Miller, and Donald E. Stokes. 1960. *The American Voter.* New York: Wiley.

Campbell, Angus, Gerald Gurrin, and Warren E. Miller. 1954. *The Voter Decides.* Evanston, Ill.: Row, Peterson.

Campbell, Tom. 1993. "A Preference for the Future," 42–52 in *The Clintons of Arkansas: An Introduction by Those Who Know Them Best,* edited by Ernest Dumas. Fayetteville: University of Arkansas Press.

Cath, Stanley H., Alan Gurwitt, and Linda Gunsberg, eds. 1989. *Fathers and Their Families.* New York: Analytic Press.

Cath, Stanley H., Alan Gurwitt, and John M. Ross, eds. 1982. *Father and Child.* Boston: Little, Brown.

Chartrand, Sabra. 1993. "Administration Backs Race Based Scholarships," *New York Times,* 27 October, B8.

Church, George J. 1992. "Questions, Questions, Questions," *Time,* 20 April, 38–44.

Citrin, Jack. 1974. "Comment: The Political Relevance of Trust in Government," *American Political Science Review* 68:973–1001.

Clark, Jeffrey. 1993. "Debacle in Somalia: Failure of the Collective Response" 205–39 in *Enforcing Restraint: Collective Intervention in Internal Conflict,* edited by L. F. Damrosch. New York: Council on Foreign Relations.

———. 1992–93. "Debacle in Somalia," *Foreign Affairs* 72:109–23.

Clift, Eleanor. 1993. "Playing Hardball," *Newsweek,* 19 April, 24.

———. 1992. "Political Ambitions, Personal Choices: Bill Clinton Talks about Work, Love and Faith," *Newsweek*, 9 March, 36–37.

Clift, Eleanor, and Jonathan Alter. 1992. "You Don't Reveal Your Pain: Clinton Reflects on the Turmoil of His Childhood," *Newsweek*, 30 March, 37.

Clift, Eleanor, and Bob Cohn, with Jonathan Alter and Joe Klein. 1993. "Seven Days," *Newsweek*, 12 July, 19–29.

Clinton, Hillary Rodham. 1994. "Excerpts from Hillary Clinton's New Session on Whitewater," *New York Times*, 23 April, A11–A12.

———. 1996. *It Takes a Village and Other Lessons Children Teach Us*. New York: Simon and Schuster.

Clinton, William J. 1995a. "Exchange with Reporters on Air Force One (September 22, 1995)," *Weekly Compilation of Presidential Documents*, 2 October, 39:1674–85.

———. 1995b. "I Know What I Believe," *Newsweek*, 9 January, 43–45.

———. 1995c. "Interview with Bob Edwards and Mara Liasson of National Public Radio (August 7, 1995)," *Weekly Compilation of Presidential Documents*, 14 August, 32:1385–93.

———. 1995d. "Interview with Larry King in Culver City, California (September 21, 1995)," *Weekly Compilation of Presidential Documents*, 25 September, 38:1641–54.

———. 1995e. "Interview with Tabitha Soren of MTV (August 11, 1995)," *Weekly Compilation of Presidential Documents*, 14 August, 32:1426–32.

———. 1995f. "Remarks and Question and Answer Session with Students at Abraham Lincoln Middle School in Selma, Calfornia (September 5, 1995), *Weekly Compilation of Presidential Documents*, 11 September, 31:36, 1492–1500.

———. 1995g. "Remarks at a Clinton/Gore '96 Fundraising Dinner (September 7, 1995)," *Weekly Compilation of Presidential Documents*, 11 September, 36:1515–21.

———. 1995h. "Remarks at a Fundraiser in San Francisco (September 21, 1995)," *Weekly Compilation of Presidential Documents*, 25 September, 38:1634–40.

———. 1995i. "Remarks at a Town Meeting in Billings (June 1, 1995)," *Weekly Compilation of Presidential Documents*, 5 June, 22:950–62.

———. 1995j. "Remarks to the National Governors' Association in Burlington, Vermont (July 31, 1995)," *Weekly Compilation of Presidential Documents*, 7 August, 31:1342–49.

———. 1994a. "Clinton: Voters Are Demanding That the Parties Work Together," *New York Times*, 10 November, B8.

———. 1994b. "Interview with John Brummett," 274–85 in John Brummett, *Highwire: From the Back Roads to the Beltway—The Education of Bill Clinton*. New York: Hyperion.

———. 1994c. "Transcript of President's News Conference on Whitewater Affair, *New York Times*, 25 March, A18–A19.

———. 1993a. "Remarks to the National Governors' Association in Tulsa, Oklahoma (August 16, 1993)," *Weekly Compilation of Presidential Documents,* 23 August, 33:1629–38.

———. 1993b. "Excerpts from an Interview with President-Elect Clinton after the Air Strikes," *New York Times,* 14 January, A10.

———. 1993c. "Excerpts from Clinton News Conference: 'The U.S. Should Lead' on Bosnia," *New York Times,* 24 April, A7.

———. 1993d. "Excerpts from Clinton's News Conference in the Rose Garden," *New York Times,* 15 May, A8.

———. 1993e. "Excerpts from Clinton's Question and Answer Session in the Rose Garden," *New York Times,* 28 May, A14.

———. 1993f. "Exchange with Reporters Prior to a Meeting with House Democratic Leaders (May 25, 1993)," *Weekly Compilation of Presidential Documents,* 31 May, 29:21, 942.

———. 1993g. "Inaugural Address (January 29, 1993)," *Weekly Compilation of Presidential Documents,* 25 January, 29:75–77.

———. 1993h. Interview Transcript: *Meet the Press,* NBC News, 7 November, 1–25.

———. 1993i. "Interview with Dan Rather of CBS News, (March 24, 1993)," *Weekly Compilation of Presidential Documents,* 29 March, 29:12, 479.

———. 1993j. "The President's News Conference (January 29, 1993)," *Weekly Compilation of Presidential Documents,* 1 February, 29:4, 109.

———. 1993k. "The President's News Conference (June 15, 1993)," *Weekly Compilation of Presidential Documents,* 21 June, 29:4, 1083.

———. 1993l. "Remarks Announcing Withdrawal of the Nomination of Lani Guinier and an Exchange with Reporters (June 3, 1993)," *Weekly Compilation of Presidential Documents,* 7 June, 29:22, 1028.

———. 1992. "A Letter by Clinton on His Draft Deferment: 'A War I Opposed and Despised,' " *New York Times,* 13 February, A25.

Clinton, William J., and Albert Gore. 1992. *Putting People First: How We All Change America.* New York: New York Times Books.

Clymer, Adam. 1995. "G.O.P. Revises a Budget Rule to Help Banks," *New York Times,* 20 August, A1.

———. 1994a. "Clinton Insists He Won't Retreat on Coverage for All," *New York Times,* 21 July, B9.

———. 1994b. "Hillary Clinton Says Veto Is Possible on Health Care," *New York Times,* 21 June, A1.

———. 1994c. "When a Technical Point for Some Is a Major Issue for Others," *New York Times,* 9 February, A16.

———. 1993a. "Administration Offers New Math to Bolster Plan's Appeal," *New York Times,* 5 November, A1.

———. 1993b. "Americans Have High Hopes for Clinton, Poll Finds," *New York Times,* 19 January, A13.

———. 1993c. "Attacked, White House Defends Proposal," *New York Times,* 13 September, A16.

———. 1993d. "In Campaign for the Health Care Plan, Hillary Clinton Is the Top Candidate," *New York Times,* 11 October, A12.

———. 1992. "Leadership and Its Limits," *New York Times,* 1 May, A1.

Coleman, William T., III. 1993. "Don't You Know Whose Table This Is?" 53–61 in *The Clintons of Arkansas: An Introduction by Those Who Know Them Best,* edited by Ernest Dumas. Fayetteville: University of Arkansas Press.

Cronin, Thomas. 1975. *The State of the Presidency.* 2d. ed. Boston: Little, Brown.

Cushman, John H., Jr. 1994. "Administration Gives Up on Raising Grazing Fees," *New York Times,* 22 December, B12.

DeMause, Lloyd. 1977. "Jimmy Carter and the American Fantasy," 9–31 in *Jimmy Carter and the American Fantasy,* edited by Lloyd DeMause and Henry Edel. New York: Two Continents/Psychohistory Press.

DeParle, Jason. 1994a. "Clinton Plan Sees Welfare Costing $6 Billion a Year," *New York Times,* 10 March, A1.

———. 1994b. "Old Flame Burns the Housing Secretary," *New York Times,* 22 September, A18.

———. 1994c. "Report to Clinton Sees Vast Extent of Homelessness," *New York Times,* 16 February, A1.

———. 1993a. "Free Vaccine Program Creates Unusual Array of Skeptics," *New York Times,* 22 April, A1.

———. 1993b. "Reports Warning of H.U.D. Problems," *New York Times,* 11 March, A21.

———. 1993c. "Social Investment Programs: Comparing the Past with the Promised Payoff," *New York Times,* 1 March, A18.

———. 1993d. "With Shots, It's Not Only About Costs, but Stories," *New York Times,* 16 May, A18.

———. 1992. "Arkansas Pushes Plan to Break the Welfare Cycle," *New York Times,* 14 March, A10.

Devroy, Ann, and Pierre Thomas. 1995. "Barging through the Caution Signs," *Washington Post Weekly Edition,* 20–26 March, 14.

Dowd, Maureen. 1994a. "Inner Circle Is Shrinking," *New York Times,* 15 March, A1.

———. 1994b. " 'Sorry' As a Political Weapon in the TV Age," *New York Times,* 22 April, A1.

———. 1993. "On Health, Clinton Finds Heaven in the Details," *New York Times,* 25 September, A1.

Drew, Elizabeth. 1994. *On the Edge: The Clinton Presidency.* New York: Simon & Schuster.

Dugger, Celia A. 1993a. "A Roof for All, Made of Rulings and Red Tape," *New York Times,* 4 July, A1.

———. 1993b. "Setbacks and Surprise Temper a Mayor's Hopes to House All," *New York Times,* 5 July, A1.

Dumas, Ernest, ed. and comp. 1993. *The Clintons of Arkansas: An Introduction by Those Who Know Them Best.* Fayetteville: University of Arkansas Press.

Dye, Thomas. 1993. "The Friends of Bill and Hillary," *Political Science and Politics* 26:693–95.

Elwood, Paul M. 1993. "Balance the Health Budget," *New York Times,* 6 December, A17.

Engelberg, Stephen. 1995a. "The Man Clinton Turns to in Times of Turmoil and Moments of Doubt," *New York Times,* 5 July, A9.

———. 1995b. "Bosnia Highlights a Republican Split," *New York Times,* 10 December, E6.

———. 1994a. "Clinton's Investment Loss Disputed, *New York Times,* 16 March, B6.

———. 1994b. "Hillary Clinton Escaped Collapse in the Markets that Cost Many Fortunes," *New York Times,* 3 April, A16.

———. 1994c. "New Records Outline Favor for Hillary Clinton in Trades, *New York Times,* 26 May, A20.

———. 1994d. "Untangling the Threads of the Whitewater Affair," *New York Times,* 14 March, sec. 4, 6.

Engelberg, Stephen, and Jeff Gerth 1994. "The Whitewater Case: Finding the Connections," *New York Times,* 16 January, A12.

English, Art. 1993. "Bill Clinton: His Promise and His Methods," Paper Presented to the Annual Meeting of the Arkansas Political Science Association, Conway, Arkansas, 27 February.

Erikson, Erik H. 1959 [1980]. *Identity and the Life Cycle.* New York: Norton.

Evans, Ernest. 1993. "The U.S. Military and Peacekeeping Operations," *World Affairs* 155:143–63.

Evans, Rowland, and Robert Novak. 1966. *Lyndon B. Johnson: The Exercise of Power.* New York: New American Library.

Fick, Paul. 1995. *The Dysfunctional President: Inside the Mind of Bill Clinton.* New York: Birch Lane.

Fineman, Howard, and Mark Miller. 1993. "Hillary's Role," *Newsweek,* 15 February, 18–23.

Franklin, Daniel. 1995. "He's No Bill Clinton," *Washington Monthly* (May):10–15.

Freedman, Lawrence. 1994–95. "Why the West Failed," *Foreign Policy* 97:53–69.

Freud, Anna. 1965. *Normality and Pathology in Childhood.* New Haven: Yale University Press.

Freud, Sigmund. 1921. "Group Psychology and the Analysis of the Ego." *Standard Edition* 18:69–143.

———. 1918. "From the History of an Infantile Neurosis," *Standard Edition* 17:7–122.

Freudenheim, Milt. 1995. "Drug Prices Overstated, G.A.O. Says," *New York Times,* 30 May, D9.

———. 1993. "Drug Makers Defend Prices for Vaccines," *New York Times,* 13 February, A29.

Friedman, Thomas L. 1993a. "Clinton Aide Demurs on White House Staff Cuts and Reductions," *New York Times,* 12 January, A17.

———. 1993b. "Clinton's Foreign Policy: Top Advisor Speaks Up," *New York Times,* 31 October, A8.

———. 1993c. "Clinton Rules Out Delay in Unveiling Health-Care Plan, *New York Times,* 28 April, A1.

———. 1993d. "Doing More Than Bush, Less Than Advertised," *New York Times,* 14 February, sec. 4, 1.

———. 1993e. "White House Retreats on Ouster at Travel Office, Reinstating Five," *New York Times,* 26 May, A1.

———. 1992. "Professor Elect on T.V.: More Than Just a Talk Show," *New York Times,* 18 December, B12.

Friedman, Thomas L., with Maureen Dowd. 1993. "Amid Setbacks, Clinton Team Seeks to Shake Off the Blues," *New York Times,* 25 April, A1.

Frisby, Michael K. 1995. "Clinton Recruits Campaign Team of 'Nasty Boys' with Reputations as Tough, Savvy Hired Guns," *Wall Street Journal,* 16 October, A16.

Gates, Henry Louis, Jr. 1995. "Powell and the Black Elite," *New Yorker,* 25 September, 64–80.

Gelb, Leslie. 1993. "Clinton as Carter?" *New York Times,* 12 January, A15

———. 1992. "Three Wine Mice," *New York Times,* 12 January, A15

General Accounting Office (GAO). 1995a. *National Service Programs: Ameri-Corps*USA-Early Program Resource and Benefit Information (GAO/HEMS-95–222),* Washington, D.C.: U.S. General Accounting Office, 29 August, 1–71.

———. 1995b. Vaccines for Children: Reexamination of Program Goals Needed to Insure Vaccination *(GAO/PEMD-95–22),* Washington, D.C.: U.S. General Accounting Office, 15 June, 1–43.

———. 1994a. *Vaccines for Children: Critical Issues in Design and Implementation (GAO/PEMD-94–28),* Washington, D.C.: U.S. General Accounting Office, 18 July, 1–21.

———. 1994b. White House Travel Office Operations, Report to the Congress, *(GAO/GGD-94–132),* 2 May.

George, Alexander L. 1980. *Presidential Decision Making in Foreign Policy: The Effective Use of Information and Advice.* Boulder, Colo.: Westview.

———. 1974. "Assessing Presidential Character," *World Politics* 26:234–82.

———. 1971. "Some Use of Dynamic Psychology in Political Biography: Case Materials on Woodrow Wilson," 78–98 in *A Source Book for the Study of Personality and Politics,* edited by Fred I. Greenstein and Michael Lerner. Chicago: Markham.

George, Alexander L., and Juliette George. 1956. *Woodrow Wilson and Colonel House: A Personality Study.* New York: John Day.

Gergen, Kenneth. 1991. *The Saturated Self.* New York: Basic Books.

Gerth, Jeff. 1994a. "Clintons Release Tax Data Showing Land Deal Losses," *New York Times,* 26 March, A1.

———. 1994b. "Top Arkansas Lawyer Helped Hillary Clinton Turn Big Profit," *New York Times,* 18 March, A1.

———. 1992. "Policies under Clinton Are a Boon to Industry," *New York Times,* 2 April, A20.

Gerth, Jeff and Stephen Engelberg. 1995. "Documents Show Clintons Got Vast Benefits from Their Partnership in Whitewater Deal," *New York Times,* 16 July, A18.

———. 1993. "Head of Failing S.& L. Helped Clinton Pay a $50,000 Personal Debt in 1985," *New York Times,* 15 December, B8.

Goldberg, Arnold. 1988. *A Fresh Look at Psychoanalysis: The View from Self Psychology.* Hillsdale, N.J.: Analytic Press.

Goldberg, Robert M. 1995. "The Vaccine Scare That Wasn't," *Washington Post Weekly Edition,* 26 June-2 July, 23.

Goldman, Peter, Thomas M. DeFrank, Mark Miller, Andrew Murr, and Tom Mathews. 1994. *Quest for the Presidency 1992.* College Station: Texas A & M Press.

Gravitz, H. L., and J. D. Bowden. 1985. *Recovery: A Guide for Adult Children of Alcoholics.* Holmes Beach, Fla.: Learning Publications.

Greenberg, Jay R., and Stephen A. Mitchell. 1983. *Object Relations in Psychoanalytic Theory.* Cambridge, Mass.: Harvard University Press.

Greenhouse, Linda. 1994. "U.S. Opposes Lifting Segregation Controls," *New York Times,* 24 November, B10.

———. 1993. "Justices Plan to Delve Anew into Race and Voting Rights," *New York Times,* 11 July, A1.

Greenhouse, Steven. 1994. "Clinton Is Faulted on Political Choices for Envoy Posts," *New York Times,* 13 April, A15.

———. 1993a. "Clinton Delays Push to Increase Minimum Wage," *New York Times,* 3 June, A1.

———. 1993b. "Many Experts Say Health Plan Would Fall Far Short on Savings," *New York Times,* 21 September, A1.

Greenstein, Fred I. 1995. "Political Style and Political Leadership: The Case of Bill Clinton," 137–47 in *The Clinton Presidency: Campaigning, Governing and the Psychology of Leadership,* edited by Stanley A. Renshon. Boulder, Colo.: Westview.

———. 1993–94. "The Political Leadership Style of Bill Clinton: An Early Appraisal," *Political Science Quarterly* 108:589–601.

———. 1982. *The Hidden-Hand Presidency: Eisenhower As Leader.* New York: Basic Books.

———. 1969. *Personality and Politics: Problems of Evidence, Inference, and Conceptualization*. Chicago: Markham.

Guinier, Lani. 1994. "Who's Afraid of Lani Guinier?" *New York Times Magazine*, 27 February, 40–43, 54–55.

Hall, Calvin S., and Gardner Lindzey. 1978. *Theories of Personality*. 3d. ed. New York: Wiley.

Hames, Tim. 1994. "Searching for the New World Order: The Clinton Administration and Foreign Policy in 1993," *International Relations* 12:109–27.

Harris, John F. 1995. "President Revises Stand on '93 Taxes," *Washington Post*, 19 October, 1.

Hart, John. 1995. "President Clinton and the Politics of Symbolism," *Political Science Quarterly* 110:385–403.

Heifetz, Ronald. 1994. "Some Strategic Implications of William Clinton's Strengths and Weaknesses," *Political Psychology* 15:763–69.

Herbers, John. 1980. "Panel Blames Lawmakers for Aid Crisis," *New York Times*, 25 August, A24.

Herbert, Bob. 1994. "The Truth Sculptor," *New York Times*, 12 January, A21.

Hermann, Margaret G. 1986. "Ingredients of Leadership," 167–92 in *Political Psychology*, edited by Margaret G. Hermann. San Francisco: Jossey-Bass.

Hershey, Robert D., Jr. 1994. "Friend Did Futures Trades for Hillary Clinton," *New York Times*, 11 April, D10.

Hilts, Philip J. 1993. "U.S. Study of Drug Makers Criticizes 'Excess Profits,' " *New York Times*, 26 February, D1.

Hilzenrath, David S., and Ruth Marcus. 1993. "Senators Rewrite Energy Tax Plan," *Washington Post*, 10 June, A1.

Holmes, Steven A. 1992. "Race Relations in Arkansas Reflect Gains for Clinton, but Raise Questions," *New York Times*, 3 April, A14.

Hook, Sidney. 1943. *The Hero in History*. Boston: Beacon.

Horney, Karen. 1937. *The Neurotic Personality of Our Times*. New York: Norton.

Housing and Urban Development (HUD). 1994. *Priority Home! The Federal Plan to Break the Cycle of Homelessness (HUD-1454–CDP(1)*. Washington D.C.: U.S. Government Printing Office, i-126.

Ifill, Gwen. 1994a. "Clintons Campaigning to Scuttle Endorsement of Rival Health Plan," *New York Times*, 2 February, A1.

———. 1994b. "Hillary Clinton Didn't Report $6,498 Profit in '80 Commodity Account, White House Says," *New York Times*, 11 April, A15.

———. 1994c. "Using Clinton's Helicopter Costs an Aide His Job," *New York Times*, 27 May, A20.

———. 1994d. "Clinton and Japan Chief Say Trade Talks Fail; U.S. Threatens Action," *New York Times*, 12 February, A1.

———. 1993a. "A Campaigner Adjusts to Life As the President," *New York Times*, 15 January, C6.

———. 1993b. "Fifty-six Long Days of Coordinated Persuasion," *New York Times*, 19 November, A28.

———. 1993c. "Making Deals, Not Waves, Is Strategy for Health Plan," *New York Times*, 28 September, B10.

———. 1993d. "Making His Way Out of the Muddle He Made," *New York Times*, 16 May, A1, E4.

———. 1993e. "One Clinton Promise Fits All Issues," *New York Times*, 17 October, sec. 4, 3.

———. 1993f. "President Defends His Policies As Adding to Personal Security," *New York Times*, 13 October, A22.

———. 1993g. "Social Security Won't Be Subject to Freeze, White House Decides," *New York Times*, 9 February, A1.

———. 1993h. "Globe-Trotting Clinton Faces Trip's Side Effects," *New York Times*, 9 July, A8.

———. 1992a. "Questioned about Trust, Clinton Turns Angry," *New York Times*, 24 April, A21.

———. 1992b. "Tenacity and Change in a Son of the South: William Jefferson Clinton," *New York Times*, 16 July, A1.

———. 1992c. "Vietnam War Draft Status Becomes Issue for Clinton," *New York Times*, 17 February, A16.

———. 1992d. "A Front Runner in Trouble, Clinton Portrays Himself As a Victim of Attacks," *New York Times*, 10 February, A14.

———. 1992e. "Clinton Resists Being Labeled a Liberal," *New York Times*, 28 July, A11.

———. 1992f. "Clinton Expands Position on the Draft," *New York Times*, 20 September, A26.

———. 1992g. "Democrats Drop Donor's Session with President," *New York Times*, 2 May, A1.

James, Caryn. 1994. "Memoir of a First Mother More Warm Than Saintly," *New York Times*, 4 May, C21.

Jehl, Douglas. 1995. "On Morning After the White House Is Back on the Defensive," *New York Times*, 29 January, A19.

———. 1994a. "Clinton Aides Often Used Helicopter," *New York Times*, 1 June, A12.

———. 1994b. "Clinton Calls Show to Assail Press, Falwell and Limbaugh," *New York Times*, 25 June, A1.

———. 1994c. "Clinton, Unlike Recent Predecessors, Leaves the Experts at Home," *New York Times*, 8 February, A14.

———. 1994d. "Coverage of 95% Might Be Enough, Clinton Concedes," *New York Times*, 20 July, A1.

———. 1994e. "White House Aide Who Failed to Pay Tax Is Punished," *New York Times*, 23 March, A1.

———. 1994f. "Packing for Europe, Clinton Hopes to Find a Boost in Ratings," *New York Times*, 1 June, A13.

————. 1993. "Bill, Hillary and Other Plain Folks Are All Set for One Heady Weekend," *New York Times*, 31 December, A20.

Jenks, Christopher. 1994. *The Homeless*. New York: Basic Books.

Johnson, David. 1994a. "Clinton Associate Quits Justice Post As Pressure Rises," *New York Times*, 15 March, A1.

————. 1994b. "Clintons Create Fund to Accept Gifts to Pay Their Rising Legal Costs," *New York Times*, 29 June, A18.

————. 1994c. "Panel Names Chief Counsel for Inquiry in Epsy Case," *New York Times*, 10 September, A6.

Johnson, Phyllis Finton. 1983. *Bill Clinton's Public Policy for Arkansas: 1979–1980*. Little Rock, Ark.: August House.

Jones, Charles O., ed. 1988. *The Reagan Legacy: Promise and Performance*. Chatham, N.J.: Chatham House.

Kakutani, Michiko. 1995. "Books of the Times: Retracing a Path That Led to the Presidential Trail," *New York Times*, 10 February, C30.

Kaplan, Abraham. 1964. *The Conduct of Inquiry*. San Francisco: Chandler.

Kearns, Doris. 1976. *Lyndon Johnson and the American Dream*. New York: Harper & Row.

Kellerman, Barbara. 1983. "Introversion in the Oval Office," *Presidential Studies Quarterly* (spring):383–99.

Kelley, Virginia [with James Morgan]. 1994a. *Leading with My Heart: My Life*. New York: Simon & Schuster.

Kelley, Virginia. 1994b. Transcript of Interview with Connie Chung on CBS Eye to Eye, 6 January, 20.

————. 1992. Transcript of Interview with Katherine Couric on NBC Today, 15 July, 33–36.

Kelly, Michael. 1995. "Letter from Washington: A Place Called Fear." *New Yorker*, 13 April, 38–44.

————. 1994. "The President's Past," *New York Times Sunday Magazine*, 31 July, 20–29, 34, 40–41.

————. 1993a. "Clinton Myth of Nonideological Politics," *New York Times*, 6 June, A26.

————. 1993b. "The First Couple: A Union of Mind and Ambition," *New York Times*, 20 January, A13.

————. 1993c. "Hillary Clinton Rejects Delays in Health Care Plan," *New York Times*, 29 April, B12.

————. 1993d. "Hillary Clinton's Health Panel Invites Ideas From the Invited," *New York Times*, 12 March, A7.

————. 1993e. "Hillary Rodham Clinton and The Politics of Virtue," *New York Times Magazine*, 23 May, 22–25, 63–66.

————. 1993f. "Loophole Left Open, Clinton Weighs Tax on Middle Class," *New York Times*, 26 January, A1.

————. 1992a. "Clinton's 4–Day Holiday: Exhaustive Relaxation," *New York Times*, 1 September, B9.

———. 1992b. "Given a Good Lead, Clinton Is No Longer Talking Tough," *New York Times,* 18 September, A20.

———. 1992c. "The Making of the First Family: A Blueprint," *New York Times,* 14 November, A1.

———. 1992d. "A Man Who Wants to Be Liked, and Is: William Jefferson Blythe Clinton," *New York Times,* 4 November, A1.

———. 1992e. "Though Advisors Differ, Clinton's in Tune with Them All," *New York Times,* 13 September, A1.

———. 1992f. "Day After 'Final Word on Draft,' Clinton Faces Renewed Questions," *New York Times,* 3 September, A20.

———. 1992g. "Clinton Readies Answer to Bush on Draft Issue," *New York Times,* 15 September, A1.

———. 1992h. "Clinton Says He Was Told of Draft Aid," *New York Times,* 5 September, A7.

———. 1992i. "Clinton Again Faces Draft Issues As He Returns to New Hampshire," *New York Times,* 27 September, A20.

———. 1992j. "After 13 Months, Clinton Relaxes," *New York Times,* 8 November, A29.

Kelly, Michael, and David Johnson. 1992. "Campaign Focuses on Vietnam, Reviving Debates of the 60's," *New York Times,* 9 October, A1.

Kilborn, Peter T. 1994. "Jobs Program May Become the Casualty of Its Success," *New York Times,* 11 April, A14.

Klein, Joe. 1993a. "Clinton's Value Problem," *Newsweek,* 26 April, 35.

———. 1993b. "A High Risk Presidency," *Newsweek,* 3 May, 32–38.

———. 1993c. "Slow Motion," *Newsweek,* 24 May, 16.

———. 1993d. "What's Wrong?" *Newsweek,* 7 June, 16–19.

———. 1992a. "The Bill Clinton Show," *Newsweek,* 26 October, 35.

———. 1992b. "Bill Clinton: Who Is This Guy?" *New York,* 20 January, 29–35.

Kohut, Heinz. 1984. *How Does Analysis Cure?* Chicago: University of Chicago Press.

———. 1979. "The Two Analyses of Mr. Z," *International Journal of Psychoanalysis* 60:3–27.

———. 1977. *The Restoration of the Self.* New York: International Universities Press.

———. 1972. "Thoughts on Narcissism and Narcissistic Rage," *Psychoanalytic Study of the Child* 27:360–400.

———. 1971. *The Analysis of the Self.* New York: International Universities Press.

Kolbert, Elizabeth. 1992. "Early Loss Casts Clinton As a Leader by Consensus," *New York Times,* 28 September, A1.

Kranish, Michael. 1993. "Clinton Didn't Skirt Limelight," *Boston Globe,* 9 June, A8.

Krauss, Clifford. 1993. "Skeptics and Lobbyists Besiege Student Loan Plan," *New York Times,* 2 June, A14.

Kritsberg, Wayne. 1988. *The Adult Children of Alcoholics Syndrome: From Discovery to Recovery.* Pompano Beach, Fla.: Health Communications.

Kroft, Steve. 1992. "Interview with Governor and Mrs. Clinton," Transcript of *60 Minutes,* CBS News, 26 January, 1–5.

Kurtz, Howard. 1995. "Yesterday's 'Sleaze,' Today's 'Character Issue,' " *Washington Post Weekly Edition,* 3–9 April, 24.

Labaton, Stephen. 1995. "Clinton Rebuffs a Senate Demand over Whitewater," *New York Times,* 9 December, A1.

———. 1994a. "Aide Is Said to Contradict Bentsen about Whitewater," *New York Times,* 23 July, A9.

———. 1994b. "A Clinton Friend Admits Mail Fraud and Tax Evasion," *New York Times,* 7 December, A1.

———. 1994c. "Clinton Loans in Arkansas Were Paid Off By Donors," *New York Times,* 14 July, D23.

———. 1994d. "Commodities Broker Has History of Legal Trouble," *New York Times,* 31 March, A18.

———. 1994e. "Diary Says White House Wanted Treasury Official on Whitewater," *New York Times,* 25 July, A1.

———. 1994f. "House Committee Told of Contacts over Whitewater," *New York Times,* 27 July, A1.

———. 1994g. "Regulator Briefed White House Aides in Inquiry into S. & L.," *New York Times,* 25 February, A1.

———. 1994h. "Treasury Aide Denies Pressure to Intervene in S. & L. Case," *New York Times,* 31 March, A1.

———. 1993a. "Ron Brown Gala Raises Questions," *New York Times,* 13 January, A1.

———. 1993b. "Commerce Nominee Cancels Party Planned by Companies," *New York Times,* 14 January, A1.

Ladd, E. C. 1993. "The 1992 Vote for President Clinton: Another Brittle Mandate?" *Political Science Quarterly* 108:1–28.

Lamb, Michael E., ed. 1976a. *The Role of the Father in Child Development.* New York: Wiley.

———. 1976b. "The Role of the Father, an Overview," 1–61 in *The Role of the Father in Child Development,* edited by Michael Lamb. New York: Wiley.

———. 1975. "Fathers: Forgotten Contributors to Child Development," *Human Development* 18:235–266.

Lamb, Michael E., and David Oppenheim. 1989. "Father and Father-Child Relationships: Five Years of Research," 11–26 in *Fathers and Their Families,* edited by Stanley H. Cath, Alan Gurwitt, and Linda Gunsberg. New York: Analytic Press.

Laningham, Van. 1987. "Arkansas Won't Take a Back Seat to Any Presidential Drive, Clinton Vows," *Arkansas Gazette,* 22 April, 1.

Lansky, M. R. 1980. "On Blame," *International Journal of Psychoanalytic Psychotherapy* 8:429–55.

Lasswell, Harold D. 1968. "A Note on 'Types' of Political Personality: Nuclear, Corelational, Developmental," *Journal of Social Issues* 24:81–91.

———. 1948. *Power and Personality.* New York: Norton.

———. 1930. *Psychopathology and Politics.* Chicago: University of Chicago Press.

Layne, Christopher, and Benjamin Schwarz. 1993. "American Hegemony—Without an Enemy," *Foreign Policy* 92:5–23.

Lehmann-Haupt, Christopher. 1994. "Low Shock Threshold in White House Exposé," *New York Times,* 9 June, C18.

Levin, Robert E. 1992. *Bill Clinton: The Inside Story.* New York: S.P.I. Books.

Lewis, Anthony. 1993a. "Now, Be the President," *New York Times,* 19 November, A32.

———. 1993b. "Bill Clinton's Center," *New York Times,* 7 June, A17.

Lind, Michael. 1995. "The Out-of-Control Presidency," *New Republic,* 14 August, 18–23.

Lowi, Theodore. 1984. *The Personal President: Power Invested, Promise Unfulfilled.* Ithaca, N.Y.: Cornell University Press.

Mächtlinger, Veronica J. 1976. "Psychoanalytic Theory: Pre-oedipal and Oedipal Phases, with Special Reference to the Father," 277–305 in *The Role of the Father in Child Development,* edited by Michael Lamb. New York: Wiley.

Mahler, Margaret. 1968. *On Human Symbiosis and the Vicissitudes of Individuation.* New York: International Universities Press.

Mahler, Margaret, Fred Pine, and Anni Bergman. 1975. *The Psychological Birth of the Human Infant.* New York: Basic Books.

Mandelbaum, Michael. 1994. "The Reluctance to Intervene," *Foreign Policy* 95:3–18.

Manning, Robert A. 1994. "Clinton and China: Beyond Human Rights," *Orbis* (spring):193–205.

Mansfield, Harvey C., Jr. 1989. *Taming the Prince: The Ambivalence of Modern Executive Power.* New York: Free Press.

Maraniss, David. 1995. *First in His Class: A Biography of Bill Clinton.* New York: Simon & Schuster.

Marks, Peter. 1993. "Vaccinations Are Often Free, But Many Children Miss Out," *New York Times,* 14 February, A1.

Martin, Ian. 1994. "Haiti: Mangled Multilateralism," *Foreign Policy* 95:73–91.

Masterson, James F. 1988. *The Search for the Real Self.* New York: Free Press.

Matalin, Mary, and James Carville [with Peter Knobler]. 1994. *All's Fair: Love, War, and Running for President.* New York: Simon & Schuster.

Mathews, Tom. 1993. "Clinton's Growing Pains," *Newsweek,* 3 May, 34–38, 40.

Mayer, Jane. 1995. "Lonely Guy: Is Alienating Friends the Way to Be Reelected?" *New Yorker,* 30 October, 58–63.

Maynes, Charles William. 1993–94. "A Workable Clinton Doctrine," *Foreign Policy* 93:3–20.

Mazlish, Bruce. 1994. "Some Observations on Political Leadership," *Political Psychology* 15:745–53.

McNamara, Robert S. 1995. *In Retrospect: The Tragedy and Lessons of Vietnam.* New York: Times Books.

McWilliams, Wilson Carey. 1993. "The Meaning of the Election," 190–219 in *The Election of 1992,* edited by Gerald M. Pomper, F. Christopher Arterton, Ross K. Baker, Walter Dean Burnham, Kathleen A. Frankovic, Marjorie Randon Hershey, and Wilson Carey McWilliams. Chatham, N.J.: Chatham House.

Meyerson, Harold. 1994. "Clinton At an Impasse," *Dissent* (fall): 453–56.

Miller, A. H. 1974. "Trust in Government 1964-70," *American Political Science Review* 68:951-72.

Mitchell, Alison. 1995a. "U.S. Grants Vietnam Full Ties; Time for Healing, Clinton Says," *New York Times,* 12 July, A1.

———. 1995b. "Panetta's Sure Step in a High-Wire Job," *New York Times,* 17 August, B12.

Moore, Jim [with Rick Ihde]. 1992. *Clinton: Young Man in a Hurry.* Ft. Worth, Tex.: Summit Group.

Moore, Rudi. 1993. "They're Killing Me Out Here," 85–94 in *The Clintons of Arkansas: An Introduction by Those Who Know Them Best,* edited by Ernest Dumas. Fayetteville: University of Arkansas Press.

Moritz, Charles. 1988. "Bill Clinton," 119–21 in *Current Biography Yearbook 1988,* edited by Charles Moritz. New York: H. W. Wilson.

Moynihan, Daniel P. 1969. *Maximum Feasible Misunderstanding.* New York: Macmillan.

Muir, Roy. 1989. "Fatherhood from the Perspective of Object Relations Theory and Relational Systems Theory," 47–61 in *Fathers and Their Families,* edited by Stanley H. Cath, Alan Gurwitt, and Linda Gunsberg. New York: Analytic Press.

Murray, Charles. 1984. *Losing Ground.* New York: Basic Books.

Myerson, Allen R. 1994. "Oil-Patch Congressmen Seek Deal with Clinton," *New York Times,* 14 June, D2.

Nardulli, Peter F., and Jon K. Dalanger. 1993. "The Presidential Election of 1992 in Historical Perspective," 149–67 in *America's Choice: The Election of 1992,* edited by William Gotty. Guilford, Conn.: Dushkin.

Neubauer, Peter B. 1989. "Fathers As Single Parents: Object Relations Theory Beyond Mother," 63–75 in *Fathers and Their Families,* edited by Stanley H. Cath, Alan Gurwitt, and Linda Gunsberg. New York: Analytic Press.

———. 1960. "The One Parent Child and His Oedipal Development," *Psychoanalytic Study of the Child* 37:201–21.

Neustadt, Richard E. 1990 [1960]. *Presidential Power and the Modern Presidents: The Politics of Leadership From Roosevelt to Reagan.* New York: Free Press.

New York Times. 1994a. "Editorial: Arkansas Secrets," 31 March, A20.

————. 1994b. "Editorial: Bill Clinton's Vital Signs," 25 January, A18.

————. 1994c. "Editorial: Mr. Clinton's Whitewater Contact," 21 July, A22.

————. 1994d. "Editorial: The Tainted Defense Fund," 30 May, A22.

————. 1994e. "Editorial: The Vaccine Debacle," 24 August, A16.

————. 1994f. "Editorial: Whitewater Disinformation," 26 July, A18.

————. 1994g. "Excerpts from Clinton's Comments on Cynicism and the Press," 25 June, A12.

————. 1994h. "Now It Can Be Told: The Task Force Was Bold and Naive and Collegial," 18 September, E7.

————. 1993a. "Editorial: Clinton Plugs In," 12 February, A16.

————. 1993b. "Editorial: A Dawn of Promise," 21 January, A24.

————. 1993c. "Clinton Pledges Open Fund-Raisers," 13 October, A22.

————. 1992a. "Transcript of 2nd TV Debate between Bush, Clinton, and Perot," 16 October, A11–A14.

————. 1992b. "Verbatim—Heckler Stirs Clinton Anger: Excerpts From the Exchange," 28 March, D9.

Oakley, Meredith L. 1994. *On the Make: The Rise of Bill Clinton*. Washington, D.C.: Regnery.

Oates, Joyce Carol. 1994. "The Woman Before Hillary," *New York Times Sunday Book Review*, 8 May, 14.

Osborne, David, and Ted Gaebler. 1992. *Reinventing Government: How the Entrepreneurial Spirit Is Transforming the Public Sector*. Reading, Mass.: Addison-Wesley.

Osborne, T. 1988. *Laboratories of Democracy*. Cambridge: MIT Press.

Page, Susan. 1993. "Clinton's First Year," *Newsday*, 19 December, 7, 70.

Parker, Richard. 1994. "Clintonomics for the East," *Foreign Policy* 94:53–68.

Pear, Robert. 1994a. "Architect of Health Plan Could Face Charges," *New York Times*, 22 December, B12.

————. 1994b. "Clinton Aides Seek New Review Board for Drug Pricing," *New York Times*, 16 May, A1.

————. 1994c. "Clinton Criticized As Too Ambitious with Vaccine Plan," *New York Times*, 30 May, A1.

————. 1994d. "Clinton Health Plan: Testimony Reveals the Government's Hand," *New York Times*, 10 February, D20.

————. 1994e. "Clinton's Plan for Immunization of Children Suffers a New Blow," *New York Times*, 22 August, A1.

————. 1994f. "Treasury Had Doubts about Health Plan, Papers Show," *New York Times*, 7 Setember, A22.

————. 1993a. "Clinton Backs Off His Pledge to Cut the Budget in Half," *New York Times*, 7 January, A1.

————. 1993b. "Clinton May Not Meet Deadline on Health Plan," *New York Times*, 2 May, A20.

———. 1993c. "Clinton Offering Health Plan with Guarantee of Coverage and Curb on Private Spending," *New York Times,* 11 September, A1.

———. 1993d. "Clinton Seeks to Regulate Medical Specialties," *New York Times,* 15 September, A22.

———. 1993e. "Democratic Senators Press Cabinet Choice on Welfare," *New York Times,* 15 January, A15.

———. 1993f. "Health-Care Plan to Be Delayed Further," *New York Times,* 6 May, A18.

———. 1993g. "Hillary Clinton Attacks Health Plans Offerred by Conservative Democrats," *New York Times,* 9 November, A12.

———. 1993h. "Hillary Clinton Sees Hurdles in Forging Health-Care Plan," *New York Times,* 12 February, A11.

———. 1993i. "President Again Postpones Unveiling of a Health Plan," *New York Times,* 3 June, A20.

———. 1993j. "U.S. to Guarantee Free Immunization for Poor Children," *New York Times,* 15 August, A1.

Peters, Charles. 1994. "Whitewater, and Other Thin Ice," *New York Times,* 12 January, A21.

Pious, Richard M. 1979. *The American Presidency.* New York: Basic Books.

Pollock, Andrew. 1993. "U.S. Appears to Retreat from Setting Targets to Increase Japan's Imports," *New York Times,* 10 July, A4.

Pomper, Gerald. 1993. "The Presidential Election," 132–56 in *The Election of 1992,* edited by Gerald M. Pomper, F. Christopher Arterton, Ross K. Baker, Walter Dean Burnham, Kathleen A. Frankovic, Marjorie Randon Hershey, and Willson Carey McWilliams. Chatham, N.J.: Chatham House.

Posner, Michael. 1994–95. "Rally Round Human Rights," *Foreign Policy* 97:133–39.

Pryor, David. 1992. Introduction to *Bill Clinton: The Inside Story,* by Robert E. Levin. New York: SPI Books.

Purdum, Todd S. 1995a. "Clinton Angers Friend and Foe Alike in Tax Remark," *New York Times,* 19 October, A1.

———. 1995b. "Clinton Feels Vindicated on Vietnam by McNamara Book," *New York Times,* 15 April, A7.

———. 1995c. "Clinton Plans to Lift Public out of 'Funk,' " *New York Times,* 24 September, A1.

———. 1995d. "Hard Choice for White House on Hillary Clinton and China," *New York Times,* 17 August, A1.

———. 1995e. "In Brief Visit, Clinton Schmoozes at Renaissance Meeting," *New York Times,* 1 January, A18.

———. 1995f. "President Will Seek a Higher Minimum Wage, Senior Aides Say," *New York Times,* 24 January, B14.

———. 1994. "From Mother to Son: Grit, But No Taste for Bad News," *New York Times,* 9 January, A2.

———. 1992. "Bets Dark Horses: Raised One, Too," *New York Times,* 13 August, C1.

Quindlen, Anna. 1994. "In Hot Water," *New York Times,* 5 March, A23.

———. 1992. "And Now, Pragmatism," *New York Times,* 8 April, A25.

Radcliffe, Donnie. 1993. *Hillary Rodham Clinton: A First Lady for Our Time.* New York: Warner.

Rein, Irving J. 1994. "Imagining the Image: Reinventing the Clintons," 187–200 in *Bill Clinton on Stump, State, and Stage: The Rhetorical Road to the White House,* edited by Stephen A. Smith. Fayetteville: University of Arkansas Press.

Reischauer, Robert. 1994. "An Analysis of the Administration's Health Proposal," Congressional Budget Office, February: xi-81.

———. 1993. Letter to Richard A. Gephardt with Budgetary Analysis," Congressional Budget Office, November 15, 1–8.

Renshon, Stanley A. 1996. *The Psychological Assessment of Presidential Candidates.* New York: New York University Press.

———, ed. 1995. *The Clinton Presidency: Campaigning, Governing and the Psychology of Leadership.* Boulder, Colo.: Westview.

———. 1993a. "Good Judgment and the Lack Thereof in the Gulf War: A Preliminary Psychological Model with Some Applications," 67–105 in *The Political Psychology of the Gulf War: Leaders, Publics and the Process of Conflict,* edited by Stanley A. Renshon. Pittsburgh, Pa.: University of Pittsburgh Press.

———. 1993b. " 'How to Select a Good President'—Some Observations," *Political Psychology* 14:549–54.

———. 1989. "Psychological Perspectives on Theories of Adult Development and the Political Socialization of Leaders," 203–64 in *Adult Political Socialization: A Sourcebook,* edited by Roberta I. Sigel. Chicago: University of Chicago Press.

———. 1974. *Psychological Needs and Political Behavior: A Theory of Personality and Political Efficacy.* New York: Free Press.

Rich, Frank. 1994a. "The Other Agenda," *New York Times,* 12 June, A17.

———. 1994b. "I Am Not a Comedian," *New York Times,* 28 April, A22.

Rose, Richard. 1988. *The Postmodern Presidency.* Chatham, N.J.: Chatham House.

Rosenbaum, David E. 1995. "Clinton Plan Keeps Deficit, Study Shows," *New York Times,* 17 January, A8.

———. 1993a. "Bentsen Suggests Broad Energy Tax Will Be Proposed," *New York Times,* 25 January, A1.

———. 1993b. "Clinton Backs Off Plan for New Tax on Heat in Fuels," *New York Times,* 8 June, A1.

———. 1993c. "Clinton Calls Packed Agenda One Goal," *New York Times,* 5 September, A38.

———. 1993d. "Clinton Weighing Freeze or New Tax for Social Security," *New York Times,* 31 January, A1.

———. 1993e. "Clinton's Bright Ideas Get to Meet Ugly Facts," *New York Times,* 11 January, sec. 4, 1.

———. 1992. "Clinton Could Have Known Draft Was Unlikely for Him," *New York Times,* 14 February, A1.

Rosenthal, A. M. 1994. "The First Ladyship," *New York Times,* 11 March, A31.

———. 1993. "Defining Bill Clinton," *New York Times,* 19 November, A33.

Rosenthal, Andrew. 1995. "Seeking to Avoid Carter Comparisons, President Refines Comments," *New York Times,* 26 September, A20.

Rosenthal, Elizabeth. 1993. "Claims and Counterclaims on Vaccine Costs Generate Heat but Little Light," *New York Times,* 15 March, A16.

Rosteck, Thomas. 1994. "The Intertextuality of 'The Man from Hope': Bill Clinton As Person, As Persona, As Star?," 223–48 in *Bill Clinton on Stump, State, and Stage: The Rhetorical Road to the White House,* edited by Stephen A. Smith. Fayetteville: University of Arkansas Press.

Ryan, William P. 1991. "Treatment Issues with Adult Children of Alcoholics," *Psychoanalytic Psychology* 8:69–82.

Safire, William. 1993. "Who's Got Clout?" *New York Times Magazine,* 20 June, 25–28, 33–34.

Samuelson, Robert J. 1995. "Clinton, the Deficit, and the Truth," *Washington Post National Weekly Edition,* November 27–December 3, 5.

———. 1993a. "Clinton As Roosevelt," *Newsweek,* 24 May, 49.

———. 1993b. "Clinton's Nemesis," *Newsweek,* February 1, 51.

Sanger, David E. 1993. "Clinton Achieves Trade Framework in Japanese Pact," *New York Times,* 10 July, 1.

Schlesinger, Arthur, Jr. 1974. "Can Psychiatry Save the Republic?" *Saturday Review,* September 7, 10–16.

———. 1973. *The Imperial Presidency.* Boston: Houghton Mifflin.

Schmalz, Jeffrey. 1993. "Letting Go of Hope As Clinton Softens Pledges," *New York Times,* 18 January, A13.

Sciolino, Elaine. 1993. "Three Players Seek a Director for Foreign Policy Story," *New York Times,* 8 November, A9.

Shalala, Donna E. 1995. "Cheap Shot at the Vaccine Program," *Washington Post National Edition,* 3–9 July, 29.

Sheehy, Gail. 1992. "What Hillary Wants," *Vanity Fair,* May, 140–47, 212–17.

Simonton, Dean Keith. 1993. "Putting the Best Leaders in the White House: Personality, Policies and Performance," *Political Psychology* 14:537–48.

———. 1986. "Presidential Greatness: The Historical Consensus and Its Implications," *Political Psychology* 7:259–83.

Skowronek, Stephen. 1993. *The Politics That Presidents Make: Leadership from John Adams to George Bush.* Cambridge: Harvard University Press.

Smith, Stephen. 1993. "Compromise, Consensus, and Consistency," 1–16 in *The Clintons of Arkansas: An Introduction by Those Who Know Them Best,* edited by Ernest Dumas. Fayetteville: University of Arkansas Press.

Smith, Tony. 1993. "Making the World Safe for Democracy," *Washington Quarterly* 16:197–214.

Solomon, Burt. 1993. "Clinton—Every Man but His Own?" *National Journal,* 11 September, 2206.

Specter, Arlen. 1993. "Just What the Doctor Ordered . . . Big Government?" *Washington Post,* 22 December, A21.

Sperlich, Peter W. 1975. "Bargaining and Overload: An Essay on Presidential Power," 406–30 in *Perspectives on the Presidency,* edited by Aaron Wildavsky. Boston: Little, Brown.

Staley, Carolyn. 1993. "The Music of Friendship," 34–41 in *The Clintons of Arkansas: An Introduction by Those Who Know Them Best,* edited by Ernest Dumas. Fayetteville: University of Arkansas Press.

Stedman, Stephen John. 1992–93. "The New Interventionists," *Foreign Affairs* 72:3–16.

Stemlau, John. 1994. "Clinton's Dollar Diplomacy," *Foreign Policy* 97:18–35.

Stencel, Mark. 1993. "Clinton's Pledges," *Washington Post,* 20 January, A19.

Stevenson, Jonathan. 1993. "Hope Restored in Somalia?" *Foreign Policy* 91:138–54.

Stone, Roger. 1994. "Nixon as Clinton," *New York Times,* 28 April, A23.

Storr, Anthony. 1990. *Solitude.* New York: Free Press.

Stuckey, Mary E. 1991. *The President As Interpreter-in-Chief.* Chatham, N.J.: Chatham House.

Suedfeld, Peter. 1994. "President Clinton's Policy Dilemmas: A Cognitive Analysis," *Political Psychology* 15:337–50.

———. 1985. "APA Presidential Address: The Relationship of Integrative Complexity to Historical, Professional and Personality Factors," *Jounal of Personality and Social Psychology* 49:1643–51.

Suedfeld, Peter, and Michael D. Wallace. 1995. "President Clinton as a Cognitive Manager," 215–33 in *The Clinton Presidency: Campaigning, Governing, and the Psychology of Leadership,* edited by Stanley Renshon. Boulder, Colo.: Westview.

Sullivan, Andrew. 1994. "All the President's Problems," *New York Times Book Review,* 3 July, 2, 11.

Sullivan, Harry S. 1953. *The Interpersonal Theory of Psychiatry.* New York: Norton.

Suro, Robert. 1992. "Senate Office Helped Clinton on Draft, Aides Acknowledge," *New York Times,* 19 September, A1.

Szamuely, George. 1994. "Clinton's Clumsy Encounter with the World," *Orbis* 38:373–94.

Tetlock, Philip E. 1992. "Good Judgment in International Politics: Three Psychological Perspectives," *Political Psychology* 13:517–40.

Tierney, John. 1992. "Grace Under Pressure? It's Working for Clinton," *New York Times,* 2 March, A20.

Tonelson, Alan. 1994–95. "Jettison the Policy," *Foreign Policy* 97:121–32.

———. 1993. "Superpower without a Sword," *Foreign Affairs* 2:166–80.

Toner, Robin. 1993. "Clinton Orders Reversal of Abortion Restrictions Left by Reagan and Bush," *New York Times,* 23 January, A1.

———. 1992. "AIDS Protester Provokes Clinton's Anger," *New York Times,* 27 March, D21.

Treaster, Joseph B. 1994. "President Plans to Raise Drug Treatment Budget," *New York Times,* 8 February, B9.

Tucker, Robert C. 1981. *Politics As Leadership.* Columbia: University of Missouri Press.

Tucker, Robert W. 1993–94. "The Triumph of Wilsonianism?" *World Policy Journal* 10: 83–99.

Tyler, Patrick E. 1994. "Textile Accord with China Averts Trade Clash," *New York Times,* 18 January, D1.

Vagelos, P. Roy. 1993. "A Shot in the (Wrong) Arm," *New York Times,* 20 April, A29.

Vaillant, George E. 1977. *Adaptation to Life.* Boston: Little, Brown.

Verhovek, Sam Howe. 1994. "Past Sheds Light on Clinton and School Prayer," *New York Times,* 24 November, A28.

Walt, Stephen M. 1989. "The Case for Finite Containment: Analyzing a US Grand Strategy," *International Security* 14:5–49.

Warner, Judith. 1993. *Hillary Clinton: The Inside Story.* New York: Signet.

Washington Post National Weekly Edition. 1995. "Editorial: The Acquittal of Billy Dale," 27 November-3 December, 25.

Wattenberg, Martin P. 1991. *The Rise of Candidate Centered Politics: Presidential Elections of the 1980's.* Cambridge, Mass.: Harvard University Press.

———. 1990. *The Decline of American Political Parties, 1952–1988.* Cambridge, Mass.: Harvard University Press.

Weinrod, W. Bruce. 1993. "The US Role in Peacekeeping-Related Activities," *World Affairs* 155:148–55.

Weissberg, Jacob. 1994. "Why Bill Clinton Is a Great American President: No, Really," *New York,* September 5, 17–20.

Wenner, Jann S., and William Greider. 1993. "President Clinton: The Rolling Stone Interview," *Rolling Stone,* 9 December, 40–45, 80–81.

Whillock, Carl. 1993. "Change Has Never Been Easy," 78–84 in *The Clintons of Arkansas: An Introduction by Those Who Know Them Best,* edited by Ernest Dumas. Fayetteville: University of Arkansas Press.

White, Ralph K. 1983. "Empathizing with the U.S.S.R." *Political Psychology* 4:121–37.

Wills, Garry. 1994. "Clinton's Troubles," *New York Review of Books,* 22 September, 4, 6, 7, 8.

———. 1993. "Clinton's Year at Sea," *New York Times,* 9 January, A21.

———. 1992. "Mr. Clinton's Forgotten Childhood," *Time,* 8 June, 62–63.

Wilson, James Q. 1994. "Reinventing Public Adminstration: The 1994 John Gaus Lecture," *PS: Political Science and Politics* 36:667–73.

Wines, Michael. 1994. "Clinton, on the Stump, Opens a Final Health Care Push," *New York Times,* 16 July, A9.

——. 1993a. "A 'Bazaar' Way of Rounding up Votes," *New York Times,* 11 November, A23.

——. 1993b. "Clinton Now Seems Prepared to Drop Any Wide Fuel Tax," *New York Times,* 9 June, A1.

——. 1993c. "Clinton, Who Opposed 'Soft Money,' Got Plenty," *New York Times,* 19 March, A19.

Winnicott, D. W. 1975. *Through Pediatrics to Psychoanalysis.* New York: Basic Books.

——. 1965. *The Maturational Process and the Facilitating Environment.* London: Hogarth Press.

——. 1958. "The Capacity to Be Alone," *International Journal of Psychoanalysis* 39:416–20.

Winter, David G. 1995. "Presidential Psychology and Governing Styles: A Comparative Psychological Analysis of the 1992 Presidential Candidates," 113–34 in *The Clinton Presidency: Campaigning, Governing, and the Psychology of Leadership,* edited by Stanley A. Renshon. Boulder, Colo.: Westview.

Wolf, Ernest S. 1988. *Treating the Self: Elements of Clinical Self Psychology.* New York: Guilford.

Wolf, Naomi. 1995. "Our Bodies, Our Souls: Rethinking Pro-choice Rhetoric," *New Republic,* 16 October, 26–29, 32–35.

Wolfowitz, Paul D. 1994. "Clinton's First Year," *Foreign Affairs* (January-February):28–43.

Wood, B. L. 1987. *Children of Alcoholism: The Struggle for Self and Intimacy in Adult Life.* New York: New York University Press.

Woodward, Bob. 1994. *The Agenda: Inside the Clinton White House.* New York: Simon & Schuster.

Wright, George, Jr. 1993. "Everybody's Friend," 28–29 in *The Clintons of Arkansas: An Introduction by Those Who Know Them Best,* edited by Ernest Dumas. Fayetteville: University of Arkansas Press.

Zoellick, Robert B. 1994. "The Reluctant Wilsonian: President Clinton and Foreign Policy," *SAIS Review* 14:1–14.

★ ───────────────────────────────────────

SUBJECT INDEX

Abortion issue, 232, 264; Administration support of federal financing for, 298

Activity levels of presidents: need to set limits and, 57; political functions of, 56; psychological functions of, 58;

Adult child of an alcoholic (ACOA) theory, elastic nature of, 195–96

Affirmative action: Clinton and, 75, 265; in Clinton health care program, 232; Clinton's cabinet and, 277; George Bush's views on, 23

Ambition: as basic character element, 39–40; both necessary for, but suspect in presidency, 52; politics of, 1, 2; ideals and, 43; negative connotation of, 39; role of parents in regulating childhood grandiosity and, 272; shaped by relationships to others, 46; shaped by character integrity, 40, 43

American political culture, 23

AmeriCorps. See National Service Program

Basic public dilemma, 14, 19, 72; Clinton's, 31. Clinton's strengths and, 7; decline of public trust and, 30; definition of, 30; Franklin D. Roosevelt's, 31; international context and, 19; judgment and, 249; Lyndon Johnson's, 31; Ronald Reagan's, 31

Bosnia, 21, 31, 33, 80, 133, 316. See also Foreign policy

Budget caps, 61

Campaign promises, 77

Candidate-centered politics, 30. See also Trust in leaders

Character, 3; attacks on, 30; and choice, 37; definition of, 38; the development of, 37; distinguished from other psychological concepts, 38–39; external world and, 4; Clinton's view of, 37; talents as embedded in, 7; as a vertical and horizontal concept, 4

Character integrity, 12; as a basic character element, 40–44; as definition of, 41; drawing of boundaries and, 69; effects of parents' ideals on development of, 179–80; ethics in relation to, 77; fidelity of interpersonal relations and, 187; role of parents in setting firm, loving boundaries and development of, 172–73, 178, 197; origin of the sense of entitlement and, 198; political persona and, 44; reflected in policy

Character integrity (Continued)
  choices, 70–71; self-confidence and, 73;
  self-esteem and, 41; values and, 40
Character style: definition of, 47; motivations and, 48–49
China, 79. See also Foreign affairs
Civil-rights programs, 31
Clinton, Hillary Rodham: ability to focus,
  221, 227, 230; ability to be independent
  of others, 228, 233; ambition of, 51, 220,
  223–24, 230–31, 233; attendance at major
  meeting, 218–19; basic fit of the Clintons'
  psychologies now, 230; basic fit of the
  Clintons' psychologies when they first married, 220–22; Bill Clinton's view of political role of, 216; change in political views
  in college, 225; character integrity of,
  224–25, 236; chronology of early family
  life, 222–23; college involvement in social
  and political issues, 225; combativeness
  of, 221, 228; confidence in her self and her
  views, 224, 225–27, 229, 233; as Co-President for Domestic Policy, 217; criticizing
  Wellesley commencement speaker, 226–
  27; desire to do good, 225; desire to do
  something important, 224; development of
  the Clinton marriage over time, 220; directness of, 220; effect on husband's ambitions, 230, 302; first meeting with Virginia
  Kelley, 155, 162; high school involvement
  in social and political issues, 224; ideals
  versus political interests, 236–38; idyllic
  childhood of, 222; intelligence of, 221,
  226, 230; interpersonal skepticism of,
  221; issues with boundaries, 233–36, 242;
  as liberal, 221; Little Rock segregation
  case and, 233–34; political partnership
  with husband as a rationale for attention
  to her role, 216–19; "politics of meaning,"
  and 233; pragmatism of, 221, 232; psychology of marriage in relation to the Clintons' relationship, 219–22, 233; public
  comfort with her role, 219; relationship
  with press, 220–30; Rodham family focus
  on competition and excelling, 223; Rodham family focus on education, 222; role
  in Arkansas nuclear power station disengagement, 234; role in developing "war
  room," 219; role of religion and, 224–25;
  role in selecting cabinet, 218; segregation
  of fees earned at Rose law firm, 239; seriousness of, 224, 227; shared ambition

with husband, 225; shifting explanations
  of futures trading, 239–41, 279; shifting
  explanations regarding the Whitewater development, 241; stability of Rodham family, 222; staff innovations as reflection of
  power, 218; strong personality of, 220,
  228; temper of, 228–29, 231–32; as tough
  on others, 228; use of public meetings to
  promote policies, 237; view of her own
  ideology as transcending Left-Right, 221–
  22; views on wealth, 238–39; and
  Whitewater, 279; as wishing to have it
  both ways, 233; work on behalf of Beverly
  nursing homes buy out, 238–39; work on
  behalf of Madison Guaranty, 234–35; wry
  sense of humor, 224
Clinton, William J., and family life: as
  adored child, 198; as adult child of an alcoholic (ACOA), 173, 186, 195–98; annotated chronology of, 147–48; boundary
  problems and, 179, 180, 199; confrontations with stepfather, 182; experience of
  two different mothers, 194; as golden boy
  in high school, 148; grandmother's feelings toward, 193–94; hiring of nanny,
  176, 179; household rules, 182; impact of
  grandmother (Edith Cassidy) on, 174; lack
  of reliable figures to impart ideals, 196;
  loss of father, 13, 122, 151, 166–69, 186;
  "The Man from Hope" film and, 145–46;
  mother's autobiography as source for, 311;
  mother's early absence, 166, 174, 186,
  309; mother's remarriage to Roger, 188–
  89; myth of, 145–47, 166–67, 179, 190,
  311–12; as parent to himself, 296; role as
  caretaker for his brother, 181; role as caretaker for his mother, 181–82, 188; role of
  grandparents in, 189–95; role of religion
  in, 163, 180–81; the shrine, 170; as special
  child, 182; stepfather (Roger Clinton) as
  alcoholic, 13, 181–82, 197; stepfather's reliability, 175, 187; view of mother, 183–84
Clinton, William J., psychology of: ability to
  do several things at once, 60; ability to focus, 57, 259; ability to learn from mistakes, 8, 65, 68, 137; abusiveness with
  aides, 12; accomplishments as "educational governor" and, 246, 247; achievement motivation, 124–25, 307; activities
  at Georgetown and, 55–56; activities in
  high school and, 55; activity levels, 39, 58,
  262; activity levels, psychological meaning

of, 57–59; aides' views of core values, 76; ambition, xi, 8, 43–44, 50–56, 287, 300; anger, 12, 51, 100, 109–11, 303; appointment of Henry Foster, Jr., and, 8; appointment of Lani Guinier and, 8, 75, 140, 296, 316; attention to details, 125, 260; backtracking, xi, 114, 304; bargaining skills, 135; belief that he can convince others, 91, 104, 274, 316–17; belief that he knows what is best, 66; candor, 33, 78, 114, 131–32, 136, 138–40, 212; campaign promises and, 32, 78–80; capability of making basic errors, 60–61, 91–92, 252; capacity to be alone, 58–59, 198; capacity for introspection, 68, 141; character integrity, 70–73, 114–15; charm, 88, 104, 285; chemistry, importance of, 93; as "comeback kid," 45, 120; commitment to change, 66–67; competitiveness, 125–28; controversial nature of his presidency, 32, 51; decision to run against George Bush, 134; desire to be in charge, 260; difficulties in being prepared, 62; difficulties in maintaining boundaries and limits, 12, 90, 131, 260, 282, 296; early ambition, 52–53; empathy, 106–8, 253; energy, 11, 54–55; enormous appetites, 6; excitement of working for, 7; fidelity to ideals, 42, 124, 210; fidelity to others, 105, 111–16, 134, 212–13; foreign policy and, 21, 136–37; "Friends of Bill" and, 97–99; funds to support Arkansas legislative program as governor and, 235; grandiosity, 90; honesty, 70; identification with the public, 130; impatience, 121–24; impressive memory, 98; inconsistencies, 3, 5–9; indecisiveness, and "unveto" story, 315–16; intelligence, 7, 9, 11, 12, 59, 265; intelligence, limits of, 61–68; intense but episodic interests, 270; investment in his activities, 55–56; as kaleidoscope, 82, 83; as masked active-negative type, 103–4; meeting John F. Kennedy and, 53, 300; mother as "character" and, 13; movement toward others, 96–97, 186; NAFTA and, 56; need for approval, 11; need to be liked, 12–13; need to be liked, difficulties of theory and, 99–100, 115; need for validation, 50, 100; 1994 election as a repudiation of, xii, 100; permanent campaign and, 56, 272–73; persistence of, 88, 120–21; political identity of, 23, 44; popular vote of, in 1992, 21; as pragmatic

leader, 33; public's distrust of, 9, 30; public's hopes for, 1, 79; public's strong ambivalent feelings toward, xi, 3, 94, 245, 269, 285; promise of, 1, 7, 8–9, 259, 285; questions regarding core values, 75–76, 81; reconciling Left-Right issues, 83, 116, 296; rectifying errors, 64; relationship with Hillary Clinton, 133; relationship with the media, 140, 286, 316; resemblance to Richard Nixon, xii, 103, 117–18; response to 1994 election and, 68; response to others when they don't agree and, 110, 214; risk taking, 92, 134–38; as robust and complex, 307; *Rolling Stone* interview and, 86, 102–3, 110, 130, 314; as Roosevelt, 116–17; self-absorption, 108; self-confidence, 87–90, 120–21, 287; self-idealization, 50, 85–87, 122, 130; self-imposed deadlines and, 123, 129; sense of being special, 128–30, 211–12; sense of own correctness, 87, 214–15, 269; short-term flexibility of, 65; as skilled political strategist, 99; strategic empathy and, 107; substantial talents of, 7, 9, 40, 53–54, 99; success, importance of, to, 101; success of, academic, 51–52; success of, paradoxical consequences, 39; success of, political, 52–53; taking responsibility, 65, 85, 118, 138–41; trust in others, 105, 186, 188–89; use of connections, 53, 98–99, 206–8, 213–14; use of loopholes, 81, 214; verbal ability, 88–89; view of own ambitions, 51, 85, 130, 301; view of own character integrity, 84–87; view of own values, 76, 82; as wishing to have it both ways, 65, 130–34, 139, 215, 278. *See also* Clinton, William J., presidency of

Clinton, William J., presidency of: ability to integrate diverse policy views, 265; activist president in an age of public distrust, 270; ambition and public overload, 269; ambition fulfilled by second term, 300–301; ambitious agenda of, 91–92, 121, 125, 141, 266, 270; ambitious agenda of, and aides' worries, 267; ambitious agenda of, compared to agenda as governor, 268; appointment of ambassadors, 78; attempts to bypass press, 263; basic contradictions of, 131, 297–99; basic public dilemma of, 249, 268, 271, 299, 305; bolstering a sense of public urgency, 292, 295; cabinet appointments reflecting conflicting views,

Clinton, William J. (Continued)
260; candor regarding policies, 271–72,
275–76, 297–98, 304; centralization of
power, 261; commitment to cut White
House staff, 132–32; commitment to social change, 294–96; compared with leadership as governor, 67; concern with appearances, 277–78; danger of frustration
in a possible second term, 303; decision
making style, 82–83, 84, 90, 250, 260,
262; demonization of enemies, 100, 292,
299; domestic uncertainty and, 2; early
conflict of interest guidelines, 278; educating the public, 268–69; emphasis on domestic policy, 137; endurance, 262; ethical
standards, 132, 278–82; evidence of expansive thinking, 261, 262; forced resignation of key administration officials, 279–
80; foreign policy advisors and problems
of collegiality, 264; inconsistent policy
stands, 264, 297; inexperience of White
house aides, 67–68, 264; institutional setting and, 19; lack of trust in public, 295–
96; legal defense fund set up for, 281; lost
opportunities of first term, 299; mismatch
between administration and public ambitions, 286–87, 298; as "New Democrat,"
23, 33, 67, 69, 71, 74–75, 81, 82, 118,
131, 271, 287, 289, 296, 299; order banning replacement of striking workers, 79;
paradox of legislative success and public
doubt, 267, 286; persistence and determination, 268; political center and, 296,
297–99, 303; possibility of statement in a
second term, 304; possible nature of a second term, 300–306; post cold-war period
and, 2, 5, 21; problem of focus, 261; public's hopes for, 286–87; resolving policy dilemmas, 264–66, 302; role of political consultants, 67, 273; selection of advisors on
the basis of chemistry, 263; selling policies
versus educating the public, 255, 272–74,
276; shifting public response to, 269; skill
in selling programs, 272; staff as serving
not constraining, 301; "triangulation"
strategy, 305; "trust deficit" and, 271; use
of questionable financial calculations for
public policies, 271, 274–75; Whitewater
investigations and, 279, 280. See also Clinton, William J., psychology of; Political
leadership; Presidential psychology
Conservatives, 22; Jimmy Carter as, 23, 74

Constitutional Convention, 23; ambivalence
toward presidential power, 24
Crime bill, 75, 245

Deficit reduction, 75, 267, 275
Democratic party, 21, 32, 111, 132, 280,
300, 304; effect of control in both houses
on Clinton, 280, 301
"Democrats only" strategy, 126–27
Draft controversy, 85, 99, 138; chronology
of crisis, 201, 203; Clinton as a victim of
partisan attacks, 202; Clinton's explanations during, 201, 205, 207, 210, 213;
Clinton's role in anti-war movement, 209–
10; Clinton's view of his special treatment,
213–14; as a crisis of ambition versus ideals, 210–15; as a developmental crisis for
Clinton, 201; difficulties of reconstruction,
201; dilemma of the war, 200; issue of receiving draft notice, 208–9; issue of special
treatment, 206–10; letter to draft board,
202; relatedness as an element of, 212–13;
role of ambition, 211; ROTC deferment,
202–4; sense of entitlement in, 211–12

Earned income credit program, 269
Economic stimulus program, 71, 75, 111–
12, 113, 127, 255, 266
Economic Summit (Little Rock), 60, 129,
276–77
Empathy: functions of, 254; in the regulation
of childhood narcissism, 41; strategic,
253. See also Relatedness
Energy tax, 112–13, 219
Ethics, 41, 77. See also Character integrity

Family leave bill, 79, 245, 267, 297
Federal Reserve Board, 60–61
Fidelity: capacity to endure loss and, 43; to
ideals, 41, 76. See also Character integrity;
Ideals
Foreign policy, 5; America as remaining a super power, 6, 20; cold war, xi, 20; decisions to use force, 21; limits of American
power, 25; "New World Order," 20–21
Free trade, 264, 265; G-7 summit with Japan, 278. See also NAFTA

Government waste, and decline of public
support for programs, 27
Grandiosity, childhood and ambition, 39
"Great Man" theories of leadership, 4

Haiti, xi, 21, 33, 78, 86, 133. *See also* Foreign policy
Head start program, 71, 269
Health-care plan, 31, 79, 80, 88, 113, 123, 128, 136, 217, 231, 232, 236, 237, 255, 271–72, 274, 281; administration's view of, 287; scope of, 297
Homelessness, 25; Clinton program for, 297–98; New York City policy and, 26
Homosexuals in military, xii, 75, 108, 139, 287

Ideals: and character integrity, 41; development of, 42; identity and, 43; the role of others in shaping, 46. *See also* Character integrity; Fidelity to ideals
Intelligence, 7; applications of, and judgments about, 11; and judgment, 63
Iraq, 31. *See also* Foreign policy

Judgment, good, 5, 12, 28, 30; ability to learn and, 252; analytic skills and, 48; character integrity and, 251; complex thinking and, 249–50; definition of, 248; effects of character on, 250–52; effects of high ambition on, 136; empathy and, 253–54; end of cold war and, 20; framing decisions and, 20, integrative complexity and, 265; means of implementing, 251–52; political calculations and, 251; reflective insight and, 250; self-confidence and, 90, 136, 250, 252; self-interest and, 253; sense of entitlement and, 253; situations and judgments, 249; understanding the problem and, 252; wishful thinking and, 252. *See also* Political leadership; Presidential performance

Kelley, Virginia, 145; as an abandoning mother, 173–76; as an adoring, doting mother, 170–71, 173; ambition of, 156–57, 164–65; attraction to charming, narcissistic men, 152–54, 160, 163, 192; attraction to drinking and night life, 159, 161–63, 175–76, 180, 184, 193, 196; attunement to her children, 173, 176–78, 185; Auntie Mame persona of, 149–50, 158, 162; belief that she knew best, 158–59; conflict with mother over Bill, 174, 192–193; dates her son's political ambitions, 52–53, 300; decision to leave Hope to get advanced training, 175, 184; desire to be noticed, 154–55, 162–63; difficulties with boundaries, conventions, and rules, 160–61, 163, 171, 182; fidelity to others, 186–89, ideals and values of, 154–156, 159, 163; importance of attractiveness to, 155; importance in Bill Clinton's life of, 149; importance of pleasure versus work, 162, 180; influence on her son's competitiveness, 125; judgment of, 177–78; lack of self-reflection, 150; marriage to William Blythe (first husband), 147; narcissism of, 157, 162, 165, 173, 184; relationship with father, 156, 162, 190–91; relationship with mother, 156–57, 160, 190–91; relationship with George J. "Jeff" Dwire (fourth husband), 148, 153, 154, 155; relationship with Richard Fenwick (first boyfriend), 187–88; relationship with Richard W. Kelley (fifth husband), 148, 156; relationship with Roger "Dude" Clinton (second and third husband), 147–48, 152, 155, 161, 164; relationship with son Roger, 164, 176–77; role of crisis in the life of, 150; self-esteem of, 157; use of appropriate theories to understand, 309; use of denial, 151–52, 164, 169, 176; usefulness of autobiography, 311–12; usefulness of interviews with, 310; view of herself as a doting mother, 171, 184; view of herself as soft hearted, 151, 185; view of her own life, 150; work as instrumental for, 159–60
Korea, 25. *See also* Foreign policy

Leadership. *See* Political leadership
Liberals, 22, 305; Jimmy Carter as, 23, 74–75

Middle class tax cut, 64, 78, 80–81, 316
Middle East, 25. *See also* Foreign policy
Minimum wage, 80
"Motor voter" Bill, 79

Narcissism: ambition as a byproduct of normal, 39, 52; parents and the moderation of, 40; political style influenced by, 49
National Educational Goals, 269
National service program, 67, 71, 267, 269, 293; differing administration and GAO estimates of costs, 298
National Urban League, 74

North American Free Trade Agreement (NAFTA), xii, 31, 56. 75, 127, 134–35, 245, 267, 269, 270
1992 election, alternative meanings of, 32
1994 election: Clinton's response to, 287; Clinton's understanding of, 286; meaning of, 66, 285; providing opportunity for Clinton to more clearly define himself, 302–3

Persona: definition of, 44; functions of, 45
Personality, distinguished from character, 38. See also Presidential psychology
Political identity: consolidation of, 73; distinguished from persona, 44; political functions of flexible, 83; political ideology and, 74; reconciling Left-Right issues and, 84
Political leadership, xi, 5; ambition and, 257; consolidation and, 256, 266; decline of faith in public policies and, 27; definition of, 254; differing views of, 254; education as a primary function of, 255, 256, 257; empathy and, 253; fidelity to commitments and, 257; fidelity to ideals as a political resource, 77; focus and, 256; good intentions and, 72; identity and, 73; mobilization and, 255–56, 266; orchestration and, 256, 266; policy experimentation and, 72; as relationship, 27; reputation as resource, 305; task of managing social and political change, 296–97; time demands and, 57; trust and, 256–57. See also Judgment, good; Presidential performance; Trust in leaders
Political parties: functions as filters, 21–22; moderation of, in general elections, 22
Political psychology: limits of, 4; limits of focus on childhood and, 13; linking psychological development to theories of, 13; theories of, and Clinton presidency, 2; traits theories and, 11, 12
Politics of Reconstruction, 3
Presidency: alternative centers of power as check on presumptive presidency, 302; as deflated institution, 24; as engine of progress, 24; failure of incumbents to gain reelection, 24; imperial, 24; increasing expectations for, 248; psychological source of legitimacy, 28; public expectations and, 5, 24; requirements of the modern, 6; role construction and, 5; self-interest versus public's interest, 28

Presidential performance: achievement motivation and, 124; ambition and, 52; ambition versus ideals and, 43; character and, 37; character style and, 47; consequential behaviors and, 314–15; context and, 30; dangers of using crisis as a pretext, 295; influence of the assessment of childhood on, 312; functions of impatience and, 121; functions of knowledge and, 129; functions of persistence and, 120; high self-esteem and, 87; judgment as key pillar of, 247; key means versus outcomes in evaluation of, 247; leadership as second key pillar of, 247; as measured by legislative victories, 245–46; relatedness to others and, 96; role of competitiveness in, 126–27; search for greatness and, 246–47. See also Ambition; Character integrity; Character style; Presidential psychology; Public psychology; Relatedness
Presidential psychology: character-based personality traits and, 119–20; distinguished from character, 119; effects of not living in the real world, 88; importance of, in the presidency, 24; presidential traits and, 307–8; reactions to circumstances and, 5; relationship of context to, 308
Public policies: Americans' views of the fairness of, 31; candor of advocates and, 26–27; consequences of, 72; decline of public confidence in, 25, 31; trust in, as basic public dilemma, 31; unintended consequences of, 26, 31
Public psychology, 1, 19; anxiety regarding social, political, and economic change, 294–95; decline of identification with major parties, 2; decline of optimism, 25; decline of confidence, 3, 26; hope, 79; suspiciousness, 3; third party candidates and, 3

Relatedness: as basic character element, 45–46; as central element of presidential performance, 94–95; character integrity and, 77; definition of, 46; distinguished from affiliation motive, 93; functions of charm and, 105; Lyndon Johnson's style of, 49; object relations and, 95; obtaining evidence regarding, 96; presidential performance and, 47–48; role of parents in regulating boundaries, 171; strategic empathy distinguished from empathetic attunement, 106–7

Reinventing government program, 33, 84, 255, 267; new health-care regulation and, 297; White house estimate of savings from, 275

Republican Party, xi, 22, 127, 128, 139–40, 267; attacked by Clinton on Medicare, 299; as Clinton's salvation, 285, 302; possible effect of major 1996 losses on a possible Clinton second term, 303

Research methods, and Clinton presidency: analyst's stance toward, 317–18; anecdotal evidence, uses and limits of, 11, 313–16; basic assumptions of theories used, 309; behind-the-scenes accounts, 312–13; comparative psychoanalytic theory as an approach to presidential psychology, 308–9; facts and their meaning, 309–10; idealization by friends and problem for researchers, 317; issue of objectivity, 316–17; three levels of analysis, 309; use of other biographies, 309; usefulness of descriptive accounts, 312–13

Rwanda, 25. See also Foreign policy

Sea-Wolf submarine, 264
School prayer amendment, 78
Somalia, 21, 33. See also Foreign policy
Soviet Union, 25, 31. See also Foreign policy
Student loan program, 80, 267; White House and CBO estimates of savings from, 275–76

Third-party candidates, 3, 21
Traits, 11; complications of using, 12; development of, 12; documenting Clinton's, 12. See also Presidential psychology; Research methods
Travel office, White House, 139
Trust in government, 27, 29

Trust in leaders: decline of, 29; as psychological cement of leadership and governance, 28; relationship of hope to, 29. See also Political leadership

U.N. peacekeeping operations, 21. See also Foreign policy

Vaccine program (The Comprehensive Child Immunization Program of 1993), 67, 231, 233; administration distribution system for vaccines, 291–92; AmeriCorps participation in, 293; bolstering a sense of urgency to enlist support for, 292, 295; Clinton Administration response to July 1994 GAO report, 291; conflicting data on immunization costs and rates, 289, 292, 293; as emblematic and cautionary tale, 288, 293–94; GAO July 1994 evaluation of program, 290–91; GAO June 1995 evaluation of program, 292–93; high costs of vaccines as cause of low immunization rates, 288, 289; Hillary Clinton's view of program as a major domestic achievement, 294; laudable goals of, 267, 290; "neglectful parents" as cause of lot immunization rates, 290–91; as new entitlement program, 289, 293; results of, 293

Vietnam War, 25. See also Foreign policy, Clinton, William J.

Waco, Texas, 138–39
Welfare reform programs, 25, 267, 295; adequacy of the evaluations of early programs, 26; Clinton's views on, 23; compatibility with Clinton as "New Democrat," 298; compatibility of Clinton welfare program with RIGO, 84; decline of public support for, 27; promise to "end welfare as we know it," 79; Richard Nixon and, 22; unspecified savings as the basis of, 274

★ ──────────────────────────────────────

NAME INDEX

Allen, Charles, Flynn, 122, 169, 183
Allport, Gordon, 38
Altman, Roger C., 279–80, 282
Apple, R. W., 8
Aristide, Jean Bertrand, 86–87
al-Assad, Hafez, 79

Baird, Zoe, 269
Baker, Gerald, 226
Baker, Jim, 263
Balint, Michael, 150
Barber, James David, 49, 103
Bassett, Woody, 97–98
Becker, J. Bill, 115
Begala, Paul, 76, 273
Bentsen, Lloyd, 57, 114, 260, 264, 267
Bersin, Alan, 228
Blair, Diane, 246
Blair, James B., 240
Blythe, William, 147, 152, 157, 161, 180, 187
Bone, Robert L., 240
Boren, David L., 127
Bradley, Bill, 2
Brantley, Ellen, 229
Brooke, Edward, 226–27
Brown, Floyd, 9

Brown, Ronald, 132, 270, 280
Brummett, John, 8–9, 59, 66, 81, 88, 104, 111, 315–16
Bumpers, Dale, 291
Burns, James McGregor, 268
Bush, George, 2, 21, 23–24, 61, 71, 74, 79, 91, 106, 109, 116, 124, 135, 256, 307

Campbell, Tom, 97,
Carter, Jimmy, 2, 23–24, 31, 48, 71, 74, 103, 116–17, 124, 269
Carville, James, 76, 149, 272–73
Cassidy, Edith (Grisham), 147, 174, 190–94, 310
Cassidy, Eldridge, 147, 174, 190–94, 310
Christopher, Warren, 137, 218, 274
Cisneros, Henry, 260, 270, 279–80
Clinton, Hillary Rodham, 15, 51, 60, 65, 89, 128, 133, 155, 215–42, 263, 273, 279, 288, 302, 304, 313, 317
Clinton, Raymond, 53, 98, 206
Clinton, Roger, 147–48, 152–53, 155, 162–63, 167, 174–76, 178, 186, 188, 192–93, 196–97, 310
Clinton, Roger Cassidy, 148, 151, 176–77, 181, 188, 194–96
Cohen, Steven, 220

Coleman, William T., III, 62, 97
Cooper, Jim, 128
Cronin, Thomas, 26
Cutler, Lloyd N., 282

Danforth, William, 291
Dole, Robert, 127, 299
Drake, Dale, 170
Drew, Elizabeth, 9, 60, 83, 90, 92, 104, 109–10, 114–15, 131, 140, 149, 263, 267, 312–14
Dukakis, Michael, 23, 48, 88
Dumas, Ernest, 8–9, 317
Dwire, George J. "Jeff," 148, 153–55, 164

Eagleton, Thomas, 214
Eakeley, Douglas, 106, 220
Edelman, Marian Wright, 288
Eisenhower, Dwight D., 20, 45, 71–72, 110–11, 130, 305
Elders, Dr. Joycelyn, 270
Ellis, Trice, Jr., 206–7
Elwood, Paul, 232
Enthoven, Alan, 237
Erickson, Erik, 41
Erickson, Kai, 237
Espy, Michael, 270, 280
Falwell, Jerry, 110

Fenwick, Richard, 187
Fiske, Robert, 280
Ford, Gerald, 2, 24, 31, 71, 116
Flanigan, Pat, 105
Flowers, Gennifer, 149, 274, 312
Foster, Dr. Henry, 269, 281
Francis, Dru, 52
Freud, Sigmund, 46, 307
Frye, Nurse, 155
Fulbright, J. William, 53, 98–99, 207, 210, 214

Gaebler, Ted, 32
Gearan, Mark D., 270, 287
George, Alexander, 314
George, Juliette, 314
Gergen, David, 64, 89
Ginsburg, Ruth Bader, 109
Giroir, C. Joseph, Jr., 239
Gittleson, Mort, 62
Goldstein, Joe, 225
Goldwater, Barry, 22, 74, 225

Gore, Al, 79, 127, 140, 217–18, 263–64, 274–75
Greenberg, Stan, 273
Greenspan, Alan, 56, 60–61, 263
Greenstein, Fred, 64
Greider, William, 102–3
Grunwald, Mandy, 273
Guinier, Lani, 8, 75, 105, 140, 229, 269, 296, 316

Hanson, Jean E., 279
Hart, Gary, 93, 133
Hatch, Orrin, 123
Hawkins, Willard A., 208
Helms, Jesse, 86
Holmes, Eugene, 134, 202–5, 207–13
Holt, Frank, 98–99
Holt, Jack, Sr., 98
Horney, Karen, 46
Hubbell, Webster, 270, 279–80
Hussein, Saddam, 91, 104

Inman, Bobby Ray, 269
Irons, Edith, 52, 55, 185

Jackson, Clifford, 206, 209
Jackson, Jesse, 100
Jaffe, Morris, 280
James, Caryn, 311
Jefferson, Thomas, 246
Jenks, Christopher, 26
Johnson, J. Bennet, 8, 317
Johnson, Lyndon, 20, 22, 24, 29, 31, 49, 64, 72, 74, 77–78, 110, 116, 261
Jones, Clinton D., 208
Jordan, Vernon, 132, 278

Kakutani, Michiko, 11
Katz, Jay, 225
Kearns, Doris, 49
Kellerman, Barbara, 48
Kelley, Richard W., 148, 156
Kelley, Virginia, 52, 126, 145–65, 169–71, 173–94, 196, 309–11
Kennedy, John F., 2, 20, 53, 71, 74, 77, 103, 116–17, 300
Kennedy, William H., III, 279, 281
King, Larry, 296
King, Martin Luther, Jr., 210
Klugh, Dr. "Buddy," 159
Kohut, Heinz, 39–40, 110, 172, 201
Koppel, Ted, 63, 204

Lake, Anthony, 137, 263
Lancaster, Martin, 236
Lasswell, Harold D., 215
Lehmann-Haupt, Christopher, 313
Leopoulos, David, 170
Levin, Robert, 66, 98–99, 179, 317
Lincoln, Abraham, 79, 246
Lindsey, Bev, 227
Lindsey, Bruce, 90, 218, 261, 282
Ludwig, Eugene A., 282
Lyons, James, 241

Mackey, Johnnie Mae, 55, 185
Magaziner, Ira G., 232, 237, 281
Maraniss, David, 11, 59, 98, 317
Martin, Marsha A., 26
Mathews, David, 121
McCarthy, Eugene, 225
McCurry, Michael, 138
McDougal, James, 235, 241
McGovern, George, 214, 225
McLarty, Thomas, 111, 261–62, 282
McNamara, Robert, 200, 214–15
McWilliams, Wilson, 31–32
Miller, Mark, 109
Mitchell, Andrea, 139
Mitchell, George, 127
Mixner, David, 209
Miyazawa, Prime Minister Kiichi, 54–55, 278
Mondale, Walter, 22
Moore, Jim, 98
Moore, Rudi, Jr., 66, 88, 221
Morgan, James, 311
Morris, Dick, 65, 81, 305
Moyers, Bill, 167
Moynihan, Daniel, 27, 79
Murdoch, Ellen Press, 226
Myers, Dee Dee, 281

Neuman, Joe, 61
Neustadt, Richard, 47
Nixon, Richard, 2, 20, 22–24, 31, 45, 48, 64, 72, 74, 93, 96, 103, 117–18, 130, 203, 226, 261
Nunn, Sam, 108, 139
Nussbaum, Bernard W., 279, 281

Oakley, Meredith, 8, 59, 62, 100, 105, 317
Oates, Joyce Carol, 311
Osborne, David, 32, 66
Oxman, Stephen, 97

Panetta, Leon E., 123, 275
Parker, Max, 207
Paster, Howard, 273
Perot, Ross, 3, 21, 124, 307
Peters, Charles, 9
Piercy, Jan, 229
Pious, Richard, 24
Powell, General Colin, 3, 108
Purvis, Joe, 170

Quindlen, Anna, 104

Rangel, Charles, 112
Rather, Dan, 121
Reagan, Ronald, 24, 31, 45, 47, 71, 79, 92, 116, 130, 238, 305
Reese, Kenneth, 226
Reich, Robert, 61, 114, 219, 260
Reno, Janet, 139, 260, 281
Rice, Condoleeza, 128
Rivlin, Alice, 263, 279
Rodham, Dorothy, 222
Rodham, Hillary. *See* Clinton, Hillary Rodham
Rodham, Hugh, 222
Roosevelt, Eleanor, 216, 219
Roosevelt, Franklin Delano, 6, 31, 56, 72, 79, 101, 116–17, 216, 246–47, 260, 272, 291, 305
Roosevelt, Theodore, 21
Rosco, Carol, 218
Rubin, Robert, 219

Schaffer, Beverly Basset, 234–35
Schlesinger, Arthur, Jr., 302
Schroeder, Patricia, 112
Shalala, Donna, 79, 218, 260, 289–90
Sheehy, Gail, 185
Smith, Stephen, 114
Spurlin, Virgil, 52
Staley, Carolyn (Yeldell), 55, 97, 126, 170–71, 180–82, 210
Stephanopoulos, George, 76, 78, 82–83, 92, 131, 135, 217, 275
Sullivan, Andrew, 312
Sullivan, Harry Stack, 242

Taylor, Donna, 97, 186
Toricelli, Robert, 113
Truman, Harry, 20, 133, 139, 305

Walters, Mrs., 179
Warner, Judith, 227

Watkins, David, 270
Wattenberg, Martin P., 29–30
Wenner, Jann S., 102–3
Wesley, John, 224–25
White, Frank, 238–39
White, Randy, 108
Williams, Lee, 98
Williams, Margaret, 218
Wills, Gary, 310
Wilson, Edith, 216
Wilson, Woodrow, 20–21, 64, 124, 314, 317

Winnicott, D. W., 172
Winter, David G., 307
Wood, Kimba, 105, 269, 316
Woods, Henry, 234
Woodward, Bob, 56–57, 76, 109, 267, 272, 312–14
Wright, Betsey, 207
Wright, George, Jr., 96, 115–16

Yeltsin, Boris N., 54, 261
Young, Buddy, 282